Cousin Felix
Meets the
Buddha

Cousin Felix Meets the Buddha

And Other Encounters in China and Tibet

LINCOLN KAYE

Illustrated by Mei-lang Hsu

FARRAR, STRAUS AND GIROUX

NEW YORK

Farrar, Straus and Giroux
19 Union Square West, New York 10003

Copyright © 2003 by Lincoln Kaye
Illustrations copyright © 2003 by Mei-lang Hsu
All rights reserved
Distributed in Canada by Douglas & McIntyre Ltd.
Printed in the United States of America
First edition, 2003

Library of Congress Cataloging-in-Publication Data
Kaye, Lincoln, 1947–
      Cousin Felix meets the Buddha and other encounters in China and
      Tibet / Lincoln Kaye ; illustrated by Mei-lang Hsu.
          p.   cm.
      ISBN 0-374-29998-6 (hc : alk. paper)
          1. Kaye, Lincoln, 1947—Journeys—China.   2. China—
Description and travel.   I. Title.

DS712 .K39 2003
915.104'6—dc21

                                                                        2002022967

Designed by Cassandra J. Pappas

www.fsgbooks.com

10   9   8   7   6   5   4   3   2   1

For my parents and Townsend Brewster

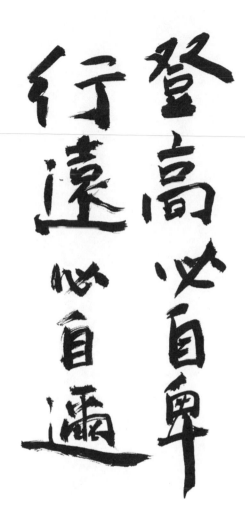

To climb high, take yourself down a peg;
To range far, home in on yourself.

Contents

Preface:

Homing In

OVER TEA AND MELON SEEDS, Yeh Yan-tu pens the *xu*, or epigraph, for this book. It's a ceremonial moment and Yan-tu is the ideal celebrant: a science-fiction author and senior editor of Taiwan's foremost daily newspaper, he's my oldest and best Chinese literary friend. The room we're sitting in, his den, befits the occasion. He's decorated it as a classic Chinese scholar's studio, lined with bamboo bookshelves and framed calligraphy.

Even the fishing trophies on the wall (Yan-tu is an avid angler) are rendered in ink and paper, rather than sawdust and shellac. When he lands a prize catch, he lightly brushes the still-living fish with calligraphy ink and imprints the whole length of it on rice vellum. After adding a commemorative verse or two and a vermilion seal, the trophy is ready to hang in the study. Rather than a wall-mounted mummy, Yan-tu preserves just a suggestive trace of the climactic moment of capture, the creature as it might have loomed up toward the gunwale, spine still arched in struggle, eye wide with astonishment. (As for the actual fish, it's long since either been steamed with ginger and scallions or else—likelier—thrown compassionately back into the sea.)

Finding an appropriate *xu* is an angling expedition of another sort. The manuscript is finally finished and ready to be considered as a whole, rather than in piecemeal chapters. Yan-tu trawls the deep sea of his learning and comes up with an apt epigram to sum up the entirety of the book. The quote, he swears, comes from the *Analects*, although he never does manage, despite my repeated nagging, to provide a precise chapter-and-verse citation. Not that it matters, really. The aphorism *sounds* like Confucius, anyway, with the sage's characteristic tone of riddling hortation: a paradoxical prescription for how to undertake a pilgrimage.

Most of the focal characters in this book are pilgrims—true believers, propelled across the Chinese landscape by the force of some overriding idea. The background scenery varies from pilgrim to pilgrim, and so does the motivating creed, be it Maoism, Buddhism, animism, humanism, jingoism, or mercantilism. My pilgrims include a death-dealing paramedic, a Taiwanese huckster, a *qi gong* guru, a troupe of itinerant actors, a careerist policeman, a Tibetan lama, a muckraking lawyer, a die-hard revolutionary agitator, a reform-minded bureaucrat, a suicidal commissar, and many others whom I came to know in my five-year stint as China correspondent of the *Far Eastern Economic Review*.

For panoramic social portraiture, pilgrimage remains as sturdy a narrative vehicle today as it was in Chaucer's time. Pilgrims still regale each other with roundelays of storytelling; autobiographic confession comes naturally on journeys of self-discovery. Besides revealing the storytellers as characters in their own right, such tales also highlight the ideas that drive them. And the pilgrims' progress unfurls for us a pageant of backdrop landscapes. We set out from Beijing and pass through the factory enclaves and migrant camps of China's "economic miracle." We cross the loess plateau of the heartland, cradle of both Chinese prehistory and Mao's revolution. In the Himalayan foothills of the Far West, we trace the lines of ethnic confrontation between Han Chinese and the people of Central Asia.

But the pilgrimage motif is more than just a handy way of stringing together characters, themes, and locales. It captures the peculiarly nostalgic restlessness of today's China. In Yeh Yan-tu's *xu*, the verb I've translated as "home in" is the same word used in, say, calculus to describe an asymptotic convergence upon a limit. Its ideogram features a fine-mesh net, to signify involution, and a stylized foot, denoting a journey. This introspective "homing in" is what distinguishes a pilgrim from a tourist, explorer, or expeditionary.

Unlike, say, Huck Finn "lightin' out for the territories," the pilgrim knows exactly where he's going, even though he's never been there. He knows it by faith, by looking inward—or backward—to something he's heard or read or dreamt. Only by first withdrawing into himself can he find the strength to then turn around and face the outer world. Despairing of the present, the mind seeks refuge in a purity it thinks it once knew. Given freedom and resources to travel, the pilgrim then sets out in search of a sacred precinct where his inner vision may be realized.

This psychological two-step well suits the mood of contemporary China, where, for much of the past century, nostalgia for bygone glory has grown apace with despair about present realities. But only in the past couple of decades have enough Chinese enjoyed the freedom or mobility to vote their discontents with their feet, which makes for an age of pilgrimage.

My own American strain of restless nostalgia propelled me, as a preteen in suburban New York, to first set my sights on China. Like a proper pilgrim, I knew exactly where I was going, even though I'd never been there. China, for me, was the Sunday funnies world of "Terry and the Pirates," peopled entirely by gung ho heroes, shifty villains, and femmes fatales. Nor did my vision of China lose any of its comic-strip luster even during my brief collegiate fling, a decade later, with Chairman Mao's "perpetual revolution." To pass through the ideological looking glass, all it took was a facile reshuffle of good-guy/bad-guy tags: Terry joins the Pirates.

But by that time, I'd already glimpsed the rich civilization behind the cartoon. My first inkling came from a one-time China missionary, Father Thomas Berry. He has since become a celebrated sage of the "deep ecology" movement, but in those days he taught philosophy at

Fordham and Saint John's universities, with a specialty in non-Western thought. Yet for all his academic eminence, he was still not above occasional doorkeeper duty at the Passionist Monastery up behind our neighborhood subway station. It was in this role that I happened to meet him when I stumbled upon the monastery while playing hooky from high school.

Upon learning of his background, I must have popped him some idle question about the Mysterious East. He responded with a dazzling introductory lecture on Chinese intellectual history. He pitched his talk precisely to the level of an impressionable fifteen-year-old, even illustrating his points with lavish art books from his personal library. I was hooked. The monastery became my venue of choice for high school truancy. Father Thomas fed me plenty of stirring historic stories, literary texts, and classic artwork. But beyond that, he gradually unfolded for me his sense of China's special take on reality and man's place in it.

To the Confucian mind, Father Thomas wrote, all things great or small are drawn to each other with a "mutual attraction [that] functions as the interior binding force of cosmic, social and personal life." Humanity, as witness of this "intercommunion," unites heaven and earth in consciousness.

The word *shih* (±) sums it up: a horizontal line for heaven, another underneath for earth, and a bold, upright stroke for the consciousness linking the two. The ideogram, one of the simplest (and, presumably, oldest) in Chinese, originally designated a civil or military official. Later it came to represent any accomplished and dedicated person, whether a warrior or a scholar. To become a *shih* is a Confucian ideal. Each "pilgrim" in these pages is a *shih* of sorts, embodying some compelling vision that animates for him the mundane surrounding landscape.

As a Hindu thirsts for transcendence or a Christian for redemption, so, according to Father Thomas, does the Confucian *shih* prize the "meta-virtue" of *cheng*, or "authenticity." The more spontaneously and sincerely you can be yourself, the more fully you reflect "cosmic integrity." But that's hardly an invitation to go-it-alone or let-it-all-hang-out. You can truly "be yourself" only in context; human inter-relationships mirror and sustain the affective harmonies of the universe—hence the Confucian stress on hierarchy and family. In the analytical West, by contrast, we take a much more atomized approach, Father Thomas feels. Our God stands apart from His creation—a moody Personality Who "covenants" with His "chosen" elect. No wonder we're so obsessed with differentiation and individuality.

Such concepts were way out of my depth back in high school. (Maybe they still are; reencountering Father Thomas lately, I found him, well into his eighties, as intellectually challenging as ever.) But to him I owe my earliest inkling of China's deep-down "otherness" even at the most fundamental level, where thoughts are formed.

For me, the language itself epitomized this enticing mystery, but I never got a chance to study Chinese until years later, after I'd already flunked out of college and started working as a reporter on U.S. dailies. Finding myself between jobs, I shipped out on a passenger freighter to Taiwan. (Mainland China was still off-limits in those Cold War times.)

I never meant to stay in Taiwan more than a couple of months, just long enough for an introductory Chinese course. But language study proved so rewarding (and so affordable even on my modest income as a freelance English teacher) that I wound up hanging on. It wasn't until my third year there that I felt ready to try out my Chinese in my own métier: reporting feature stories. Moving up to Taipei, the capital, I took a job with *Echo Magazine*, a cultural monthly in English. The office was a hive of immensely talented Taiwanese journalists. I was the only full-time foreign staffer.

It was at *Echo* that I finally made the breakthrough I had been waiting for. My language had reached a stage (just barely) where I could go beyond formal pleasantries to tap into deeper thoughts and feelings. Over lots of mountaineering weekends and midnight curbside noodle feasts, I finally got a firsthand sense of the Chinese "affective genius" that Father Thomas talked about. Colleagues from those days, including Yeh Yan-tu, remain cherished friends even now.

But the bond that transformed me most was with my wife, Hsu Mei-lang (or Ah-loong, as she's called in Taiwanese), whom I first met when we were both starting out at *Echo*. For me, she is the touchstone of Confucian *cheng*, the springtime spontaneity that resonates in every facet of Chinese life. In her, I personalized all my long fascination with China. The "otherness" of China merged with the otherness of Ah-loong to captivate me.

To conflate Ah-loong with China, though, is an unpardonable fallacy, as she herself never hesitates to remind me. By disposition she's a secessionist, one of a kind, unconstrained by clan or nation. Such a stance puts her at odds with mainstream Chinese values of personal submissiveness and cultural chauvinism. Yet much as a renegade Catholic might remain irreducibly papist even in apostasy, so Ah-loong goes about her many rebellions with a wholly Confucian earnestness—a paradoxical mix of focused tenacity and "big-picture" lucidity of perspective; the mind of a *shih*.

Such a mind sees actualities far beyond the reach of mere, plodding reportage like mine. Covering stories with her over the years, I've come to rely on her as much more than an interpreter. Her gift of empathy unburdens the tongue-tied. Her fine-tuned ear for language and her cultured sensibility capture the subtlest nuance. Her sketchbook (a few leaves of which appear here) complements my notebook to bring out characters and landscapes in stereoscopic relief. When we venture out together (which we do every chance we get), we constantly pool recollections and compare notes. Although, for narrative convenience, I have written these pages in the first person singular, Ah-loong is a co-observer and co-author in the fullest sense. This may not be the most dispassionately objective way to go about a story, but this shortfall is more than offset by the judicious sympathy and responsibility that Ah-loong brings to our coverage.

Responsibility to our subjects has guided our decision to obscure certain specifics of virtually everybody depicted here except for ourselves. Despite all the ballyhoo about its economic liberalization, China remains a dangerous place for anyone who chances to embarrass one or another of its innumerable face-obsessed satraps, great or petty. Many who appear in these pages could fall under suspicion merely for openly interacting with the likes of us. So we have deliberately falsified all our characters' names along with other particulars.

Everything in the book is based on our actual, firsthand encounters in China. We wrote and sketched from copious notes, photos, and even videotapes. Those who know their China (or who knew us during our years there) may think they recognize some of the descriptions here. They may guess right, too, but only in part, for we have gone out of our way to mix and match portraits so as to keep them unidentifiable. We're not aiming for lifelike taxidermy, rather just lightly brushed imprints, much in the spirit of Yeh Yan-tu's elegant angling souvenirs. We're too grateful to our characters to reveal them too forthrightly; they still swim in China's surging human sea.

Some helpers, already high and dry, can be safely acknowledged by name. First thanks are due to my colleagues at the *Far Eastern Economic Review*: to Derek Davies, who hired me and entrusted me as a correspondent in six different Asian countries over fifteen years, and to Philip Bowring, who enriched the magazine with a wealth of sections and formats on which I learned my writing and reporting craft. L. Gordon Crovitz, Jim MacGregor, and Karen Elliot House of Dow Jones humored me through the early onset of my book-writing pretensions; Nayan Chanda, now publications director of Yale's Center for the Study of Globalization, provided a timely impetus to my graduation from journalism to authorship.

My Beijing understudy, Anthony Kuhn, used his incomparable language and liaison skills to steer us to many a choice encounter; he's now come impressively into his own as China bureau chief for National Public Radio. Lynn Pan, a seasoned author with a definitive shelf-ful of China tomes to her credit, gently warned me away from crowding my chapters with much needless clutter. Toby Brown, of General Oriental Investments, offered plenty of practical advice without waiting for it to be solicited. Don Cohn, who has blazed far ahead of me on the New York–to-China track, has been unstintingly generous with his trail lore.

Poet-financier Ajit Dayal encouraged Ah-loong and me from the start and lent us a writing haven in Bangalore. Ramgopal Agarwala, head of the economics unit at the World Bank's China mission, helped place some of our grassroots anecdotes in a fitting macro-context. Our wonderful Beijing neighbors, Yunchong and Hengching Pan of the Canadian International Development Agency, provided crucial background and contacts. Jürgen Kremb and Chou Su-hsi of *Der Spiegel* generously opened up their files and Rolodex to us and served as sounding boards throughout. So did Citibanker John Law (Luo Qiang), my old *jiu rou pengyou* (roistering buddy) from student days in Taiwan, who retains his uncanny lifelong ability to crop up with a morale boost just when most needed.

Rone Tempest of the *Los Angeles Times* and Laura Richardson of *Jiao Liu Magazine* also tided us through many a slump and took on the chancy role of the manuscript's first readers. Another early reader was Ian Buruma, who graciously forwarded our drafts to his publishing friends. Our Indian agent, Amrita Chak, went through some chapters from the crucial perspective of a highly cultured reader without any particular background or *a priori* interest in China. A similar take, from an American angle, was offered by my sister, Amity Horowitz, and her philosopher-son Eli. Dr. Alexander Berzin of the Aryatara Institut, Berlin, vetted the lama chapter from the standpoint of Tibetology.

Jonathan Spence, Sterling Professor of History at Yale, generously read the antepenultimate draft and offered invaluable suggestions, which we've tried to reflect in the finished product. Librarians Kung Wen-kai and Calvin Hsu at Yale's Sterling Library helped us track down some key references and taught us the ins and outs of Chinese net-surfing.

Special thanks to our editor, Jonathan Galassi, who bore with us through all the heavy breathing of this book's long gestation; to our New York agent, Jeff Posternak of the Wylie Agency, who nervously paced the corridor outside the delivery room; and to Farrar, Straus and Giroux's Lorin Stein, who deftly midwifed us through the final production stages.

Our deepest debt of gratitude, though, remains to our children, Anna, Ted, and Melati, who, with evident élan, survived adolescence largely on their own, while we busied ourselves with this, their balky sibling.

Cousin Felix
Meets the
Buddha

Prologue:
The Forest for the Trees

THE BEIJING we first moved to, in the wake of the 1989 Tiananmen Square Massacre, was in a state of deep hibernation. The economy stagnated, investment shriveled, the reform process had ground to a halt. People were sullen, cowed. News sources clammed up. There was nothing to cover but official lies and bluster.

With so light a workload, we had plenty of time to settle in. What most impressed us, at the time, was the relative bikeability of our new hometown. Compared with Hong Kong, where we had come from, the Chinese capital was languid and low-rise, with an infinity of back alleys (*hutongs*) to explore. As per official rules, we had to live and work in government-allotted apartment blocks, but between home and office was a heady expanse of free space. In our first year of cycle-commuting, I'd chart a fresh route almost daily through the maze of lanes that made up Chaoyang Hutong, a warren of traditional courtyard houses, some dating back as early as the Qing dynasty (1644–1911).

In the process of learning my way around, I gradually tuned in to the anatomy of the neighborhood and its seasons. I came to know which windowsill would display an array of ripening persimmons in the autumn and which would sport potted irises in the spring; where the elders practiced *kungfu* in the mornings; where to buy fresh tofu. I bumbled into the crossfire of schoolboy snowball fights. More than once I inadvertently surprised courting couples shyly hand-holding in what they'd assumed to be an unfrequented byway. I established my patronage of a particular street barber, a bike mechanic, a breakfast-dumpling stall. I was on nodding terms, at least, with several of the curbside grannies of the "Neighborhood Watch," who were assigned by the Communist Party Block Committees to keep an eye on inter-lopers.

Even so, I never exactly felt like a Chaoyang insider. Such a status could hardly be attained through any amount of accumulated street smarts, since the real life of the quarter was off the streets, hidden be-hind the high house walls. It was within the courtyards that people played out their affections, jealousies, and ambitions. In each house, all rooms turned their backs to the street. Instead, their doors and win-dows issued onto central, open-air "sky wells." These pocket gardens once boasted rockeries, bonsai, or topiary shrubs—back in the days when each grand courtyard house sheltered the ingrown world of a single, wealthy extended family all under one roof. Since the 1950s, however, the sky wells have become more utilitarian as Communist housing reforms carved up these houses into ever-tinier apartments to be parceled out by bureaucratic fiat. Random strangers wound up sardine-packed into precincts originally designed for an unrushed, un-crowded, private sarabande of family intimates. But the courtyards came to foster intimacy of a different kind in their new incarnation as public spaces, the micro-plazas of mini-neighborhoods. From a pass-ing bicycle, the ornately gabled gateways of the *hutong* houses offered glimpses of the relaxed jumble of courtyard life inside: laundry lines, communal water taps, parked bikes and barrows, potted plants, un-kempt shrubs, chicken coops, pickle jars, old men bent over chess-

boards, children playing hopscotch, gossiping matrons under shade trees, house cats sprawled in the sun.

By contrast, the narrow alleys between houses seemed somber, hemmed in by the back walls of the courtyards. Daubed gray or ochre or cinnamon red, the featureless masonry provided a backdrop to dramatically silhouette any passerby. Not that there were a lot of casual strollers to watch. Most pedestrians would hurry through without pause or nod, intent on private purposes. The only ones who'd linger in the lanes would be pushcart vendors, door-to-door peddlers, street sweepers and the Neighborhood Watch grannies. At night, even these few "street people" would vanish and I'd have the *hutong* completely to myself. With the front doors drawn shut, all that emanated from the courtyards were cooking smells, snatches of murmured conversation, and the occasional shaft of light from a frosted-glass windowpane. Hardly any greenery on the streets, at least not at eye level. But where branches overtopped the courtyard walls, streetlamps cast fitful tree shadows on the blank brickwork. Racing alongside me, my own bicycle shadow hurtled through the ghost foliage. I came to cherish the loneliness of these alleys, the silence and solitude amid the teeming—though hidden—life of the neighborhood.

China, as a newsbeat, perked up after a while. The Soviet collapse raised the stakes for policy-makers in Beijing and abroad. On Deng Xiaoping's personal command, the business feeding frenzy resumed. The resulting free-for-all combined with the lingering resentments of the Tiananmen massacre to rend whatever was left of social cohesion. After decades of enforced conformity, Chinese were left—for better or worse—to shift for themselves, economically and spiritually. Such moments are rare in China's long history, which is mostly written in terms of broad social aggregates rather than individual protagonists. But periodically—often at the interstices of dynasties, when the "Mandate of Heaven" is ready to change hands—there recur lapses when group-think breaks down and vividly original personalities emerge. To cover such an interlude as a reporter is an exciting privilege.

Yet each time I ventured out of the capital on a news safari, I found myself missing the languid rhythms of the *hutong*. As soon as I got back to Beijing, I'd relish once more my home-to-office commute. So it went, right up to my last ride through Chaoyang's back alleys.

It was early autumn, the period marked "White Dew" in the Chinese Farmers' Almanac. I'd just returned from a circuit through South China, where the summer heat still blazed and burgeoning new highrise construction already bespoke the onset of a business rebound. Upbeat as it was, the southern climate—both economic and meteorological—could get a bit enervating after a while. I felt ready for the more muted colors and tempo of the capital.

High clouds feathered the purple dusk. In the fortnight that I'd been gone, I noticed, most of my fellow cyclists in the rush-hour bike lanes had already switched from cottons to flannels. Along the broad Workers' Stadium Road, no trace remained of last month's melon stalls. Vendors now trundled portable braziers to roast chestnuts and yams. That meant, I knew from experience, that even more elaborate al fresco snacks must by now have made their seasonal debut in the back alleys: grilled kebabs, candied crabapples, fried bread. Eager to spoil my appetite for dinner, I steered straight for Chaoyang. But, cutting across the boulevard, I spotted none of the usual street theater at the mouth of the *hutong*. No strings of naked lightbulbs, no bamboo stools, no billows of smoke. Instead of pungent cookfires, there was only the incongruous smell of plowed loam. Baffled, I nosed my bike into the lane.

The streets remained, but the houses were gone. The two-hundred-year-old courtyards—still aswarm with jumbled, secret life when I'd set out just last month—had been reduced in the meantime to a plain of scattered masonry. In fact, most of the stonework and salvageable bricks had already been carted off for reuse. Only fragmentary debris was left, already crumbling back into the yellow dust that underlies Beijing. How could a whole, richly textured world vanish so suddenly and so completely? I traced a couple of remembered lanes, following the remnants of intact flagstone pavement between the tidy quadrants of rubble. But after a few zigzags, the sheer pointlessness of my progress brought me up short.

At a fork in the road near where (I think) my barber used to be, I found myself at a loss for any reason to choose one direction over the other. All I could do was brake and straddle my bike, staring at the ground. The place had been picked so clean it lacked even the usual detritus of demolition sites—no coins, no potsherds or scraps of paper mixed in with the stones. On a flatbed cart in the next lane, someone had stacked a half-dozen weather-beaten latticework window frames. The little donkey, standing—perhaps sleeping—in the traces, steamed visibly. A hundred yards away, at what was once a blind corner of the alley, a lone figure sat slumped on a low stool, surveying the broken stones. The salvage man stopping for a smoke? The last of the Neighborhood Watch crones? Or maybe no human soul at all, just a ragpicker's bundle waiting to be carted away.

But, unpeopled as it was, the rubble plain was far from lifeless. The walls had come down, but not the trees: gnarled pines, sprawling plane trees, dog eared persimmons, lacy willows. Each one of them bore hallmarks of domestication, having flourished theretofore only in the isolated context of its own courtyard. Some of them had been carefully pruned and trellised. A few were daubed with anti-termite lime. One gingko wore a tin collar around its base, presumably to guard against rats and squirrels. Other treetrunks still bore tacked-on bits of plastic hardware—toiletry shelves, shaving mirrors, dishracks, chopstick holders. Scraps of residual clothesline turned one maple into a bedraggled May-pole. Improvised prosthetics propped up a venerable cedar: support cables between the upper branches, putty to seal up clefts in the bark, bamboo crutches for the outlying boughs.

The trees loomed in the gathering dusk, bereft of human society and cast, for the first time in their long lives, into an arboreal milieu all their own. A homelier grove I have never seen—sparse and stunted, with only brick shards for an understory. Yet, straddling my bike at the canceled crossroad, I could almost convince myself that the Chaoyang arboretum *did* amount to a forest of sorts. The moiré of superimposed foliage, the first stir of night wind in the branches, the

onset of evening crickets—all added up to the semblance of an airy copse at sunset.

Even before the courtyard walls had come down, I realized, any passing sparrow would have taken this *hutong* for an oasis of woodland amid the surrounding high-rises. If, as per the tenets of Chinese *feng shui*, plants pulse life force through the unseen acupunctural meridians of the earth, then these trees must have been communing with each other all along, like prisoners tapping out secret codes on the cellblock plumbing. Yet here I'd been cycling through this boscage, oblivious, for over a year now, unable to see the forest *or* the trees.

Within a week, nursery crews descended on what was left of Chaoyang to dig up the more presentable trees. They trucked them off, roots swaddled in burlap, for transplantation on freeway medians, golf-links, and condominium lawns out beyond the new Ring Road. After that came the backhoes and bulldozers. Before long, the erstwhile *hutong* had turned into a chrome-and-glass shopping mall.

Crossing the River by
Feeling the Stones

NOTHING BESPEAKS China's antiquity so eloquently as its dust—or at least so it seems in the depths of a Beijing winter funk. By late March, Gobi dust coats every cranny of the city: the frames and sills and roof tiles, the bare trunks of plane trees, the grim concrete cornices.

Even my eyeballs feel begrimed, and my tonsils and my daintiest alveoli. Too long I've been breathing the curdled smog of coal fires and the recycled steam of Soviet-era central heating. Newspapers get repetitious, winter cuisine palls, and social rituals grow stale. Details of daily Beijing life start to take on the consistency of Gobi dust—atomized, pervasive, inert. Can anything grow in such a medium? Cabin fever sets in. Travel brochures that I'd hardly deign to look at back in high autumn now linger for a week on my desk. Not that I get such a lot of brochures anymore. The cruise lines gave up on me long ago.

But here's something from the state-run China International Travel Service: a travel agents' notice about vacation packages for *huaqiao* (overseas Chinese) to Huangdi Ling, the tomb of the Yellow Emperor, founding father of the Chinese race. On the Qing Ming grave-sweeping festival day, April 5, Shaanxi provincial authorities will be offering cultural performances and a trade fair there.

"Warmly welcome overseas Chinese visitor to venerate our primordial ancestor in exclusive ceremony. Central government dignitaries to preside, including members of the Chinese People's Political Consultative Committee. Three-star accommodation at Provincial Guest House."

That sounds like niche marketing at its most recherché. Shaanbei—northern Shaanxi—gritty, arid, dirt-poor, at least a half-day's bone-jarring bus ride from the nearest airport. Not everybody's idea of a lightsome spring weekend. Still, Qing Ming in Huangdi Ling is not an invitation to be overlooked. For a *huaqiao*-in-law like me, it might offer clues to just what kind of tribe I've married into.

Ah-loong, my sole familial link with the Yellow Emperor, turns out to be game for the trip. After all, it gets us out of town and up into the Ordos Loop, where the Yellow River jogs north and then south again to stake out a tenuous agrarian toehold upon the Gobi. Spring supposedly comes a few weeks earlier to the loess hills—a welcome respite from the last throes of a Beijing winter.

Besides, we'll get a chance to transit Xian, a tourist mecca that we've somehow missed in all our years in China. Train tickets prove no problem at this time of year, and with twenty-four hours of "hard sleeper" ahead of us, we'll have plenty of time to ponder our itinerary and prime ourselves to do right by our ancestors.

EVERYBODY'S GOT ANCESTORS and reveres them, more or less, but no place can match China for elaborating this universal sentiment into a full-blown cult. To share in these ancestor rites is to probe the roots of China's self-conception. How to draw the line between Chinese civilization and the engulfing barbarity of the rest of the world? What is the touchstone for membership in the Middle Kingdom? Where is the boundary between history and chaos?

No better site than Huangdi Ling for mulling such questions, and no better occasion than Qing Ming ("Clear and Bright"). Unique among traditional Chinese holidays, it's calculated on the solar rather than the lunar calendar—a vernal equinox festival. Like spring rites all over the world, it must have originated as a lusty romp through the hedgerows. It was also the occasion for burning off the stubble of the winter fields in preparation for spring planting.

But once it got mixed up with the ancestor cult, Qing Ming took on a more somber cast. The scorching of the croplands became the occasion for renewing all domestic flames, which meant first letting the hearth fires go out. That, in turn, translated into a day of penitential cold baths and uncooked meals—a token reversion to the fireless simplicity of Paleolithic prehistory, before the Yellow Emperor "civilized" the Chinese.

Sobered by these austerities, families gather on Qing Ming to tend the graves of their lineal forebears. In Taiwan, Hong Kong, and parts of the *huaqiao* diaspora, the festival triggers contests of funerary one-upmanship as mourners strive to outdo each other in ostentatious display of tangible grief. But in mainland China, Qing Ming remains an intimate, almost furtive affair.

Descendants rake and prune and trim around the grave mounds, smoothing the channels of *feng shui* (literally "wind and water"), the invisible but all-powerful energy currents that link the fortunes of the living and the dead. A properly sited grave, with the right disposition of trees and streams, can prosper a clan for generations. Ideally, even the surrounding hills should bear the shapes of auspicious animals—a tiger to the west, a bird to the south, and so forth.

Feng shui flows along hidden channels in the earth, analogous to the invisible meridians of the living body that are used in acupuncture. This reflects the world's origin as the metamorphosed corpse of Pan Gu—he who was born from the dark egg of chaos. For the first 18,000 years of measurable time, Pan Gu single-handedly propped up the heavens and kept them apart from the underworld. When at last he died, his breath became the wind, his voice the thunder, his eyes the sun and moon. The four cardinal directions are his limbs; his trunk formed the mountains. As for humanity, we're his body lice—or so says the first-century B.C. *Classic of Mountains and Seas.*

Aside from keeping Pan Gu's meridians unbunged, the graveside worshipers tend to their more immediate ancestors, too. They lay out a spread of steamer buns, dried mushrooms, meats, and bean curd—nothing too appetizing, lest it attract the envy of malevolent "hungry ghosts," who hang around graveyards and have no duly filial descendants of their own to look after them.

Qing Ming is the time to top up the ancestral bankroll of "spirit money." Historically this currency was made of coarse, hand-pressed paper, maybe embossed with a wisp of gold leaf or a crude woodblock print. Nowadays, China is awash in rotogravured "hell banknotes" strangely reminiscent of Hong Kong dollar bills, complete with copperplate flutes and scrolls, auspicious serial numbers, and pompous "bank manager" signatures. It's a giddily hyperinflated currency; the sole denomination is H$100 million (that's 100 million "hell dollars"), but nobody seems worried about having to make change. In the weeks leading up to Qing Ming, peddlers sell off thick wads of both new- and old-style spirit money at open-air markets. You can transmute the scrip into negotiable netherworld tender by burning it at graveside. Or else you can roll the banknotes into spindly paper "spirit trees" to plant at your family tomb.

Even such low-profile, private observations as these would have been squelched fifteen or twenty years ago. Since "Liberation," Qing Ming has been publicly celebrated with no more than perfunctory memorial services centered around state-run cemeteries for "revolutionary martyrs." For the most part, though, the regime has given short shrift to the tomb-sweeping festival—and no wonder. Family observances of any kind could hardly thrive under founding Red dynast Mao Zedong's injunction to "smash the old" in the name of radical collectivization. "Class background" was considered a matter of heredity; a "negative" one could stigmatize you for life. To pamper your august forebears might harm, rather than help, your worldly prospects. Better to come from a nameless, undistinguished lineage. If not so favored, at least don't tout your pedigree. Totalitarian snitch culture encouraged betrayal of your living intimates; how much easier to forsake your dead ones.

Long after Mao's demise, Qing Ming still remains a loaded occasion for the Communist leadership. Considering the cruelty of many a death in recent Chinese history, a day given over to requiem rites risks reopening still-raw wounds.

In 1976, just months after the death of premier Zhou Enlai, the Qing Ming festival served as the trigger for Communist China's first pro-democracy demonstrations in Tiananmen Square. Zhou had been widely revered as a buffer against the worst depredations of the Cultural Revolution, so mourners laid unauthorized wreaths for him at the foot of the Martyrs' Monument in implicit protest against the excesses of Mao and his ultra-leftist heirs. After gathering momentum for a few days, the demonstration was put down even more brutally than the famous Tiananmen student protests thirteen years later, according to veteran activists who witnessed both massacres firsthand.

To this day, Qing Ming kicks off the annual season of official paranoia in Beijing. For three months, right up through June 4 (date of the 1989 Tiananmen massacre), plainclothes and uniformed police blanket Tiananmen and the surrounding city, ready to squelch any commemoration of a series of awkward anniversaries. Private Qing Ming ceremonies may be tolerated nowadays, but public observances remain dicey.

All the more brazen, then, the regime's gall in officially staging Qing Ming rites at Huangdi Ling. Maybe it's because the primordial ancestor is remote enough in time and dubious enough in authenticity that he's deemed safe: the kind of Big Lie that an authoritarian regime can live with. If people can be induced to believe in the Yellow Emperor's historicity, so much the better. And even if they can't, so long as they pay dutiful lip service to an officially promoted nonsense, the regime's authority is reaffirmed. Such vehicles prove ideal for the Party's coalition-building "United Front" cooptation drives, and *huaqiao* are especially susceptible to such appeals. Keen to cash in on

China's current development boom, overseas Chinese show themselves more avid than ever these days for opportunities to display their fealty to the fatherland.

So for a *huaqiao* fund-raising gala, the Yellow Emperor could prove just the ticket. He's the vanishing point of Chinese historical perspective, the place where all parallel lines (or lineages) converge. He occupies a position all his own at the intersection of godhead and humankind. Legend ranks him as the last of the prehistoric Three Sovereigns. Of the three, the Yellow Emperor was the only unequivocal hominid. The earlier two featured a dragon's tail and an ox's head, respectively.

On the other hand, China's earliest historian, Si-Ma Qian, counts the Yellow Emperor not among the mythic Three Sovereigns but rather as the first of the avowedly historical Five Rulers. Si-Ma Qian launches his *Historical Records* with a recital of Huangdi's inventions: boats, carts, pottery, armor, writing, medicine, divination, silk weaving, surnames, ball games, calendars, and lots more. Without such amenities, Si-Ma Qian seems to imply, people can hardly be deemed human, let alone Chinese.

COUNT ON CHINA to begin its account of itself with a practical tinkerer rather than a cosmic creator. By some Gresham's law of religiosity, ancestor worship crowds out other more "spiritual" faiths, much to the despair of missionaries over the millennia. Ethereal saints, sublime abstractions, revealed truths—none of them can vie in China with the appeal of a flesh-and-blood bridge of forebears from here to eternity.

By extending the whole Confucian web of interlocking social obligations backward through time, the ancestor cult lends a quasi-religious buzz to the bonds between parents and children, spouses, siblings, students and teachers, rulers and ruled. With thousands of years of historic resonance, such social relationships take on a rightness, an inevitability beyond challenge. But if the past lends *gravitas* to current social arrangements, the reverse also holds true: ancestor worship serves to "domesticate" history by analogy with the present. Even the dead draw pay, in the form of memorial rites. And, like other "salarymen," they face wage hikes or cuts; they're subject to periodic "personnel review" through the vagaries of historic reassessment.

Few other civilizations display a greater volume—or a narrower range—of historic records than China. Since feudal times, historiography has been the exclusive privilege of the same tiny elite of scholar-bureaucrats who commanded the armies and ran the civil administration. The result (with a few notable exceptions) is a mandarin's-eye view of the past: lots of statistics, episode, and protocol, but precious little causal analysis. Instead of a period-specific *Zeitgeist*, official historics account for events in terms of self righteously eternal moral verities. Each successive dynasty gets to draft its own chronicles and rewrite those of its predecessors so as to justify its own rise to power.

Not just the professed moral values, but even the form of historiography remains timeless. Since ideographs offer no obvious clues to the phonetic evolution of the language, written prose style was able to remain frozen right up through the 1920s in a self-consciously classical mode divorced from everyday spoken usage. Chinese grammar doesn't even provide for verb tenses to demarcate past from present. Casually perusing a historic chronicle, a reader might be hard-pressed to tell at a glance whether the author or the events described date from a hundred or three thousand years ago. It's as though a page of Herodotus were stylistically indistinguishable from one of Toynbee, both posing equal claims of immediacy and relevance.

Nor is this burden of the ever-present past confined only to lofty dynastic history. Every Chinese household has its own ancestor shrine. It may be a whole roomful of gilt-brushed name plaques or just a single calligraphic scroll of the clan surname tacked up over a shelf for daily wine-and-incense offerings. Grand or simple, the ancestral altar stands at the center of family life, as homely and familiar as a kitchen table, yet implicitly exalted. At festivals and anniversaries, the ancestors are served first, absorbing spiritual nutriment from the choicest tidbits (after which the clan's living elders get to polish off the mundane leftovers). Instead of getting sent to stand in the corner when they've been bad, Chinese children are made to kneel in front of the family altar and ponder the impossibility of ever discharging their debt to a facelessly stern infinitude of ancestors.

The effect, as Ah-loong recalls, can be utterly chilling: "You feel like you're at the wrong end of a telescope. There are all your ancestors, unimaginably great and remote. And from *their* perspective, you're shrunk down to nothing—a bug, a mote, a flyspeck."

Yet some kids—the stiff-necked, ill-bred, or hyperimaginative ones—manage to retain doubts. If these ancestors are all so high-minded and solemn and pure, the young reprobate wonders, how come, after so many aeons, they'd only wind up producing a loser like *me*? Could the whole ancestor cult be no more than a grown-ups' plot to cow me? What if each forebear was just as unruly as I am, just as selfish and kinky?

And all at once the little mote is staring back up the telescope of time. Gone are the undifferentiated nebulae of ancestral rectitude, the dizzying infinity of cumulative obligation. The far-off, fixed stars click into focus as teeming worlds, not unlike our own. Our lens may not have high enough resolution to discern much detail, but at least we can make out enough to infer that the whole genealogical constellation is actually a gaudy crowd of wastrels, rebels, grifters, drifters, nebbishes, fops, and fussy old aunts—all of them spinning off on orbits of their own. Of *course* our forebears must have been driven by dark demiurges of their own. How *else* would they ever get to be anyone's progenitors at all?

Surely not, as Confucian orthodoxy would have it, out of an altruistic solicitude to keep up ancestral rites. Save *that* tale for your sour old schoolmarms. Vulgar wisdom knows better, which is why lumpen China keeps grafting unseemly sprigs onto the Yellow Emperor's family tree: hecklers, heretics, vixens, mutineers, warlocks—even barbarians like me.

For nothing focuses the genealogical telescope so sharply as romance, as Ah-loong and I discovered in the surprise onset of our courtship on a camping trip way back in our twenties. It started out as a perfectly prosaic junket to Taiwan's central highlands, the sort of outing we routinely enjoyed with fellow staffers on a Taipei cultural monthly magazine. But when I showed up at the bus depot, the only familiar face I encountered at the departure gate was that soignée little debutante from circulation, a semi-stranger. Other office colleagues had finked out at the last moment; no choice but for the two of us to set out on our own.

We'd each been up to Taroko Gorge before, along the cliff-hanging road carved by mainland Chinese civil war refugees deep into Taiwan's aboriginal heartland. But this time, the place impinged with a new urgency. It wasn't just the imposing landscape—the silky waterfalls threading between bamboo-furred slopes, the icy torrent below, tumbling through its marble canyon, the sulphurous steam of hot-springs, the firefly-spangled night and sonic lace of crickets. Refracted through this lens of poetry, the human context of the scene also subtly shifted in perspective. The tourist crowds around us, instead of obtruding with forced jollity, faded into a poignantly hopeful ambiance of generalized merrymaking.

And against this backdrop, the unseen immanences of Taroko loomed all the more imposingly—the daredevil road-building crews of mainlanders, with their exiled dreams; the ousted tribals, with their disconsolate mountain gods. Never mind how, in life, these spirits would have been pitted against each other more often than not. As ghosts, they colluded in the wordlessly elegiac sense of shared loneliness that drove Ah-loong and me together. And together, we suddenly—astonishingly—sensed ourselves transformed into what neither of us, alone, could ever be: potential ancestors-in-the-making.

This was news too exciting to keep secret. So, upon returning from the mountains, Ah-loong rushed straight home to tell her family that she intended to marry. To her hurt surprise, they couldn't quite join in her wonder at the sweet mystery, the improbable inevitability, the slapstick solemnity of human generation. Everybody *knows* what sort of girl goes with foreigners, Mother Hsu warned, and everybody knows the inevitable upshot: the divorce, the unfilial children, the lifelong alienation, never sure of where you belong. But worst of all was the disgrace. What would the neighbors say? What about your aunts? Thank the gods that your father isn't here to see you now. Nor *his* father, nor . . .

But the girl was already gone. She'd caught her telescope-glimpse of the genealogical firmament; no plea or bluster could get her to kneel contritely at the family altar anymore. After our elopement, the Hsu elders could only comfort themselves with the consolations of Taiwan chauvinism: "At least it's a foreign devil. Better *that* than one of those mainland Chinese swine."

SO AH-LOONG REMAINS, even now, a little uneasy about sharing a roost with some of the fellow-nestlings that perch in the Yellow Emperor's family tree. As for me, I'm long past any illusions about my own inclusion in the Greater Chinese lineage. But, on our genealogical safari to Shaanxi, I come equipped with an alternative "ancestor" of my own: Edgar Snow, patron saint of American journalism in China.

Snow's 1937 masterpiece *Red Star Over China* offered the first internationally credible eyewitness account of Mao's "soviet" guerrilla base. Ever since 1927, the then-reigning dictator of Kuomintang (KMT) "Nationalist" China, Chiang Kai-shek, had harried the Communists into remote rural redoubts where they were sealed off behind cordons of government troops and official disinformation. Braving the blockade, Snow discovered a Red insurgency that had, during its decade-long news blackout, already gathered world-shaking momentum. This was the hottest of scoops, not just abroad but even within China. According to sinologist John K. Fairbank, the publication of *Red Star* "was in itself an event in modern Chinese history."

And this Shaanxi itinerary of ours covers the very ground that Snow traversed, as recounted in the opening chapters of *Red Star*. A long rail-haul from Beijing brought him to Xian, last bastion of KMT control at the edge of Mao's "soviet." Snow found the frontline city rumbling with undercurrents of resentment and intrigue. After linking up with his clandestine Xian contacts, Snow threaded his way northward by truck, foot, and horseback into the forbidden Red heartland. We mean to retrace pretty much the same route.

Of course, to presume even the remotest kinship with such a heroic "ancestor" puts me back again at what Ah-loong called the "wrong end of the telescope, shrunk down to nothing." Who could ever live up to a legacy like Snow's—his courage, his influence, his literary force? Yet who can deny his inspiring example of honest, open-eyed, grassroots reportage, regardless of the risks?

In the isolationist climate of the 1930s, when *Red Star* first came out, America's nightmare was that Japanese aggression in China would drag the United States into war. Chiang's Nationalists had shown themselves useless against the Japanese onslaught. So stateside readers welcomed Snow's news that at least *one* Chinese force—Mao's Reds—had the gumption to fight its own anti-Japanese battles, thereby possibly sparing America the trouble. Barely a decade later— with Mao victorious on the mainland, Chiang in exile on Taiwan, and Washington in the grip of McCarthyite paranoia—the same American public would blame Snow for having unduly "humanized" the Chinese Reds as harmless "agrarian reformers." But no objective reading of Snow's fifteen-year civil war coverage can support such a charge. He nowhere depicts Mao or his minions as anything other than out-and-out Communists. Nor does it make any sense to praise or blame his work according to how well it fit America's mood of the hour. Mao's star rose to meet Chinese needs, not American whims; *Red Star* simply chronicled the fact.

No such rejoinder, however, could cut much ice in the prevailing Cold War climate of the time. Editors, once avid for his copy, now "spiked" Snow's story proposals. Even his casual acquaintances could wind up facing press smears or tendentious congressional grillings. Chiang's KMT, from its island toehold, kept up its disinformation campaign. Beijing and Washington spiraled ever deeper into mutual isolation and incomprehension, and just when Snow's informed inputs were most needed, he was frozen out of U.S. public discourse and policy-making on China.

"Being American," he optimistically wrote, "I have an incurable tendency to expect the United States to grow slightly up." No such luck, he was finally forced to conclude; the U.S. media "refused to publish any reports by eyewitnesses of the China scene except those which confirm their own wishful thinking and self-deception." Over the years, he ruefully learned to reinvent himself as a "world citizen." He died in Switzerland, in 1972, in self-imposed exile, at the age of sixty-seven.

Yet, as an ancestral spirit, Snow's still very much with us, Ah-loong and I feel as we ride our "hard sleeper" over the Longhai Line, the same railway that he took at the start of *Red Star*. Snow describes his train as "new and very comfortable." Ours is more rickety, with tea stains on the lace curtains and cigarette burns in the gray vinyl seat covers. The passing landscape remains much as Snow describes it: "weird levels of loess hills," tier on tier of them as the wind deposits ever-finer dust particles in successive ridges. But the moral landscape seems far more cluttered and equivocal now than in the 1930s—or so I'd like to think, anyway.

One of the charms of ancestor worship is the legend of a Golden Age. Under the guise of reverencing bygone heroes, this cult slyly lets us off the hook. Our forebears outshone us, we self-servingly suppose, because they enjoyed favored times. We're born too late; tough luck. If only we'd been around back *then*. So, half-dozing along the Longhai Line, I catch myself envying Snow the clear-cut imperatives of war reporting. He knew just where he had to go to get *the* China scoop of the century; he had "only" to muster the courage and contacts to get there. Grandmaster that he was, Snow still had at least an intelligible chessboard to play on, with properly demarcated red and white squares. Nowadays, China comes on in such a rush and jumble that it's hard to tell even the name of the game, much less the identity of the pieces or which side they're playing on.

Our arrival in Xian highlights the contrast. Snow, in his time, proceeded straight from the "recent and handsome" railway station to a quiet guest house, where he was to meet the undercover couriers who would slip him through KMT lines. While waiting, he passed his time in courtesy calls on top provincial officials and rummy games with George Hatem, M.D., an American fellow traveler also bound for Red China.

No such recuperative interlude awaits us in Xian. Hardly do we get out of the crumbling, sooty depot than the touts descend on us with their wares. Tour the imperial tombs and temples? You can do it in a five-stop, one-day itinerary. Dining out? Try the seven-course Han Court Banquet, accompanied by an antique musical ensemble and acrobatics show. A theme park for the kiddies? Journey-to-the-West Playland recreates in thrilling rides and animated dioramas the Buddhist pilgrim Hsüan-tsang's seventh-century trek from Xian to India in search of sutras.

Some calligraphy? A suit of "jade" armor? Erotic paintings? How about a pinup of celebrated Tang courtesan Yang Gui-fei fresh from her hot spring bath?

In Xian, history is an extractive industry. The rich cultural deposits of the past accrue in buried layers, just waiting to be stripmined.

SUCCUMBING TO a tour-bus tout, we head out to Xian's richest historic mother lode: the tomb of Shihuangdi, the first emperor to preside over a unified China. In fact, the very name "China" derives from the short-lived Ch'in dynasty (nowadays romanized as *Qin*), which he founded twenty-three centuries ago. As his royal flacks kept reiterating, he brought new glory to "the Yellow Emperor's seed—the black-haired people."

No mean ancestor, this: the First Emperor standardized China's written script, weights and measures, laws and bureaucracy. Yet, despite his accomplishments, history reviles him for the harshly authoritarian "legalist" philosophy that underwrote his military conquests and such prodigious civil works as the Great Wall and the Grand Canal.

To disarm ideological adversaries, Shihuangdi famously burned the books of all opposing philosophic schools and buried Confucian scholars alive. As a public-relations ploy, this proved counterproductive. The Qin dynasty fell just four years after the First Emperor's death, leaving subsequent historiography in the hands of what remained of the Confucian elite. And the Confucians lost no chance to avenge themselves upon him and blacken his name posthumously.

Still, interspersed amid centuries of shrill demonization, Shihuangdi has had the occasional defender, too. His latest rehabilitation came in 1971, when he was suddenly drafted to spearhead an "anti-Confucian" campaign in official media. The epithet "Confucian," at the time, was a cipher for anyone who dared to oppose Maoist absolutism, with the result that political players of all stripes sought to claim the mantle of Shihuangdi, the nemesis of all things Confucian. Radical communards saw him as a paragon of collectivism. Pro-democracy agitators, in a celebrated wall poster, hailed him as an advocate of impartial law over despotic whim. Technocrats identified with him as a social engineer. Then Mao died, the anti-Confucian campaign faded, and Shihuangdi sank back into his customary disrepute.

But not in Shaanxi. Whatever his posthumous ups and downs in Greater China, Shihuangdi's stock has remained consistently high in Xian ever since 1974. That was when a farmer, digging a well forty miles outside the city, stumbled upon the first of what turned out to be nearly 6,000 life-sized terra-cotta warriors that comprise the First Emperor's otherworldly Praetorian guard. This trove soon became the mainstay of a thriving local tourism industry, Shihuangdi's generous bequest to his Xian descendants.

Sad to say, he neglected to deposit his mortal remains in a convenient downtown location. From the railroad station, our bus skirts the old city wall and wends through rows of grim concrete apartment blocks before striking out across bare, sandy fields. The landscape is flat and boring enough to snooze through, especially after a rough night of "hard sleeper." I don't wake up until we're already slowing down for Shihuangdi's tomb mound.

China's first historian, Si-Ma Qian, writing not long after the Qin collapse, waxes on about the splendor of the First Emperor's tomb: gem-studded palaces and courtyards, gold and silver pavements following a swan motif, a mock sun of pearl inlaid in the ceiling, rivers of mercury flowing between jeweled banks. The artisans who made these wonders wound up interred amid their own handiwork so as to preserve its secrets. Si-Ma Qian warns that the whole necropolis is booby-trapped with spring-drawn, automatic-release crossbows to protect against grave robbers.

The traps also seem to fend off archaeologists: the tomb remains unexcavated to this day, despite aerial-imaging confirmation that there is, indeed, a vast funerary complex buried here. To dig it out would be prohibitively costly and politically fraught. Better, for now, just to hold it in trust in the national portfolio of relics for future generations to unearth whenever they feel ready.

In the meantime, the only visible trace of the tomb is a blunt little hillock, a quarter-mile long and about 150 feet high, with goats grazing at its base. We hardly even notice the mound until our tour guide, a prim little martinet in a vaguely military black pants suit, stands up at the front of the bus to announce it over her karaoke mike. A bit of a letdown; so *that's* all it comes down to, after centuries of abrasion by Gobi dust and Confucian disparagement. Even a volcano of egotism like the First Emperor leaves only a little bump like this: "Look on my works, ye Mighty, and despair!"

But at least the bleakness is somewhat relieved by upbeat commercial hucksterism. Unlike the "colossal wreck" of Ozymandias's monument, Shihuangdi's tomb is hardly surrounded by "boundless and bare . . . lone and level sands." Instead, less than a mile beyond the tumulus, we pull up to what looks like a county fairground, complete with banners, barkers, and Port-a-Potties. Our guide proclaims a fifteen-minute "shopping break," after which we're to reconvene at the bus.

Ah-loong and I had left the Longhai Line and Xian station without breakfast, so we hit the first snack bar we find and greedily devour a whole roll of pineapple crème cookies, washed down with bottled soya milk. Refueled, we're ready to browse the ingenious offerings of the souvenir stalls: miniaturized terra-cotta warriors of every variety, even a brightly colored plastic model with removable armor (I wonder what's underneath). A bronze replica of a Qin warhorse doubles as a cigarette lighter, snorting flame when you tweak its tail. Children can outfit themselves for Iron Age mayhem with a complete range of half-sized crossbows, daggers, and halberds.

At a photographer's kiosk, we find a stack of postcards featuring newsreel stills from the initial archaeological digs back in the 1970s. The black-and-white images emphasize the starkness of the land-scape. Excavations pock the otherwise unblemished plain, the flat line of the horizon broken only by the ridgelines of the archaeologists' tents. A close-up shows identifiable bits of terra-cotta anatomy still half-buried in dust that's cross-hatched with modern-day sneaker prints. Two armies from different millennia confront each other in a broad panoramic view: hundreds of peasant excavators swarm over the pits, from which emerge the terra-cotta legions of Qin.

Behind the kiosk, life-sized cardboard blowups depict a row of terra-cotta warriors—kneeling archers, lancers, and a single cavalry-man. They're all left headless; customers are invited to insert their own faces atop the armored shoulders for souvenir portraits. A young couple from our bus tries out a few of these cutouts, beaming and rolling their eyes at each other. But before the kiosk photographer can swoop in to immortalize them, our guide whistles us back to the bus, waving an orange pennant emblazoned with the tour company's logo.

RALLIED AROUND this flag, we troop into the stadium-sized shed that covers the exhumed Qin infantry. No tourist stragglers delay us, no eager beavers try to jump queue at the entrance; a pretty orderly group we are, for a couple dozen passengers randomly recruited from a railroad station. But any self-congratulatory impulse is nipped in the bud by the spectacle that confronts us as we fan out along the con-crete loggia overlooking the excavation. Compared to the preternatu-ral discipline of this 6,000-strong battalion, our little bus platoon seems a ragtag shambles.

The warrior array fills a pit about the size of four Olympic pools laid side by side. From our vantage, the pit also looks about as deep as a swimming pool, and the filtered light from the clerestory windows of the giant shed imparts a chill, grayish, subaqueous tint to the loess clay of the statues and the pit walls. The terra-cotta eyes look drowned, too, fishlike, without iris or pupil.

The figures are frozen in motion—archers about to shoot, lancers ready to lunge, cavalrymen reining in their spirited horses. No matter where you move on the loggia, all 12,000 eyes seem to track you, all ears to await your command. Faced with such a trimly rectangular reflecting pool of obedient attention, none of us tourists dares to utter a word. A hush falls over the balcony—broken only by our guide, who must be quite inured by now to this spectacle.

She waits for us to fall in at ease, then crisply informs us, "You are standing in front of the Eighth Wonder of the Ancient World, the biggest and completest collection of antique statuary ever unearthed." She paces the loggia with deliberation, her furled pennant tucked under her arm like a swagger stick. "The terra-cotta legions of Qin present a whole world of their own, the world of our forefathers as they first came together under a single Chinese state. Note the artistry of the figures, the expressiveness: no two of them are alike, each stamped with its own individuality."

Though you wouldn't know it from looking at them. There's a repetitiousness about the terra-cotta warriors that you'd be hard-pressed to find in real life among even the most robotic of color-guard drill teams on Tiananmen Square.

To be sure, the Qin warriors *do* display disparities of height and girth, as well as variations in posture and costume according to job and rank. The faces, too, are somewhat distinctive. Some bespeak an admixture of Turkic recruits from Central Asia among the Qin forces. Nonetheless, all wear the same livery and the same indrawn, abstracted, *golem* expression of mindless submission.

The faces all reduce to ten basic shapes, as our guide is now explaining with the help of a wall chart. Within these broad parameters, the sculptors mixed and matched particular features from a limited set of prototypical noses, eyes, ears, mouths, brows, and chins. The limitations of this physiognomic "alphabet" allow for about as wide a range of expression among the terra-cotta ancestors as you'd find among 6,000 Cabbage Patch dolls—the sort of "individuality" that can be computer-generated by a permutational randomizing algorithm.

The trivial differences between the Qin warriors only emphasize their sameness, as though the quirks were introduced just to highlight the overriding discipline of the solemn military cortège. Such merging of distinctions lay at the heart of Shihuangdi's genius—the Great Unifier, the Standardizer, the Legalist Sage. No wonder he chose to face eternity girded amid a human *fasces*, an unbreakably tight-bound bundle of individual, yet interchangeable, "black-haired people."

Yet the terra-cotta legion "represents a humane advance," our guide assures us. Despite the vast cost in man-hours of corvée labor, at least "it's a lot better than the previous practice of burying a real army alive with each dead king." Fair enough. Your measured rate of humanitarian "progress" all depends on your baseline, as China continues to remind us.

Still, scanning this sea of affectless faces, I catch myself wondering whether ancestors, too, might not warrant the basic human right of a richer individuation.

"Anybody out there you know?" I nudge Ah-loong.

"Hmmm. How about that fourth archer from the left," she whispers. "Kind of a Hsu nose, don't you think?"

Our guide shushes us, rapping peremptorily on another wall chart with her swagger stick. "Structurally," she expounds, "the terra-cotta warriors are all hollow."

AFTER THE DAUNTINGLY DISCIPLINED underground city of the dead, it's a relief to plunge into the underground city of the living, where raucous anarchy rules.

On our ride back to downtown, we jump off the tour bus at the Bell Tower, Xian's central plaza. The traffic circle is far too tumultuous for us to broach at street level, so we duck down a grimy little stairwell into what we take for a pedestrian underpass. This unassuming portal turns out to open onto a subterranean crossroads even more convoluted than the daylit street plan upstairs. Tunnels branch off in every direction. This, we realize, must be the hub of the city's celebrated bomb-shelter network.

In the early years of Communist rule, Xian became a showcase of state-sponsored industrialization. Mao set out to shift heavy production westward from the seaboard and the central river valleys to a "Third Line" of economic defense deep in interior China, beyond the reach of American and Taiwanese bombers. Thousands of state enterprises were launched within the first post-Liberation decade; millions of workers and dependents were shipped inland.

In keeping with the strategic rationale of the whole project, Xian and other "Third Line" cities were honeycombed with underground shelters to shield the workforce in case of enemy air raids. As ancestor-in-chief of the People's Republic, Mao could often adopt an unnervingly long view of his progeny's prospects. If even a fraction of China's multitude could live through a global nuclear holocaust, he reasoned, it would still be enough to swamp the surviving Western populations and usher in a new Red millennium—hence his oft-quoted dismissal of America's nuclear arsenal as a "paper tiger."

Mercifully, his calculus was never put to the test. In the event of an actual conflagration, Mao's molehills might have turned into mass graves incomparably grislier than any imperial necropolis. Instead, with the ebb of Cold War nuclear paranoia, the bomb shelters have now become prime underground real estate, rented out to amusement arcades, video parlors, karaoke dens, and such. In Xian, the tunnels bore heedlessly through some of the richest archaeological strata in China to link the Bell Tower with each of the four main gates in the city wall.

The underground "boulevards" feel far more mobbed than the sidewalks above. Maybe it's just a claustrophobic illusion, a trick of low-wattage half-light and echoing footfalls, but a lot more people seem to have midday errands down here than in the shops and offices upstairs. Passersby dart through the miasma of cigarette smoke without making eye contact, avoiding collisions by sheer sonar, I suppose. We choose a tunnel at random and head away from the Bell Tower hub.

The subterranean honky-tonk crowd is as exclusively male as the terra-cotta legions of Qin. But the catacombs must have some feminine habituées, too, judging from the signage. Karaoke joints display glossy photos of the "hostesses" within, curiously demure in tight-fitting *qi pao* sheaths buttoned primly up to the neck. A hole-in-the-wall peep show promises a "Scientific Contortional Display." The star scientist of the show is painted in peachy flesh tones on the velveteen entry flap with a very few sequins strategically stitched onto her for scintillating concealment. A fawning barker offers to draw the curtain for me; Ah-loong quickens her pace.

The neon pulse and the contrapuntal blare of Cantonese pop tunes and techno-rock hurry us along until the whole throbbing corridor births us up through a stairwell. We emerge gasping and blinking, like beached Jonahs, to find ourselves amid a dusty plain of demolition debris. Nobody in sight and no trace of habitation—just some boarded-up storefronts and Qing-era gateways attest to what once must have been a densely packed traditional neighborhood. A few half-intact brick walls support makeshift tarpaulin shelters. At least there's still electricity, evidently; a nearby loudspeaker barks something strident, repetitious, and unintelligible.

We follow this sound, for want of any other point of orientation. But before we can locate the squawk-box, we come upon a noodle vendor incongruously crying his wares along the obliterated "street." His spruce little pushcart contrasts strikingly with the surrounding desolation: hand-stretched spinach noodles nestle in a glass case, tomatoes, peppers, and onions gleam alongside his cutting board, his wok steams briskly on a charcoal brazier. His white pillbox hat, starchy as a chef's toque, identifies him as a Hui Muslim.

"Where in the world are we?" I ask, relieved to find some guide in this wasteland.

"Where do you want to be?" he shrugs. "That way to Town Hall," he nods to the left. "This way's the City Wall," he waves off to the right. "And here's lunch," he adds, grandly unlimbering a couple of wooden stools for us from his cart. Seems like the best hospitality we're likely to run into in the immediate vicinity, so we take him up on his offer.

The noodles turn out to be excellent, topped with a kind of tomato chutney. Ah-loong compliments the chef, but then asks the obvious: "What are you *doing* here?"

"Well, I live here. This is where I was born and raised," the Hui replies, pointing out a blue plastic lean-to nearby. The brick wall it's attached to, he relates, is all that's left of an old courtyard house where his parents were assigned a "temporary" room upon relocating from Henan in the 1950s to take up work in a state-run roller bearing factory. The family lived there for decades, waiting for permanent work-unit housing on the plant site. The wait went on even after the parents retired and the son inherited the factory job. And then, two years ago, the plant went under; not officially bankrupt, but unable to meet its payroll or to continue production.

"So now we've got no work unit *and* no housing," he laughs. Much as I admire his aplomb in the face of disaster, I still don't get the joke. I can see how the collapse of a public enterprise could blast his livelihood and his permanent housing prospects, but how could it wipe out a whole neighborhood like this, which must have "temporarily" housed families from a variety of units?

"Oh, *that's* another story. It's all thanks to you foreigners," he affably explains. "Once the tourists started coming, downtown real estate became too valuable to waste on the likes of us." Taiwan and Hong Kong interests bought up large tracts to develop into shopping malls and condominia. But, when successive financial crises slashed credit to the property sector, many of these grandiose plans got shelved. The development freeze hit after the old neighborhoods were flattened but before the promised replacement housing could be built. That left evicted tenants in a drawn-out limbo, with no place to live.

"But at least I've got a pushcart and I can stretch some noodles," he brightly concludes.

"So how's the noodle business?" I ask.

"Not great, but not so bad, either," he allows. "I've still got some customers right here in the neighborhood. There are more of us hanging on around here than you'd ever guess just by looking at the place. Besides, there's always the picket trade."

"Pickets?" I ponder. Living in Beijing, even my vocabulary of dissent has grown rusty.

"You know," he coaxes, "demonstrators, protest marchers. These days we average a rally a week around here. Sometimes it's to protest housing evictions. Sometimes it's about work-unit lockouts. Now and then the imam calls us out to denounce some anti-Islamic slur in a school textbook or a newspaper. Whenever there's a demonstration, I just pile on some extra stools and roll my cart down there to Town Hall. You get hundreds of people at a time and, if the march goes on long enough, everybody gets hungry sooner or later.

"Not that our protests ever make any difference. And we can't go on forever selling noodles to each other when nobody around here's getting paid . . ."

Ah-loong and I split an extra bowl of noodles between us—just to enhance his cash flow, we tell ourselves. Then, carbo-loaded, we follow the noodle man's directions to the City Wall. Climbing the zigzag path up to the ramparts, we look back over Xian. The skyline is still low-rise, in cobweb-colored brick, interspersed with concrete or stucco office blocks. Off on the other side of town, a couple of chrome-and-glass hotels or department stores have already sprung up, overtopping the Bell Tower. Here and there a construction crane gangles, ominously unmoving. All over Xian, broad swathes of rubble scar the vista.

Even from up here we can still make out the slogans spray-painted on the few surviving walls in the streets we just came from: "Snails Without Shells—No Home to Return To." On boarded-up shop windows, the local residents' association has plastered handbills demanding relocation help from the city government and the overseas Chinese tycoons who demolished the neighborhood.

At last we spot the source of the electronic yammer that's been dogging us all afternoon: a solitary loudspeaker strung high on a lamp-post. And now we can finally decipher its tape-loop harangue. It's a grassroots appeal to the real estate developers for redress: "Hong Kong and Taiwan brothers—how can you ignore us? Aren't we all sons of the Yellow Emperor?"

"SONS AND BROTHERS, emperors and troopers," Ah-loong sighs. "Enough machismo for one morning, don't you think? And enough trudging in the dust. Isn't there anyplace a girl can get a bath around here?"

No point in my disclaiming personal responsibility for the pulverization of inner-city Xian. Sticky, train-weary, and footsore after the morning's exertion, Ah-loong has had about all she can take of backpack travel for now. And it's all my fault for dreaming up this hyperactive weekend junket and patriarchally quick-marching her around the tourist circuit. When such a mood overtakes her, experience has taught me, there's no use protesting.

The best bet, instead, is a quick change of pace. Our view from the city wall hardly tempts us back into Xian's ruined precincts, anyway. I bury my nose in our Shaanxi guidebook, looking for a more congenial spot to stay the night. "How about here?" I propose, flipping to the page about suburban Li Shan, some twenty miles out of town. The book describes a landscaped hillside park surrounding a provincial government spa, Huaqing Hot Spring.

What's more, as an antidote to the all-male Qin necropolis and the bomb shelter honky-tonks, Li Shan enshrines a pair of formidable women. A temple at the top is dedicated to the primordial Earth Mother, Nu Wa, while the thermal pool at the base was where the Tang dynasty imperial concubine Yang Gui-fei had her poetically celebrated bath. Two more dissimilar icons of femininity would be hard to imagine.

Nu Wa, half woman and half snake, must derive, like the biblical Lilith, from a goddess figure of matriarchal prehistory. Her cult is so ancient and so much at odds with the subsequent patriarchal pantheon that her origins have long since been forgotten. She just appears, sui generis, at the beginning of time, patching up cracks in the leaky primordial firmament to prevent an inundation of Chaos from swamping the nascent cosmos.

She's so lonely on the uninhabited earth that she takes to molding people out of mud, just to have someone to talk to. Soon Nu Wa has a retinue of high-toned, aristocratic courtiers, but there are still not enough of them to satisfy her very Chinese craving for crowds. So she invokes another proto-Chinese penchant of hers—a genius for mass production—to fill out the populace. Instead of handcrafting each person, she trails a vine in the primordial ooze and then flails it about like a bullwhip to spatter the world with mud droplets that turn into a plebian human multitude. Which may be why, to this day, the Chinese refer to uncouth yokels as "dirt dumplings."

Nothing so earthy about Yang Gui-fei, on the other hand. Her dazzling beauty precipitated the sudden eclipse of China's most glorious dynasty at the very apogee of its power. Her fateful bath at Huaqing Hot Spring, immortalized by the contemporary poet Po Chu-yi, is the Chinese literary equivalent of the "face that launched a thousand ships." Nor does Po Chu-yi stop at the neck in his panegyric. He goes on to dotingly detail the rest of her: "hot spring water, limpid, rinsing the dewy flesh," etcetera, etcetera.

These charms so beguiled the Tang emperor Ming Huang that, just to indulge her, he willingly turned over command of his crack armies to Yang Gui-fei's favorite court buffoon, a fat and uncouth Turk. No sooner did he consolidate his generalship, though, than the Turk turned upon his royal patrons and marched on Xian, forcing the emperor and consort to flee. The dispirited imperial guard, in full retreat, mutinied against Ming Huang, demanding the death of the fateful temptress who'd precipitated the whole disaster.

When it came down to a choice between offering up her head or his own, the emperor tearfully consented to the execution of Yang Gui-fei—the "everlasting wrong" mourned in Po Chu-yi's title and in countless operatic perorations ever since. Legend has thoroughly glamorized what may have struck Tang court insiders at the time as no more than a tawdry "wag-the-dog" scandal. Such is the romantically soft focus of a millennium of historic hindsight.

EVEN A FEW DECADES of hindsight can do wonders for some historic pariahs, as we discover upon arrival at Li Shan. Alighting from the highway bus, we step right into what feels like a time warp: the spa gardens swarm with troops in 1930s uniforms. Those in gray tunics sport the starburst insignia of Chiang Kai-shek's KMT. Dun fatigues denote warlord troops from Manchuria. For a moment we stare agog at what looks like a ghostly coup d'état by long-dead regiments. The slap-happy fraternization of the two armies, though, belies any sense of military emergency.

I sidle up to an incongruously gum-chewing "Manchurian" officer, quaintly uniformed in garrison belt and puttees. Ever so politely, in deference to the outsized revolver holstered at his hip, I ask him, "Excuse me, Lieutenant, sir, but I wonder what unit might you belong to?"

"Shaanxi People's Militia," he grins, puffing a faint whiff of Juicy Fruit my way. To ease my evident bafflement, he explains that he is an extra in a TV movie: *The Xian Incident*.

Perfect—yet another remake of what has to be the most spin-doctored episode in modern Chinese history. Yet oddly appropriate, too, for the Qing Ming weekend—a chance for the Party to spruce up the posthumous memorials of its own ancestors while at the same time maybe appeasing a Hungry Ghost or two from the Other Side.

The Xian crisis of 1936 was precipitated by "Young Marshal" Zhang Xueliang, a progressive warlord whom the KMT regime placed in command of Shaanxi after he'd been ousted from his hereditary Manchurian stronghold by the invading Japanese. As far as Chiang Kai-shek was concerned, Zhang's main mission was to contain Mao's Yenan base. Generalissimo Chiang would just as soon downplay resistance to the Japanese invasion and stockpile his Western-donated ordnance for later use against his Chinese factional foes on the left.

But the headstrong warlord had other priorities: a patriotic "United Front" with Mao to drive Japan from Chinese soil. When Chiang visited Xian to urge a concerted "final push" against the Communists, the Young Marshal had him kidnapped from his holiday villa here at Hua Qing. The Manchurian troops held their nominal commander in chief hostage until he verbally agreed to a civil war truce and a joint campaign with the Reds against the foreign invaders.

The United Front interlude gave Mao enough breathing room to rebuild his forces from a battered remnant of about ten thousand Long March veterans into a tidal wave of nearly a million regular troops and twice as many militia by V-J Day in 1945. But it wasn't so much the tactical setback as the humiliation that most galled the Generalissimo; he never forgave his Xian captor. Zhang would remain under house arrest for the next five decades, first in China (as long as the KMT held out there) and later in Taiwan (after Chiang's rout).

As a magazine correspondent in Taipei, I got to meet the Young Marshal on the occasion of his ninetieth birthday reception. It was his first unmediated contact with outsiders in fifty-three years. Prior to that, his last public appearance had been on Christmas, 1936, when he'd freed Chiang and flown with his erstwhile hostage to the KMT's wartime capital in Sichuan. By the time of his ninetieth birthday, the once fiery warlord could barely slice his own cake—a far cry from the dashing figure he must once have cut.

But on this Hua Qing film set, the glamour of the 1930s lives on undimmed, at least to judge by the crowd of enthusiastic day-trippers craning for a glimpse. The fans swarm around the original bungalow where Chiang was kidnapped, waiting for the actors to finish shooting an indoor sequence. The door jamb still bears bullet holes, I note, presumably from Manchurian troops' commando assault. Klieg lights inside the villa project silhouettes against the frosted-glass windows. Then the lights click off and the doors swing open.

"Chiang Kai-shek" emerges through the heavy, lacquered portal, fanning himself with a handkerchief to keep the residual heat of the arclamps from sweat-streaking his makeup. Ah-loong, beside me, gasps audibly—the reflexive heart clutch of suddenly meeting a dead and unwelcome relative in a waking nightmare.

For it was as a relative that Chiang was presented to her throughout her childhood in Taiwan: Jiang Gong, "Venerable Uncle Chiang." He was so designated in her schoolbooks, full of heartwarming accounts of his selfless dedication to his "national family." Thus was he introduced on the radio when, in his unintelligible Zhejiang dialect, he'd offer his annual New Year felicitations to his subjects. Even his portrait, beaming from every banknote, billboard, and classroom wall, was somehow made to look all twinkly and avuncular, despite its innately sharp and foxy little features.

And this is the benign visage that now appears in the doorway   a far cry from Chiang's usual movie portrayal in mainland historical epics, as a petulant, cunning little runt, smirky and scowly by turns. Gone are the customary eye shadow, the sallow pancake makeup, and archly penciled brows. Now it's all silver hair and silver smiles, just as the Generalissimo is depicted in his Taipei mausoleum. The people around us note, without enthusiasm, the deviation from established norms of Chiang Kai-shekery.

"*Wah!* He's actually *grinning!*"

"Gruesome, isn't it?"

"Who *is* that, anyway?" I ask the middle-aged movie buff in front of us. He explains that the same actor, a mini-star named Sun, has specialized for decades in playing the Generalissimo in mainland costume dramas. China cranks out so many of these historic epics that any ham can attain minor celebrity merely by physical resemblance to some past luminary. Stick with it long enough and an actor can even aspire to a certain histrionic range; in the current production, Sun graduates from Chiang-as-villain to Chiang-as-hero. According to cinema fanzines, our movie buff tells us, this latest update of *The Xian Incident* will stress how, when the chips were down, Chiang altruistically buried his differences with the Communists for the sake of the nation.

But why, just at this juncture, would the Party choose to rehabilitate its old arch rival, Chiang? Must be aimed at Taiwan, I speculate, especially now that TV movies like this can be distributed on both sides of the strait. Compared to Taiwan's current crop of "splittist" politicians, even the Generalissimo must seem to the Beijing regime these days a very paragon of filial devotion to the Chinese fatherland.

If such an ideal could inspire "Venerable Uncle Chiang," then it ought still to resonate—so this new *Xian Incident* remake might wish to imply—with his devoted nieces and nephews on Taiwan today. Meanwhile, to mainland viewers, refurbishing the Generalissimo can be projected as a gesture of reconciliation toward the "renegade province." And if it's spurned by the Taiwanese ingrates, at least Beijing gets credit for trying.

The only trouble with such reasoning is that, on either side of the Taiwan Strait, there hardly remains enough of a Chiang Kai-shek constituency to be worth coopting anymore. Among Taiwan's 85-percent island-born majority, his name mainly evokes memories of martial law, cultural repression, civilian massacres, and "white terror" police methods. He's a relative, all right, but an abusive one who is now widely rejected and despised by his estranged "national family." Mainlanders, for their part, may not nurse quite so lively an animus against Chiang, but neither do they care much about him. He's already been reduced to a set piece, just a prop in the Party's self-aggrandizing mythology of its own pre-Liberation heroics—a subject that most modern viewers find boring or, at best, campy, as evinced by the crowd's reaction when Sun appears in the doorway in his Chiang Kai-shek makeup.

Evidently the film crew has been shooting only close-ups inside the bungalow, for the actor's not in costume. Instead, he's decked out in fashionably casual blue jeans, workshirt, and loafers (no socks). The incongruity sends titters through the crowd, since most historic images show the preening, foppish Generalissimo either in a floor-length Confucian scholar's gown or else on horseback with swagger stick, kepi, and military cape. The snickers turn to guffaws when, in a waspish, nasal whine quite like Chiang's actual recorded voice, Sun turns to his retinue of studio flunkies behind him and demands, "Where are my pajamas?"

It's no idle movie-star rant, though. The actor will be needing a pair of pajamas for his climactic scene. Chiang, hearing the rifle fire outside and fearing the worst, bolts from his bed and out the bungalow's back window without pausing to dress. In his haste, he even leaves his false teeth in a bedside glass, as every Chinese pupil learns in gradeschool (on the mainland, anyhow, though not in Taiwan). Barefoot, the Generalissimo runs half a mile or more up a steep and brambly mountainside. Coming upon a chimneylike crevasse in the cliff, he scrambles straight up the sheer rock and cowers there until the Manchurian troops come and yank him out by his heels.

RATHER THAN WAIT around for Sun's costume change, Ah-loong and I decide to head up the mountainside to view the sunset. Our route retraces Chiang's panicked flight, except that nowadays the path is nicely paved with flagstones and lined with trinket vendors. The crevasse where Chiang once cringed has now been fitted out with iron banisters to help tourists clamber up. The stone is worn smooth and black by sixty-odd years of knees and backsides.

Gum wrappers and cigarette butts silt up on the narrow rock shelf of his roost. No time today, though, for anybody to enjoy a leisurely smoke: weekend day-trippers perch there one after another, briskly popping their snapshots and making way for the next in line. Gawky schoolboys, doddering grandmas, uniformed soldiers, high-heeled fashion plates—the place is as crowded as a downtown boulevard. At the mouth of the crevasse, picnickers avail themselves of a little pagoda-style gazebo.

A freshly painted signboard dubs this the "Pavilion of Soldierly Remonstrance," and explains how the Manchurian officers' hortations so stirred the Generalissimo's patriotism that he agreed, there and then, to enter into an anti-Japanese United Front. This version of events would seem to be part of the same Chiang-rehabilitation effort as the film-shoot we've just seen. Contemporary accounts relate that it took weeks of tense negotiation to bring the crisis to its highly equivocal Christmas Day resolution. Even the gazebo has been re-named, evidently: older guidebooks, like the one we've got, refer to it as the "Grab Chiang Pavilion," using a dismissive verb whose ideogram depicts a hand holding someone by the feet.

Back at the base of the hill, we'd declined the offer of bamboo sedan chairs, preferring to go under our own steam and at our own pace. Still, even this leisurely stroll leaves us soaked with sweat by the time we reach Chiang's hiding place. What a lather of fear must have propelled the hyperfastidious Generalissimo, unshod and toothless, and already fifty years old at the time, to cover this distance pell-mell in his nightshirt. And how he'd chafe now to see what a carnival had sprung up around the locus of his chagrin.

"Poor old Venerable Uncle," Ah-loong murmurs, feeling her first twinge of sympathy for Chiang since gradeschool. Ancestors, even estranged ones, still seem entitled to at least a little dignity in death. They may have sloughed off their bodies, but they still have "face" to preserve.

Right now, though, we're more concerned about preserving our own feet, as our incipient corns are starting to remind us after a long day's touristic walkabout. We decide to skip the Nu Wa temple and head downhill to the spa. The thought of a thermal soak sounds pretty attractive by now, especially in the same mineral spring that once lapped the delectable Yang Gui-fei.

Same spring, perhaps, but hardly the same tub. Nowadays, the thermal flow debouches into a down-at-the-heels Stalinist sanatorium. After persuading a suspicious matron that we're really married enough to be allowed to share a bath, we're assigned a concrete basin in a white tile cubicle. Sprawled side-by-side in the fluoride-laden water, we stare at the mildewed ceiling. I find it easier to conjure up Po Chu-yi's verses if I turn my back on the swinging, naked sixty-watt bulb overhead. I flip over on my belly to contemplate Ah-loong through a scrim of fluoridated steam. Now *that's* more like it. Limpid water. Dewy flesh. Etcetera.

THAT HOT SPRING must contain some secret ingredient beyond plain old fluorides, for we wake up feeling marvelously scrubbed, sleek, and revitalized, with all our kinks smoothed out. Morning light limns the bamboos and boxwoods in the Hua Qing garden. After a last thermal dip, we emerge, slightly steaming, into the cool April air. To preserve our mood of morning freshness, we stop on our way into town at the Banpo archaeological dig for a glimpse at what our guide-book describes as the "dawn of the Chinese race."

Researchers have unearthed there a complete Neolithic village nes-tled in an unassuming riverbend—some forty-five houses, six pottery kilns, and nearly 250 graves. The site is now roofed over and engulfed in a nondescript suburb of Xian barely a mile off the main road in from Li Shan. To get there, we jump off our bus at the Chan River bridge and follow the banks as best we can, skirting factory walls and residential compounds.

At this early hour, before the influx of horn-blaring tour buses, we can still hear the purling of the river and the cries of waterbirds. The suburban streets, offset from the bank, contribute a muffled over-lay of neighborhood wake-up sounds—laughter, scolding, spitting, gargling, and kitchen clatter. If we ignore the occasional burst of radio music, we could almost convince ourselves that little has changed from the bustling Banpo of 4,000 B.C., at least as concerns the sonic landscape.

Not so the sights and smells. In those days, this place would have been a steaming marshland surrounded by dense forest. Geologic evi-dence suggests the Shaanxi loess plains were hotter in Neolithic times and much more humid. These climatic differences are reflected in the excavated house sites—round or rectangular pits, half-sunk into the ground, with pediments for wooden frameworks to support conical canopies. Such structures would never withstand the frosts or dust storms of modern-day Xian. No evidence of a stockade around Neo-lithic Banpo; just a shallow drainage ditch to mark the periphery of the village.

A diorama in the Provincial Museum brings home to us how dras-tic an environmental and cultural transformation separates historic China from its earliest traceable antecedents. The village, as depicted, looks more Polynesian than anything we'd think of as Chinese—

thatched roofs on airy log-frame houses, lissome maidens in grass skirts, naked children and rooting piglets.

Family groups lounge around cookfires. Klatches of women plait beads into each other's tresses. An old grandpa dandles a toddler. Younger men busy themselves hand-molding clay urns or trimming logs for new houseframes. A stout crone, elaborately coifed and supported on the arms of two younger matrons, advances to meet a returning party of hunters—the village matriarch? Some children play with the capering dogs. Others tote water jars or firewood bundles. The hunters parade a trussed boar down the main "street," trying (in vain, it seems) to catch the attention of the flower-bedecked *wahines*.

The whole tableau evokes in me a sense of déjà vu—not so much race memory, I realize, as a reawakening of preadolescent fantasies. I think of myself on a sixth-grade school trip, nose pressed to the glass of the Quaternary Gallery at the Natural History Museum in New York, mentally disporting with the bare-breasted root-gatherers on some prehistoric savanna. But the last place I'd expect to find my soft-porn daydreams echoed would be a Chinese government shrine to Han ancestral grandeur. I wonder if Ah-loong shares any such erotic reveries.

"So which of these people do you think would be our Neolithic incarnations?" I ask her, noting a handsome, spear-toting hunter as he hands over a game bird to a raven-haired beauty at the door of what must be their connubial hut. But my wife has other ideas. "*That* would have been me"—she points out a harried mother, crouched over her cookfire with a squalling baby strapped to her back. "And that one's you"—she indicates a half-recumbent slacker fishing by the riverbank.

Ha! Fat chance she'd ever let me get away with such a distribution of labor, least of all in the Stone Age world of Banpo. Our guidebook assures us that women ruled the roost here, according to the archaeological evidence. In the earliest Neolithic burial sites, bodies were sorted by gender rather than kinship groups. Each corpse was accompanied by its own modest set of tools and ornaments, with women marginally better-adorned than men. Only later came such innovations as family burial plots with elaborate, class-differentiated grave goods. Next came improved weaponry, larger domesticated animals, and defensive village walls. And by then, anthropologists theorize, China had already evolved the rudiments of a rigidly patriarchical, authoritarian, clan-based society.

So how did the stern sons of the Yellow Emperor evolve from those easygoing daughters of Nu Wa? What centuries of skulduggery and browbeating, what genocides and eco-catastrophes must have intervened? Ah-loong and I, each for our own reasons, sigh for the lost idyll of prehistory as we survey the diorama's pastel, Gauguinesque village vignette.

Nothing pastel, though, about the actual Banpo pottery on display in the next gallery: burnished red-and-black ware, the same color scheme as classic Grecian urns. Except instead of graceful nymphs and satyrs, the Neolithic Chinese emblazoned their pottery with violent loops and whorls or eerily expressionless masklike faces and totemic animals too hybridized to name. Wizened little runes incised on the vessels are supposed to be the precursors of modern Chinese ideograms. These pots hardly strike me as artifacts from the sunny morning of the world; more like the somber vestiges of a hardscrabble culture with a grim pantheon to propitiate.

Who knows what ancient and implacable forces are depicted in those masks and swirls? Maybe these ancestors had ancestors to worry about, too.

BOARDING THE BUS for Huangdi Ling, we find the Xian depot as densely packed with bodies as the terra-cotta warrior pits in the Qin necropolis. Much the same ethnic mix, too, as the terra-cotta legions, with Uighurs and Hui seeded among the Han. Even the facial features might be reducible to the ten basic physiognomic types our guide had described. Except, instead of the unnerving terra-cotta passivity of the tomb guardians, these bus depot visages are frantically animated. Funereal decorum and soldierly discipline are conspicuous in their absence.

Elbowing and shoving, a phalanx of passengers tries to squeeze through the door. Others attempt a flanking action, either diving in head first through the open bus windows or tossing in bundles to serve as proxies in the scramble for seats. The desperate scrum is joined without acrimony or quarter—just a single-minded concentration on staking out some chair space, a perch on the baggage mounds, or at least a patch of standing room and a strap to hang from.

Somehow all the people and bundles get stowed aboard and the ancient bus shakes itself awake. We wheeze our way out of the depot and strike north from the corner of the city wall. Ah-loong and I roost just behind the driver, thanks to the reserved tickets we'd bought the previous day. Not that seat numbers necessarily count for much in the predeparture scrimmage, but my alien face earns us a wider berth than most passengers.

So we ride in state, enjoying the cinematically unfolding landscape: broad fields of newly sprouted spring wheat interspersed with blue-green garlic and flamboyant mustard flowers. We cross the Wei, a Yellow River tributary, and then mount a rise through steeply terraced fields. At first, it looks like much the same tidy topography you find all over China—slabs of cropland bordered by a mosaic of terraces, then more fields atop the butte.

But deep fissures score some of the higher terraces, and the tableland is pocked with intermittent sinkholes. We thread our way down the far side of one mesa and up the next one. With each successive butte the blemishes become more pronounced. The fields shear off in great naps and folds of splintery earth. The crops grow sparser and the tableland narrower until we hardly even feel like we're mesa-hopping anymore; rather just teetering along a raised spine of roadbed between precipitous gorges. In this most friable of soils, what starts off as an unassuming little gully up here at the top of the ridge unravels into a broad talus slope by the time it reaches the valley floor. Looking across the gorge, we can trace the scars and gashes on the opposite saddle-rise.

Nothing can grow on these ruined hillsides except a few gnarled, tenacious trees. Just at this time of year, though, they're in their glory—wild plum and almond, all in bloom. Against the consumptive yellow of the wasted soil, the blossoms stand out wraithlike, white as paper spirit trees. The only other dab of color is the colicky green of new wheat in scattered terraces. For the rest—the earth, the stream courses, even the sky—everything is daubed in various shades of dun.

This is the so-called yellow which has lent its name to the central China plateau, the river of "China's sorrow," and the primordial "Yellow Emperor" himself. It's one of the tiredest colors in the world. Not depressing, really; even cozy, in its way, like the tatty fuzz of a well-worn teddy bear or a thoroughly broken-in old camel. But after just an hour of the loess lands, an expectation of monotony sets in. The narrow palette leaves the eye jaundiced.

To liven up the ride, we take up a peculiarly Shaanbei road game: the search for the Edgar point. Ever since we passed through the Xian city gate, we've been on the same road that Snow took to his fateful tryst with the Reds. At some point along the way—he never reveals just where—he passed from Chiang Kai-shek's "White" zone into Mao's soviet. As far as Snow was concerned, he was voyaging into an alternative reality: "People's China," more vivid and original, more compassionate and pure than the callously exploitative empire of the ruling KMT.

Behind him lay the cities, where "the well-fed foreigners could live in their own little never-never land . . . quite unaware of the pulse of humanity outside." Ahead was a "strange iron brotherhood . . . that levelled out individuals, lost them, made them really forget their own identity and yet find it somehow in the kind of fierce freedom and rigor and hardship they shared."

But Snow is coy, in *Red Star*, about just where lay the frontier between these two realities. "To state precisely the manner in which, just as I had hoped, I did pass the last sentry and enter no man's land might have caused serious difficulties," he writes. "Suffice it to say that my experience proved once more that anything is possible in China, if it is done in the Chinese manner."

In that same oblique manner, I'm convinced, it's *still* possible to touch earth in People's China. And only so can we escape the cynical bamboozlement and crass get-rich-is-glorious ethos of the current imperium, which ironically now styles itself Red.

So, finding that mysterious frontier—the Edgar point—becomes our bus game. Just where along this road did Snow actually cross over and enter that zone of heightened authenticity? Was it behind that ridge? Up this valley? And where can *we* cross over and access the secret, subversive heart of the land? Inside this cave? Via that village? For in every age, for every traveler, there's always an Edgar point—or so I'd like to believe—even if it's constantly shifting from one moment to the next.

OUR GAME KEEPS US alert to the wilder possibilities of the landscape. We scan every copse, hut, and gully, every roadside bystander, as a potential window to the "other side." But about three hours out of Xian, instead of our finding alternative reality through our watchfulness, alternative reality comes dancing straight down the highway to find us.

Just as our bus is chugging in first gear to the top of yet another rise, our ambulatory Edgar point appears in sackcloth, squarely in the middle of the road. He hunkers in a semi-crouch, sweeping the potholes with a short-handled broom. His scraggly beard flaps as though he's muttering something to himself. His sparse ponytail is done up in a topknot, half-unraveled. The ingrained black of his burlap swaddling could betoken Taoist religious vestments. Or, then again, it could be just a deeper accretion of the same streaky patina that coats his face, neck, and spindly legs.

At the sound of our claxon, he rises up on one leg, tucking the other one beneath him, stork-wise. He raises his broom in a solemn present-arms, then tucks it smartly under his left elbow with the handle clutched to his chest, like a drum major. His right arm shoots straight out at us, waving in an elaborate series of finger-wiggling, wrist-rolling gestures. The whites of his eyeballs gleam against his grimy complexion as he stares down the bus, sighting over his right shoulder.

"*Ta ma-de!* [mother-jump!]—it's him again!" our driver curses, simultaneously working the brake, clutch, and horn for all he's worth. The road dancer doesn't budge, except to swing his broom once over his head in a slow, triumphant arc. Our engine sputters, coughs, and dies. The face in the windshield, now barely two yards in front of us, blinks in delighted surprise. The jaw snaps shut, beard waggling, in a tight little grimace of satisfaction. Then he shoulders his broom with great deliberation and struts in a kind of fluid goose step right past the stalled bus and on down the road.

Nobody seems greatly upset. Passengers go on chatting, snoozing, or eating as before. Our driver can't even bother to hurl imprecations; he's too busy standing on the brake pedal and cranking the starter motor in hopes of reviving the engine before it goes cold. No luck. At last he gives up, locks the transmission in gear, and sends his conductor out to block the wheels with stones.

Shooing a few squatters off the engine hump beside the driver's seat, he throws open the metal cover and starts tapping experimentally with a box wrench. Only then, as steam and fumes roll down the aisle, do the passengers begin to shamble out the bus doors, still without missing a beat in their ongoing conversations. Such contretemps must be pretty humdrum around here, judging from the general equanimity.

People unlimber their bundles from the luggage racks and line them up on the road shoulder. A family finds a knoll for a picnic. A young mother sits on the front bumper, calmly nursing her baby. The driver has already given up tinkering with the carburetor from inside the bus. Now he lies flat on his back under the chassis, handtesting the various levers and connecting rods. A few young men slide under the bus to kibitz and linger there to nap. I try it out myself: very restful, shady and cool, with an interesting, upside-down, worm's-eye view of the surrounding loess hills and the milling passengers—alternative reality, indeed.

My reverie is shattered, though, by a sudden stir in the crowd around me. Someone's spotted a bus coming our way, presumably the next one to have left Xian after our departure. Our driver emerges, grease-spattered, to flag down his colleague in the other vehicle. The teenagers who had been snoring beside me now casually distribute themselves across the road, just to help the next driver resist any temptation to roll on past us. People shoulder their bags as though ready to hurl them at the oncoming bus like catapult stones.

The new bus, already as packed as ours had been, rolls to a halt amid clouds of dust and exhaust. Its driver keeps his engine revving lest he be caught in the same sort of stall-out that idled us here. Before our driver can even finish shouting his story over the engine din, our fellow passengers have already pried the doors open and started cramming in. I can't imagine how this overstuffed vehicle could possibly accommodate a double-charge of humanity. Already, heads and elbows are starting to ooze out all the windows like runnels of toothpaste leaking from a burst tube.

"Hey, what are we making here—sausage?" a voice rings out in the flat, nasal accent of Shaanbei. The owner of this commanding baritone appears at the bus door, bespectacled and pomaded, to bar the way of a five-foot-tall peasant with a six-foot-long duffel. "*How* are you going to cram a great big wad like that into a tight little nook like this, Grandpa?" he laughs. The old man backs off with a sheepish smile.

The young baritone steps down off the bus. For such a short man, he is tautly muscled under his crisp, white polyester shirt. He hardly looks like a Shaanbei bumpkin, but he reels off the local dialect with disarming fluency. "How about we stash this stuff up there on the roof rack?" he proposes, relieving "Grandpa" of his duffel. He surveys the crowd through his horn-rims and picks out a couple of lanky kids. "You two climb up to stow things snugly. And you"—this to a sturdy farmer—"stand on the bumper and help pass things up to them."

The designated stevedores assume their posts without even a shadow of hesitancy. A human chain of baggage handlers is set up. People meekly surrender their bundles to be passed hand-to-hand up to the roof rack. The bespectacled baritone directs the whole operation without barking any orders, just suggesting solutions and joshing people into compliance.

After all the baggage is loaded from the roadside, he starts in on the people already aboard the bus, persuading them to commit their bundles, too, to the roof rack. That way, he explains, we'll have room to fit all the extra passengers. Three more boys clamber up to the roof to receive another round of luggage passed up through the windows—cardboard suitcases, flour sacks, plastic buckets, even a bamboo cage full of live chickens. The driver of our defunct bus produces a striped plastic tarpaulin and the whole tottering mound of chattel is tied down with a tow rope.

Now to reshuffle the seating inside the bus. Laps are found for all the children. A uniformed schoolboy yields his seat to the nursing mother. People scrunch over to accommodate elders. "Slender as you are, don't you think you could make a little more space?" our self-appointed factotum flatters a delighted matron. Some teenage standees are dispatched to "keep an eye on things" by self-importantly riding upstairs with the freight.

And, as the last piece in the jigsaw puzzle, a precarious perch is found on the engine hump up front for Ah-loong and me, "our foreign friends." Our master of ceremonies plants himself on the dashboard facing us, with his back propped against the windshield.

WE'RE BOWLED OVER by his take-charge style. "How did you *do* that, anyway?" I ask.

He replies in perfect radio-announcer Mandarin, without a trace of Shaanbei twang. "Well, I'm only 'crossing the river by feeling the stones,' " he pronounces, citing Deng Xiaoping's favorite homily for improvisatory social engineering. "You know, just seeing whatever works and going with it. Then, too, of course, I come from here. These are my people, and I know how to handle them. You don't get far pushing them around. They're poor and they're stubborn. They *will* survive, against any odds, and they'll grab whatever it takes to do so.

"Left to their own devices, they'll climb over each other like scorpions in a pit. But, properly coordinated, they can also work together like an anthill to achieve prodigious things. They mean well and they love to laugh. Sometimes you can joke them into cooperation. Or shame them. Or awe them.

"It also helps that I'm a cop in the culture section of the Provincial Public Security. Detective Hong Guoxing," he introduces himself, and adds that "not too many of our hometown boys get jobs like that, so it *does* count for something with these folks."

It counts with us, too. Knowing we're in the presence of a police officer, we instinctively sit up straighter and try to behave. No more road games.

"Thanks for finding us seats," Ah-loong offers. "It would have been a rough ride, strap-hanging all the way to Huangdi Ling."

"No need to thank me," he demurs. "It's my job. I'm just planting you where I can keep an eye on you. You know, you two aren't even supposed to *be* here without permission. This whole area's under martial law for the duration of Qing Ming."

"Nobody told us . . ." Ah-loong stammers. I, for my part, dumbly echo, "Martial *law* . . . ?"

"Happens all the time," the cop waves, deprecatingly. "Whenever there's an influx of VVIPs. Do promise me, won't you, not to assassinate the entire Provincial People's Political Consultative Committee?"

This strikes me as a macabre joke under the circumstances. Here we are, after all, riding into a proscribed corner of interior China under police observation.

"Well, what should we do *now*?" I wonder aloud.

"Nothing at all," he reassures me. "Just enjoy your ride, since you're already on the bus. We'll decide when we get there." He eyes me up and down once more. "By the way," he inquires, "*Sprechen Sie Deutsch?*"

Not really, I have to admit, but how come *he* does?

"I took up German for my language requirement back at Zhong Shan," he says, naming a top-drawer Canton university as his alma mater. "Mass Communications Department, international news major," he adds with evident pride.

"German's a tough language," I allow, admiringly.

"Nowhere near as hard for me as Cantonese," he laughs. "Not just the language, either, but the whole style. Those southern dandies don't readily take to us 'dirt dumplings' from the interior. You've got to do twice as well as the others just to measure up. I managed to fit in all right, though, after a while. Learned a lot—extracurricular stuff like how to dress, how to dance, how to use a fork and knife. Even how to demonstrate; I joined the student protests in '89. And after graduation, I stayed on for a couple of years, reporting for the *Yangcheng Daily News*."

"Then, how come . . . ?" Ah-loong casts about for a delicate way to pose her question, but Hong anticipates her.

"You mean, why would anyone quit the Canton press corps to become a Shaanxi cop?" he nods. "I did it for love. What else?" His high school sweetheart, daughter of a policeman, had finished law school back in Xian and was now working in the Propaganda Department of the Provincial *Gong An*, the Public Security Bureau.

"That's sweet," Ah-loong beams. "So you came back to get married."

"Nothing moves so fast in the civil service," he sighs. "Our bureau has an eight-year queue for married quarters. And 'No apartment, no wedding,' she says."

"That sounds like a long and lonely wait," I commiserate.

"Long, for sure. But not exactly lonely. While waiting for my apartment, I get to share a barracks with hundreds of others. And, you know what? After Canton, it's a relief in a way. A simple life, and a clean one."

Ah-loong and I just nod, noncommittally, in no mood, under the circumstances, to challenge anything he says. Nevertheless, he feels somehow obliged to defend his assertion.

"I know, 'clean' may not be the first word that comes to mind when you think of life in the *Gong An*. Back in my university days, and even when I was newspapering, I, too, took it for granted that any policeman must automatically be on the take. I forgot what every Shaanbei farmboy ought to know: that no matter how good your seed, if you want your crop to grow tall and straight, you've first got to manure the field.

"Look at your basic beat cop, the way he's paid. Who can raise a family on that kind of money? And doesn't a cop have a right to family life, same as anyone else? How can you ask him to be enlightened when you don't give him the material foundation?"

The word he uses for "enlightened," *wen ming*, translates literally as "bright and cultured," while "material foundation" is a Marxist shibboleth revived by latter-day Chinese economic reformers to justify business-friendly policies. Clearly we're dealing with someone who knows his sociological jargon. He rolls on with more buzzwords, drawing on the lexicon of China's intellectual salons of the reformist 1980s.

"Civil society, rule of law—all those slogans we used to rattle off in university—the only way to make them happen is through building up the material foundation. That's what I've finally figured out since my protest days in '89. We had it all turned around back then. We wanted democracy right away. It doesn't work like that. First you need economic development. Which is what I now tell any student hotheads I run into. Not that I come upon a whole lot of radicals these days, even though my unit's in charge of policing campuses."

As a police intellectual—a relatively rare breed—Hong naturally got assigned to the bureau's Cultural Section, handling (besides campuses) such issues as copyright protection, pornography, and religious affairs. I guess police attention to these topics must be sporadic at best, judging from what we'd come across in just a couple of days' casual, touristic rubber-necking in Xian: pirated books and tapes, X-rated peep shows, and curbside displays of zany millennial tracts.

"So which of these missions takes up most of your time?" I gingerly inquire.

"Oh, none of *those* jobs," Hong allows. "In a place like Xian, our main task is relic preservation. Not just defending designated monuments—that's the easy part. But Shaanbei is so strewn with archaeological treasures that nobody really knows what to protect or where. Why, even the famous terra-cotta warriors themselves only came to light when the commune just happened to dig a well out there. How can we send a cop every time somebody decides to dowse for water?

Let's not even *mention* the grave robbers and antique forgers. They get better and busier by the month."

These crooks, he says, have been spurred to new heights by the flow of tourists and the spread of collection fever in Hong Kong, Taiwan, and Chinatowns around the world. "We've got to really know our material to monitor the antiques markets. Some of the forgeries are good enough to fool top experts. And some of the genuine artifacts that go missing are so important that you start to wonder if there isn't some kind of organized plot to smuggle our cultural heritage overseas.

"Which is why we need to be extra vigilant," he adds, eyeing us appraisingly from his dashboard perch, "every time we draw large numbers of you foreigners to our archaeological sites for an occasion like this."

On this wary note, we roll into Huangdi Ling.

AS IT TURNS OUT, here in Shaanxi, "martial law" doesn't quite mean the bristling array of tanks and bayonets that the phrase would connote in Beijing; rather, just a solitary police jeep blocking the empty highway. Our bus judders to a halt with an indignant claxon blast. A pudgy constable saunters over to parlay with our driver, who's already snorting invective, building up a head of steam. Hong, steering us out the bus door, heads off the impending confrontation by commandeering the jeep.

"That'll do, Old Chua," he soothes the cop. "Why don't you just pull off the road and let the bus pass? Then you can run us down to headquarters." The constable offers Hong a fine-tuned salute—snappy enough to betoken their difference in rank, yet just tardy enough to suit their disparity in age. He holds the door for us officiously as we climb into the backseat.

I can't quite make out whether we're being bundled into a paddy wagon or riding in VIP pomp. Either way, we rate a siren and rooftop beacon as our jeep careens down the lone boulevard of Huangdi Ling. We get through the mad ride without blood on our fenders only because, eerily enough, there's not a pedestrian to be seen for the entire length of the town. We brake in front of City Hall so abruptly that Ah-loong and I half-tumble into each other. Our constable climbs out from behind the wheel and opens the door for us, impassive as a liveried footman.

As we make our wobbly way across the sidewalk, Hong bounds ahead of us through the entryway, scouting the bunkerish concrete "lobby" for any responsible functionary to turn us over to. We catch up with him as he's craning up a stairwell hollering "Anybody home?" No response. The four-story building seems as deserted as the streets outside.

Just as he's about to give up, a middle-aged watchman comes shuffling groggily out of the toilet down the hall, still buttoning his rumpled tunic.

"Oh, it's *you*, Guoxing." He sounds relieved at spotting Hong. "How'd you get here?"

"Morning bus. Where *is* everybody?"

"Off to the opening ceremony. Plenty of big shots came up here from the capital."

"Well, can't we find anybody in the Foreign Affairs Division? I've got these two," he nods our way. "Ran into them on the bus. Who can take charge of them?"

"Hmm. That's not an easy one," the watchman pronounces dubiously. "The Foreign Affairs people have gone off with the rest. Let's see who we can turn up . . ."

Unhooking his walkie-talkie from his belt, he squawks a series of numerically coded queries, but gets only static in response. "Why not take them over to the guest house, where they've put the rest of the foreigners?" he proposes in the end. "Maybe the tour agents there can figure out what to do with them."

Back on the street we are relieved to find our jeep gone, so we walk the half-block down to the Provincial Guest House. It turns out to be another concrete bunker, much like City Hall, but incongruously Mediterraneanized with whitewash and red-tile trim on the lintels. A bald clerk on a high stool spraddles his elbows across the front desk, his head in his hands, lightly snoring. Behind him, an array of wall clocks purport to tell the time in Moscow, Cairo, Amsterdam, New York, Sydney, and Tokyo. All these places are evidently on Beijing time—11:15 A.M.

Hong finds a service bell at the edge of the counter and bangs it twice. Without lifting his head, the clerk opens his eyes and languidly fields the detective's brusque queries. No, there's nobody here from the municipal government or its Foreign Affairs Section. Nor from the state tourist authority. And, no, there aren't any rooms available in the guest house; full up with *huaqiao* since yesterday.

"Come on," Hong sighs and ushers us, blinking, out into the noon sunshine of the treeless plaza. "Back we go to the main highway," he announces.

"To send us back to Xian?" I ask, bracing for the worst.

"Wouldn't make much sense, would it?" he muses. "Seeing as how you're here already, I mean." He peers up and down the deserted boulevard, scratching his head. "Nah," he shrugs. "I've got an aunt who lives up there by the road. She can put you up for a night or two."

This proposition leaves us too astonished to reply at first. Few in China could take on such a commitment even for themselves, let alone on behalf of their relatives. Most residential quarters are way too cramped to readily accommodate guests. Under dire necessity, an unexpected family member can always be squeezed in. But strangers are another matter, both logistically and culturally. Not to mention the "foreign" factor; harboring unregistered aliens like us at home is against regulations for any ordinary Chinese citizen, much less a policeman. Or is it precisely *because* he's police that Hong can even consider bending the rules so?

Far be it from us, in any case, to question his generosity, considering our total lack of alternatives. But, as we pad along meekly behind him on a pedestrian shortcut back to the highway, we keep running into fresh confirmation of the boldness of his invitation and the potential awkwardness it creates for him. We hardly slip through town unseen; acquaintances hail Hong every block or so, eyeballing Ahloong and me with unabashed curiosity. Our escort pretends not to notice their ogling and never, throughout all the inevitable chitchat, even alludes to our incongruous presence on the scene.

Unlike the deserted boulevard we drove in on, these back alleys remain impervious to the official Yellow Emperor ceremonies. Instead, they teem with private preparations for tomorrow's family Qing Ming observances. Through wide-flung shutters we spot housewives airing their kitchens and scouring the crockery, spring-cleaning before the symbolic extinction and rekindling of the stove fires. Quilts and long johns hang on courtyard clotheslines. Squalling babies endure baths alfresco in plastic washtubs. Husbands hurry back from market with last-minute groceries for the Qing Ming graveside picnics. Peddlers hawk spirit money door-to-door.

Hong stops for brief colloquies with a cigarette vendor, a street-sweeping granny, a schoolteacher, a couple of gum-chewing teenage loiterers and a public-toilet attendant, all of whom seem to be itching to know—but uneasy to ask—about his mysterious foreign sidekicks. At the end of this gauntlet, on the edge of town, we emerge into the courtyard of the local public works department's dormitory complex: low-rise motel-style row houses flanking a two-story redbrick central block.

We brush past a black plastic curtain into a dingy stairwell. The stairs sound and feel creaky enough that I find myself straining my eyes through the gloom to see where I'm going. Hong, on the other hand, tosses off an ebullient, over-the-shoulder commentary while taking the steps two at a time with all the sleepwalking insouciance of someone who grew up here.

Which, in fact, he did, as he's now explaining. After he lost his parents at age three, his widowed aunt raised him and his sister here, along with three children of her own. "So Auntie won't have any problem putting you up," he assures us. "She's used to a full house."

He pauses at the door of a corner apartment and asks, as a last-minute afterthought, "Who *are* you, by the way?" We introduce ourselves by name, but he apparently needs more than that to present us to Auntie. "And *what* are you?" he presses. "I mean what brings you here?"

"*Huaqiao*," I declare with a flourish. "In search of our Chinese roots."

He eyes me quizzically, with his hand on the doorknob, but ventures a nod of reassurance—as much to himself, perhaps, as to us. He raps out one long knock and three short, like the opening bars of "The East Is Red." Whoever's inside makes it to the door in no time at all, but then has to fumble a few seconds with multiple locks. The door is hinged to open out into the hallway; no room in the cramped flat for it to swing inward.

"Auntie, I've brought you a couple of *huaqiao*. They're seeking their roots," he announces, matter-of-factly. "Do you think we can find a place for them?"

She can barely find space for her own square and stolid bulk. The kitchen alcove she withdraws to has just room enough for Auntie, a plastic washbasin, and a single-ring gas stove. Around the "parlor" table in the entryway, six people can sit—but not stand; a sleeping loft, suspended from the ceiling, truncates the headway. A triple-decker bunk bed can accommodate more sleepers in a windowless closet off the "parlor."

Auntie eyes us from under her straight-cut, steel-gray bangs: "Well, they don't look too oversized," she assesses us, approvingly. "We can put them across the hall and let Xiou-lian stay here with us."

"Lucky you," Hong congratulates us. "You get the honeymoon suite." The family was allocated an extra room a few doors down, he explains, when Auntie's eldest daughter married an electric lineman. But, since her husband's out on the line this week, the daughter might just as well stay back here in her girlhood home.

We couldn't possibly evict her from her own bedroom, Ah-loong protests. "Don't worry," Auntie interrupts. "We're all used to sleeping with each other here, but not with you." This irrefutable clincher of an argument effectively cuts off any further objections.

Like proper honeymooners, we can look forward to a close snuggle tonight. Our allotted "suite" has just room enough for a desk, a steel armoire, and a single bed; communal bathroom down the hall. We stash our backpacks, rinse off the road dust, and repair to the Public

Works departmental canteen downstairs, where we've invited Hong to join us for dinner.

THE RESTAURANT HAS no menu, so we ask Hong—presumably a regular—to suggest some dishes. "Their Mother Smallpox Bean Curd's pretty good," he recommends. "So are the Tiger Spotted Chilies and the Twice-Cooked Pork." We follow his tips. All quite standard canteen entrées, but rarely ordered together since they're all highly spiced. Is that typical Shaanbei taste? I wonder.

"Well, I can't speak for all of Shaanbei," he laughs, "but it's *my* taste. I like things flavored strongly enough to stick with you for a while. At university, I could never get used to that bland Cantonese stuff. Maybe it's a holdover from when I was growing up. Back then I'd have to stretch out the memory of each meal as long as I could before allowing myself to get hungry again."

"Was food so scarce here then?" Ah-loong asks.

"Not for everyone, not all the time," Hong relates. "At least it didn't have to be. Shaanbei's quite capable of feeding itself. You've heard of Nanniwan?" he asks, alluding to a once-marginal farming district north of here that, through the miracle of agricultural collectivization, famously blossomed into the breadbasket of Mao's soviet after the Long March.

"My father came from that part of Shaanxi. As a teenager, he had a hand in transforming that valley, according to his sister, my aunt. But he was too hot-blooded to live out his life as a farmer. He joined the Red Army and served under Peng De-huai." That affiliation assured him a rapid rise in the Communist ranks—followed by an even more precipitate fall, Hong relates.

Peng was a star commander during the civil war and went on to further distinguish himself as minister of defense in overall charge of China's world-shakingly successful offensive during the Korean War. He was renowned for his rectitude, his loyalty, his valor—and his stubbornness. As Peng's protégé, Hong's father joined the party while still in his teens and had attained a military status equivalent to a colonel by the time his patron was purged for criticizing Mao's quixotic Great Leap Forward in the late 1950s. That pretty much checked the elder Hong's further career advancement, but he was still an officer in good standing when his two children were born. Only with the 1966 onset of the Cultural Revolution was he targeted for complete annihilation.

"All I know about him is what I heard from my aunt," Hong admits. "I have no firsthand recollection, since I was just two years old at the time. My mother was hounded into abandoning her 'bad element' family just forty days after my kid sister was born. That, my aunt says, shattered my father even more than the repeated beatings he got at his 'self-criticism' sessions.

"Not that the Red Guards were exactly sparing with their blows, either. On my father's last day, Auntie says, they thrashed him from morning until afternoon, when he finally died of a heart attack. His head was so bruised that they couldn't even pry off the dunce cap they'd stuck on him. The paper was fused on his brow with dried blood and hair and bone and brain—can you imagine?"

Hong pauses a moment to shudder off the horrific picture. "So that's how they buried him, dunce cap and all, back up in his village near Nanniwan," he quietly resumes his tale. "And that's where I'll go after this VIP ceremony, to burn a few 'hell notes' of my own this Qing Ming."

The dunce cap wasn't the only stigma irremovably attached to the family. Even after Hong and his sister had moved down here to Huangdi Ling, the "counterrevolutionary" label stuck to the two children. Auntie's work unit, the electric utility, offered no increase in food rations for her enlarged household, "which is why we all had to learn to stretch out our meals with salt and chilies," Hong smiles ruefully. Nor was there any extra subsidy to educate such suspect orphans.

"Auntie was already overburdened with three older kids of her own in school," Hong explains. "My sister and I couldn't ask her for books and slates and fees. We couldn't even tell her about how the town kids called us 'bad elements' and refused to play with us. We didn't know *what* to do with ourselves—just hung around the schoolhouse, looking in. After a while the teachers felt so sorry for us that they took up a collection on their own and, between them, raised the few *kuai* it took for us to go to school. Auntie never knew about it until years later."

He still remembers that original classroom as grandly imposing, although he now realizes objectively it was anything but. The grade school occupied an outbuilding of Huangdi Temple, which was then a far cry from the lavishly restored tourist attraction it has since become. But even in its ramshackle state, the temple fared a lot better than the systematically demolished shrines of other sects. As a Chinese race hero, the Yellow Emperor escaped most of the "snake demon, cow devil" opprobrium reserved for the icons of Confucianism, Taoism, or Buddhism. Rather, Huangdi was blessedly ignored—like the Huangdi Ling grade school his temple harbored.

That benign neglect allowed Hong to flourish under the tutelage of a couple of quietly heroic teachers. He did well enough in his studies that, upon the death of Mao and the consequent revival of the education system, he was one of just three Huangdi Ling students to earn a place in the provincial high school in Xian.

By the time he finished high school, the university examination system had already been restored. But, with his younger sister still to support through school, Hong was in no position, financially, to avail himself of the exams right away. He had to work fully two years as a house painter before he was free to apply to university. The wait paid off, though: he finally placed into Zhong Shan and, in a separate exam, won a government scholarship. With a study stipend of 30 renminbi a month (that's RMB 30, or about $6.00 at then-current exchange rates) and a further RMB 28 living allowance, he could just about hand-to-mouth his way through his first two undergraduate years.

And then, in Hong's third year of college, the government formally "reversed the verdict" on his father, posthumously exonerated him of counterrevolution, and restored his Party membership. "I felt insulted at first, to tell the truth," Hong admits. "After all his suffering and ours, all those tears, all those chilies and studies and hard work, what do they finally offer in recompense? A little slip of paper with red stars."

Along with the certificate, however, came a partial reimbursement of his father's back pension. That finally relieved some of the economic pressure on Hong and his sister. (She's just finished her degree in electrical engineering at Xibei University and accepted an appointment at a power plant, Hong relates with evident pride, although he adds that he'd rather she'd been able to go abroad for graduate studies.)

"In our final year of the mass communications course at Zhong Shan," Hong recalls, "we all had to turn in an essay on 'The Character I Most Admire.' Some classmates picked revolutionary heroes like Mao or Zhou or even Lei Feng. Others sang the praises of capitalists like Bill Gates. One brave soul even wrote about Peng De-huai. But I chose my father. After all, he's somebody real, unlike these historical figures that hardly touch me.

"Not that I concretely remember anything at all about him, really—not even his face or his smell. But what a journey he made! From farmboy to Red Army fighter to 'counterrevolutionary' to rehabilitated martyr. He never shrank back, never stood on the sidelines. He seized his times, era by era, faced it all, took things as they came. He 'crossed the river by feeling the stones'—*every* stone, all the way across. Directly or indirectly, his way has determined my own."

"How so?" I ask. "Did you have him in mind when you went into journalism? Or when you switched from reporter to policeman?"

"He influenced both those choices," Hong nods. "Because of him, I felt I had to escape from here as a kid. And later to come back as a man. It's a small place, Huangdi Ling; everybody knows everyone else's history. All the while that I was growing up here, and every time I come home here even now, I always encounter people that I *know* had a hand in hounding my father to death. It's unavoidable; one just naturally runs into them, or their relatives or their descendants, on the street, at school, on the job.

"So how do I handle it? How would *you* handle it? What's the point of nursing a grudge, whether against the individuals involved or against the system as a whole? After all, the Party formally recognized its mistake, rectified the verdict on my father, even paid some kind of so-called compensation.

"And then, a couple of years ago, I myself joined the Party. It still helps your career, you know. And I'm *entitled* to get along, aren't I? My credentials are impeccable: I'm the son of a pre-Liberation veteran cadre in posthumous good standing. He suffered horrors, but he emerged with honor. At Qing Ming, I dress in mourning clothes and burn him some 'hell notes.' But then I get back into my uniform and pin on my badge.

"As a *huaqiao*," he asks Ah-loong, "didn't they ever teach you that Du Mu poem about the Almond Blossom Village? Back in our Huangdi Temple classroom, every schoolchild had to memorize it." He recites:

> Qing Ming festival. Pelting rain
> Drives roadside passersby to distraction;
> "Might I ask where to find a wine shop?"
> A herdboy points to Almond Blossom Village.

"The landscape he's describing, you know, is right here in Shaanxi," he points out, "somewhere around the Tang dynasty capital, the modern-day Xian. We were taught that poem as just a mood piece, but I always thought there was more to it than that. Symbolic, in its way: the weeping heavens, the mourners swooning in their grief. And the poet, himself, looking for a wine shop—a way to forget, to move on past his sorrows and return to the world of the living.

"So whom does he ask? A youth, a symbol of the future. And where is he sent? To the faraway village with the poetic, inviting, springlike name."

EMERGING FROM the canteen, we step into an arid spring gloaming that's a far cry from Du Mu's fraught downpour. The road that was so empty before noon, when we arrived, now teems with overnight traffic bound for Inner Mongolia. Smog-belching trucks thrum down the blacktop, kicking up a scrim of loess dust that reduces the sun to a blanched disc over Jiao Shan to the west. Hong spells out the trail to the summit for our sunset walk to the Yellow Emperor's tomb. He has to shout his directions to make himself heard over the din.

"That lane right across from us takes you to the temple where I went to grade school. From there you have your choice of footpaths to the actual tomb. It's pretty sparse forest all the way to the top; you practically can't get lost as long as you keep heading uphill. And, coming down, the town lights will guide you. Better go see the tomb now; you won't be able to tomorrow. We'll have police out in force to keep you or anyone else from getting anywhere *near* it without an invitation."

A military convoy pelts past, stranding us for a few minutes on the parched road shoulder. But once we get over the highway and onto the wooded lane, the cypress shade enfolds us in a deeper, richer twilight. In the temple courtyard, elephantine trees soar up into the gloom of blue-black foliage high above the tiled rooftops. One cedar, flanking the temple entrance, still bears ancient iron nails on which the original Yellow Emperor is said to have hung his armor after his campaigns—proof positive of the primordial ancestor's historicity, according to the souvenir pamphlet we buy at the temple schlock stall.

Farther up the slope, the trees become shorter and less regal. Unlike the stiff, standoffish giants of the temple courtyard, these hillside cypresses stoop to accost us with their gestures, beckoning along the loess-scuffed pathways, silver in the sunset afterglow. Just as the dusk finally gives way to night, we pass through the dragon-emblazoned entry arch to the Yellow Emperor's tomb precinct.

The tourists and trinket vendors have long since left for the day. The courtyard is deserted now except for a photographer who has set up his tripod in front of the giant bronze incense burner to catch a night shot of Huangdi's commemorative stone stele through a picturesque foreground of flame and smoke. To improve the effect, he feeds bits of litter into the smoldering incense ash until he achieves a suitably photogenic flare. The glow makes the surrounding cypresses writhe. Silhouetted against the burial mound, spindly "hell dollar" paper trees flicker like ghostly emanations.

Ah-loong stands transfixed by the uncanny scene, her Chinese *qi chang*, or force field, finely attuned to the ambiance. I'm less susceptible to the lensman's pyrotechnics; I'd just as soon use the flickering fire glow to get in a peek at what's behind the tumulus. I make my way through a moon gate at the back of the compound, Ah-loong tagging along behind me at a distance. All we find is a maze of seemingly aimless trails. We stumble in the dark, without signpost or pavement to guide us. Nothing out here but a couple of twisted cypress trunks inexplicably ringed with low iron railings whose only point seems to be to scrape our shins.

Just as I'm ready to turn back, a lank silhouette slips from behind a tree above our trail. At the first audible crack of a twig, Ah-loong jumps like a rabbit. My guts clench with an adrenal rush. Only our new companion seems unflapped. He coolly strolls our way, babbling on in midsentence as though he were just resuming a momentarily interrupted conversation.

". . . as well as the horns. The dragon's horns, I mean—you saw them, right? Those trees, you know, the little trees with the railings." By now he's close enough to register our apprehensive gaze up the slope where he so inexplicably appeared. "No, no, not this way," he chides us, trying to redirect our attention back to the "horns" he's talking about. "They're behind you, not up here. This mound up here is the *crown*, not the horns."

As though recapping a lesson for especially slow schoolchildren, he singsongs, "The mound is the crown and the trees are the horns. The tomb is the pearl in the dragon's mouth. The incense-burning terrace is the tip of the tongue. It's all right here."

From some sort of portfolio under his arm he pulls out a sheet of paper and hands it to me. It feels much-fingered, greasy, and creased. No way to make out the details of the image in the forest gloom, illumined only by hazy starlight and the dust-refracted glow of the town below. But at least the black-on-white outline is marginally more discernable than the shadowed features of our gaunt interlocutor.

It seems to be some sort of chart: four unidentifiable animals (or, at any rate, blobs with heads and feet), drawn in a ring and divided into two paired groupings with a lazy S-curve meandering between them. Tapping a spiral rosette-looking thing at the top of the page, the presumptive author of this diagram resumes his explication in the same didactic drone: "We're here, on the dragon. You see the tiger, over on the south side of the river? And there's the phoenix to the east, right opposite the turtle to the west."

He nods to the three compass points before us, where vague protuberances blot out the ascendant constellations. And, sure enough, a few glints of reflected starlight hint at a streamcourse meandering across the middle of the panorama. Returning to his map, he taps again on the rosette at the top of the page. "Here on Jiao Shan, you see, the ridges are the dragon's nine coils, and the flanks of the mountain are his outspread claws."

Whereupon he illustratively splays his arms, palms out-thrust and fingers curled like talons—a gesture so sudden and forceful that the night air reverberates with little sonic boomlets, which he underscores with falsetto whoops, "Piang! Piang!"

I recoil; Ah-loong rocks back on her heels. "Yai!" she gasps. "Where'd *you* come from?"

"*Come* from?" he echoes, bemused. "Why, I didn't *come* from anywhere. I've been right here all along—same as you. But we're not here as personalities, you know; rather, we're all here as *qi*—force, energy, potential. And this is the world's most powerful *qi chang*. Why else would the Yellow Emperor choose this place, out of all his vast realm, to be buried?"

THAT QUESTION PREYED upon him after his former Work Unit went broke. The bankruptcy ended his "previous incarnation" as a shift foreman in a state-run coal mine, he relates. (Never mind his discarded name from that era, he adds. It doesn't matter—"the shadow of a shadow.")

All at once production stopped and so did his livelihood. He had nothing but time on his hands and doubts on his mind. The *qi*, the energy of the earth, was still there, bound up in undepleted coal. And people still needed to cook and eat, smelt steel and fire turbines. So why had the mine—the mainstay of life in Huangdi Ling—suddenly ground to a halt?

His mates all had to shift for themselves, migrating or taking up peddling of one sort or another. But he couldn't shake the Big Questions. He just devoted his days to pacing the hills and pondering about *qi* and the Yellow Emperor. Why do things happen the way they happen? What force drives them? What inevitability? Why now? Why here?

No answers came to him until ("Piak! Just like that") he saw the dragon embedded in the mountain—a sudden vision that all at once summed up his lengthy ramblings on Jiao Shan. Subsequent researches in history, archaeology, geomancy, and numerology only served to confirm his insight and fill in additional detail. He divined the surrounding tiger, phoenix, and turtle in the same instantaneous way.

"I offered to tell the authorities about it, the Landmarks Preservation people, but nobody wanted to know. Why should they listen to cosmology from a laid-off collier? Some 'authorities' they turned out to be," he snorts, derisively. "Look what a mess they made of this tomb restoration. They've got the pearl—that is, the burial mound—half-submerged in the ground. And there's the incense terrace—the tongue—stuck *outside* the compound wall—the jaws. Who ever heard of a dragon with his tongue hanging out of his mouth? It's preposterous, undignified."

So he took upon himself the private, unofficial, round-the-clock stewardship of Jiao Shan and its *qi chang*. He sermonizes day-trippers and shares their picnics, recycles cans and bottles for pocket change, and incinerates the daily haul of paper trash in the incense burner. He's become the scourge of drunks and vandals, but courting couples he leaves alone since they only enhance the *qi*.

To anyone who'll listen, he expounds the inner architecture and occult power of this place. A passing *huaqiao*, for instance, was so impressed with his exegesis of the dragon's horns that he donated the shin-bruising railings we'd stumbled against earlier. And every morning in the predawn, when the *qi chang* is at its clearest, he rehearses the *qi gong* exercises he's devised to restore to humankind the inner balance of prehistoric antiquity.

"The Yellow Emperor himself quested after that lost balance. *He* learned it, in turn, from his own teacher, Qi Po. In his *Classic of Inner Healing*, the Yellow Emperor says, 'In former times, man lived among birds, beasts and reptiles . . . Within him were no family ties which bound him with love; on the outside were no officials who could guide out and correct him . . . Evil influences could not penetrate deeply . . . Hence it was sufficient to transmit the Essence and to invoke the gods.'

"That's all that I'm trying to do up here," our companion shrugs, switching out of his declamatory, quotational mode back into a chattier voice. "People come up here to do *qi gong* with me, more and more of them each day, some from a long way off. It's a powerful *kungfu*—Piang! Piak!"—he cuts a few more sonic-boomlet flourishes. "But there's nothing weird or supernatural about it. Just a matter of opening yourself up to the *qi*.

"And *qi* is in you and around you all the time, the most basic essence of your everyday experience. Anyone can feel the *qi chang. You* can, right now. Sit down," he directs us.

Not that we're exactly in the habit of taking orders from conspicuously skittish strangers on dark, deserted mountaintops, but his mesmeric tone brooks no contradiction. The dust feels cool under my palms and the ground chill seeps right through my corduroys.

"Back straight," our instructor admonishes. "Hands in your lap. Close your eyes." He gives us a minute to settle in. The cypresses creak as the wind seethes through the valley. "Don't listen to anything," the voice warns, seemingly lower and closer now. "Don't think. And don't try *not* to think, either. No need to stamp out any thoughts or sounds that come. Just let them pass without hanging on to them. Feel yourself breathing. Pay attention to your breath. No special stunt-breathing. Just ordinary, relaxed breath. Going out. Coming in."

No sooner does he mention it, of course, than my heretofore perfectly natural breathing becomes excruciatingly self-conscious. Either

I'm hyperventilating or I'm holding my breath like a pearl diver, unable to escape either extreme without falling immediately into its opposite. What am I doing here? Why am I listening to this guy?

Don't think, I shush myself. And don't try *not* to. I distract myself with memories, gossip, poetry, ditties. When I catch myself at it, I try to distract myself from my distractions. Amid all the internal blather, at last my breathing subsides to normal. The breaths mark time far more easily and naturally than any ticking clock. As the breath relaxes, time subtly expands.

Only then do I register the voice again. "Now shift your attention to your own body. Settle down comfortably and then hold still. Feel every bit of your body the same way you felt your breath. Move your attention up and down your body; move it left and right. Start off slow, feeling every part in turn. After a while, you may naturally speed up until you feel the whole body at once."

Same torrent of internal gibber as before: where I'd been sitting perfectly comfortably a moment ago, suddenly I'm tormented with itches, a charley horse, lumbago. Lest I scratch or squirm, I try to jam the signals with all kinds of psychobabble, then re-collect myself and try to jam my own jamming *ad delirium*. Eventually—I have no idea how long it actually takes, in clock time—I bore myself into submission. I sit still and relaxed without any mental dialogue at all. For once I'm all *here*, all in the present. And the moment feels spacious, unhemmed by past or future.

"It's cold, did you notice?" the voice is now so near and so soft that it almost seems inside my head. "This close to the desert, the temperature drops fast at night. But you don't *feel* cold, do you? There's some kind of layer that surrounds you, some envelope between you and the cold. You can feel your way out into that envelope, just as you did with your body, bit by bit at first, and then all at once. Feel where it meets the night air. Feel how any passing breeze flaps it ever so lightly, and how it settles back into place."

He gives us a moment to play with this new sensation. I'm so lulled by his voice at this stage that what he's saying strikes me as perfectly natural and tangible, at least until he himself points out the novelty.

"What you're feeling now, you know, is *not* your body. It is you, to be sure, but not in the way that you're used to thinking of yourself. It's something else: your *qi chang*. Tune into it some more and you'll find how tightly it's braided into the great *qi chang* of everything.

"I mean *everything*, from the bug on your nose to the Yellow Emperor, from your earliest ancestors to your unborn descendants, from the outermost stars to your innermost dreams. Not to mention the Huangdi Ling Dragon, the Phoenix, the Tiger, and Turtle, and the river that links them all into a great, swirling, inseparable *yin-yang*. Can you put all that together? Can you yourself become the *tai-chi*? Can you find a way to be on both sides of that river at once?"

He lapses back into his earlier singsong. "Crossing the river by feeling the stones. Under the river, weighted by stones. Rolling downriver, smooth as a stone. Damming the river, as firm as stone. Over the river, pelted by stones." He rings all these changes in Chinese just by varying the verbs, then pauses to sigh. "Word games. See through them, to reality. There's a river; there are stones—that's all. Always changing, always the same, that river. The stones, too."

The voice trails off and says no more. We stay there, unmoving, for I don't know how much longer. When we finally open our eyes, our companion is nowhere in sight. Yet I sense he's not far off, which I find curiously comforting considering how much his first appearance had unnerved us. On the ground in front of us, he's left us his map, weighted with a smooth, round river-bottom rock.

WE HARDLY NEED a map to find our way back to Huangdi Ling. As Hong promised, it's enough just to aim our steps downhill and follow the glimmer of streetlights below. Not much to trip us up in this sparse cypress forest; the ground's a good deal smoother than many a village road in rural China. Our approach to the town is almost imperceptible—a thinning of the trees, a thickening of the dust, a hint of a ruined mud-packed wall, a bare bulb dangling from a sagging post. Gradually, the rocks in our path coalesce into a pattern of rough-hewn flagstones paving steeply inclined lanes.

A toddler on a tricycle careens out of a doorway and slaloms a few yards down the road before skidding to a well-practiced stop. A diminutive granny minces arthritically down the pitched cobbles, supported by dutiful young matrons in an unconscious echo of the Banpo diorama. A couple of grade-school kids bring up the rear, lugging low wooden stools.

We overtake them and ask where they're heading. "There's an opera, tonight," the old lady replies excitedly. The very fact that we'd ask such an elementary question brands us as clueless outsiders, so she deputes a daughter-in-law to lead us to the site of this evening's alfresco performance—a concrete bandshell on the town's central fairground. This stage is expressly dedicated to *qin qiang*, Shaanbei's earthy indigenous form of musical theater, as our escort explains.

Even in this age of karaoke and cable TV, the stylized old plays still seem to enjoy a mass following; fully an hour before showtime, the field's already filling up. Vendors of spiced melon seeds and fizzy drinks line the entrance to the fairground. Tractors snort down the entry ramp, towing flatbeds full of farmgirls in their best town finery. They park in the rear, drive-in movie style, so the girls can survey the audience as well as the stage. Denim-jacketed fops motorcycle slowly past the flatbeds, three and even four gallants piled atop each 125-cc Honda.

Standees crowd closer to the stage—young families, bachelor loafers, permanently coal-begrimed ex-miners. Knots of old men mill around with long-stemmed pipes tucked in their waistbands. Their heavy, brass-mounted spectacles lend them an air of owlish intellectuality, even though the rock-crystal lenses are meant as dust goggles rather than for reading. In front of the old men, perched on low wooden stools, gossiping old ladies fill the innermost rows. Children pile right onto the proscenium, the little girls' pigtails silhouetted against the spotlit curtain.

The expectant chatter builds in the audience as the musicians start tuning up. Then one of the children spots my foreign face way in the back. The cry goes up: "*Lao wai!*"—Old outsider! Everyone's gaze immediately swivels around our way, the grannies' stools scraping, the elders' spectacles flashing, the kids craning over the footlights into outer darkness. Suddenly, we're the show. To escape all the unwanted attention, we bolt into the most sequestered spot we can find hereabouts—backstage. As the percussive overture strikes up, we skirt around the edge of the crowd and duck, unchallenged, past a canvas flap into a kind of concrete bunker under the bandshell.

If we thought to get away from stares, though, we soon learn otherwise. The moment we burst into the "greenroom," we're once again the focus of all eyes—twenty-odd pairs of them, this time all heavily embellished with eyeliner and greasepaint. After a split-second lapse of frozen astonishment, the actors recover their professional poise and ad lib a reaction to our sudden appearance in their midst. All in unison, as though on cue, they break into a flutter of light applause.

An old "general" in his undershirt, his face an asymmetric whorl of white, red, and black paint, swaggers toward us on wooden platform shoes, bellowing a stagey, stentorian "Welcome" through his horsehair beard. With this ceremony disposed of, everybody turns back to business. A courtesan resumes her makeup. Another picks up her knitting. A group of footsoldiers—all portrayed by middle-aged women—replenish their tea mugs from a thermos flask. Children play hide-and-seek among the embroidered robes hanging in the wardrobes.

The humdrum, threadbare domesticity of the greenroom contrasts with the overwrought caterwauling and opulent pageantry of the opera stage. A gray-beard clown makes room for me beside him on a prop chest. His minimalist makeup—just a zinc-white trapezoid across the bridge of his nose—gives him a look of fixed quizzicality. He asks how county drama troupes support themselves back where I come from. I try to explain that most American counties get by without drama troupes at all, but that U.S. theater companies in general rely on ticket sales.

"We tried selling tickets a couple of times," he sighs. "Nobody came. But when it's free like this, look how they throng to watch us! You see, we're still part of the planned economy."

As per the annual plan, he explains, Qing Ming is the troupe's busy season: a dozen shows in a row, all different plays, running noon and night for six consecutive days to coincide with the county fair. The rest of the year, it's hard to get a performance commissioned. The seventy-odd members of the troupe, including a couple dozen retirees, all draw fixed stipends of under RMB 200 a month, plus RMB 2 a shot for the occasional rehearsal to keep up the repertoire.

That's all the county can afford anymore, he adds. With the mine going broke, the local administration would far rather devote any remaining revenue to touristifying the Yellow Emperor's tomb. Opera's a frill they'd love to chop from the budget if they could get away with it. But the locals won't let them. "Shaanbei old-timers are so devoted to *qin qiang* that we don't dare deviate one word from the old, stock scripts. Our audiences know them by heart—even better than we do."

It's easy to see why, watching the stage action from behind the wings. Mannered and oblique as it is, the traditional opera still serves up a patent mixture of sly satire, tear-jerking melodrama, and earthy double-entendre that could never get past the mainstream film and broadcast censors. Take, for instance, tonight's offering: *Two Dragons Chasing One Pearl*, a quirky tragi-farce that meanders through three hours of plot twists. Basically, it's a "wisdom of Solomon" courtroom conundrum, but with peculiarly Chinese overtones of ancestor worship.

The story opens with our heroine, Li Qian Niang (Dimples Li), rather raunchily bemoaning her forced celibacy. She's been left a virtual widow for the past eight years. Her husband, Liu Yu, godson of the commander in chief of the imperial legions, went missing in a remote frontier garrison and is presumed dead. Yeo Jin, the emperor's nephew-in-law, takes a shine to her. He browbeats her clansmen into offering her up for remarriage. The prospect so revolts her that she tries to kill herself at her wedding ceremony. She's saved by the last-minute reappearance of her long-lost husband, who reclaims his bride. The only trouble is, she's just been formally plighted to someone else.

Liu and Yeo bring suit against each other on charges of wife-stealing. The conflicting claims throw the imperial entourage into a panic. The courtiers don't know which way to turn, since both sides are equally well-connected. Even the emperor himself is at a loss what

to do. The thankless question gets sloughed off upon an obscure bu-reaucrat: Xu Jiujing, a humpbacked little county magistrate whose gauche appearance and sardonic turn of mind have long barred him from preferment. Xu suddenly finds himself called to the capital and decked in ministerial finery. First case on his docket is the Liu-Yeo imbroglio.

Casting about for a way out of his dilemma, Xu decides to slip Dimples a dose of drugged wine that throws her into a deathlike coma. The question then comes down to which of the contending families wants to assume responsibility for her burial. The House of Yeo abruptly loses interest, while the Lius stand ready to accord her full rites. That settles the matter for Xu. As soon as the drug wears off, he awards the revived Dimples to Liu Yu. But the whole proceed-ing leaves the judge so disillusioned with the law that he sheds his court robes and goes off to open a humble, rustic wine shop.

Our backstage vantage affords us an actor's perspective on the crowd. A gratifyingly responsive audience it is, too. There's an audible intake of breath at Li Qian Niang's suicide bid, loud guffaws at the bumbling pusillanimity of the courtiers, snickers at Xu's wry asides, belly laughs when the magistrate gratuitously cuffs his bailiff, and loud cheers for the denouement.

"Only in China," I nudge Ah-loong. "Anywhere else the aspiring swain would have to slay a dragon or kiss a toad or write a sonnet— *something*, at any rate, to suggest he can make a life with his beloved. Only here would the ultimate proof of true love be his readiness to plant her corpse among his ancestors. How's *that* for backward-looking ghoulishness?"

"Mister Sinologist," she nods gravely. "What they're *really* cheering for, you know, is the way Xu gives up his government job and 'plunges into the sea' "—Beijing slang for an entrepreneurial start-up. "What could be more Chinese than *that* nowadays?"

Two Dragons Chasing One Pearl may draw cheers from its human audience, but not necessarily from the Yellow Emperor, presumptive guest of honor at the Qing Ming drama fest. The god's reaction is rather more equivocal, at least judging from the weather he sends. Lightning frisks about the horizon, briefly silhouetting Jiao Shan. A few fat raindrops dapple the dustbowl of the fairground. We hurry back to our dormitory to escape the threatened storm, arriving just ahead of the first cloudbursts.

With the rain clattering against our windowpane, we're all the more grateful for our snug little room. The narrow dormitory cell seems as much a closet as a boudoir. Into this cubby, Hong's newlywed cousin has crammed her entire dowry: a color TV, still in its packing crate; a Flying Pigeon bicycle, still swaddled in bubble-wrap; a stack of neon-colored quilts, tightly baled with twine. After storing all these durables, there's barely space left for a trestle bed, an enamel washstand, and a pint-sized school desk. Half the desktop is taken up by a fluorescent table lamp; the rest is buried under a fat Zhou Enlai biography, some film magazines, and a vinyl-bound high school autograph album, class of '92.

Our hosts have thoughtfully left us a thermos of hot water by our bedside. We pour off a few inches into the washbasin for a sponge bath. Then we fish out our mountaintop guru's *feng shui* diagram for a closer, fluorescent-lit look. Considering that they represent great cardinal pillars of creation, the four guardian animals seem disarmingly cuddly. The tiger snoozes on folded paws, his tail demurely tucked under him; the turtle casts a knowing, smirky, backward glance; the phoenix looks feminine and broody; even the dragon peers cross-eyed at his own flared nostrils.

Just as we're settling down to ponder these cosmic personalities, Hong Guoxing comes by to pay us a goodnight visit. As soon as we open the door and he spots the *feng shui* map spread out on our bed, he pronounces, "You've run into Gao Xinyang, I see."

We don't even know the name of the man who gave us the chart, we admit, but we sketch in a brief description of our meeting with him. "Uh-huh, that's Xinyang all right," the cop nods. "Not that he ever introduces himself by name anymore. He's beyond all that now, isn't he? And without a proper name to call him by, people can give him any puffed-up title they like."

We're a bit taken aback by the rancor of his tone. "So you know him?" I ask.

"How could I not know him? Huangdi Ling's a tiny place, like I said. When I was a kid, Xinyang was already a Model Worker at the coal mines. A true 'Labor Hero,' no doubt about it, but something of a draft horse who worked just for the sake of working. No understanding at all of the material foundations of life.

"He never got over it when they closed the pits. He just couldn't see it as part of the bigger picture. Until he wandered up the hills there. *Then* he started seeing pictures so big that they dizzied a lot of people here.

"Townsfolk would seek him out in the mountains to practice his so-called *qi gong.* All he taught, really, was just some normal calisthenics for breathing and balance, but it *seemed* special when he'd put you through your paces in that voice of his. After a while, word got around and people started coming from outside.

"And soon we started finding *these* things," he waves contemptuously at the *feng shui* map. "Not just in Huangdi Ling, either. They'd crop up from Xian all the way into Inner Mongolia, following the truck roads. Other handbills, too; he's written dozens. Migrant workers would carry them as far as Canton or Shenzhen. Housewives would plaster them in their kitchens as good-luck charms. Old people would wrap them around their knees to cure their rheumatism. Craziness!"

"Well, what's the harm if it makes people feel better?" Ah-loong asks.

"People *don't* feel better," the cop explodes. "They just *think* they do! How can you cure a disease with a cartoon or a homily? It's unscientific. And how does Xinyang survive up there without money, anyway? How are his followers supposed to get along if they really go in for the spiritual life full-time, without material foundation? Or maybe does Xinyang have some other sort of crooked material foundation of his own?

"Let's not even talk of the names that people dream up to call him: Master, Sage, Bodhisatva, Old Man Jiao Shan. What happens to social order when just *anyone* can set himself up like that as some sort of super-authority? But his worst presumption is to usurp the authority of Time itself. All this 'live for the moment' nonsense of his; it undermines history and hope for the future, it saps pride and duty and loyalty. Race and nation, ancestry and family—all fantasies, according to Xinyang's logic. I *know* his message. I have my informants. I've got an inch-thick dossier on him. I keep telling my bosses down in Xian that we should pick him up, but nobody listens."

"Well, what could you charge him with?" I ask.

"Oh, plenty of infractions," he smiles, ticking them off on his fingers with relish. "Loitering, vagrancy, desecration of monuments. Unauthorized assembly, unlicensed publishing. Fraud, deceit, subornation. Misleading minors. Not to mention the religious laws."

"So why do they ignore your warnings about him down in Xian?" I wonder.

The question brakes the momentum of his tirade. "Perhaps they don't take Shaanbei seriously," he shrugs. "Maybe they don't believe that anything really important or dangerous could come from such an out-of-the-way place as this. If so, then they're forgetting Chairman Mao's advice that 'a single spark can start a prairie fire.' They're forgetting the Yenan soviet, the 'cradle of revolution,' right up the road from here. And they're forgetting about the powerful *feng shui* channels that link up everyplace in the country to the Yellow Emperor's tomb, the very hub of the whole Chinese *qi chang*."

AFTER A NIGHT of wind and rain and prairie-fire dreams, we wake to a predawn quiet that really feels, for a fleeting instant, like the still hub of the reeling Chinese cosmos. It doesn't last long, though. A chattering of sparrows nibbles away at the edges of the silence, followed by the repetitive yelp of a lone and distant farm dog. Which, in turn, triggers a contrapuntal yammering of every local street cur in Huangdi Ling. Finally a self-important rooster gets around to announcing the daybreak as his own original discovery.

Our dormitory courtyard echoes with wake-up sounds: hocking and wheezing, then the swizzle and sploosh of a hundred simultaneous toothbrushers. We pull the covers over our heads in a vain effort to blot out the clang of kettles onto gas rings and the rattle of crockery in the neighbors' kitchen alcoves. But there's no escaping the high-pitched rev of a jeep downstairs or the grinding of gears as it noses its way out the courtyard gate. One after another, the creaky cars of the public works' motor pool set out for the day. By the time the sun is just tipping over the "phoenix" mountain to the east, a cement mixer starts churning in the courtyard and construction workers totter onto the scaffolding of a new dormitory block right opposite our window.

Nothing for it but to get out of bed and make our way to the toilet down the hall. Joining the queue there, we attract stares but no conversation. Another quick sponge bath from the tea thermos and we hit the road. From a curbside stall by the bus stop we grab a couple of flatbreads en route to the temple at the entrance to Jiao Shan.

That's about as far up the hill as we're likely to get this morning. The actual tomb and the summit are reserved for dignitaries: overseas Chinese benefactors and party brass from Xian. The rest of us, ordinary townspeople and unofficial visitors alike, are left to pile up at the base of the hill, like a jumbled talus slope of cast-off humanity.

Not that anybody down here seems much bothered about being relegated to the bottom of the hill. Everybody is too busy with market-day bustle. The hucksterish mood at the temple is a far cry from the contemplative hush of our sunset visit to this same spot only last night. Now, at barely eight A.M., the courtyard's already aswarm with peddlers. Stalls flog everything from latex girdles to rat poison to singing crickets. Filmy pastel nighties dangle from clotheslines strung up on the iron nails supposedly driven by the Yellow Emperor into the temple's giant cedars.

Open-air barbers and masseurs ply their trade under shade trees. A family of contortionists—mother, father, and two teenage daughters—draw few spectators for their ad hoc street circus. A dancing monkey attracts more onlookers. Bettors crowd around a gladiatorial combat between two fighting beetles in a bamboo cage. Curbside soothsayers offer a broad palette of divination styles: cards, dice, palmistry, physiognomy, astrology, graphology, numerology. A disheveled Taoist, squatting by the footpath, hails us as we pass: "From Tai Shan [a sacred mountain hermitage in Eastern China] I heard you were coming, so I rushed here to bring you good fortune."

Passing up this sales pitch, we settle for a more downscale purchase of good luck. We add our own five-jiao bill (roughly a U.S. nickel) to the confetti of low-denomination banknotes silted up in the Yellow Emperor's purported footprints—spraddle-toed depressions, each a yard long, stamped into a courtyard pavement. Standing on the temple steps, we can survey the entire sweep of the alfresco market, from the highway, over the "toes" of Jiao Shan and on down to the opera bandshell in the central fairground.

Wherever the eye may fall, somebody's buying, selling, flirting, preening, gawking, eating, pushing, pulling, haggling, or praying—an infinitude of fleeting, one-on-one transactions. It's a tableau of hyperfocused vignettes, no one of which claims precedence over any other; a composition without any natural center of attention, like a Brueghel skating scene.

Yet in this genre Brueghel would have little to teach a Song dynasty virtuoso like Chang Tse-tuan. Consider the swoon of particularity in his masterpiece *Ascending the River at the Qing Ming Festival*. In its seventeen-foot length, the horizontal scroll crams over five hundred individual figures. Although painted nine centuries ago, it renders exactly the same occasion we're witnessing today—a mass influx from a far-flung hinterland to attend a lively street fair on the occasion of Qing Ming.

Many of the wares, services, and amusements depicted in the scroll are still available now, hardly changed, at the Huangdi Ling fairground. Whether in the ancient painting or the modern street scene, the closer you look, the richer the detail. Yet then as now, the whole of the scene is greater than the sum of its parts. The individual figures and vignettes are as distinctively discrete as streambed rocks, but the overall swirl of the crowd rolls inexorably on like a river in spate.

Against such a flood, no weir avails for long. Pedestrians completely ignore the crosswalk where the road from the Yellow Emperor's tomb intersects the row of market stalls. Nobody even tries to clear the blacktop until it's time for the VIPs to descend from the morning ceremonies at the summit. Then a few dozen constables mosey up from the highway, where their police van is parked. They slouch into position on either side of the road, parting the crowd. Behind the police cordons, bystanders just wait, with the stoical incuriosity of cows at a railroad crossing.

The motorcade barely bothers to slow down for a hairpin curve in the road, let alone to greet the public. These limousines, we're told, bear the members of the People's Political Consultative Committee, the highest "representative" politicians in the province. Yet none of the PPCC pooh-bahs so much as waves to his "constituents" and few in the crowd care to crane through the mirrored windows of the passing BMWs and Volgas for a glimpse of their "favorite sons."

The cars whiz on past like a flotilla of flying saucers, leaving nothing behind but dust and fumes. Yet still the police remain in place. What are we waiting for? Another burst of limos? Perhaps a procession of *huaqiao* tour buses? Minutes drag by and the crowd grows restive. A toddler ducks under a constable's outstretched baton. Her mother dashes out onto the macadam to retrieve her. On the opposite side of the road, the line of the police picket buckles. A half-dozen teenagers caper across the pavement with a middle-aged sergeant in waddling pursuit.

Down by the police van, a young officer (Hong Guoxing? Can't tell for sure from up here) paces the highway, barking urgent orders into a walkie-talkie—all to no avail. The cordon gives way completely and the pedestrians course through. The constables flail helplessly in their midst like Pharaoh's drowning legions in the resurgent Red Sea.

We flow along with the crowd across the blacktop and on down toward the provincial guest house. It takes us over an hour to run this gauntlet of market stalls, pausing to enjoy some more street theater along the way: a weight-guesser, a puppeteer, a self-flagellant strongman advertising patent medicine, a sugar-sculptor who dribbles syrup onto a griddle to make zoomorphic lollypops. Young Uighurs accost us with furtive offers of fake Rolexes and French ticklers, as well as purportedly aphrodisiac tidbits culled from endangered wildlife: tiger claws, bear gallbladders, and deer musk glands.

ARRIVING AT the guest house, it's a bit of a shock to find the same off-color wares for sale at the provincial tourism authority's souvenir counter. The only differences seem to be in the pricing (up to eight times higher than what the Uighurs ask) and the packaging. Everything's shrink-wrapped and branded with the Yellow Emperor's name: Yellow Emperor Wristwatch, Yellow Emperor Erotic Aids, Yellow Emperor Reindeer Antlers, *inter alia*. Candies, T-shirts, and rice wine all bear the Yellow Emperor's supposed likeness—a smooth and smiling visage more like an urbane board chairman than a prehistoric demiurge.

A dowager in a taffeta pants suit tries out a whiff of Yellow Emperor Cologne from a sample aerosol. "What a name for a perfume," she grumbles to the salesgirl. "Couldn't you come up with a classier name? 'Primordial Essence' or 'Eau de Yore,' or something." She sniffs her freshly daubed wrist and wrinkles her nose: "Who ever heard of ginseng-smelling cologne, anyway?"

Turning away from the souvenirs, she starts rhythmically banging the service bell on the front desk. "Checkout, checkout, please," she sings, slapping her Netherlands passport on the counter. Drawing no response, she drums her fuchsia-lacquered nails in frustration, then busies herself running a censorious finger over every available surface—the house phone, the table lamp, the cashier's window—to check for dust.

The deskclerk is far too preoccupied to heed her. Milling *huaqiao* line the entire length of the counter, each one wanting his room receipt, his key drop, his onward transport *right now*. But the clerk—the same balding snorer whose nap we'd interrupted yesterday—is not one to be rushed. For each guest, he calmly totals up the room bill on an abacus and fills in all the blanks in his multicolumned room registry, taking his time.

Skirting this logjam, we cross the lobby to try our luck instead at the provincial travel agency's kiosk. But here, too, the booking agent is torn between the conflicting demands of her customers. A pair of thirty-something business partners—American *huaqiao*, from the look of them—want to charter a taxi back to Xian, but can't agree on the itinerary. They argue in Shandong-accented Mandarin.

The beefy type in the golfing togs wants to rush back to the capital in time for the provincial governor's Business Round-Table tonight. But his bow-tied partner, armed with a list of worthy charities, keeps proposing a stop at this orphanage or that school on the way.

"Look, I know it's important to show your commitment to the country," the golfer grudgingly concedes, as though humoring a child. "Yes, it scores points with the locals, opens doors for us, and all that. But let's not lose sight of the main point, okay? This is the *governor* we're talking about. Plus a whole roomful of top investors. Contacts. Swapping business cards. *Networking.* How can we come late? Besides, there's no place decent to stay or to eat this side of Xian. First things first, all right?"

"No, *you* keep first things first," his partner retorts, flushing. "Why'd we come back to China, anyway? For contacts? For money?

For dinner? Or to give something back to the country, like we said when we started? And *this*," he waves his list over his head, "is how we pay back. Not in business cards!"

The travel agent glances nervously from one to the other, at a loss how to proceed. When we approach the counter, she seems relieved to let them work out their philosophical differences while she fields our far simpler query: Any more tours heading up Jiao Shan to the tomb? The last busload just left, she says—a miscellany of *huaqiao*. If we hurry, we might still be able to catch them in the driveway.

We charge out of the lobby and across the parking lot after the bus. It's an ultra-modern super-deluxe tour coach, the streamlined kind with its seating area riding high over its luggage compartment and its windows tinted to blend in with its gunmetal-blue paint job. It's even christened with a name—*Enterprise*—emblazoned above the windshield. To head off this imposing starship, we have to virtually fling ourselves across the hotel's gateway. Only then does the bus glide silently to a halt and the door open for us with a pneumatic sigh.

The driver collects our fare and waves us in to find seats wherever we can. The interior lighting is as tastefully subdued as a first-class airline cabin—more suitable for luxurious catnapping, it would seem, than for sight-seeing. Yet even in this plush twilight, I can *feel* all eyes fixed on us, the latecoming interlopers who've delayed the tour. Making our way down the aisle, I catch snatches of murmured conversation in English, French, Spanish, Malay, and a few more languages I can't identify—but no Chinese.

The only seats left are in the very last row, and even there we're too late to get a window. A suntanned, silver-rinsed couple occupies the left-hand corner of the bus, opposite a solitary old man scrunched over to the right. As we settle into the middle of the row, the lady to my right asks, with exaggerated enunciation, whether I can speak English. As soon as the couple can peg me for an American, the two of them hail me with spontaneous tribal solidarity. "We're Sol and Sylvia Chew," the man introduces, "from Monterey Park, California."

Handshakes all around.

"Well, fancy meeting *you* here," Sylvia chimes in, brightly. "*Really* off the beaten track, now, aren't you? Don't worry. Even the boonies are okay in China if you know how to handle them. Drink only hot tea. When bargaining for stuff, never pay any more than half their opening offer. And always bring your own TP."

"TP?"

"Toilet paper," Sol translates. They learned these maxims through experience, he adds, having already visited the country four times before. Ever since he retired from the roofing supply business some fifteen years ago, the Chews have enjoyed yearly excursions overseas. They just choose package tours out of the *Chinatown Shoppers' News* classified ads. Eastern Europe, Thailand, the Greek Islands, Peru, the Trans-Siberian Railroad whatever seems the best value at the time

"But China's the one place we keep coming back to," he adds. "The dollar goes a long way here and we can get around in the language. They roll out the red carpet for overseas Chinese, so we can really feel like celebrities here, which is a lot more than you can say for some of these other countries. Only trouble is, after four visits to China, you start to run out of new destinations. I mean, by the time you get around to a place like Shaanxi . . ."

While I'm busy bonding with Sol and Sylvia, Ah-loong's engaged in a sidelong assessment of the old man next to her: the familiar terry-cloth sun hat, the starched and pressed blue jeans, the down-to-the-nubs crewcut, the suede sneakers, the cotton jersey buttoned up to the neck. The meticulously casual ensemble seems almost Japanese, yet the face is somehow too candid for that, peering about at everything with genial, unabashed interest. "Ah-Bei [Elder Uncle] . . . ?" Ah-loong ventures in Taiwanese.

"Wah! Where do you come from?" he beams in delighted surprise. He speaks in Taiwanese, but with a heavy mainland accent. Ah-loong identifies herself as a down-island Taiwanese, then reciprocates her seatmate's question: Where's *he* from?

"Keelung," he automatically responds, naming Taiwan's northernmost harbor. "Although I'm really from Hunan," he adds, naming a landlocked province of the mainland. "I mean . . . well, it's complicated."

The complication is more in his mind than in the biographical details, to hear him tell the tale. The man's personal trajectory, convoluted though it may be, is also so commonplace that it's practically a cliché on either side of the Taiwan Strait. Press-ganged at age fourteen into the KMT armies, he got swept up in an incomprehensible (to him) civil war that eventually deposited him in Taiwan. There he remained his entire adult life: marrying a Taiwanese, raising children, working a civil service job, retiring on a pension.

"I hardly remember anything about my life on the mainland," he admits. "Just a lot of dirt-digging and then some scary shoot-outs. I guess I must have had a family, once. I half-recall a mother, some brothers. But I lost all contact with them when the army took me away. Now I'm not even sure what particular village I'm from; I only know that I speak native Hunanese. What with farmwork and fighting, I guess I never even *had* a childhood, really, so my life pretty much began as a grown-up, in Taiwan."

A full enough life it's been, too, he relates. Through his children and in-laws, he's built up family ties such as he'd never known in China. He so thoroughly identifies with the island that, for the last several elections, he's voted with the independence-minded Democratic Progressive Party. And yet he's of an age now—seventy-one, to be precise—where he finds himself inclined to view the overall arc of his life, beyond just the transient episodes. So he took a three-month "leave of absence" from his family for this solitary mainland journey, the first time he's set foot in China in half a century.

"And did you find what you were looking for?" Ah-loong asks.

"I don't even *know* what I'm looking for," he laughs. "Roots? Relatives? Impossible, with such scanty facts as I have to go on. All I can do is just travel around, watching people. It's still as much of a muddle here as I remember it, though not quite as scary as it seemed in wartime. But now, with almost everyone I see in China, I think, 'There, but for luck . . .'

"And I start to wonder where luck ends and I begin. Or where luck ends and *they* begin, the strangers I run into here. Which is just another way of asking where *I* end and *they* begin. That line gets blurrier the longer I look at it. In seventy-one years, I think I've never felt lonelier than on this trip. Yet never so connected, either."

BY NOW, the *Enterprise* has already reached the summit of Jiao Shan. The *huaqiao* on board pile out to view the tomb. Ah-loong and her newfound friend, absorbed in their conversation, stroll off together, chatting in Taiwanese. Sol and Sylvia decide to stay on the bus, preferring to conserve energy for their scheduled stroll on the Xian city wall later tonight. So I'm left on my own for a turn about the grounds.

The day-lit tomb hardly matches the evocative power of our twilight visit yesterday. Under the dust diffused afternoon sun, every shadowless rock or tree looks somehow diminished. The incense-burning terrace with its bronze brazier, the ceremonial entry arch, the tomb mound itself—all take on a tired, loess-yellow hue.

Wandering out through the moon gate behind the tomb, I'm somehow relieved *not* to run into Gao Xinyang, last night's *feng shui* guru. The "dragon horns" he pointed out to us now reveal themselves as withered cypress trunks, stripped of bark or branches. The surrounding hills look bare and lumpy as *wo-wo tou*—steamed corn dumplings. I'm at a loss to see in them the promised dragon, phoenix, and turtle. Perhaps, if I sat down and attended to my breathing for a while, the whole *feng shui* menagerie would reveal itself.

No time for that, though; the *Enterprise* is already revving its engine for our return downhill. Just a mild intimation, so far—the driver has yet to even touch his horn. Still, it's none too soon to start drifting back into the tomb compound. On my way to the parking lot, a pair of stocky *huaqiao* burghers hand me an Instamatic to snap their portrait in front of the entry arch.

They parlay in Malay about how to pose the picture. "How about over here, Adik"—Little Brother—"so as to include this carving?" "But if we stand there in the center, Abang"—Big Brother—"we can fit the whole archway within a horizontal frame."

I dredge up my long-disused Indonesian to ask, "Abang? Adik? You're siblings, then?"

They seem quite tickled by my query (or is it my brash assault upon their language?). "But of course-*lah*," Abang pronounces in a slightly clipped Oxbridge English. "Can't you tell?"

Now that he mentions it, there *is* a resemblance of sorts. Posed side-by-side, they look like a hair-transplant surgeon's "before-and-after" ad. Adik is fully and frankly bald, with just a graying fringe to ring his gleaming, nut-brown pate. Abang sports a rich plantation of jet-black hair culminating in a widow's peak that highlights his lofty, ivory brow. The elder brother wears a quietly elegant blazer; the younger sports a batik shirt resplendent with fern fronds and peacock fans. Yet despite these differences of fashion, both share the same quizzical smile (Adik's with perhaps an extra hint of world-weariness; Abang's with an overtone of anxious solicitude).

They introduce themselves as the Brothers Kwek, Aloysius and Johannes, Catholic Peranaakans (thoroughly assimilated Sino-Malay creoles of the Indonesian archipelago). They're heirs to a long-established trading empire in cloves and batik. Upon coming of age, Johannes, the elder, took over the family's warehouse and shop on the Singapore waterfront. Aloysius inherited the "factory" in Cirebon, North Central Java.

The Singapore warehouse didn't last for long, though, before it was taken over by the island republic's Housing Development Board for conversion into a high-rise block of offices and condominia. That was fine with Abang; he wound up with a "fair sum" in monetary compensation plus an airy, modern duplex flat in the new high-rise.

Adik, on the other hand, saw no reason to alter his traditional life in Cirebon. The old family retainers (or their children and grandchildren) continued to polish the pewter, wax the mahogany floors, and serve up multicourse creole banquets. Jesuits schooled a new generation of Peranaakans, from the same old chapbooks. The Kweks took good care of their Indonesian military patrons, who duly reciprocated their solicitude.

And then, suddenly, the Suharto regime fell and the whole archipelago convulsed. Fires raged, mobs roved. The strife circled all around the Cirebon factory, withdrew awhile, then lapped nearer still.

Inconsistent and unconfirmable rumors kept Aloysius constantly on edge. Ongoing army patrols brought scant reassurance, since there was no telling from day to day who commanded the commanders. Out-of-uniform paratroopers could just as easily turn into lynch mobs. With 3 percent of the population controlling an estimated half the national wealth, popular resentment could flare at any moment. As always in Indonesia, the handiest scapegoats were ethnic Chinese.

So now, for the first time in many years, Aloysius had to think of himself as Chinese. It hardly came naturally to him. He'd never laid eyes on China, had no known relatives there, spoke not a word of any Chinese dialect, didn't even particularly like Chinese cuisine. Over centuries of settlement in Java, the Peranaakans had evolved into a distinctive culture. They considered themselves as "indigenous" as any other strand in the multiethnic fabric of Indonesian life—but try telling *that* to a mob, when push comes to shove. It might be the better part of valor, the Brothers Kwek decided, for Aloysius to come stay with Johannes for a while.

"It worked out pretty well to start with," Abang relates. "But my Adik's been kind of a jumpy sort ever since we were little."

"Everything in Singapore was so clean, so bright, so simple," Aloysius sighs. "And, meanwhile, we had no really intelligible news from Indonesia. I had plenty of worries and nothing to do with my time. I just sat around all day, watching television with the grandchildren. I began to feel like I was already *living* in *Sesame Street*."

"So we decided to take a trip here," Johannes picks up the story. "We went first to the coast, to the Singapore-sponsored investment park in Suzhou. Then we came to Shaanxi. Since there's no getting away from being Chinese, we thought we might as well find out more about China. Maybe consider shifting some family assets away from Indonesia. After all, 'When you drink the water, remember the source,' " he intones, quoting a Chinese platitude much cited in charitable appeals to *huaqiao*.

"Anything *we've* been drinking these many years has its source ultimately in Cirebon," Aloysius shakes his head dubiously. "Here they can't even make a decent cup of coffee."

"But whatever we became in Cirebon, the original source is here," Johannes counters. "We Kweks must have *learned* how to make coffee, at some stage. Our original ancestors never dreamt of such a thing. Everything can be learned. China could learn how to become a gigantic version of Singapore, someday."

"Now *there's* a thought," Aloysius shudders. " '*Guru kencing berdiri, murid akan kencing berlari,*' " he quotes—"If the teacher pisses standing up, the pupil will surely piss on the run,"—an Indonesian proverb that reflects the Malay Muslim taboo against urinating in anything but a squatting position.

By now our driver's already honking to summon us back to the bus. The Kweks and I exit the tomb compound via the incense terrace, where a harried matron is struggling to light a last few joss sticks with a Zippo.

"Cut it out, Mom," her teenage son admonishes in a nasal New York English. "The driver's already calling."

"Just one more joss stick," she replies in Mandarin. "Take those plugs out of your ears and come block the wind while I hold the lighter."

He ignores her summons, defiantly cranking up the volume of his Walkman until it's audible even to passersby like us. "You really believe there's somebody *in* that grave?" he taunts.

"It's not a body, it's a force," she retorts as her incense finally catches flame. She jabs the joss sticks into the smoldering cauldron. "This is your ancestry, your heritage, your birthright. It's the only thing that protects you from being ignored and pushed aside by the whole world. It's something very ancient, very powerful. And it wants worship. So *feed* it."

She bundles the hapless teen down the path to the parking lot and throws me a withering glance as she cuts ahead of us into the line to board the bus. "Do you *mind*?"

WE GET OFF at the base of the hill and watch the *Enterprise* spin away down the road in a cloud of loess dust. We scuff our own way across the fairground toward the farmers' market and amusement stalls, relieved to be off the high-gloss bus and back in touch with ground reality among the earthier scions of the Yellow Emperor.

In a spirit of salt-of-the-earth solidarity, we beam our *bonhomie* at everyone we see: the ring-toss carnies, basket and farm-tool vendors, noodle chefs, gawkers, gapers, and rubes. Nobody exactly beams back, but at least we draw from most people a brief glance of disinterested curiosity, which we construe as a kind of acceptance.

At the far side of the fairground, a crudely painted freak-show banner displays an array of two-headed babies, fur-covered naked ladies, elephants, giraffes, and flying pigs. Outside the tent, a barker hails passersby with a manic verve that's belied by his perfectly expressionless face. Without exactly promising quite such extravagant attractions as the banner depicts, he invites the public to come inspect his proprietary store of "zoological, cultural, and historical wonders. Instructional and amazing. Here for one week only. Don't miss the chance! Step inside, step inside . . ."

We pay our half-renminbi admission and duck under the tent flap.

Inside, we find a few jars with sad, poached-looking fetuses floating in cloudy formaldehyde; a woodchuck (labeled "King Rat") in a cage so tight that his fur bristles up through the chicken wire; a glass box full of crumbling moths skewered on pushpins; and assorted yellowing photos. That's all.

Through the canvas, we hear the barker blabbering on. Without missing a beat, he subtly alters his spiel: "Amazing and instructional, see the Old Outsider. Fresh from foreign parts, wide-eyed and fuzzy-faced. Here for a limited engagement. Don't miss the chance—step inside, step inside . . ."

The Golden Spike

IT MAY BE humdrum in an American mall, but there's nothing prosaic about a McDonald's branch in Beijing. Here, a franchised burger stand epitomizes exotic dining. The bright lights, obsessive hygiene, brisk service, and rote cheerfulness all contrast sharply with the tone of the greasy neighborhood dives that set the baseline of Chinese sidewalk gastronomy. Never mind that most everyday Beijing street stall food tastes a lot better than a hamburger, and at a fraction of the price. Chinese crowds still pack into McDonald's for the totemic significance. It's more than just a meal; it's a quick, affordable jolt of American energy and optimism.

I recognize the impulse that draws the Beijing McCrowds, the yearning for expanded horizons. In the lower-middle-class Long Island subdivision where I grew up in the fifties, we'd flock to Chinese noodle joints for a touch of exotic class on the cheap. People in Taoranting, a southwestern suburb of Beijing, have a lot in common with the Long Islanders of the 1950s: overbooked schedules, a modicum of newly disposable income, and a nascent taste for sanitized exotica. Now Beijing families at the same "liftoff" stage of their own economic development turn to McDonald's for an instant connection to what passes for cosmopolitan culture.

Each burger franchise offers a total-immersion synergy of sights, sounds, and tastes, like a mini–theme park. Whatever the decor, from Riverboat Rococo to Nevada Neon, every McDonald's strikes the same underlying note of brassy American triumphalism. Here at the Taoranting branch, the motif happens to be Moonprobe Modern. Day-Glo comets and stars emblazon the midnight-blue ceiling. On the rivet-studded aluminum walls, porthole-shaped picture frames display glossy NASA posters—drifting nebulae, lumbering astronauts in space suits, Old Glory stiffly staked out against an airless lunar sky. Blown up larger than life-size, on a pillar over the ketchup dispensers, a lone footprint in moondust: "One small step for man, one giant leap for mankind."

From my table by the street-side plate-glass window, I survey the Chinese gastronauts broaching their introductory steps on Planet Fast Food. A harried mother tries to appease her squirmy twin toddlers with fudge sundaes. Half a dozen high school boys in unkempt khaki uniforms dispatch a bucket of Chicken McNuggets. A shy young couple—fresh from a matinee date at the cinema across the street?—share a vanilla shake. Chirpy office girls meet for Cokes. Moonlighting shopclerks dash in to bolt a burger between their day jobs and their night jobs.

The comfortingly familiar scene reinforces the hope that prosperity can transform the Chinese masses into folks "just like us." If McDonald's can establish a beachhead in Taoranting, could democracy, humanism, and rule of law be far behind? Will the turn-of-the-century economic boom sweep away all trace of Oriental inscrutability and make the Middle Kingdom easier for us to fathom and to live with? It would be heartening to believe that, left to run its course, prosperity will sooner or later give rise to an engaged and moderate citizenry.

And, of course, such a public must eventually rein in any "rogue" tendencies of the Beijing regime—an outcome so inevitable that one wonders why it shouldn't be as obvious to China's leadership as it is to our own. Are the successors of Deng and Mao simply too atavistic even to conceive of such a thing as an aroused populace? Or are the Chinese bosses closet liberals secretly scheming to usher in democratic checks on their own power? Or are they fully aware of the risks they run, but fresh out of any better alternatives to shore up their legitimacy? Is the Communist Party already too committed to economic hypergrowth to climb down?

Or have "Asian authoritarians" had it right all along: material well-being plays out differently in "Confucian" cultures, blunting rather than sharpening middle-class demands for political participation?

JUST WHAT the Chinese leaders have in mind we'll never know until we can telepathically wire-tap the entire Politburo. But, short of that, I have a friend, Xu Zhenhui, with whom I periodically check in to sound out Party thinking about political reform and representative government. He is a midlevel official in the Civil Affairs ministry who has spent nearly a decade supervising implementation of China's 1987 election law. I haven't seen him in over a year now, so I'm looking forward to catching up with him today.

The Taoranting McDonald's, just down the block from Xu's 500-square-foot civil service apartment, is our usual meeting place. Since he's a ranking bureaucrat and I, as an accredited foreign correspondent, am a known lackey of Western propaganda media, it seems the better part of valor for us to meet on neutral ground like this rather than at his place or mine. Here we're anonymous; in the context of a McDonald's, there's nothing unusual about either a homesick American like me or an upwardly mobile Chinese suburbanite like him.

Yet unbeknownst to most of the Big Mac crowd, Xu is far from typical. His official brief was one of the strangest in Chinese government. Starting just a couple of months after the 1989 Tiananmen massacre, Xu, a Party member since his early twenties, took on the full-time mission of promoting free and fair grassroots elections across the land. He went at it with missionary zeal, jetting off every couple of weeks to supervise polls in some remote corner of China. Each time, he'd come back to regale his press-corps friends with a fresh crop of anecdotes—ad hoc electoral innovations; bold campaign rhetoric from the hustings; entrenched local potentates overturned.

A legend began to build up around him as a kind of Johnny Appleseed of democracy—an itinerant enthusiast, obsessively bent on mono-cropping elections in every cranny of the political landscape. He looks the part of a Johnny Appleseed, too—wide-eyed and manic and somehow rumpled even in his worsted gray office suit. After decades in Beijing, there's still something rustic about him, a throwback to his peasant origins (a rare pedigree, for a Chinese bureaucrat, since the post-Maoist suspension of class-based affirmative action in civil service promotion).

But Xu is no political *naïf*. There's a canny, strategic side of him, with a long-term agenda for promoting democracy. He aims to start small, with the humblest villages, and gradually work his way up to bigger, richer communities and higher echelons of government. The goal, he freely admits, is to apply Mao's old guerrilla doctrine to modern politics: "Use the countryside to encircle the cities."

No coincidence, then, that Xu has achieved his best results so far in the same out-of-the-way, impoverished backwaters where Mao and company once set up their original Red guerrilla bases back in civil war times. Voters there routinely churn their village councils and innovate new modes of electioneering. On the other hand, the booming Special Economic Zones (SEZs) of the southeast coast resist all of Xu's inroads—the opposite of what you'd expect from the supposed link between democratic yearnings and newfound wealth.

This paradox may perplex Western "bourgeois liberals," but it comes as no surprise to die-hard Communists. Party leftists know that China's boom is built on the backs of exploited migrants from the depressed interior. Legions of "guest workers" toil in and around the SEZs, but they cannot vote there. Registered voters along the coast comprise a privileged minority with vested interests in the status quo. They can be counted on not to tamper with the established order. Migrant workers, on the other hand, can only vote their discontent back home in the heartland, where they're registered. They form a natural constituency for Communist detractors of the economic "miracle." So the deeper democracy penetrates into interior China, the better the Party's left wing can shore up its support base. That's why Xu's staunchest backers in the Politburo have always been elderly hard-liners derided by Western sinologists for their quaint last-ditch resistance to the inroads of economic liberalization.

Yet the same diplomats and journalists who dismiss Xu's Communist patrons are the ones most smitten by his Johnny Appleseed charisma. The U.S. Information Agency even sponsored him to attend a six-month graduate seminar for "future leaders" at an Ivy League campus. Returning from America with a collection of button-down shirts and a fresh appreciation of how media "spin" shapes public opinion in the West, he set out to drum up international news coverage for his program. I signed on for one of his first poll-watching press junkets.

We went to Liaoning, Manchuria, in the dead of January. I remember the trip as a series of prolix town meetings around glowing potbelly stoves. One after another, the villagers, androgynously lumpy in greatcoats, got up to proclaim their earnest concern for town welfare. Nobody delved much into programmatic particulars. In their (lack of) substance and their halting, rough-hewn cadences, the speeches sounded much alike to my untutored ear. Yet some drew rousing ovations, others loud guffaws, while a few evoked stony silence.

It hardly looked like a paradigm of lively debate or issue-based decision-making. We were shown the scrupulously secret balloting and the upset election results. Yet I couldn't shake my vague unease that there was some sort of subtle Potemkin going on. The campaign process was anything but transparent. The brief and stilted one-day period of official electioneering had little visible bearing upon the outcome. Clearly the real action all happened behind the scenes.

When, over McNuggets, I asked Xu about it upon my return from Liaoning, he couldn't fathom my qualms. What *else* did I expect, after all, in a mini-electorate like that, where everybody knows everyone else? But in that case, I pressed, how can you project such "democracy" up to the next higher echelon, say the district or county? Beyond the level of face-to-face electioneering in open meetings, you get into a whole new order of media campaign to align disparate voters behind a candidate's image and positions. And isn't that the slippery slope to multi-party politics?

No such risk, Xu assured me. Higher-level democracy will serve just like the grassroots elections to recruit new talent for the ruling Party's long-overdue renovation. It's not a matter of the Party putting up competitive election candidates for government office. Rather, let the competitive government election process winnow out candidates for Party membership.

For half a century, in Xu's view, the Party has been frozen in the mold of an underground revolutionary guerrilla army—clandestine, self-sufficient, designed for total control of all social functions, unchecked by either law or public oversight. Government has been reduced to mere window dressing for the Party. Such a structure might make sense in a civil war situation, where the Party, as "vanguard of the proletariat," needed maximum freedom for flexible response to fluid situations. But it doesn't work for the complex trading economy of an emerging world power.

Now, just to get on with business, both the Chinese and the international public look for the reassurance of a coherent, predictable Chinese state answerable to known, stable, and visible imperatives. To create such confidence, Xu is convinced, regulatory power must shift to an elected government subject to law.

"Then what becomes of the Party?" I wondered. Xu's answer was pat and well-rehearsed: even if it's no longer the entire ship of state, the Party is still the guidance system. It serves as a moral gyroscope, rather than a full-blown administrative apparatus. So it becomes more sensitive than ever to the quality of its membership—hence his stress on trial by election.

"Wouldn't you get even better-quality recruits through multi-party elections?"

He turned the question back on me: "How much headway will a ship make with a lot of competing guidance systems? . . . Let's get sundaes. The pineapple's good," he proposed, with the confidence of a man who knows his way around a McDonald's.

THIS TIME AROUND, though, he looks a lot less confident. From my seat by the window, I catch sight of him before he sees me. There's a split-second quaver in each stride as he crosses the Taoranting Road. He keeps glancing left and right even though he's got a "walk" signal and the traffic's held up for him by a stoplight.

Entering McDonald's, he seems momentarily startled by the automatic sliding glass panels. He pauses in the doorway, slightly rocking on his heels, taking in the scene. No telling if he's spotted me yet. He makes for the counter and orders a medium coffee, then wends his way through the tables as though hunting for a congenial spot. After some show of deliberation, he casually drops into a chair at the table next to mine. Coincidentally, like.

"Well, fancy meeting *you* here," I venture.

Xu seems fascinated with the Day-Glo space scenes on the wall. "Hmm . . . fancy," he addresses a passing comet. "Listen. Things have changed a little." He half-swivels toward me. "First, I had a car accident. Up in Liaoning, with all the snow—you know what it's like there. Our jeep went into a skid and I landed in the hospital for a couple of months."

He dismisses my expressions of sympathy. "No big deal. I'm over it now. Just some physiotherapy for lingering joint problems. But when I got out of the hospital, I found I'd been transferred to another section of our ministry. Disaster Relief." He pauses for my reaction, but I'm at a loss for what to say.

"Well, aren't you going to congratulate me?" he prods, sarcastically. "It's a promotion, you know. I jumped two pay grades. Ministry colleagues, my cadre-school classmates, they're all *dying* to get into that section. After all, it's a 'wet' job"—civil service slang for a bureaucratic berth rich in graft opportunities. "Now I get to handle valuable shipments of materiel. Not like the 'dry,' dead-end election job I was stuck in before."

"What happened?" I stammer, appalled at his evident bitterness. It's impossible for me to imagine him doing anything but promoting elections.

"I guess I was getting too caught up in the role. I'd forgotten I was only a piece of apparatus. In our Party, even when you've been installed somewhere as a moral 'guidance system,' you can always be manually overridden by the pilots in charge."

"So now what do they have you doing?"

"I still travel a lot," he shrugs. "Wherever there's misery and despair. Earthquakes, floods, droughts. A bumper crop of them this year. I bring in relief personnel and supplies, but there's never enough and everything needs to be done yesterday. The perpetual state of emergency makes it hard to keep track of resources deployed, so predators swarm over whatever's stealable. I spend half my time just struggling to brush flies off the carrion.

"Whoever banished me to Disaster Relief had a sense of irony. After a decade of pushing for grassroots self-determination, I'm now forced to learn firsthand all about the constraints on democracy: scarcity of resources, urgency of needs, and sheer greed."

"And what about your old section? Who took over?"

"Oh, they had one of my juniors all groomed to step in. A good, solid piece of apparatus, he is, too. He'll show his worth soon enough and get himself promoted on out of there. But the work goes on. It's unstoppable. Amazing things are happening.

"Listen—do you have any friends in Chinese media? Broadcast journalists? There's a film in circulation, *The Wolf Fang File*. You won't be able to get it officially, it'll take some digging. But find it and see it. It's important."

He cuts off my stream of queries. "Just *find* it." He resumes inspection of the comet on the wall. "Gotta lay off this stuff," he sighs, crumpling his styrofoam coffee cup. "Bad for you."

VIDEO SAMIZDAT, copied from copies, takes on a washed-out look. Colors come up lighter and outlines blurrier. The effect can be incongruous, daubing even the heaviest subject matter in airy impressionist brushstrokes. So we don't know what to expect when our friend (after first shutting the blinds and sending his child out to play) pulls out an unmarked cassette from behind his bookcase and feeds it into his VCR. What are these pink polka dots scrolling languidly down the blank white screen? Plum petals on a snowbank? Bloodstains on a shroud?

It takes a few seconds of narration for us to realize we're looking at inked thumbprints on a petition—the only way illiterate villagers know how to sign their names. Cut to a frozen lakefront to establish the locale: the village of Wolf Fang, in the Taihang Mountains, nearly 120 miles southwest of Beijing. Artsy focus on some picturesque whorls of lake ice.

The voiceover tells how Wolf Fang's cropland was flooded in 1960 for a reservoir. Ever since then, the village has had to depend on monthly relief grain rations to keep its 417 families fed. Except, for nearly two decades now, a clique of entrenched village cadres has been skimming the relief grain. Protests made through Party and government channels only get villagers beaten and jailed.

Zoom in for a series of head-and-shoulders portraits of villagers. Whether it's the effect of a worn video or a life of care, the faces look doughy and featureless, wiped clean of expression. The local brogue takes a little getting used to. Vowel sounds all come out darker than in standard Mandarin. Sentence endings are inflected with a fatalistic, dying fall. The villagers tell an off-camera interviewer about their rage, fear, and helplessness.

"For years, we never had enough to eat," an elderly couple complains. "People got so upset with the cadres here that village social work ground to a halt," says a Women's Association leader. "Just asking questions could earn you weeks of house arrest," a peasant complains.

The villagers mass in the schoolhouse courtyard. "Enough!" they shout. "Oust the thieves!" Pan across a tableau of dumpy figures in quilted cotton jackets, fists raised against a backdrop of gray brick walls and dusty lattice windows. The whole scene looks like a stylized set piece from any of a dozen "revolutionary" theatricals I've seen over the years in China.

"What *is* this?" I ask our host. "Some kind of historical melodrama? A TV soap opera? Some slanderous Western propaganda film?"

"Nothing of the sort," he laughs. "It's pure documentary. These are real people and events. And it was made by a top production team from the government's own Chinese Central Television station, CCTV. Keep watching. We're just getting to the interesting part."

The villagers hire a Beijing lawyer to plead their case in court—a radical notion. In China, a citizen-initiated lawsuit (much less a class action against the government) is practically unheard of. Such rights may exist on paper, but it's a rash plaintiff or lawyer who'd risk official wrath to exercise them. Half a dozen lawyers turned down the Wolf Fang brief before one Luo Ruiliang of a firm called New Dawn Law Practice agreed to take it on.

On camera, however, Luo hardly looks like a firebrand. The epaulets of his gray trenchcoat emphasize the stoop of his narrow shoulders. A lank strand of pompadour keeps drooping across his bony brow only to be repeatedly brushed away like a pesky horsefly. His wall-eyed stare gives him an owlish Jean-Paul Sartre look, accented by his sardonically lopsided smile.

He's got plenty to smirk about. The more Luo presses cadres for an account of the missing relief grain, the more outrageous their comebacks. What's the big deal, one of them scoffs. A mere 40,000-pound shortfall of grain fits well within the normal statistical discrepancy over a period of ten years. Another cadre declares that he'd really love to let the lawyer see the village account books for the past decade. Alas, the ledgers have all been eaten by goats.

The sheer effrontery of this whopper cracks up our host. I don't know how many times he's seen this tape, but it still leaves him rocking in his chair slapping his knee. As for me, I'm lost in admiration for the TV journalists.

"How'd they get him to *say* a thing like that on camera?" I wonder.

"Wait, it gets better. Or worse, I suppose."

Luo advises the villagers to sue the county administration for free-

and-fair grassroots elections in Wolf Fang, as specified in China's 1987 Organic Law on Village Committees. He's collected 132 thumbprint signatures—well over the 20-percent quorum of village households required to call an election. He tries to present his papers to the uniformed policeman in charge of the township's public security. The man can't figure out what he's called upon to do in such a case. With plodding bafflement, he rehashes the steps of a syllogism that refuses to add up: "You're a lawyer, right? And I'm the law around here. So doesn't that mean you're working for *me*?" After some head-scratching, he simply refuses the papers. "No thanks. I won't go to court with you."

By now, I'm fairly gaping in amazement. "That's right," my friend nods. "They're really *that* clueless about law. But they've still got some tricks in store. Look at this next bit."

The narrator introduces Shih Liguo, described as "a Wolf Fang intellectual who acquainted the villagers with their rights." After decades as a political commissar in the People's Liberation Army, Shih had chosen this idyllic corner of his native Yi county to retire to. But he was shocked at the exploitation he found there. "This can't be allowed to go on in a People's Republic," he declaims in his ringing tenor, glaring straight into the lens. It was his arrival on the scene that galvanized village resistance and led to the hiring of the lawyer.

On camera, Shih looks a little like the conventional icon of Sun Yat-sen, "father" of the 1911 revolution that overthrew the Manchu Qing, China's last imperial dynasty. A long face, smooth, with skin drawn taut over high cheekbones. Bushy, motile brows. His eyes would seem fanatical in their intensity, except for the laugh lines at the corners. A pencil mustache and jutting jaw reinforce the curt certitude of his speech. He delivers his dicta in a clipped, educated version of the local dialect.

To break the back of the Wolf Fang agitation, county officials decide to remove Shih, its presumptive leader. They dispatch a blue-and-white Public Security squad car to fetch him back to the county seat. But to forestall any flare-up in the village, they assign a Wolf Fang native son to the task: Cai Peilian, Shih's own brother-in-law, who's "made good" as a police constable and deputy party secretary at the county level. This is no arrest, Cai tries to assure the townspeople. He just wants to bring Shih home for a family chat.

The strategy backfires. Villagers surround the squad car and upbraid Cai. The stocky official, red in the face, denounces his Wolf Fang compatriots as a mob. He shrilly orders the TV crew to stop filming; the cameras roll on without missing a beat. A microphone boom bobs visibly over Cai's head in the surge and crush. Shih is spirited off to the walled courtyard house of a scrappy Wolf Fang elder, who promises to shelter the old commissar "for as long as it takes." The villagers draw up a cordon in front of the courtyard.

"In all my adult life, I've only cried twice," Shih confides in the off-camera interviewer. "Once was when Premier Zhou Enlai died in 1976. The second time was today when the whole village rallied around me."

Lawyer Luo appears in the courtyard door, beleaguered. Behind him looms the house where Shih is holed up. Before him mills an angry, restive crowd. In his floppy trenchcoat, he's dwarfed by the stolid masonry of the gateway lintels. He's scared, and he doesn't try to hide it.

"If we make a mistake now," Luo warns the villagers, "we'll lose all we've fought for. Powerful forces oppose us. They'd love nothing more than for us to clash with the authorities. Then they could crush us as rebels and throw out our lawsuit. Don't let that happen.

"Look, I've trusted you this far," Luo implores the crowd. "Now it's your turn to trust me. I've talked with Old Shih and he understands, too. Give an inch of ground this time. Go back to your homes. That way we can win. In court. By law. The big victory, the one that counts."

Cai withdraws, empty-handed, on the promise that Shih will present himself in the Yi county seat of his own accord. "He'd better be there within three days," Cai mutters darkly. "Or else." The squad car edges its way through the crowd and disappears down the road. But a couple of days later, Shih has no choice but to leave the village. Wolf Fang's morale sinks to a low ebb, the narrator relates (as the video cuts back to the lakefront, this time a bleak winter sunset over hummocks of opaque ice).

Wolf Fang loses not only Shih but also Luo. The lawyer, too, has to go back where he came from. Villagers surround his departing van. Some reach through the windows to pump his hand in gratitude. Some kneel by the roadside. An old lady presses her face against the glass, begging him to stay. "You're our only hope, our savior," she pleads, tearfully.

"It's time," he gently chides her. "My place is in the courthouse. That's where I can do you the most good. I'll come back after we've won."

True to his word, the next time he shows up in the village is on election day, April 6. Barely a fortnight before Luo's announced deadline for filing his writ, the county administration has "spontaneously" scheduled council elections for Wolf Fang. Nothing to do with lawsuits, officials let it be known; simply a routine exercise as specified in the Organic Law. Coincidentally, the election will be the first in any of Yi county's 300-odd villages in the decade since the law was passed. Luo withdraws his petition.

Zoom in for yet another artsy lakefront shot: crystalline arabesques of ice dissolving into leaping freshets of meltwater. In the rinsed light of a spring morning, a town crier picks his way through the rutted mud lanes calling all household representatives to a nominating session of the village assembly.

The assembly names a slate of eight candidates to stand for six posts in the general election. With odds like that, the poll sounds about as sporty as shooting fish in a barrel. The real thrill must lie not in picking winners but in repudiating losers. All nominees but one are stalwarts of the petition drive. The lone exception: Wolf Fang's old Party secretary, who had presided over the decades of kleptocracy.

"This amounts to a public lynching," I murmur.

"Sure," my host cheerfully agrees, "and one that's been well-earned by all the parties involved. But better to do it this way than with bludgeons or dynamite."

At least this kind of lynching takes on the festive air of a village fair. The camera pans over billows of red bunting on all the walls and doorposts. Atop a table in the middle of the schoolhouse courtyard, the ballot box sits surmounted by a red crepe rosette. Villagers pour in from all the surrounding alleys. A bandy-legged old man, propped between grandsons, totters up to cast his ballot. A beaming mother with a baby strapped on her back lines up to vote. When her turn comes, the baby stuffs the ballot into the slot on the mother's behalf. Villagers mill about the courtyard, decked out in their Sunday best. Nothing fancy; just workaday tunics, but well-scrubbed and meticulously patched. Matrons plait ribbons into their braids. Younger women sport plastic hairbands with sequins. Spring sunshine glints from the finery.

The camera homes in on a few faces in the crowd. "We've waited years for this day," a grizzled yeoman nods in satisfaction. "Maybe things will finally start looking up for us," a shy yokel ventures to hope. The TV interviewer asks one boisterous hulk of a man whether he could accept a council that included candidates he'd voted against. "Of course not," the giant laughs. "Then what would be the point of holding an election?"

Luo weaves from group to group in the courtyard, exchanging congratulations with the villagers, nodding and smiling like a debutante at a cotillion. He's traded in his trenchcoat for a natty blue windbreaker. His lopsided smile has widened into a toothy grin. On this triumphal note, the scene fades to one last artsy pan of the lakefront. Sunbeams shimmer on the waters under the bluest of springtime skies. The credits roll.

"And they all lived happily ever after?" I ask.

"Who knows?" shrugs our host. "It's just one of literally a million villages in China. No way to keep track of them all."

"But Wolf Fang can't just sink from sight," I protest. "Not after all this fanfare. A program like this on the official TV station doesn't just happen by itself. Someone in the leadership must have taken an interest. Surely it stirred up a lot of reaction when it was aired?"

"It never *got* aired," our friend says. "It was all set to run about a year ago. It was already announced in the *People's Daily*, and in the station's own coming attractions. People turned on their TVs to see it and instead found some bland pap about marriage counseling."

"How'd *that* happen?"

He points straight up and raises his eyes skyward as though in prayer. "Last-minute orders from the top. *Way* up there, it must have been, too, to override the high-level approval that CCTV had already gotten."

"But why?"

"Take a guess. That's all anyone can do about decisions so high up. So now you can only see this film in scratchy home copies like this one." He stashes the rewound tape back behind a row of dictionaries.

"Where'd *you* get it from?"

"Don't ask me that."

"But this is preposterous," I sputter. "Every time China's denounced as authoritarian, the regime retorts by touting its advances in grassroots democracy and rule of law. A case like this only makes them look good."

"Look good to whom? This film wasn't made for you. It's not for a foreign audience. We're talking about hundreds of millions of Chinese TV viewers. If you broadcast a story like this nationwide, it's like promising that what happened in Wolf Fang will happen everywhere."

He glances reverently skyward again. "Whoever decided to squelch this film had to ask himself: Can we really deliver democracy and rule of law all over China?"

"Could they really deliver those things, for that matter, in Wolf Fang itself?" I wonder.

"You'll never find out just by watching TV," our friend admonishes, reopening the blinds. The smog-blotted evening sun drags its way listlessly between apartment blocks that stretch as far as the western horizon. "The village is out there somewhere," he muses. "So's the lawyer."

NEITHER OF THESE QUARRIES proves easy to find. We riffle through a few Hebei guidebooks and manage to locate Lake Solidarity, the reservoir depicted in the film. But no trace of Wolf Fang—nothing there of touristic interest, I guess. As for the lawyer, our phone call to New Dawn Law Practice draws a blank. He left the firm nearly a year back, we're told. Any forwarding address? "Who's calling?" demands a wary receptionist. "Just a friend," Ah-loong stammers. That doesn't cut it. We're assured, implausibly, that Luo has vanished without a trace.

Chastened, we recruit an ally for our next gambit—a friend of ours who, in the course of two decades' experience as a Beijing office manager, has cultivated an invincible telephone voice. It's a joy to listen to him as he rings up the Chinese Bar Association and asks where to find attorney Luo Ruiliang. Our friend has perfectly mastered the cadre tone—an amalgam of formality, boredom, and contempt that signals he could turn nasty very fast unless he gets what he wants. Nobody would dream of challenging such a voice. The Bar Association clerk runs an instant mental cost-benefit calculation and meekly pads off to get the information. Within minutes, we've tracked Luo to his new firm, the Keystone Partnership.

Our luck holds good on the next call: Luo himself picks up the line. We're so used to hacking our way through thickets of telephonic flak-catchers that we're a bit nonplussed at first. We feel like stage-door groupies suddenly and unexpectedly face-to-face with a matinee idol. After all, this is someone we've only encountered before on a TV screen.

But we can't admit that to Luo, at least not in an introductory phone call. By rights we're not even supposed to have seen the Wolf Fang film, since it's officially banned. And we're sworn to secrecy about the host and venue of our screening. So Ah-loong can only stammer out "We've heard a lot about the great things you've done."

Instead of asking "Like what?" Luo only offers a noncommittal "Hmm . . . ?" He keeps his voice as studiously dispassionate as a shrink's or a banker's.

"So we were hoping to meet you and find out more about your work," Ah-loong presses. She speaks in a rush, eager to get to the point of her call before Luo has a chance to cut her off.

"It can't hurt to get together," he replies after just the barest split-second of silence. He agrees to a late afternoon appointment and Ah-loong proposes a nearby hotel lobby. Luo considers for a moment and suggests, "Maybe we'd better meet here, in my office, instead."

After she hangs up we stare at each other, flabbergasted. We've never encountered such a willing interviewee in China. "He didn't even ask who I am or where I'm from," Ah-loong marvels. "Maybe he took you for a potential client," I suggest. "A pleader-for-hire like Luo must get plenty of calls from people in distress. Victims of persecution wouldn't want to give details on the phone, so Luo knows not to press for them. A lawyer can't afford to shut anyone out."

Even so, Luo's uncritical openness signals something new under the Chinese sun—an advocate-at-large. In such a closed society, what happens when a class of professionals assumes a private vocation to take up the troubles of others? It's easy enough, in the litigious West, to sneer about ghoulish, lawyerly ambulance chasers. But in a police state, to champion a stranger's grievance amounts to sheer knight-errantry.

Still, Luo makes it a point to size things up before charging into the fray. He's called us to his office, the better to check us out, we realize when we go to keep our afternoon appointment.

Just locating the place is our first test. No such address among the low-rise shopfronts that line this stretch of Chaoyang Road. It takes us a few passes up and down the block to notice the narrow gateway wedged between a beauty salon and a hardware store. This modest portal turns out to be the main entry to the vast and muddy court-yard of a decommissioned factory. Most of the plant buildings lie empty. Only a few ground-floor suites have been turned into makeshift offices. We stumble upon an accounting firm, a VD clinic, and two trading companies before we find the signboard we're looking for.

Keystone Law Partnership comprises a dozen battleship-gray steel desks, each enclosed in its own Formica-and-glass cubicle. Luo is wait-ing for us in the unadorned reception room. Engulfed in an outsized leatherette swivel chair, he looks even smaller than he did on TV. He offers a stiff handshake, head cocked quizzically to one side. His twitchy marionette gestures lend him an air of antic pugnacity. As you'd expect of a knight-errant, his belt is slung with holstered weapons: a pager and a mobile phone.

Our diminutive knight comes complete with his own squire—a ruddy, rotund, balding colleague whom he introduces only as Lawyer Zeng. The two of them stare at us expectantly as we settle into the reception-room sofa. They make no offer to launch the conversation themselves. We apologize for our tardiness.

Luo seems unsurprised at our babbled excuses about missing the gateway. "I know," he nods sympathetically. "I still can't find my own way sometimes to this place. Now and then I need to phone Old Zeng here to come out and find me on the street."

"Oh, then you're new here?" I ask. "We tried to find you through New Dawn Law Practice, but they said they'd no idea where you'd gone." The two lawyers exchange a cautionary glance. "Old Luo's been with us a couple of months," Zeng offers noncommittally. That seems about as far as we'll get on this line of conversation. Better raise our bid to call them out.

"We saw the film of your Wolf Fang case," I venture.

Luo beams and relaxes visibly. As far as he's concerned, that's explanation enough of why we're here: anyone aware of his Wolf Fang derring-do would naturally come seek him out. But Zeng seems nervous at the mere mention of the film. He's evidently dying to ask us how and where we saw it. Ah-loong heads him off with a flood of enthusiasm.

"What a victory," she gushes to Luo. "You must have been so proud."

Luo warms to the topic. "Election day was the high point. After that, though, I hardly got much chance to revel in it," he smiles ruefully.

"What went wrong?"

"Maybe I talked too much. The week they were due to air the Wolf Fang program, I went around telling everybody I knew not to miss the broadcast—my wife and son, my brothers, neighbors and colleagues. They all tuned in. Imagine the letdown when the show was canceled."

"Well, it wasn't *your* fault," Ah-loong protests.

"My office didn't quite see it that way," Luo sighs. "As long as CCTV was with us in Wolf Fang, my bosses over at New Dawn backed me totally. Nationwide TV exposure, they knew, would bring the firm a lot of face. But the last-minute cancellation scared them. If higher-ups had such problems with the Wolf Fang story, my bosses worried, then maybe New Dawn had better disown me. Not only did they fire me, they also took away my professional certification."

Ah-loong is scandalized. "How could they do that? Isn't it *yours*?"

"You'd think so, wouldn't you? But in fact, they claimed it belonged to the firm. What could I say? New Dawn's a state outfit, after all. Government firms were the only type of law practice allowed until just last year. It took me months of fighting to get back my license from them. Only with that certificate in my hand could I persuade any of the new private law partnerships like Keystone to even look at me."

"Now don't start that again," Zeng admonishes. "You know how we respect your achievements and stand behind you."

"No doubt," Luo tartly agrees. "But when it came right down to it, even you had no use for a lawyer who was, in effect, disbarred and politically suspect." The memory still rankles apparently, for Luo adds, "I won't let myself get stymied like that again. From now on, I hang on to my license myself. I worked hard enough to get it in the first place."

"How *did* you two become lawyers, anyway?" I ask, trying to keep the conversation moving and smooth over the rift that has opened up between them.

"Self-taught," Luo replies with evident pride. "We did it by mail," Zeng elaborates, grateful to reestablish common ground with his colleague after their momentary sparring. Correspondence courses, they explain, were the only way for "first-generation" lawyers to prep for the bar exam after the Cultural Revolution. They slogged through a decade of coursework, studying in snatches while holding down menial full-time jobs. Luo spent most of the 1980s carrying sacks in a flour mill; Zeng worked as a machinist. It took them until 1989 to graduate.

"And even then," Zeng adds, "we couldn't take our actual bar exams until a year later, thanks to the 'counterrevolutionary disturbances' in Tiananmen."

"What a different story *that* would have been if we'd had more lawyers in those days," Luo conjectures. "Suppose there'd been, say, eight thousand members of the Beijing bar at the time; *then* you might have seen something." In fact, he laments, there were barely a few hundred in 1989, half of them old pre–Cultural Revolution warhorses who'd been pretty well broken down in the meanwhile. Even now, there are only four or five thousand lawyers in Beijing, he adds, and not even thirty thousand in the whole of China.

The numbers are rising fast, though, Zeng notes. "Nowadays, they come fresh out of the fancy new law schools and walk straight into well-paid commercial jobs. But they lack the kind of fire that drove us into this profession in the 1980s."

"SO WHAT WAS IT that lit such a fire under you?" I ask Luo.

"Mao Zedong Thought," he replies without batting an eye. I'm at a loss to see how the Great Helmsman's sloganeering could ever inspire anyone to pursue a career in law. Sensing my puzzlement, Luo tries to explain. He starts with an autobiographical digression.

"At the onset of the whole Cultural Revolution nightmare, it was easy to regard Mao and his Thought as our enemies. After all, wasn't it in the name of Mao that Mother and I were 'sent down' to the countryside?"

Before "Liberation," Luo's grandfather had fled the squalor of his ancestral Hebei village to set up a trading house in Beijing. That was enough to make the family "class enemies," by Maoist logic. When the Communists came to power, they confiscated the Luos' four-courtyard Beijing mansion and filled it with worker households—all but a small rear-corner room where the Luos were allowed to remain.

But even this toehold they lost when the Red Guards came in 1966. Luo was just fourteen at the time and his mother nearly fifty. Two elder brothers were already on their own, ensconced in factory jobs; their acquired status as "workers" placed them safely out of the fray of class warfare. But the matriarch and the schoolboy still kept their "landlord" onus. The two of them were shipped back "home" to the ancestral village—a place Luo had never even seen before—to "learn from the peasants."

Peasant pedagogical methods proved none too gentle: a lot of beatings, punitive work assignments, and sustained ostracism. Luo and other "class enemies" had no normal social contact with the rest of the villagers. They couldn't even attend the political study sessions that livened up the peasants' daily round of toil.

"Nowadays, to get out of political study is regarded as a precious perk," Luo laughs. "But back then we felt it an affront. So I organized a separate group of us 'class enemies' to study Mao Zedong Thought on our own. Nobody could deny us that. We weren't polluting anybody else's revolutionary purity, after all. We just kept to ourselves and read Maoist classics—the *Old Three Lectures*, the *Quotations*, and such."

The group's style of analysis, too, was impeccably Maoist. Everything was reduced to conflicts and "contradictions." Any issue, down to the pettiest street quarrel, could be cast in the context of a life-and-death struggle between the bourgeois versus the proletarian line. Ultimate authority rested not in reason but in Maoist holy writ; the point was to browbeat, not to persuade.

"It didn't take us too long to get good at this game," Luo boasts. "We quickly learned how to keep on the right side of Mao's distinction between 'antagonistic contradictions' versus 'contradictions among the people.' And that's when I realized that the Chairman could be my friend after all. Through Mao Zedong Thought we gradually managed to argue our way into the councils of our production brigade. We could improve our rations, our schooling, and our work assignments. We broke through the quarantine."

But how, I ask him for the third time, did all this lead you to the study of law? My obtuseness must be starting to irk him; he spells out the connection patiently, as though to a pitiably dim schoolchild.

"The beauty of Mao Zedong Thought, for an outcast like me, was that it's all down in writing." That meant that anybody could appeal to its transcendent authority, he explains. All one had to do was to master its rules of argument, crude as they were. China had never had such a written code before, at least not in Luo's lifetime. After Mao's death and the fall of his chosen successors, Mao Zedong Thought lost much of its shine. "But by then," Luo beams, "we had an even better written code to appeal to: the law."

Like much else in post-Mao China, the restoration of law dates from the Communist Party's Third Plenum in late 1978, where Deng Xiaoping unveiled his reformist agenda. To quell Maoist throwbacks, Deng needed a body of civil and administrative legislation, so he rushed through a set of stopgap legal codes. Draconian and incomplete as they seemed, they were still a lot better than no law at all. Official media launched the new codes with paeans to the "equality of all before the law." Such slogans fired the imagination of idealistic young drifters like Luo, fresh back from communes and seeking direction for their new urban lives.

Luo's two older brothers, who'd stayed in Beijing as factory workers throughout the Cultural Revolution, already had a head start on their career reorientation. After the limited restoration of property rights, his eldest brother parlayed family land holdings into a resurgent real estate and trading empire. His second brother finished his law degree by correspondence and was already a well-regarded senior partner in Beijing's leading law firm.

"Looking at the two of them, I decided that Second Brother seemed to be having much more fun, so I chose to follow his path," Luo explains.

The legal field, in those days, had all the excitement of an ever-expanding frontier. Deng and his reformists resurrected China's Justice Ministry (defunct for the past twenty years). Law schools reopened their doors for the first time since the Red Guard raids. The few surviving pre-Liberation lawyers returned from rural exile. The four-tiered court system was revamped and appeal processes spelled out.

Not that the legal revival much tempered the harshness of Party rule. Deng still had no qualms about crushing the short-lived free speech movement at Beijing's Democracy Wall in 1979 and jailing its leaders for decades. Convicts by the truckload were carted off for summary execution in the nationwide "Strike Hard" anticrime campaign that started in 1983 and continues to this day.

Nevertheless, a steady drumbeat of new legislation kept up the level of excitement among aspiring lawyers. First came the Marriage Law, then the Contract Law, followed by laws governing trademarks, patents, and inheritance—each year a major new statute throughout the early 1980s. In 1986, a bumper year, China brought out a comprehensive Code of Civil Procedures that set forth the rights and obligations of individual citizens as well as corporate entities (regarded as "legal persons"). And the next year saw passage of the Organic Law on Village Councils—the election law that was invoked in Wolf Fang.

Luo never expected to find himself arguing this statute in his first major case as a full-fledged lawyer, after completing a two-year internship at New Dawn. "I always supposed I'd wind up in contracts and property law, like most of my fellow correspondence-course graduates," he says. But when approached by the Wolf Fang villagers, he found the brief hard to resist.

"It's not every day you get a case like that," he shrugs. "Real hot issues, a chance to make a difference. As for the villagers, well, in my life I'd been forced to spend time enough in that kind of backwater to acquire a feel for them. Maybe I 'learned from the peasants' a bit after all."

Zeng shakes his head. "Only you," he scolds his friend with a mock scowl. "We all fantasize about such stunts, but only you actually go out and try one. You got away with it that time—just barely. But don't press your luck. And *don't* bore our guests with your boasts."

"But we love hearing about it," Ah-loong protests. "That's what we came for. You did a great thing in Wolf Fang."

"For pity's sake, don't goad him on," Zeng pleads. "That's the last thing he needs."

The tone is bantering, but with an underlying edge of reproach. I know that voice. It's the unmistakable note of a "chaperone." Every collectivity in China, from the smallest tenement or workshop right up to the Central Politburo, has its own set of "liaison" specialists who buffer all official contacts between its members and outsiders. The chaperone's main job is to ensure that nothing interesting ever gets seen or said. But nobody has obliged Luo to saddle himself with a chaperone on this occasion. Our contact was set up informally, outside official channels. So why does he feel the need to voluntarily call in Zeng as an inhibitor? Does he distrust his own loquacity? Or our goodwill? Or is it just a lawyerly instinct for a backup witness in case of unforeseen future problems?

Whatever the reason, Luo immediately heeds Zeng's warning to drop the subject of Wolf Fang. He nods submission, a forelock unfurling from his pompadour like a snapped watchspring.

"Well, that's all past," he concludes, heavily.

"Are you sure?" I persevere. "No next chapter to the story? What's going on in Wolf Fang now?"

"Past. All past," he sighs.

"Well, then, let's talk about the future," Ah-loong urges, trying to restart the stalled conversation. "What are your new cases here?"

"Now *those* are pretty interesting," he brightens a little. "I've even been getting death threats on a class action that I've got going down in Tianjin . . ."

"But it's still in litigation and subject to lawyer-client confidentiality," Zeng cuts him off, primly.

Luo throws up his hands with an ironic, lopsided smile. He fumbles in the pocket of his limp cardigan and hands us his business card. No card from Zeng, though, as he ushers us to the door with the usual parting pleasantries. We pick our way across the fen of the factory courtyard with a vague sense of letdown. It's rained while we were inside and the mud is now ankle-deep.

"First time I've ever been bodily 'bounced' out of a law firm," I grumble in frustration at the truncated interview. "Those guys aren't taking any chances, are they?"

"So who were you expecting to meet in there?" Ah-loong teases. "Patrick Henry? Or Bakunin, maybe?"

She's right, of course; seditious grandstanding would be a bit much to ask of a law firm. In a country run like a jail, it's no surprise to find a legal fraternity full of self-taught jailhouse lawyers—tough, driven, hypercautious, strictly goal-oriented, with little time for philosophizing. Still, in a Chinese context, to invoke an election law in a graft case is a stunning stroke of audacity. Luo knows it, too, and seems frustrated that his exploit should remain unsung.

I squint at his business card in the neon haze of a rain-slicked Chaoyang Road: Luo Ruiliang, Attorney at Law. No firm name, just a freelance lawyer. On the flip side, he's penciled his mobile phone number. I take this as an invitation.

SURE ENOUGH, when we ring his mobile later that night he sounds eager to talk more about Wolf Fang. We agree to meet the following afternoon. He dictates instructions on how to find his house: just a couple of blocks east of the Xinhua Street subway stop. Luo will wait for us on the north side of Qianmen Road, in front of what he describes as "the most deluxe public toilet in Beijing." From there he'll escort us through the back lanes.

Coming up the street, we spot Luo chatting into his cell phone as he loiters in front of the sole landmark on the nondescript block. The five-star lavatory, done up in mock-imperial style with green-tiled upturned eaves, overshadows the huddled, blank courtyard walls that flank it on either side. It dominates the district socially as well as architecturally. Most buildings in the traditional quarters of Chinese cities lack indoor plumbing, so the public toilet becomes at least one fixed point where neighbors can count on running into each other at fairly predictable times of the day. Right now it's an off-peak hour, but the midafternoon toilet traffic is still pretty brisk: parents and children on their way back from school, cyclists pausing in mid-commute, patrons from nearby eateries, stay-at-home elders.

Luo, stationed between the Ladies and Gents doors, seems to know half the passersby. Without interrupting his phone call, he nods affably to all comers. Most return his smile—clearly he's well-known and well-liked in the neighborhood. As we draw abreast, he shrugs apologetically and gestures that he'll get off the phone as fast as he can.

"No, I'm *not* turning you down," he sighs into the handset, evidently struggling to make himself clear to an obtuse caller. "I'm *happy* to take up your defense. But why not pay a half-fee to your previous lawyer and use the material he's already gathered? What's the point of starting again from scratch? Save yourself time and money."

He nods wearily as the voice on the other end recaps the proposal. "Yes . . . uh-huh . . . that's right . . . No, of *course* I won't charge you double. I'll bill you a half-fee, too . . . Right. Then you think about it and get back to me, okay? Good."

This strikes me as a pretty unlawyerly bargaining style. But Luo, when asked about it, denies he's acting out of selflessness. "In a start-up practice like mine, you simply don't do yourself any good by undercutting other lawyers and making enemies in the profession. Besides, going to court is still a pretty new idea around here, compared with other ways of settling disputes. We'll all lose business if we make the law too expensive."

He holsters his cell phone and leads us a few doors down the road, past a hole-in-the-wall noodle joint and a cigarette stall. Both shopkeepers hail him amiably and a trio of schoolgirls sing out, "Hello, Uncle." Nobody bats an eye at the sight of us, conspicuously foreign as we are. Maybe they're used to running into Luo around the neighborhood with odd outsiders in tow.

He points out a nondescript storefront office as one of his elder brother's trading concerns. His brother owns most of the *hutong* behind it, he says. We enter the alley through a circular moon gate half cataracted over with the sagging ruin of a broken steel grille. Ramshackle brick sheds jam the interior courtyards: relics of the local street committee's efforts to maximize occupancy during the decades of state-allocated housing.

Even with private real estate holdings restored, it's all but impossible to evict established tenants, Luo explains. But this central location is too good to waste. His brother hopes one day to knock down

the whole shambling ensemble of the *hutong*—shanties, Qing dynasty courtyards, and all. Then he can erect a row of smart, multistory townhouses on the site. To buy out the existing tenants he can offer them apartments in the new buildings and still have enough extra units to turn a handsome profit. Just a matter of raising capital. But meanwhile, Luo, his wife, eight-year-old son, and ninety-year-old mother all must make do with a couple of rooms in one of the older Qing buildings.

Murmuring apologies for his humble hospitality, he pushes open a flimsy plyboard door hinged between elegantly carved stone lintels. The front door opens onto a narrow kitchen—just a blackened wok on a gas-ring and a jar full of assorted cooking utensils on a Formica counter. A dingy trickle of light leaks in from a grease-encrusted flue high above the stove. The whole room is just two paces across. The opposite wall is hung with strands of garlic and chilies, the plant stems braided into ropes.

We brush aside a couple of these strands like a bead curtain to enter the windowless back "parlor." Luo switches on a fluorescent light. Two-thirds of the room is taken up with a massive double bed. Satin-covered pillows and neatly folded quilts tower almost up to the low-raftered ceiling. The walls show signs of water seepage, despite piece-meal efforts to patch them over with newsprint. A varnished pine table, a bookcase, and three folding chairs are crammed into the remaining floorspace. Opposite the bookcase, a panda-printed curtain screens off a side room that's shared by the old lady and the child.

Luo's wife and son are both away at school (she's an elementary teacher and he's in third grade). The elderly mother vegetates quietly in her bed. From time to time a snore or a snatch of guttural sleep-talk emanates from behind the curtain.

Our host plunks on the table a manila folder marked simply "Wolf Fang" in his impetuous cursive script. "Have a look at that while I fix some tea," he suggests, and goes off to busy himself in the "kitchen."

THE FIRST ITEMS in the folder stop us in our tracks. Page after page of thumbprint signatures, just like the opening scene of the TV documentary. Except instead of soft, pink smudges as they'd appeared in the samizdat film, these prints are bright vermilion, hard-edged, and differentiable; full of personality. Some of the signers place their prints with great deliberation, so that each ridge and whorl stands out clearly. Some plow into the page in overemphatic splotches. Nervous sweat drops speckle some of the thumbprints for a gouache effect. A few timid souls barely touch the paper at all, leaving only tentative red streaks.

Just handling the pages, we sense what an emotional investment these "signatures" must have cost each party to the document. Across every print, someone has neatly entered the signer's name in crabbed ballpoint characters. Wolf Fang seems to have only two surnames; whoever's not a Bai must be a Shih.

We're still poring over the thumbprints when Luo returns with a thermos and steaming tumblers of tea.

"So this is the original petition?" Ah-loong asks.

"Something even more important than that," Luo says. "The first legal instrument these people ever signed, collectively. Their point of no return. It's their initial contract with me."

He riffles past the signatures to home in on the brief half-page of text at the head of the document. It mentions no specific legal case but simply engages Luo in an advisory role.

"The point was to give me a legitimate reason even to *be* in Wolf Fang in the first place," he explains. "Without that, authorities could arrest me anytime as an 'outside agitator' and put a stop to any initiative I might try."

The contract retains him for one year at an all-inclusive fee of RMB 4,000 (about $488).

"It seems you weren't in it for the money," I venture.

"Hardly," he laughs. "But to Wolf Fang, the sum mattered. It came out to about 30 renminbi per household. That amounts to three days' wages for a migrant worker—enough to keep my villagers serious about the relationship."

Managing his own clients was more than half the battle, Luo explains—much tougher than handling the opposition. The authorities, acting upon old norms, could be counted on to behave predictably. But the villagers were grappling with new concepts: democracy, statutes, contracts, rules of evidence—all alien notions to them. Sometimes their grasp could be pretty tenuous.

"I never knew when they'd revert to form and lurch off into mob action, the only sort of group gesture they'd ever known before. Which would have suited the Yi county cadres just fine. They've seen *that* sort of uprising many times before and they're well-equipped to crush it."

The villagers were in the throes of yet another crackdown when they first sought out Luo. They'd rampaged in the Yi county seat after cadres rejected—for the fifth time in a row—their appeal for a change of local leadership. In the wake of the riot, police swooped in to round up ringleaders. To escape the dragnet, a pair of villagers—Shih Liguo and Bai Yimin—fled to Beijing. They hid out in a flophouse hotel, burying themselves in the anonymity of the capital.

"They made an unlikely pair," Luo laughs, recalling his first impression of them.

Bai, the callow peasant, had never seen a city before. He was amazed—and a little appalled—by the bright lights, traffic jams, and fancy women. Shih, an ex-commissar, cast a bilious eye on all such wonders. For him, latter-day Beijing was a sorry comedown from the revolutionary Valhalla of his youth where once, alongside a million like-minded zealots, he'd basked in the personal radiance of Chairman Mao, the Rising Red Sun of the world, in Tiananmen Square. Shih retained some Beijing contacts from those heady days—a few surviving leftists still ensconced in the army, the ideology cells, and the propaganda media. He tried, through this network, to initiate an intra-Party grievance procedure. Nobody could help him, though. Day after day, he dragged himself "home" to his Beijing flophouse, grousing about the sclerotic grievance channels.

After hearing weeks of his tirades, a hotel clerk archly suggested Shih sue for legal redress. Weren't the newspapers full of juicy court-room stories lately? The clerk tossed off the names of five prominent lawyers culled from the evening tabloids. Shih took this flippant advice to heart and trekked to one after another of these legal luminaries—all in vain. Last in the series was Luo's Second Brother, who rebuffed him like the rest but gave him Luo Ruiliang's card.

"Why didn't your brother want to take up Wolf Fang's cause himself?" I ask.

"Well, he's pretty busy," Luo begins tentatively. "He's got his firm to consider, you know. You can't very well tackle this sort of case when you're responsible for a whole organization and so many people."

We nod understandingly, which somehow makes Luo all the more defensive.

"Not that Second Brother was scared or anything," he hastens to add. "But he's got to choose his battles. He's saving up his resources for the fights that matter most."

"Like what?"

"Oh, you know . . . big environmental stuff and occupational-safety suits," he grandly proclaims. "Major class actions. Corruption cases, too. Some very hush-hush. Out-of-court settlements that he can't even talk about."

Before we can press for specifics, Luo hurries on with his story.

"So my brother has always encouraged me to take up the cases he can no longer handle. He backed me every step of the way in my studies. He's still my best sounding board for any legal move I might make."

"You mean he's grooming you as a kind of alter ego to plead touchy cases?" I suggest.

"Sometimes it feels that way," Luo nods. "He was with me on this Wolf Fang case from day one."

DAY ONE OF the Wolf Fang case stretched into a bleary, all-night marathon, the lawyer recalls. As soon as Shih got Luo's business card from Second Brother, the old commissar rang him up on his cell phone and insisted on meeting right away. Luo had no choice but to invite the Wolf Fang duo to his home that same evening. He sat them down at this very table and heard them out.

Bai just perched there, morosely homesick, wondering when—or if—he'd ever get out of this Gomorrah and back to his village. Shih, for his part, kept brooding about his beloved Party and its fall from grace. For him, victory in this affair could mean nothing short of a total overhaul of the Yi county Communist Party cell, from craven grassroots cadres to perfidious higher-ups. Luo saw right away why no other lawyer would touch the case. They must all have told Shih— sensibly enough—that there was nothing courts could do about internal Party affairs.

"And that's true, as far as it goes," Luo concedes. "But I couldn't help wondering aloud how much of this was really a Party matter, after all. If grain had actually gone missing, that's simple theft. If village records had disappeared, that's fraud." Such infractions come under the ordinary criminal code, Luo pointed out. Where was the need for even an administrative ruling, much less Party intervention?

Such talk scandalized Shih, at first. How, he demanded, could any aspect of life fall beyond the pale of the Party? But the military side of the old commissar soon warmed to the idea of a surprise attack from an unexpected quarter. Why *not* bypass Party channels to save the Party itself? It had the markings of an elegant guerrilla ploy, Shih began to appreciate—something right out of Mao's own strategic manual. "Storm the citadel," he railed, quoting the Chairman's Cultural Revolution call to arms.

Wolf Fang was rife with revolutionary discontent, Shih swore. The entrenched Party secretary and his clique managed to keep villagers seemingly intimidated. But under the cowed exterior, resentment seethed. "In that case," Luo told them, "what we need is names. Heads of households, the more the better, representing a broad cross section of the village. We need people willing to go on record for our cause. Can you get me those names?"

The concept of a petition was new to the Wolf Fang duo, but they saw no reason why it might not be feasible. "If I tell them to sign, they'll sign," Bai boasted. "I know my neighbors. They're ready to follow me up to Yi county to get their heads busted. Why wouldn't they have enough nerve to make thumbprints on a paper?"

Their talk grew more and more agitated until Luo worried it might keep his son from studying and his mother from sleeping. He finally had to usher his guests out of the house and down the block to the neighborhood noodle stall, where, between the three of them, they knocked back a pint of *erh guo tou*, a resinous, 80-proof rice wine ideal for low-budget male-bonding rites.

With this under his belt, Shih waxed grandiloquent. This occasion, he proclaimed, will live in the annals of Wolf Fang. It was as momentous in its way as the Peach Garden Oath of mutual loyalty that bound the three heroes in the opening scene of the *Romance of Three Kingdoms*, China's classic novel of chivalry. Lest anyone miss the point, he spelled out the analogy to all present (a waiter, a noodle chef, and two hapless diners at the next table). Shih cast himself as the star of the novel, Liu Pei, a bold freebooter who went on to found the Shu-

Han Kingdom twenty-one centuries ago. Bai played his right-hand man, the generous, hot-tempered general Guan Yu.

"So who does that make me? Zhang Fei?" laughed Luo, citing the third party to the oath in the novel, a loud and impetuous general. Doesn't quite fit, Shih conceded, casting about for alternatives. "I know!" he slapped the table so hard the wine cups jiggled. "Lawyer Luo here can be our Zhu Geliang," the subtle, crafty strategic counselor of the Shu-Han.

True to his assigned role, Luo kept enough wits about him to draw up a formal letter of appointment for his legal services—the contract we were shown. Getting it signed by the villagers would be the riskiest part of the whole operation.

"General" Bai took on that dangerous task. He had to infiltrate himself back into Wolf Fang by a circuitously evasive bus route, walking the last leg of the journey by moonlight. The first signature drive amounted to a lightning raid on the village. Within less than a day, Bai managed to amass more than his assigned quota of signatures and slip back out of Wolf Fang without alerting hostile notice. By the end of the week, Luo had in hand a signed contract whose terms were vague enough that his bosses at New Dawn had no qualms about authorizing his preliminary sally into the village.

The initial contract bore 132 signatures, representing well over a fifth of Wolf Fang's households. Counting up the thumbprints, Luo realized that he already had ample support for a full-fledged legal petition. With such a quorum, he could convene a formal Village Assembly—the designated forum, under the law, to take up such questions as cadre corruption and leadership changes.

Luo drafted a petition for a Village Assembly. This time the lawyer would collect the needed signatures himself. The petition drive would mark Luo's maiden voyage to Wolf Fang.

HE PLANNED his arrival carefully. There was to be no fanfare. Neither Bai nor Shih would accompany him. The object was to attract as

little attention as possible. Yet he couldn't steal in under cover of night, as Bai had done to get the contract signed. It wouldn't do for the lawyer to appear furtive. His best policy was to arrive alone, openly, by daylight, but to keep his visit as short as possible. He wanted to be in and out of the village before officials had time to react.

Luo hopped a long-distance bus to Baigoudian, the last stop on the main highway before the Yi county turnoff. There he hired a taxi to take him the rest of the way.

"That cabby really earned his pay," Luo laughs. "Those are some tortured roads down there. No matter how you enter that village, you feel devious, as though you're sneaking in." The place can only be reached via back-door approaches, twisty hill tracks. There's no longer a straightforward, front-door entry. The old main access road was drowned by the lake in 1960, along with all of Wolf Fang's original fields, streets, and houses. So villagers had to rebuild their homes in the gullies behind the new waterfront. This convoluted topography now divides Wolf Fang into five scattered hamlets, tenuously connected by lakeside trails and hillcrest goat tracks.

Luo spent half his time in Wolf Fang clambering over these paths to canvass support house by house. Only with backing from all five hamlets would his petition carry village-wide authority. Otherwise, the whole initiative could be dismissed as the factional infighting of some hamlets against the others. One of the wards was the stronghold of the Party secretary and his henchmen, but even there, a few households dared to stand up against the cadres.

Luo had to move quickly and discreetly, leaving as little trace as possible. "In all my time in Wolf Fang," he recalls, "I never slept in the same house twice in a row."

He wrapped up his first stint in the village within three days—before anyone in the Party secretary's clique could raise the alarm. At the end of his canvassing, he had nearly 150 thumbprints on his assembly petition. He made a point of getting everyone to sign twice and keeping that extra signed copy in reserve. On the way back to Beijing, he stopped in the Yi county seat to deliver his petition to the administration. The clerk in the Civil Affairs Department was too astonished to object. All he could do was to, ever so politely, receive, log, and enter the documents.

The cadres didn't stay flummoxed for long, though. Less than a week after Luo had come back from Wolf Fang, a delegation from Yi county arrived at New Dawn Law Practice to complain about the petition. A deputy magistrate, the security chief, and the head of civil affairs all showed up in an official car, complete with revolving red roof-beacon.

The delegation demanded that New Dawn bring its rogue minion Luo to heel. County cadres had gone into Wolf Fang to do a little canvassing of their own, they said. They insisted that most of the signers either denied ever having seen the document or else claimed to have been duped about its contents. Many of the thumbprints were obviously forged, the cadres asserted (without producing any physical evidence). Others were too blurred to be recognizable. And some of the signature spaces were left blank, although their names had been counted among the parties to the petition.

Luo's boss called him in on it. Luckily Luo had had the foresight to make that signed second copy of the petition. The boss himself checked it, signature by signature; everything seemed in order. So

New Dawn stood behind him, at least back then. But Luo knew that the opposition—the local cadres—were now up in arms. This was only to be expected. Still, it meant the goons would be lying in wait for him the next time he showed up in Wolf Fang. If Luo and his supporters didn't want to wind up beaten or shot, they'd better enlist some powerful backing for any further forays.

That's where Shih's propaganda contacts came in handy. The old commissar's leftist cronies may not have been the most fashionable crowd in Beijing, but they still knew their way around the corridors of media power. Through friends of friends, Shih and Luo got a chance to tell their tale to a reporter from CCTV's News Review Bureau.

This elite, semiautonomous production unit of the central television station had just been awarded an hour-long prime-time slot for a "news-magazine"-type show. They were on the lookout for promising stories, and Wolf Fang seemed to have all the right elements: noble peasants, shifty villains, idealistic crusaders, topical issues. Not to mention a scenic locale. So it didn't take much to persuade the News Review Bureau to send a five-man team—a reporter and two cameras, each with its own soundman. For CCTV, this amounted to no more than an exploratory probe. But to Wolf Fang locals, the arrival of a TV crew was as unprecedented as a UFO landing.

"Nobody down there had any idea how to act in front of a camera," Luo laughs. "The officials knew they'd better not beat us up on film. But anything short of that was okay, they figured. It never occurred to them how much they could embarrass themselves just by talking." So the cadres blustered shamelessly and the villagers recounted how they'd been terrorized. CCTV taped it all. With the camera crew in tow, Luo retraced the steps of his first visit. He needed to reaffirm his support base. Why had so many of his clients denied their own signatures? "We heard the same story in house after house," Luo recalls. "People had caved under threat, whether of beatings, blackmail, or confiscation of their property. The stories came pouring out of them. I just took down the depositions. Here they are."

From the manila folder he produces a sheaf of onionskin pages. Each one bears the spare narrative of a different "house call" by one or another Yi county cadre. The accounts go into specific detail—who came to the door, what questions were asked, the "encouragement" offered, the declarations extracted. Luo and Bai Yimin sign off as witnesses to "notarize" the thumbprint signature at the bottom of each deposition.

I heft the thin stack of documents; barely half an ounce of flimsy paper. This, I realize, represents the legal crystallization of all those impassioned interviews with villagers that we'd seen in the film. At the same time that he collected depositions, Luo also conducted his own "public opinion survey" of Wolf Fang. A one-sheet table sums up his findings. Fully 87 percent of the people he talked with said it was time for a change of village administration. Only 4 percent backed the cadres. The rest pleaded "no opinion."

With such solid support, Luo felt he could fight the case in court if need be. Nearly half of Wolf Fang's households stood ready to join as plaintiffs if he were to sue for village elections. He drew up a formal complaint. This signed document enjoys pride of place in his Wolf Fang folder.

By the time he was ready to file suit, his backers in the village had already become veteran petition-signers. No more motley jumbles of stamp-pad blotches, as there had been on his earlier filings. Now the signatures march in tidy array, boldly inked and evenly spaced, twenty to a page—a well-ordered militia of thumbprints in place of a ragtag guerrilla band. Now that he'd mustered such a credible army of supporters, Luo sought his brother's tactical advice.

"Second Brother quoted to me from Sun-tzu," Luo relates, citing a fourth-century B.C. dictum of China's master military strategist: "Avoid the enemy when he is in dashing spirit, but strike him when he is tired and withdraws." In other words, a wise commander feints and harries his foe to exhaustion before committing his own forces in earnest. By the same reckoning, Luo's brother advised, the threat of a lawsuit can be more potent than an actual court case. Defendants like these local pooh-bahs would be far more afraid of losing face than of an adverse judgment. Just putting its officials on trial would terminally embarrass the Communist Party, whatever the outcome. So by the time you bring such cadres to court, they've already suffered the worst you can do to them. They have nothing more to fear from you. You've lost your leverage. To avoid that, you've got to keep your trial threat credible without ever actually filing suit.

Following his brother's counsel, Luo made the rounds of county offices. He brandished his petition and announced that he'd file by April unless an election date was set for Wolf Fang. Cadre reactions ranged from caustic to frosty, as captured in the TV film. But in the end, the Sun-tzu gambit carried the day.

"How much of it was your strategy, do you think, and how much the presence of the TV crew?" I ask.

Luo considers judiciously. It's true, he says, that things tended to go awry as soon as the cameras looked the other way. Like the time he went canvassing in the Party secretary's home-base hamlet while the CCTV team was off filming sunset shots on the lakefront. "Five of these goons got me up against the wall of the granary. They urged me to be less inquisitive. They urged me rather emphatically. With rake handles. About the knees. We must have been . . . ah . . . debating like this for about a quarter of an hour—it felt like forever. Finally the camera crew came roaring up in our van, alerted by our friends in the hamlet."

He waves off our commiseration. Standard fare; he routinely suffered far worse, he says, during his decade of Cultural Revolution rustication. And back then, no journalists came riding to the rescue in the nick of time.

"So that's the critical difference between then and now? The journalists?" I ask.

"One of the differences, perhaps. But it's by no means the whole story. Half a dozen factors had to come together to make the Wolf Fang victory possible. We needed the 1987 election law, and some sort of a court to enforce it, and the right lawyer to argue it, and a core group of grassroots activists to push for it. Only *then* could we invoke press power to oversee the case."

Analyzed like that, the election takes on extra resonance. But if it depended on the coincidence of so many factors, might not Wolf Fang be just a unique, one-time episode? "Couldn't your victory have been canceled by wiping out any one of its ingredients?" I ask.

"Well, not in the long run," he assures me with the serene confidence of a true believer. "Not as long as there is the final, crucial ingredient: a community of people that's upset enough to take some risks."

"And once roused, they can't be lulled or cowed again?"

"Never. Not in a place like Wolf Fang. I wish you could see for yourself."

"Could we? It's just a few hours out of town. We've got a car, and tomorrow's Saturday. Let's go."

The prospect both attracts and unnerves Luo. Without any naysaying Zeng to veto the trip, he wavers.

"Nice autumn weekend," I wheedle. "It's been a while, hasn't it? Too long, really, since you've checked in with Wolf Fang."

"I'm *sure* they'd love to see you again," Ah-loong coos. "And *I'd* be so thrilled to see the original place where you made such a difference."

We press our advantage until he agrees to meet us the following morning at six in front of the deluxe toilet. With an early start, he figures, we can make it out to the village and back home the same day without having to stay overnight—a calculation right in line with his customary quick-strike approach to Wolf Fang.

"Still, bring a toothbrush," he admonishes. "Just in case."

THE SKY IS still purple when we pull up on Qianmen Road, toothbrushes at the ready. Luo paces the sidewalk briskly, the collar of his blue windbreaker upturned against the morning chill. It's rush hour at the public toilet. Luo affably greets friends on their way in. They return his salute and hurry on about their business.

Lawyer Zeng stands forlornly at curbside, unable to join in Luo's glad-handing. His home is across town and he doesn't know anyone in this neighborhood well enough to chat across toilet stalls. He looks cold, stamping from foot to foot and snorting little clouds of steam.

So we're to be lumbered with a chaperone again. Too bad. But poor Zeng looks so woebegone that the least we can do is to bundle him into the front seat of the car and ply him with coffee from a thermos we've prepared. He gratefully wraps his fingers around our enamel coffee mug and settles into the front seat beside me. Luo sits in back with Ah-loong.

This arrangement works out well: Luo has no sense of direction whatsoever, whereas Zeng turns out to be a car owner who knows his way around Beijing. He sets about his copilotry with a will, relieved, perhaps, to have some role in this journey other than censor. Like most official chaperones I've met in China, he seems torn between dutiful circumspection and a spontaneous instinct to be informative. Map-reading is an uncompromising way to make himself helpful.

And directional help we badly need. This whole corner of the city has remade itself since last we drove in Beijing. Entire neighborhoods have vanished. Flashy new high-rises rear up in their place, all bristling with fins and flanges like hot-rod Edsels. Looping swirls of freeway interlink it all, raveled in a bewildering welter of on- and off-ramps.

Yet street life thrums on, we're relieved to see, despite the changes. Dawn is always prime time for people-watching in Chinese cities—the hour when citizens hit the sidewalks for their own restorative pursuits before the start of the workday. Dotards wheel grandchildren in baby carriages. Breakfast stalls serve up steamed dumplings and sour mung bean soup. *Kungfu* clubs meet to rehearse "shadow boxing." Tango teams practice to the tune of boom-box tape decks. Conga lines of old ladies with feathered fans sashay through the paces of the raucous *ying ge* folk dance.

Such clubs and informal associations comprise the muscle and sinew of "civil society," Xu Zhenhui once explained to me, invoking a concept he'd imbibed in his Ivy League interlude. They're vital precursors of a robust democracy. Of course they've had their ups and downs in China—the now-banned Falun Gong started out as little more than a calisthenics club before its official demonization. But most such groups carry on, unmolested as long as they maintain a low profile.

We roll past a dozen *tai-chi* devotees frozen in motion on a highway median. Ballroom dancers twirl among the concrete pilings of an entry ramp. Even cruising an overpass, we can still hear the muted clangor of a *ying ge* drum-and-gong ensemble below and catch a whiff of dumplings and bean soup. But it all seems faint and far away. The steam from the breakfast stalls merges with the freeway truck exhaust, the spew of factory chimneys, and the smoke of trash fires. A curdled miasma hangs over the city, enhancing the somber morning shadows.

As the sun lumbers over the horizon, the smog fades from blue to a sallow haze that hems our vista to just a few hundred yards on either side of the freeway. This road didn't even exist just a year ago, the last time I drove out to this part of Beijing. Back then, to reach the picnic spots on this side of town—the Marco Polo Bridge, the Resting Cloud Temple, the Ten Fords Canyon—you'd have to thread your way through the tangled byways that connect the capital with its surrounding cottage gardens.

The rutted roads would jog around cornfields and follow meandering hedgerows. If you got stuck behind a tractor or a hay wagon, you might have to poke along for miles. Now and then you'd come upon a truck overturned in a ditch or wrapped around a tree like the shed husk of a locust—killer roads. On the other hand, the produce peddlers out here used to offer bargain bushels of beautiful apples and peaches. And roadside food stalls served huge, wholesome meals garnished with warm beer and local gossip. The garden townships were a world of their own—now wholly bypassed by the multilaned asphalt.

Under Zeng's guidance, I thread my way through a series of interchanges to another on-ramp that leads through a tollgate, the start of the main Beijing–Hong Kong highway. This northmost leg is only recently opened. Deep in the Chinese heartland, large segments of highway remain under construction. But someday soon this road will link the country end-to-end like the U.S. Interstate network—and will be just as symbolically important a benchmark of nation-building. Meanwhile, the Beijing segment of roadway is already humming with traffic, despite the early hour and the stiff 10 renminbi ($1.20) toll for barely half-a-dozen exits.

We nose our Toyota into the slow lane at seventy miles per hour. Cars come looming up behind in our rearview mirrors and then whip past with a descending Doppler wail of their horns. Black Audis with tinted windows and military plates seem to dominate. There's a fair leavening of jeeps, SUVs, and Mitsubishi vans thrown in for good measure.

The highway parallels our erstwhile picnic routes, but the feel of the countryside couldn't be more different. We race along a raised embankment screened off by hurricane fences. No autumn colors on this drive; the Beijing haze follows us, augmented by the fumes of new factories lining the road. Beyond the Marco Polo Bridge, a limekiln blanches the surrounding cornfields. The shadowless smoglight, industrial sprawl, and unswerving conveyor belt of a road lull us into a daze. We cruise for nearly an hour and feel as if we've hardly left town.

Ah-loong is amazed at the convenience of the road. Luo agrees. During the Cultural Revolution, he relates, when he was "sent down" to a Hebei village no farther from Beijing than Wolf Fang, never once in an entire decade did he get back to the capital. Even if he could have gotten permission from his brigade (only given in cases of direst emergency), the journey would have taken a full two days. Now villagers can make it in just four hours without asking anyone's by-your-leave. No wonder they turn to the city for everything from coolie jobs to legal services.

"So now that there's a freeway, I guess the countryside is no longer such a world apart from the city," Ah-loong enthuses.

"Well, yes and no," Zeng pronounces, expanding upon his navigational role to help us get our sociological bearings. "Instead of a geographical divide, there's now opening up a new economic divide. This freeway's not for everybody, after all. It's a rich man's road. Just look at the high tolls. Consider the mix of vehicles. Not a whole lot of tractors or run-down buses, are there? And there's a minimum speed limit—forty miles per hour—but no maximum."

I pull off to get gas. In its white-tiled antisepsis, the roadside service plaza could grace any American freeway. Pump jockeys fill our
tank, swab our windows, and bill my credit card, all with a well-oiled
efficiency undreamed of at your everyday Chinese gas station. A matron walks her Pekinese dog in the parking lot while her driver
smokes. A snack bar sells microwave dough-balls, vacuum-packed
fat flakes, and shrink-wrapped lard wads—all quite up to American
vending-machine standards, and priced accordingly.

There's a sumptuous toilet, with private stalls, no less—an amen-
ity unmatched even in the deluxe Qianmen public lavatory. But this
porcelain palace is still roped off: no water hookup yet. So, out behind
the spotless, virgin bathroom, a couple of motorists irrigate the sur
rounding cornfields through the hurricane fence: a suave cadre-type in
pinstripes, and a leather-jacketed bruiser—a fair cross section, it
strikes me, of China's car-owning classes. Zeng, farther on down the
fence, expounds earnestly into his cell phone. To whom? I wonder.

REFRESHED AND REFUELED, we coast a few more exits to our
turn-off, Baigoudian. Just a few years ago, this place earned a national
reputation as a bandits' roost. Baigoudian's late-blooming notoriety
only came after centuries of total anonymity. Before economic liberalization, it was nothing but a sleepy market town for the surrounding
farmers. Then came patriarch Deng Xiaoping's 1992 summons to
hypergrowth. In the wake of the Tiananmen massacre, Deng kicked
China into economic overdrive to refocus national attention away
from the memory of the bloodshed. Baigoudian rose eagerly to the
challenge.

In a way, its history parallels that of Wolf Fang—another forgotten rural backwater that availed itself of post-Mao reforms to take its
own destiny in hand. Except instead of focusing, like Wolf Fang, upon
such political promises as democracy and rule-of-law, Baigoudian ze-
roed in on the economic aspect of reform. No place in China more
fervently embraced Deng's famous injunction in defense of material
production incentives: "To get rich is glorious."

In its bid to get rich, Baigoudian's initial asset was its geography. Perched at the three-way border between Hebei, Beijing, and Tianjin, the town fell into a cozy limbo between adjacent police jurisdictions. Yet it was close enough to big cities and major (prefreeway) truck routes to attract a clientele. For a modest outlay of protection money, Baigoudian was able to turn itself into a supermarket for counterfeit name-brand products.

Shoppers flocked from miles around to load up on fake Guccis, Rolexes, and Nikes. The goods came fresh out of the sweatshops of North China's burgeoning industrial zones. Prices ran to just a small fraction of what customers would have to pay for genuine branded wares. Over time, even the workmanship became plausible enough to pass for original merchandise, at least upon cursory inspection.

Surfing the crest of its growing fame, Baigoudian soon branched out, from ready-made wearables and accessories to such other lines as knock-off electronics, software, and pharmaceuticals. Diversification paid off. Within a couple of years, the town was earning even wider fame as a center for drugs, guns, and whores. Beijing travel agencies began organizing weekend tour packages to the lawless enclave. Hotels and fancy restaurants sprouted up where day-trippers mingled with newly rich crime lords. Sporadic gangland wars sparked fleeting police crackdowns, but each time things would quickly settle back to business as usual.

With their newfound wealth, the city fathers began to crave respectability. They even went so far as to invent themselves a historic legacy. They opened a tourist museum lauding Baigoudian as the original locale of *All Men Are Brothers*, a classic romance about Robin Hood–like outlaws of the twelfth-century Song dynasty. Never mind that literary scholars place the saga's actual setting in Shandong, some 200 miles to the east. Such quibbles cut no ice with Baigoudian's boosters; spiritually, they saw themselves as descendants of the novel's Merry Men.

So, as we pull off the freeway, I'm expecting something like Sherwood Forest, or at least a *kungfu* movie set. Where are the rickety inns full of shady characters? Where are the tile-capped walls for assassins to vault? Where are the willow groves for sword fights, the teeming bazaars, the maze of trackless alleys?

Instead we see only bland warehouses, truck yards, and block after block of factory lofts. Smokestacks spew multicolored filth—brown and yellow and forsythia green. Restaurants are shuttered this early in the morning. The hotels, their neon signs turned off, loom gloomily in the smog. I scan the empty sidewalks in vain for swaggering high rollers, scarlet women, or lurking ninjas. Not a soul stirs except for a few Day-Glo-vested street-sweepers. In the block-long downtown, between the boxy City Hall and the new two-storied junior high, uniformed schoolchildren line up patiently behind crossing guards as convoys of trucks wheeze past.

"So *this* is the famous Baigoudian?" I sigh as we edge our way over the speed bumps.

Luo laughs at my evident disappointment. "You were hoping maybe for something a bit more lurid? I'm afraid you're too late." The local burghers put all that rough-and-tumble stuff behind them last year when the highway came through, he explains. Couldn't afford the risk; with the new road, it had become too easy for the cops to swoop down on them here. Besides, Baigoudian had already made a name for itself and amassed a little capital—enough to bankroll some small-time industry. Why turn your town into a permanent, rolling crime wave when you can do better for yourself by going straight?

Fair enough, I guess. Many a raffish casbah has taken the same stodgy turn at the first opportunity: Somerset Maugham's Singapore reinvents itself as a squeaky-clean shopping mall, Times Square becomes a Disneyland of sorts. But such transformations often paper over a seamier downside hidden from view, and Baigoudian seems no exception. As a corollary of its born-again Babbitry, the town has acquired a penumbra of slums to house the casual laborers who staff the downtown shops, factories, and pleasure palaces, as we discover when we inadvertently overshoot the bypass road.

Within a few hundred yards of City Hall, the new concrete structures give way to a fringe of tar-paper shanties. Retailers have yet to open their shutters this early in the day, but the service economy already shows signs of life. A stack of retreads identifies a tire repair shop. An electrified barber pole spins listlessly in front of the Evergreen Massage Parlor. The sidewalks peter out to narrow dirt shoulders along the road, here and there cluttered with the makeshift plastic tents of migrant worker encampments. The highway pavement itself seems less and less promising.

"Any of this look familiar to you?" I ask Luo, since he's the only one among us who's already been through these parts. But it turns out that, so far, he's only ever transited Baigoudian passively in the back of a public bus or a TV van. Zeng fishes a Hebei provincial map out of the glove compartment and busies himself checking for any possible turnoff we might have missed.

I'm so absorbed in dodging pot holes that it takes a warning shout from Ah-loong to alert me—just in time—to a writhing body in the middle of the road. All I see in the first flash is a puffy gunnysack sprawled on the blacktop. Such debris is common enough on Chinese byways to set off few alarm bells. But as I draw abreast, I realize that whoever dropped this bundle is still lying there in the road, half-hidden behind the fallen load. No telling the age or gender of the torso on the tarmac. Clothes, gunnysack, hair, and complexion—all the same gray as the roadbed dust. But as the prone body half rolls over, a pair of smoldering eyes lock onto mine for a split second and the chalky face twists into a grimace.

Too late to brake, I swerve to the right onto the road-shoulder just in time to miss the fallen figure. A migrant tent looms up before me. I wrench the wheel back to the left and then again right, narrowly avoiding a sheer drop into a drainage ditch. We careen full-speed down the road, shaken but unscathed. The bundle's already vanished from the rearview mirror before any of us can make out just what—or whom—we'd seen.

"Shouldn't we go back and do something?" Ah-loong pleads.

"Forget it!" Luo snaps with unexpected vehemence. "That's the *last* thing to do in a case like this. You'd find yourself surrounded and shaken down before you could say a word. If the victim didn't get you the bystanders would. Drivers have wound up lynched like that."

Nevertheless, Zeng mandates a U-turn, having figured out by now where we'd missed our turnoff. But for all our trepidation, as we again broach the shantytown, we see no sign of the gunnysack or the person on the road.

THE MISSED BYPASS, about a mile back, proves to be an unpaved and unmarked lane that peels off the blacktop at a hairpin angle. Not a promising start for a major truck route grandiloquently designated on the map as Provincial Highway Number 112. After a few hundred feet, though, the road takes on more of the trappings of a world-class, six-lane autobahn: concrete dividers, arc lights, gravel margins, and roadside reflectors. Some local worthy's contractor-nephew must have done very nicely on this deal. We bank around a cambered curve through a gleaming underpass that whisks us right out of Baigoudian and onto the Yi county highway.

"Now *this* is more like it," Zeng beams, with a driverly connoisseurship. I floor the accelerator, looking forward to another stretch of freeway. No such luck. Barely a mile out of town, the blacktop tapers down to a two-lane track.

One lane, really, since this traffic artery is lined with a plaque of slow-moving vehicles and pedestrians. Migrant workers scuff along in single file, while tractors and mule carts lumber through the miasma of dust on both sides of the road. That leaves just the center lane for the hurtling trucks in both directions. Splotches of roadkill and dustings of powdered windshield glass attest to the losers in this game of chicken.

I tensely steer my white-knuckled course right down the midway, now and then scrunching rightward into the donkey lanes just in time to clear oncoming traffic with barely inches to spare. Eyes riveted to the road, I take in little of the passing landscape—just fleeting, peripheral glimpses of produce stands, repair shops, billboards, and lumbering drays.

A few more miles and the roadside commerce thins out enough to afford a glimpse of rich cornfields interspersed with substantial houses—tile-roofed Iberian haciendas, half-timbered Tudor cottages, baroque mini-chateaux. One compound even surrounds itself with a crenellated palisade. The builder has evidently tried for a Cinderella Castle look with peach-colored stucco and sugar-cone spires. But the castle motif has its functional side, too, as the twenty-foot ramparts attest. Lancet windows squint down from the battlements in slit-eyed suspicion. Video cameras swivel restlessly atop the turrets, scanning the road frontage. What are they monitoring, I wonder aloud: the passing donkey carts? The trudging hoboes?

Luo sees no irony in my question. "Anybody *that* rich had *better* keep an eye on any and all passersby," he allows. "But the man in that house is probably more concerned with Jeeps than with foot traffic. Look at the cars parked in his courtyard. I'll bet he's got a regular private army in there." Through the anodized steel barbican, I glimpse a fleet of shiny new Cherokees tended by a solitary watchman in a black T-shirt. Luo assures me a dozen more bodyguards could materialize instantaneously should the need arise. "The same goes for a lot of the other big estate-owners around here," he adds. "They've got to mount a lookout just to keep track of the traffic."

I'm at a loss to fathom why simple farmers would need such legions to protect their cornfields. "What farmers?" Luo laughs. "Most of these houses must belong to top cadres from Yi county. Or else to old, pre-Liberation landlord families that have managed to reclaim part of their original estates now that we've gone back to private land holdings."

Given the history of this area, you can see where the rich might well be uneasy, he adds. The fat, well-watered countryside we're driving through may look as tranquil as any bucolic corner of China. But in fact we're right at the frontier between the prosperous, agrarian heartland and the hardscrabble wastelands of the interior. For millennia, these plains—with their garrisons, manor houses, and officialdom—have staked out the farthest reaches of the established order. And they've always been subject to raids by desperadoes from the hills. So it was during the Japanese occupation, when the Taihang was a hotbed of nationalist resistance. So it was during the civil war, when the mountains were riddled with Red bases and impassible to Kuomintang troops. And so it remains today; China's "economic miracle" ends where the hills begin.

But the area's reputation as a fault line of cultural confrontation dates back far beyond modern times, Luo points out. "See that little stream over there?" Through the haze, we can barely make out the flat glint of a drainage canal lazing across the plain. "That's the Yi River, which gives the county its name. Perhaps you've heard of it?" he asks Ah-loong. To jog her memory, he declaims in the stentorian singsong that Chinese assume for ancient texts:

> Keen the wind,
> Cold the waters of Yi . . .

But before he can finish, Ah-loong excitedly blurts out the rest of the quatrain:

> The hero, once embarked,
> Nevermore returns . . .

"You mean to say . . . this is the place . . . ?"

Luo nods. "Right here. This is where Jing Ke danced his last."

The road chatter in the Toyota subsides for a moment in tribute to the historic import of the spot. As far as my three passengers are concerned, no more need be said. But for the sake of their uncultured driver, they try to clue me in on the background to this quote and this riverbank.

The Jing Ke story dates back to the third century B.C. China, as such, did not even exist yet. It was on the verge of inventing itself as a unitary empire. Before that, in its thousand-odd years of recorded history, what we now call China had been a loose agglomeration of feudal principalities. By the time of the Warring States Period, the chivalric niceties of feudal life had already broken down under the twin population pressures of a burgeoning birthrate and nomad incursions along the inland margins of the Chinese world to the south and west.

The "civilized" Chinese states of the coasts and river valleys exhausted themselves waging ever more vicious wars upon each other. The only Chinese kingdoms exempt from the strife were the semibarbarian principalities at the inland edges of the known world. These border states were too busy fending off nomad invasions from the uncharted deserts and jungles beyond the pale. They had no time to mix in China's internecine fray. So by the time the heartland kingdoms had torn each other apart, the battle-hardened border principalities—Chu to the south and Qin in the west—were left to vie over which one of them would get to pick up the pieces.

This winner-take-all contest would determine who'd finally become the first Chinese emperor. Ambitious Qin and Chu warlords dreamed for the first time of a unified realm from the Gobi Desert to the Yellow Sea—a potential prize that spurred them to outdo each other in savagery. Statecraft degenerated into duplicitous intrigue. Death tolls ran to the hundreds of thousands per battle—body counts unprecedented anywhere else in the global history of warfare right up until World War I.

After decades of scorched-earth campaigns, the upper hand was finally ceded to the Qin, who showed themselves quicker than any other Chinese kingdom to scrap feudal scruples and adopt the no-holds-barred tactics of the nomads. This meant more than just cavalry and crossbows. The main innovations of the time were not in military technology but in social organization.

"The Qin," Zeng reminds us, "were ancient China's most ardent standard-bearers for the rule of law. Maybe we should honor them as the spiritual ancestors of all lawyers."

Behind his thick specs, Luo rolls his eyes: "Spare me such forebears, please. Although I'll grant you I've met a few *judges* in my time who could well be descendants of the Qin."

Before the Warring States Period, Luo explains, feudal court life, diplomacy, and warfare had all been governed—in theory, at least—by chivalric ethics, rather than any sort of codified law. In its earliest Chinese usage, the term "law" meant little more than a harsh roster of punishments designed to keep the peasantry in line—hardly a suitable criterion for lordly conduct. Nobles presumed to far loftier standards of loyalty and fair play, ideals that could only be internalized through aristocratic education and self-discipline, not by statute.

But the conquering Qin had little time for such norms or for the nobles who embodied them. No airy ideals of honor for them; just straightforward, across-the-board impartial application of law. Not that the Qin went beyond the old feudal legal concepts; their statutes remained as narrowly punitive as any that went before. But, in line with their reductionist social vision, they expanded the coverage of the law codes to include all orders of humanity.

Instead of a high-minded warrior caste, the Qin relied on an unquestioningly obedient professional soldiery. All subjects, regardless of class, stood to face the same brutally explicit penalties. The new order, Luo admits, brought a certain kind of egalitarianism and rule of law, as well as imperial grandeur. But it offered no justice, no freedom, and precious little personal grandeur for anyone but the absolute monarch himself. The collision between the Qin and the old nobility was a head-on clash of worldviews, Luo says. And in this cultural conflict, one main line of confrontation was right here on the banks of the Yi.

Why here? I ask. Who *was* Jing Ke, and why did he choose this spot for his "last dance"?

Because this river, Ah-loong explains, was the southwestern boundary of the feudal kingdom of Yan, one of the last holdouts against the Qin onslaught. By the time of Jing Ke, the invaders had already swept out of the mountains and deserts of the far west to subdue almost the whole of China. Only Yan stood fast, along with a few other vest-pocket states here at the western edge of the coastal plains. So the Yan capital (near present-day Beijing) became a magnet for down-at-the-heels nobility from all over China. The place stewed in militant nostalgia—perhaps a bit like Miami's Little Havana today. The mood is brilliantly captured by Si-Ma Qian (ca. 145–90 B.C.), the definitive chronicler of the time, who lived less than a century after Jing Ke—a mere eye blink away, on the scale of Chinese history.

In his *Records of the Historian*, Si-Ma Qian portrays some of the romantic revanchists hanging around Yan at the end of the Warring States Period; men like the elderly *kungfu* master Tian Guang or the embittered renegade Qin general Fan Yuqi. Most romantic of the bunch was Jing Ke himself, the paradigm of an "assassin-errant." This is the term Si-Ma Qian uses to describe the sporadic Quixotes of Chinese statecraft—lone paladins who pit themselves in single combat against the inimical forces of history. The *Records of the Historian* tells of five such assassins-errant, spread over five centuries.

Not for these champions the pride of rank or the public heroics of battle. Each assassin-errant sets out on his own, anonymously, against overwhelming odds, to change, single-handedly, the course of events with a one-time, desperate lunge. Whether they succeed or fail (two out of Si-Ma Qian's five assassins die with their mission unaccomplished), theirs is the moral victory. They win our sympathy by their purity of intent, according to Luo (who strikes me as something of a would-be assassin-errant himself).

Jing Ke, the last in Si-Ma Qian's quintet of assassins-errant, fits right into this romantic mold. A scholarly young swordsman, he spent most of his time loitering in the Yan marketplace, singing drunkenly with his wastrel friends. Nevertheless, Jing Ke's aristocratic and intellectual mien, as well as his skill with a sword, earned him the patronage of local nobles like *kungfu* master Tian Guang.

Realizing the futility of saving his realm on the battlefield, the crown prince of Yan decided to infiltrate an assassin-errant into the Qin court. At swordpoint, the prince hoped, the Qin king might be coerced to withdraw his troops. Such precedents were not unknown in feudal history. After all, the Qin king was still a nobleman. And a nobleman's word—even given under duress—was his absolute bond. The prince asked master Tian Guang to suggest a candidate for this desperate mission. After naming Jing Ke, the old *kungfu* fighter felt honor-bound to kill himself to assure the secrecy of the plan.

His was by no means the only suicide required for this scheme. Needing a pretext to present himself at the enemy's court, Jing Ke cast about for a suitable "door prize" to win his way into the Qin throne room. What better tribute to offer the would-be emperor than the severed head of the runaway Qin general Fan Yuqi? Jing Ke approached the old general to suggest he sacrifice his head as a means to simultaneously avenge himself on Qin and recompense his Yan benefactors. This seemed reasonable to Fan, who thereupon "bared his shoulder, gripped his wrist in a gesture of determination, and . . . cut his own throat," according to Si-Ma Qian.

Jing Ke packaged the head in a lacquer box and prepared an additional item of tribute: a furled map of Yan territory. Inside the map scroll he concealed the fine-honed, poison-tipped dagger with which he'd threaten the would-be emperor in the very midst of the Qin throne room.

Thus armed, the assassin-errant set off on his suicidal mission. Reaching the banks of the Yi River, he paused to bid the Yan prince farewell and declaim his famous quatrain. He sang it twice: once as a dirge in the mournful *bian-jih* scale, and again as a battle cry to the martial strains of the rousing *yu* mode. On the second rendition, he unlimbered the poison blade and solemnly, with infinite deliberation, rehearsed his swordsmanly repertoire. "And that," Luo sums up, "was Jing Ke's last dance."

AGAIN THE REVERENT SILENCE. As far as Ah-loong and the two lawyers are concerned, the story's over. The two elders, Fan and Tian, have heroically killed themselves. Jing Ke has committed himself to his noble course of action and offered his stirring valediction. And so we arrive at the moral climax of the episode. Our edification is complete. I feel a little embarrassed about it, but somehow this still doesn't quite satisfy my pedestrian, Western sense of denouement. "So what finally *happened*?" I ask.

"Happened?" Zeng mulls my question, unable for a moment to

fathom my puzzlement. "Oh, you mean the *outcome*." He sighs as though it's too obvious to go into. "Why, Jing Ke failed, of course. Otherwise there'd be no China today, would there?"

The way Zeng describes it, Jing Ke's demise unfolds as a slapstick tragedy. The lord of Qin, delighted to learn of the tribute offerings from the last holdout state, had the Yan delegation ushered right into the throne room. Upon handing over the map, the assassin-errant whipped out the concealed short-sword and leveled its poisoned tip straight at the royal throat. Jing Ke neither lunged nor spoke; he just braced himself with the unshakable steadfastness of a *qi gong* master swordsman, waiting for the king to start bargaining for his life.

The lord of Qin—the self-proclaimed Son of Heaven—lurched helplessly about the throne room, dodging around columns, waving his voluminous sleeves, and whining for help. But no support was forthcoming, since Qin's paranoid court protocol forbade anyone but the king himself to bear arms in the throne room. And the king, at that stage, was far too flustered even to use his own weapon. He some-how got his belt twisted around in front of him so that his long sword couldn't clear the scabbard.

The courtiers stood dumbfounded. The royal physician was the first to budge. He started belaboring Jing Ke about the shoulders with his medicine case. Ignoring this nuisance, the assassin-errant held his ground, his poignard implacably tracking the frantic monarch. Other throne-room courtiers started piping in with sideline advice to the hapless sovereign: back off, duck down, get your scabbard behind you.

At length, the Qin king rallied enough wit to heed them. Finally drawing his blade, he started hewing away at his assailant's legs; choppy, two-handed, arm's-length strokes, more like a woodcutter than a swordsman. The assassin-errant silently kept his short-sword aimed at his quarry while the king hacked eight deep gashes into him. Only when his feet were literally cut out from under him did Jing Ke finally slump back against a column and hurl his poisoned blade at the king. He missed.

Whereupon the assassin-errant uttered his first sound since unlimbering his sword: he laughed. "I failed because I only tried to threaten you to exact a promise I could carry back to my prince," he said. "Had I sought to kill you, it would have been otherwise." No such compunction troubled the Qin king. He couldn't even be bothered to dispatch Jing Ke in person. Instead, by special dispensation, he allowed his armed bodyguard into the throne room to finish up the butchery for him.

"As befits an emperor-to-be," Zeng nods approvingly. "Delegate your dirty work, executive-style. There's something a bit primitive—don't you think?—about all this face-to-face combat and word-of-honor stuff. Here's the Son of Heaven, about to pull together the vastest realm ever seen in human history up to that time. And Jing Ke can only think to roll back the clock and play out the whole drama according to the rules of a family squabble among blue-blooded clans. Tell me, who's the man of vision in this story and who's the petty-minded throwback?"

"And yet it's Jing Ke who goes down in history as a hero," Luo points out. "Who even *remembers* the name of any flunky that rallied at the time around your precious emperor-to-be?"

"*I* remember," Zeng retorts. "That quick-thinking physician was named Xia Wuju. It's right there in the *Records of the Historian*. He was rewarded with two hundred taels of gold. Deserved every ounce of it, too. Without him, we might not even be Chinese today. There might never have been a unified China for us to belong to."

"Couldn't it be that remembering Jing Ke and honoring his courage has more to do with our 'Chineseness' than any membership in a unified empire?" Luo asks.

CHINESENESS HARDLY SEEMS to be a *beau idéal* of the Yi county grandees who've built their strongholds along the present stretch of Provincial Highway 112, judging by the eclectic architectural whimsies that line our road: Doric porticoes, wedding-cake mansions, *Arabian Nights* palaces, Victorian gothic towers—each derivative fantasy trying to outdo the others in exotic extravagance.

But, in the last and grandest fortress in the series, chinoiserie reasserts itself with a vengeance. It looks like an entire medieval Chinese city, set well off the road in a little basin of its own. It's far enough below the highway that we can peer right over the battlements of the outer wall to see the winding lanes, shady courtyards, and market stalls within. It might be taken for a ruin from Ming times or even earlier, except that it's too trim—every rooftile intact, pennants fluttering atop the gates, window frames glinting with varnish, the gilt-brushed character for "tea" clearly visible on a shop sign. And, eerily enough, not a soul in sight.

"There's *one* big shot who's done all right for himself," Ah-loong speculates. Luo disabuses us: "Even our most creative cadres couldn't afford to go *that* far overboard." The tidy little ghost town turns out to be a studio lot built by Hong Kong movie magnates for filming *kungfu* epics. It provides, incidentally, a major source of employment for hill hamlets like Wolf Fang, Luo adds; one of the few places in Yi county where upland villagers can reliably find day-labor jobs, at least when there's a "shoot" going on. They work as movie extras, simply playing themselves—dirt-poor bumpkins, except in quaintly antique rags instead of modern tatters.

Does it gall them, I wonder, to have to play bygone starvelings in order to keep themselves fed today? "Oh, most of them are too hardpressed to worry much about the ironies of it all," Luo assures me. And besides, the Taihang villagers are quite used to trading on their own history for cash, he adds. "You could say it's always been the mainstay of their livelihood." If your forebears were born-and-bred feudal peasants, all the more reason for you to now draw a day wage as a cinematic rent-a-serf. By the same token, since every Wolf Fang household can boast a grandpa or two in Mao's Red Army, it's only natural nowadays for all registered villagers to draw "revolutionary family" stipends.

Even agriculture, in this part of the Taihang, is not so much a real, here-and-now occupation as a kind of salaried race memory. Ever since the reservoir flooded Wolf Fang's fields forty-odd years ago, villagers have received compensation allowances for their hypothetical crops. They're quite at home with the idea of getting paid *not* to farm. Back in dynastic times, when the later Qing emperors chose these hills as their burial grounds, the court gave villagers a dole of *huang jin* ("imperial gold") to keep them from tilling the soil lest it disturb the *feng shui* of the royal tombs.

What, I ask, was the point of keeping Wolf Fang intact at all after the place was needed for other purposes? Why didn't the Qing just clear the area by royal decree? Why not, even now, relocate the locals away from the Lake Solidarity dam site? Or simply deny them relief grain compensation and let the villagers move away of their own accord?

"It's a matter of face," Luo explains, "national face." Poor Wolf Fang seems fated always to be chosen for some high profile, powerfully symbolic public fetish—the repository of the dynasty's *feng shui* or the Party's nation-building infrastructure. "And in that kind of situation, you see, waste is *good*. It wouldn't do—wouldn't be grandly *imperial*—to spare any resources. So it only adds value to keep up the semblance of a viable Wolf Fang village."

By this reckoning, Luo adds, the more people are bought-off and idled, the more face accrues to the ruling power, whether an emperor or a Politburo. The Wolf Fang villagers are kind of like the retinue of paper servants that are burnt at a Chinese funeral—the more of them that go up in smoke, the greater the family's prestige.

But this wastage of peasant lives is playing with fire, in the long run, Luo adds. "These people may look sluggish, but they can nurse a grievance forever. And once they get riled, they hardly count the cost. How do you think all these villagers earned their 'revolutionary family' credentials? Not by dispassionate ideological study, I can assure you. Rather, after begging long enough for a scanty dole, they just got fed up and started taking potshots at passing KMT officials.

"Behind Wolf Fang, there's a peak called Ax Head Mountain. Five Communist Martyrs holed up there and bedeviled the Kuomintang for nearly a year before succumbing to overwhelming odds. The Ax Head Martyrs are now praised in all the schoolbooks, and their descendants get lavish pensions—a result that doubtless would have been quite unimaginable to those five yokels at the time. All they would have known was that they'd had it up to here with government patrols. They had nothing much to lose and they were angry enough to die. It's a whole other world in those hills. Things appear in a different light there. You'll see."

Even as he speaks, we sense our first inkling that we're finally broaching the edge of the plateau. Not that we actually catch sight of any recognizable mountains on the horizon—just a slight thickening of the smog. It grows rapidly more pronounced as we race westward until, all at once, we recognize that half the sky ahead comprises a wall of rock, not air.

HARDLY DOES the Taihang coalesce before us than we find ourselves already through its outermost ramparts. What looked at first like a sheer escarpment resolves itself, presently, into a series of stippled ridges. Our highway casually sidles up to the cliff and, without ado, insinuates itself into an unassuming gully. A couple of tight S-curves later, we've left the plains behind. Our straight road turns twisty and our horizons abruptly contract.

The light, the colors, the perspective all change as dramatically as if we'd just hang-glided into a cloud bank. Except instead of going all hazy, our view becomes sharper as our field of vision abruptly draws in around us. On such truncated sight lines, there's not even smog enough between us and the horizon to blear the hues or blur the outlines. What appeared from the plains as distant, dun slopes now glimmer before us in shades of pearl. Each gnarl of bracken stands etched in its own shade.

I downshift and gun the engine to take the ascent one switchback at a time. Every crook in the road reveals a new, intimate landscape of ridges, boulders, and stunted trees. Even after our highway levels out again atop the rise, jumbled bluffs still hem us in on all sides; a topography like the hollows of Appalachia. Here and there a one-room cottage presides over a hollow all its own, with barely space for a trellis of tomatoes alongside.

Only once do we come upon a plot of land flat enough to farm as a field of sorts—a lopsided lozenge of dirt wedged between boulders. The shape's too irregular for nice, straight crop rows. Instead, it's laid out in a thumbprint whorl of concentric furrows. No room here for even a mule to turn around. Only a man-drawn plow can wriggle its way between the rocks.

A two-man plow-team is turning over the field as we drive by. The tool they use looks as ancient as agriculture itself—just an asymmetrical fork of poplar, smooth and blanched like a dinosaur wishbone. A scrawny teenager pulls the plow, straining against a hempen strap slung across the chest of his pink jersey. Behind him, a wiry old gaffer rides the crux of the fork, guiding the plow blade with his foot while wrenching the other branch of the wishbone back and forth as a steering handle.

These two are the sole able-bodied males we spot anywhere along the main highway through the Taihang. Farmstead after farmstead seems semiabandoned. The only other practicing farmers to be seen are occasional women ladling nightsoil onto squash vines in their cottage gardens. Even where the scattered cottages coalesce into a village of sorts, we encounter no more than a few old ladies dozing in the doorways and some children chasing piglets through a rubble-strewn yard.

The narrow "street plan" of the village predates any notion of a motor road so the mud-and-wattle house walls now back right onto the blacktop. Little window slits peer directly into our car as we nose our way through town. We have a sense of unseen eyes watching us, but glimpse no one in the shadowy recesses of the cottages.

But if the precincts of the living look desolate in the Taihang, those of the dead show more signs of commercial bustle. Wherever there's a pine-clad bluff or a clump of bamboo—powerful *feng shui* nodes, Zeng informs us—we come upon a spanking-new columbarium, a kind of multistory condo for cremated ancestors. Through the ornamental gateways, we make out long rows of empty concrete niches awaiting their inurned tenants.

Why, I ask, would a village this sleepy and remote require such sprawling necropolitan suburbs? They're not for locals, Luo assures me. With a location like this, these columbaria can attract "cremains" from Beijing, Tianjin, and beyond. It's an offer no bereaved family could refuse—the *feng shui* of the emperors, yours for just a few hundred renminbi; easy freeway access. Since little else will grow here, *feng shui* farming is about the only way that Taihang villagers could conceivably cash in on the post-Mao decollectivization of rural lands.

Seems like an awful lot of niches to fill, Ah-loong pronounces dubiously. Never mind, says Luo; this is one crop that's a hardy perennial. Over the long run, demand is inexhaustible. That's more than can be said for Highway 112's other main industry: the noodle stalls that have sprouted up at almost every available pull-off wide enough to park a truck. Cook-shacks and picnic tables dot the road shoulder, but we spot not a single customer at any of these establishments. So hot is the competition on this thinly trafficked stretch that hostesses in miniskirts station themselves along the blacktop to beckon any passing vehicle.

Luo is baffled again about where we should turn off to reach Wolf Fang, so we stop to ask our way from one of these noodle-stall road nymphs. As we slow to a halt, she minces up to our car window as fast as her high heels will allow. But her face falls when she realizes that all we want is information. "Wolf Fang?" She pats her lacquered hairdo nervously. "I don't know about that." Then, brightening up: "I'm not sure you can get there from here. You'd better stay for lunch."

We pass up her invitation and roll on for another half-mile before taking a hairpin lurch off to the left where the ghost of a jeep track meets our highway. Zeng, poring over the map, has a hunch that this detour will take us over the saddle of a ridge and down to the lakefront. After many a pothole, though, we still seem no closer than before to the ridgecrest.

Deep-cut tire grooves in the bare, chalky slope preclude a U-turn. To back our way out would be even trickier; the rearview mirror shows nothing but our own plumes of road dust. Luo, whose navigational ineptitude got us lost in the first place, stares straight ahead in abashed silence—until something catches his eye to jar him out of his

funk. "Hey, wait," he mutters. "Isn't that . . . ? Hang on a second
. . . STOP!"

Before I can even bring the car to a full halt, he's out the door and
scurrying back down the road to inspect a small cairn of ceramic
rooftiles he's spotted by the wayside. Not much of a landmark, really,
but in a featureless dustbowl like this I guess it counts as a monument
of sorts. On the strength of this clue, Luo sets out on foot straight up
the embankment. He's too excited to wait for anyone or to offer a
word of explanation. We have no choice but to abandon the car and
tag after him as best we can.

The climb proves steeper, though shorter, than expected. After a
few minutes of scrambling, we find ourselves atop the rise. Luo's already over the ridge and well along on the downslope, but the rest of
us are momentarily stopped in our tracks by the unexpected vista that
opens before us: a panorama of lake water so blue that it shows almost
purple amid the blanched bluffs of the surrounding hills.

Noon light glints from jaunty little wavecrests. Against this dazzling background, Wolf Fang's rooflines and foliage stand out in silhouette. These shadows are all we get to see at first of the village's
architecture or greenery. Between us and the lakefront, the arid hillside is interrupted only by a few animal pens and the blank back walls
of outlying houses. A half-dozen children play a noiseless game of
hopscotch on a grid scratched into the baked clay. As the four of us
appear over the ridgecrest, the children stop their game and freeze in
place. Then, like startled gophers, they scatter down the slope and
vanish into unseen burrows.

We catch up with Luo and head for the shore. With no path to con-
fine us, we spread out, four abreast, dragging our foreshortened shadows over the barren slope. In this empty immensity, our progress
seems snail-paced. I feel, incongruously, as if I'm in a cowboy movie—
one of those ominous scenes with the posse loping wearily across
scrubland toward some silent ghost town.

And true to the spaghetti western genre, the place turns out to be
less deserted than it looks. At first Wolf Fang presents itself as no
more than a line of squat masonry. As we draw nearer, the undifferen-

tiated brickwork resolves into individual houses. We can just about make out the occasional figures flitting across the narrow gaps between courtyards—dumpy forms muffled in cotton tunics that blend into the graywashed backdrop.

The village women studiously ignore us, but there seem to be more and more of them out on the "streets" the closer we get to town. Perhaps alerted by the hopscotch children, they've timed their errands so as to catch a corner-of-the-eye glimpse at the approaching strangers.

At last we draw near enough for one of them to make out a familiar face. She abruptly changes tack. Instead of darting back into town, she veers straight out onto the parched mudflats to meet us. "Lawyer Luo," she calls out in a throaty Taihang accent. "You've come back to us!" Then she broadcasts even louder, as an over-the-shoulder reassurance for the whole town to hear, "It's Old Luo. Our lawyer's returned."

At her word, the street behind her fills with people—middle-aged women and scads of raggedy, unsmiling children. Where had they all been hiding before? So many villagers press into the narrow gap between courtyards that the overflow bulges out of the lane and into the scrubland beyond the town. Luo strides forward to meet them, pressing hands and murmuring salutations.

For all the warmth of his greeting, though, I notice that the lawyer avoids addressing anyone by name; I guess it's been some time, after all, since he was immersed in the affairs of Wolf Fang. Besides, he might not have had too much direct contact in the first place with the members of this distaff reception committee. Most of his "clients"—his thumbprint petitioners—would have been male heads of household.

But at least one woman stands out as an exception to the no-name rule: a big-boned, rangy matron whom Luo spots at the back of the crowd. He points her out to us as "Madame Bai, my local 'mother.' " Her son, Bai Yimin, was the junior partner in the Wolf Fang duo that first went up to Beijing to find a lawyer. "Now Yimin's been elected head of the village council," Luo adds with pride, "which makes Madame Bai a top matriarch around here."

The woman's splay-footed swagger clears her a path through the crowd. Luo beams at the sight of her. She returns his smile and takes both his hands. "*Long* time," she sighs. She seems on the point of leading him off somewhere—to her house?—but then she takes in the rest of us, ranged behind him. Her eyes widen, inquiringly.

"Friends of mine," Luo hastily explains. "Mei-lang, a Taiwan compatriot, and her husband, Lin-ken. And Old Zeng, here, is from my office."

Under a close-cropped helmet of iron-gray hair, Madame Bai's face passes from motherly solicitude to guarded reserve. Foreign guests in her home may be more trouble than she's prepared to undertake on such short notice. How to beg off?

"You know, Old Luo, I've got my hands kind of full these days," she confides worriedly to the lawyer. "Yimin's down with fever."

Luo's full of concern. How long has Bai been sick?

"Nearly a month now, on and off. It's his third bout of this since taking over the council."

What symptoms?

"Oh, the usual: night sweats and insomnia, then he's listless all day, bundled up with the chills. No appetite. Nothing fatal, but it wears him down. His father was the same way during the anti-Jap fight. That's how it is with these heroes, when they get off on their crazes.

"Politics," she spits the word scornfully. "Bad news for us women. Makes our menfolk useless for farmwork. Ages them early. Sometimes Yimin's so wasted he can hardly budge from the bed. But that doesn't stop people coming at him day and night with village business."

Then she comes to her punch line—our disinvitation to lunch.

"So maybe, Old Luo, you'd better first bring your friends across to see Red Ox," she suggests, naming the local Communist Party secretary. "You can come around home afterward to look in on Yimin."

She scans the gaggle of children around us and picks out a pair of barefoot twin boys. "You two run ahead and tell Comrade Secretary he's got company," she orders, like a dowager who's used to being obeyed. "And you," she directs a preteen girl with a baby sibling strapped to her back, "show our guests the way."

OUR YOUNG PILOT has plenty of helpers in her errand; half the crowd follows along with us. We're grateful for so many guides. Otherwise, given Luo's sense of direction, we'd be hard-pressed to find our own path through the disorderly sprawl of Wolf Fang.

The town is all outskirts with no center. Its original main street now lies drowned under Lake Solidarity, and no new hub has arisen to take its place. We thread our way through random lanes that intersect wherever house walls happen to abut. After a few twists and turns, the caked-mud "pavement" gives way to a boggy inlet of the reservoir. Flat-bottomed punts line the shore, each tied to a tussock of marsh grass. Farther up the bank, moss-encrusted fishnets festoon the stacked oars.

We teeter across a plank bridge and pick up our trail again on the other side of the swamp. Blank house walls line our path. The featureless masonry is broken only by gabled gateways that give onto open-air courtyards for drying and winnowing grain. But, although it is only a week or so after the midautumn harvest festival, Wolf Fang's threshing floors look bare.

It's hard to tell which houses are empty and which are not. The best indicators are the heavy padlocks on about a third of the buildings inside the courtyards. A layer of dust impartially covers all the houses, whether occupied or shuttered. The only signs of agricultural produce to be seen are odd basketsful of peppercorns or occasional piles of corncobs. The "crop" most in evidence seems to be pondweed, which dangles in limp hanks from the rafters. It's sold to Beijing bakers, who use it as an emulsifier, Luo informs us.

In a few of the courtyards, women are hanging out laundry on washlines. When they see us troop past, they amble out through the open doorways to follow along. Scattered groups of children forsake their games to join our parade. In their outsized hand-me-downs, the children look like miniature adults, an effect enhanced by their eerie decorum. No japes out of them, none of the normal, juvenile show-off antics. They hardly even dare gawp at the strangers in their midst. Instead, they keep their eyes warily on their elders and tag along apace with the crowd.

We wend through what seems like the entire length of the town, all the way to where the empty scrubland begins again. By the time we near the end of the "street," we've acquired quite a retinue. Well before we reach the last house in the row, however, our escorts bail out. Many of them just drift away; the rest hang back several doorways behind us. Odd behavior for a Chinese village, where strangers normally find their every step dogged by curiosity-seekers. What has suddenly scared off our entourage? Embarrassment? Awe at the august rank of Red Ox, the village Party boss? Or just a reluctance to get involved in other people's catering?

Nothing particularly intimidating about Red Ox's house itself; a squat, L-shaped affair in gray stone and concrete, just like all its neighbors. The weathered planks of the outer gate still bear faded scraps of Door God posters left over from last Chinese New Year. The only difference between Comrade Secretary's and any other gateway in town is that this is the sole courtyard door we've seen that's actually shut. Luo steps up to the threshold and ventures a tentative knock.

At the first tap, the portal, unused to being closed, swings wide with a groan of relief. One look inside, though, is enough to establish why the occupants had shut the door in the first place. Consternation prevails in the courtyard. We feel like we've prematurely raised a proscenium curtain in mid-overture, while stagehands are still fussing with the sets and props.

A young matron scoops half-dried sheets into a laundry basket without even bothering to fold them first. Another woman follows behind her to unstring the clotheslines. A teenager shepherds her younger siblings into the kitchen wing of the house. A bent old lady briskly sweeps the packed-earth threshing floor. Children scramble to rescue their scattered jacks from the onslaught of granny's short-handled broom. Runners dart back and forth between the kitchen door and the pantry room across the courtyard, ferrying extra sup-plies—dried shrimps, garlic, pressed bean curd, even (most prized delicacy of all) a fresh can of MSG. Judging by the clatter and sizzle emanating from the kitchen, it sounds like they've got at least three woks going simultaneously in there. A vexed chicken caroms about the yard, trying to keep out of everybody's way.

Amid all the bustle, the still hub of the tableau is Red Ox himself, a looming giant so physically imposing that it's hard to credit his seventy-plus years. His neck bulges out of his tunic collar and his bare wrists gangle well beyond his frayed sleeves. Unperturbed by the sur-rounding turmoil, he towers over the women like a maypole rearing above the frenzy of a carnival.

Since he's the only one squarely facing the front door, he's the first to note our arrival. His lofty stature allows him, with a quick glance left and right, to rake the entire courtyard with his eyes while barely turning his head. "Enough," he booms to his frantic womenfolk. "Go."

At this cue, the whole crew—granny, children, and all—with-draws pell-mell into the clangorous kitchen. Left alone at "stage cen-ter," Comrade Secretary crinkles his craggy features into a slow smile and splays his palms in a gesture of welcome. Then, with those paddle-sized hands of his, he motions us into the house as though guiding an airliner into its home berth.

THE HALL HE STEERS US INTO, the main parlor of the house, is almost as empty as an aircraft hangar, too. A *kang*—a packed-earth sleeping platform with flues underneath for charcoal heating in win-ter—dominates a third of the room, the side adjacent to the kitchen. The only other furniture is a stolid wooden table flanked by two heavy, straight-backed armchairs. The whole symmetrical ensemble, crudely carved and painted black, hunkers directly opposite the door-way in the space normally reserved in traditional Chinese houses for the family altar.

Except, instead of the usual somber interior of an ancestral hall, this room is flooded with light from a row of windows in the front wall. And over the table, the place traditionally reserved for the ancestral spirit plaque, there hangs instead a pinup calendar of a doe-eyed beauty brandishing an automatic rifle as she straddles a police motorcycle. She's in full police uniform, too—epaulettes pertly thrown back so that the buttons strain on her olive-drab tunic. A peaked Red Star cap perches jauntily atop her tousled tresses. It takes a moment to figure out from the printed legend just what it is that she's advertising: motorcycle shock absorbers.

The woman who brings us tea, coincidentally, also sports a police tunic, although one that's considerably patched and faded. She emerges from the kitchen through a bead curtain next to the *kang* and sets a thermos on the table with a tray full of glass tumblers. "My daughter-in-law," Red Ox curtly introduces her. Two more matrons follow behind her carrying rude wooden benches, which they align at the foot of the table. The three of them then withdraw to a corner of the room and busy themselves with a basket of peppercorns that need to be shelled.

Comrade Secretary automatically installs himself in the armchair to the right of the table, the place of honor, his accustomed roost. He is, after all, the unchallenged patriarch of the village (if only by default; so far we've encountered no other adult male in Wolf Fang). He steers me, the foreign guest, to the other armchair. He motions Luo and Zeng to the two benches and nudges the tea tray forward as a tacit invitation to drink. The four of us at the table each help ourselves to a steaming tumbler and solemnly contemplate the spiraling leaves and twigs.

Ah-loong's evidently barred from this silent male communion; no tea for her and no seat at the table. She'll no doubt have something to say later on about these omissions, but she's already used to such treatment in many Chinese homes and she understands that there's no deliberate rudeness intended. So, for the present, she swallows her indignation and quietly drifts over to the corner of the room to join the women.

No sooner does she hunker down to the task of shucking pepper-corns than the Wolf Fang women hit her with the stock question: How many children? This is the inevitable conversation-opener at any chance first-meeting between Chinese and foreign women, whether at a diplomatic dinner party, a supermarket checkout line, or a railway compartment.

It always makes Ah-loong cringe. What with Beijing's draconian one-child policy, our own three children somehow seem a grosser form of conspicuous consumption than if she'd come out slumming in mink. A few Chinese women she's met have been aghast at her feral fecundity, but most sound wistful for unconstrained families of their own.

Not in this group, though. "Two girls and a boy?" the woman in the police tunic nods companionably. "Same here."

"You've got three?" Ah-loong reconfirms, unsure she's heard right.

"Well, only Old Number One is officially my daughter," the woman admits. "Old Two is a so-called nephew and Old Three is a niece." These over-quota children are "souvenirs," she adds, of guest worker stints in coastal cities. Family planning, it seems, used to be a lot stricter before villagers could venture beyond Wolf Fang. But now, with couples traveling all around in search of work, who's to enforce one-child limits in the slums and rooming houses of industrial hubs?

Even when a woman comes home to her native village with an ex-cess child or two, any investigative follow-up depends upon the local Party secretary. "And Comrade Red Ox, here, has more important things than *that* to think about," she says, beaming across the room at her father-in-law. So for nearly a decade, now, Wolf Fang (and, pre-sumably, a million similar hamlets across China) has filled up with "adopted relatives" of studiously vague parentage.

"It's one luxury we've got that the city people can't afford," she laughs.

Ah-loong's stunned by this matter-of-fact recital. In all her time in China, supernumerary offspring would only be mentioned (if at all) in a whisper of guilt, longing, or vituperative gossip. Yet here's this woman dilating on the joys of serial breeding as calmly as any Soccer Mom at an American Tupperware party. Ah-loong polls the others in the pepper-shucking circle:

"How many do *you* have?"

"Also three, but they're all boys. That *really* keeps you busy!"

"And you?" she asks the youngest in the group.

"Only one girl, so far. I'd like to try for a boy or two."

If this group is any indication, Ah-loong calculates, it's no wonder China's census estimate has to include a "margin of error" of up to 100 million. How many of these hypothetical persons actually exist is anybody's guess—a population the size of Japan's, as elusive as Schroedinger's cat. Faced with that much uncertainty, could Beijing really tolerate such loopholes in its demographic policy as these women describe? Surely it can't be so easy, Ah-loong protests. There must be some downside, some additional cost to having "extra" children.

"Well, you can't enroll them in government schools," the youngest of the three women admits. "But, then, there's not much of a school here, anyway. And, besides, schooling doesn't matter so much for factory work or farming, the kinds of jobs we go for."

"While I'm tied up here with kids, I can't be outside making money," Comrade Secretary's daughter-in-law adds. "That was okay as long as my man was out there working, but now he's home sick, so there is nothing coming in. But we'll get over it," she shrugs. "And, sooner or later, the children themselves will go out to work and send back some money as well. More children, more money."

The only other drawback she can think of, she adds, is that "all these 'nieces' and 'nephews' of ours will never be able to vote here. For whatever *that's* worth."

IT MIGHT NOT BE worth all that much, judging from Comrade Secretary's dismissive tone on the subject of voting. Since the four of us at the table can't hear or join in the women's murmured colloquy, it's left to me to break the stiff, masculine silence. I pompously congratu-late Red Ox on his "bold embrace of democracy and courageous open-ness to new ideas."

The old man waves away my flattery. "*Ayah*, there's nothing *new* about democracy. We had it here in Wolf Fang way back, fifty years ago, right after Liberation."

In his first several elections, Red Ox wasn't even a voter. He was the candidate, and the two roles were incompatible, the way he de-scribes the process. The whole election lasted barely twenty minutes. All the eligible electors would assemble in the village schoolroom. Each head of household was issued a token at the door—a lima bean or a pebble or some such—signifying his family's one allotted vote.

Red Ox, as the Communist Party's designee for village chief, occu-pied a three-legged stool in the front of the room, facing the assembly. On a bench behind him perched an earthenware water jar. One by one, the electors would file past the jar and drop in their tokens.

"It all went on behind my back," he beams. "Perfectly secret bal-loting, you see."

"What if someone didn't want to vote for you?" I ask.

"Well, nobody was *forced* to drop his bean into the jar."

"But even if *you* couldn't see how anyone was voting, wasn't it per-fectly visible to the crowd facing you?"

"Of course," he nods. "That's the whole *point* of the election in the first place, isn't it? It's not enough just for people to back the village's responsible authority. Even more important is for everyone to be *seen* to be backing the authority. Only so is authority beyond all question."

"Could you have more than one candidate?"

"What for?" he asks in unfeigned perplexity. "After all, we all *know* each other here."

"But what if there were a difference of opinion?"

"Impossible. Not in *those* days. Not over anything that mattered, anyway. On the important questions—land reform, the anti–Chiang Kai-shek struggle—we were all of one mind.

"Thanks to the Party, we had just toppled the mighty Japanese Empire. We knew that *nothing* could stop us, so long as we gave our all and stood firm behind our leaders. Sitting there in front of everybody and listening to the beans pile up one by one in that jar, the surge of confidence I felt then, the sense of power—unbeatable!"

Sounds pretty heady. How, I wonder, did he get chosen for that privileged stool?

As Party secretary, he was the natural and inevitable choice for village head. And he became secretary by sheer default, as he relates it. He was simply the last survivor of the original anti-Japanese resistance cell. The rest had met their end in guerrilla skirmishes or the siege of Ax Head Mountain. The Party had deliberately kept Red Ox out of the line of fire to use as a courier and porter. That's what he'd been recruited for in the first place.

"I was young and big. I knew my way around these hills, even in the dark. And I was so dumb-looking that the daytime Jap patrols hardly even bothered to interrogate me," he adds with his goofiest grin. "That's why they called me 'Red Ox,' you see. The Party needed a brute like me for load-ferrying. And what the Party needed, Wolf Fang freely gave."

Whatever the Party needed, he stresses, listing off the sacrifices the villagers readily made for the Communist cause: "If a resistance fighter had to lie low, he could hide in any house in Wolf Fang. When rations ran short up in Ax Head, we scrounged grain from our own depleted stores. Just about every family in the village contributed a martyr or two to the armed struggle. And when it came time to give up our ancestral fields for the greater good, none of us hung back. To us, the Party's will was law, the will of the people."

He turns, almost reproachfully, to the two city-slicker attorneys at the foot of the table, as though they were personally responsible for Wolf Fang's fall from revolutionary grace. "In those days, we had no use for lawyers, Old Luo," he sighs. "We needed none of your precious rule of law, back then, to establish democracy. Rather, it worked the other way around: democracy established the rule of the Party's law, as our elections showed for all to see. As Communists, we knew that the point of everything we did, from agitprop to elections, was to create solidarity, not to divide us.

"Because when we were divided, before we had the Party, we counted for nothing. Any petty Kuomintang grafter could come here and tax-gouge us on a whim. Any Jap patrol could roar through town raping and looting and kidnapping. But after Liberation, Wolf Fang *mattered*. Because of our wartime service, we were designated as a Revolutionary Hamlet."

The official recognition energized the village, Red Ox relates. There was excitement in the air, things were happening—movements, campaigns, mass agitations. The Party brought concrete improvements, too: a once-a-week health clinic and a gradeschool.

"We felt a part of something *huge*. Wolf Fang sent heroes to Korea. We struggled against American imperialism and Moscow revisionism. We even mobilized a work brigade to help build the Lake Solidarity Dam, which was to flood our own fields. No one here ever questioned the project. It was all part of the Party's grand design; the Party would take care of us."

And true to expectations, the Party *did* come through with relief grain to make up for the forgone crops. "It was amazing, that first year after the fields were drowned," Red Ox recalls. "We reaped no harvest at all, yet nobody went hungry. Who'd ever *heard* of such a thing? Only a couple of old-timers, who remembered tales from their childhood about how the village used to get its imperial gold stipend, in fat years and lean, just for maintaining the Qing tombs."

Having brought his fellow townsmen to the verge of this Promised Land of income security, Comrade Secretary could withdraw, Moses-like, to make way for a new generation of leadership—people who actually knew how to keep account books and could even pronounce the names of all those foreign class enemies that Wolf Fang was now called upon to denounce. Red Ox handpicked his own successor, Shih Lixuan, a boy who'd shown such promise in the new village school that he'd been singled out to complete secondary studies down in the county seat.

"When Lixuan took over," Comrade Secretary recalls, "we got rid of that old clay water jar and those lima bean 'ballots.' They seemed, somehow, unscientific." What was the use of all that paraphernalia, villagers reasoned, when Lixuan's qualifications so clearly spoke for themselves? Besides, the new village chief had the solid support of the higher-ups in Yi county.

"Ah, *preferment*," Zeng intones in the florid cadence of an *I Ching* soothsayer. "The Superior Man, on horseback, fords the Great Waters. Fortune attends."

"Well, maybe it attended on Lixuan," Red Ox laughs, "but fortune sure bypassed the rest of us. First the relief grain went missing. Then the account books vanished. Next, our neighbors and comrades started disappearing, too—into the county jail—whenever they raised a murmur of complaint. Nothing we could do; Lixuan had his local gang here and his well-placed backers down in the Yi county seat. You know the rest of the story, Old Luo."

The lawyer nods sympathy. "At least it ends happily—right?— with you back in charge."

"*That's* no ending, only a stop-gap interlude," the old man snorts. "For the first time since Liberation, we've got a village administrator in Wolf Fang who's not part of the local Party hierarchy—an unnatural situation that can't last. I'm old and have no interest in hanging on to the post of secretary. Nor am I under any illusions about how I got here."

As far as Red Ox is concerned, the villagers chose themselves a clear leader: Bai Yimin. But the election victor came from outside the Party. And the Yi county leadership, after battling Yimin for so long, could hardly then just turn around and accept him as Wolf Fang's legitimate spokesman. County higher-ups wanted someone they'd already dealt with and knew and trusted; someone, above all, of their own choosing, just to prove the Party still runs the show.

"So I'm supposedly in charge again—by default, just like last time. When there are internal Party directives to enforce, when a word needs to be put in upstairs, whenever anyone's reliability has to be vouched for, it's me they call. But for ongoing paperwork—statistics, quotas, and such—the county turns to Yimin. And he's the one that villagers approach with requests.

"Did you notice, coming over here, how everybody gives my door

a wide berth? I'm old now, but I'm not stupid; I know there's a lot going on in town these days—even right here in my own house—that
people would just as soon *not* declare straight to the Party leadership.
But if you go over to Yimin's house, you'll find petitioners lined up
there at all hours."

Sounds to me like a gross mismatch of power and responsibility.
How can Yimin fulfill either the county's quotas or the villagers'
petitions when only Red Ox enjoys any credibility with the powers
that be?

"Well, luckily Yimin and I get along together," the old man explains. "So I tell him what he's got to do and he tells me what I need to
hear. And whatever has to be ignored, we just gloss over. Not an ideal
arrangement, but what can you expect from this new style of voting,
all isolated and secret, like going to the toilet?

"Instead of bolstering authority, an election like that only highlights contradictions. No wonder we're stuck with a 'two-headed' village leadership. No wonder Shih Liguo's forever able to stir up trouble
for us at the grassroots. No wonder Yimin's always ailing.

"I hope, before long, the Yi county higher-ups can learn to live
with him and induct him as our local secretary here. Nothing wrong
with Wolf Fang that can't be cured by a good old jar full of beans."

JUST AS HE'S PRONOUNCING this prescription, there materializes
before him not quite a jar full, but at least a steaming plate heaped
with beans (braised with pickled radish). More dishes join the beans
on the table, as women, in relays, ferry steaming platters through the
kitchen door: julienned potatoes with smoked bean curd, Chinese cabbage with dried shrimp, a veritable haystack of stir-fried chives, a
beansprout-and-pumpkin soup. The *pièce de résistance*: some sort of
Spam-like composition meat, sliced and garnished with mushrooms,
peppers, and a gummy brown sauce. An aluminum washtub of rice-
and-yam gruel ballasts our luncheon table.

Ushering in the procession from the kitchen, Xiao Niu, Comrade

Secretary's son, stations himself next to the bead curtain like an officious maître d' incongruously dressed in khaki fatigues and a peaked Mao cap. He's almost as tall as his father, but nowhere near as imposing—pasty-faced, and lounging against the *kang* in a stoop-shouldered slump. His waxy, sweat-beaded complexion gives a famished look to his fervid eyes as he tracks each dish from stove to table. Yet he recoils with visible queasiness from the intermittent wisps of kitchen steam that issue through the bead curtain. And when his father invites him to join us at table, Xiao Niu practically shudders his refusal, hocking diffidently into a handy spittoon.

What's *with* this guy, I catch myself wondering; he's like a Hungry Ghost of Chinese myth, forever ravenous yet unable to sit down to the feasts of the living.

But at least Ah-loong gets to feast with us after Red Ox, in a special concession, eases the ban on women at table. He beckons her over from the *kang* and motions her to share Luo's bench. The matron in the police tunic, Comrade Secretary's daughter-in-law and the wife of our maître d', passes around plastic rice bowls. We each help ourselves to chopsticks from a tumbler. Zeng offers the usual compliments about the opulence of the banquet.

"Don't thank *me*," Red Ox retorts. "This spread is brought to you by the Wolf Fang Development Promotion Foundation"—yet another brainchild of Bai Yimin's. Basically, the "Foundation" is just a grandiloquent name for an extra shelf full of village-funded groceries in Comrade Secretary's pantry. The provisions are set aside to entertain visiting dignitaries in hopes that they'll feel inspired to invest in the village.

"Has it won you a lot of investors?" Luo asks. It turns out the Foundation's only banquet so far was a few months ago, when the Yi county leadership showed up en masse escorting some hotshot in a double-breasted suit. The cadres introduced their guest as a rich overseas Chinese hotel developer from Canada (although to Red Ox's ear the man seemed to speak with a suspiciously down-home Taihang accent). That occasion used up the Foundation's entire supply of sausage. Afterward, the whole motorcade roared off, never to be heard from again in Wolf Fang.

"Maybe their '*hôtelier*' will get back to us someday," Comrade Secretary muses. "Maybe he really *was* an overseas Chinese, after all. Nowadays, Taihang people show up in all sorts of places. But anyway, that's how come we have no sausage anymore, and can only serve you this humble fare," he concludes, ruefully. "I wish we could offer you fish. Once, no Wolf Fang luncheon would have been complete without fish. In those days, any time you'd row out on Lake Solidarity, you could count on hooking three or four fat grass carp in an afternoon."

Ah-loong, herself a grass carp devotée, wonders what became of all those fish. Red Ox relates how somebody from one of the villages on the opposite shore got the bright idea of boosting the fish harvest by dynamiting the lake bed. For a week, carp were a glut on the market. Then they disappeared altogether.

"Ever since that time, we've had nothing here but little finger shrimp," he sighs, contemptuously waggling his pinkie. "Except, of course, on holidays, when everyone returns. *Then* we eat in style."

Twice a year—at the midautumn Moon Festival and at the Chinese New Year—all Wolf Fang villagers who can possibly do so head back home, no matter how far their wanderings have taken them in search of work. The same goes for every other village in the Taihang, Red Ox assures us, and, as far as he knows, the whole rest of interior China, as well.

Holiday time is a prodigal round of reunions and storytelling and dressing up in finery. (Such occasions, Luo interjects, are also ideal for holding elections, since only then is there an adequate quorum of voters in the village.)

"Dead as it is the rest of the year, this place *really* comes back to life at the Moon Festival and New Year's," Red Ox beams. "It's almost like old times, right after Liberation."

To illustrate this Brigadoon-effect, he describes Wolf Fang's fleeting biannual awakening from its economic and social coma. During the festal season, labor contractors canvass returnees to recruit work gangs for faraway factories and construction sites. Matchmakers scurry to marry off any available singles before the next migration cycle. Seasoned guest workers regale novices with travel tips.

Some of their tales are cautionary: how (and where) to shun lousy pay, dismal working conditions, hostile natives, abusive officialdom, inflated expenses, and sluggish hiring. But most of the talk is upbeat braggadocio—thousand-mile hitchhikes, heroic production deadlines met, city-slickers duped, sights seen, and (most dotingly detailed of all) banquets eaten on the road.

Food is the topic of choice, for the migrants' map of China is, above all, gastronomic. "City people call us a 'blind river,' " Red Ox laughs, citing the slang name *mang-liu*, a pejorative for migrant workers. "Well, we may be 'blind,' but you could never say we're dead in the palate."

Whatever else he may carry in his knapsack, no guest worker would launch forth from Wolf Fang minus a personal supply of home-brewed vinegar. With it, even the dingiest gruel can be made palatable to the Taihang taste—a survival necessity when road luck runs thin. But when fortune smiles, a migrant's first splurge (after remitting some money home) will always be on the local delicacies of wherever he happens to find himself. Apart from their immediate gustatory merits, these gastronomic forays also earn bragging rights for returnees on holiday sojourns back home.

Like most other Chinese, *mang-liu* are generally eclectic in their eating preferences, once freed from the enforced parochialism of their village-bound, premigration lifestyle. Now that they can venture beyond the Taihang, guest workers love to swap tales of the amazing comestibles to be found out there: the Yunan hams, the pressed duck of Sichuan, the roast dogs of Canton, snowy Shantung steamer buns, the frogs and snails of Guangxi, Fuzhou dried squid that glow in the dark, Jiangsu eels, and the soft-shelled crabs of Ningpo—the list goes on and on.

Whenever possible (given the exigencies of their budgets and their long, hot, crowded homeward journeys) the migrants like to illustrate their epicurean memoirs with fancy victuals they've brought back for the holiday feasts. "Remember the time you carried a live tortoise all the way from Yangzhou?" Red Ox prompts his son. "Or the rock cod you brought us from Qingdao?"

Xiao Niu flushes with pleasure, recalling the occasion, but then blanches again as though even the vivid memory of a braised fish were enough to nauseate him. He hocks into the spittoon and deflects his gaze from our luncheon table, turning instead to the *kang*, where his wife has resumed her pepper-shucking.

"I'll bring you another cod," he swears fervently, although his throat sounds tight. "I'll get you Hainan lobsters and thousand-year eggs from Hong Kong. Who knows?" He ventures a strained little chuckle. "I may yet bring home American hot dogs."

"*That's* it," Red Ox booms his encouragement a little too loud. His daughter-in-law nods wordlessly without looking up from her peppers. "That's the *life*."

"The *only* life for people like us," Xiao Niu agrees. "Ready money, if you're lucky. Adventure, too—a chance to go places you've never been before. Maybe where *nobody's* ever been before, at least not from these parts. If you open up new territory for Taihang workers, it's more than just prestige for you. Some of our people do so well in 'introduction fees' that they don't need to sweat anymore. They become labor contractors in their own right."

Xiao Niu himself was well along on this career path, he wants us to know, before his present minor health problems. He'd already traversed all of China, from the Russian frontier to the Golden Triangle of Southeast Asia. He'd even crossed international borders to work with Chinese construction gangs in Siberia and Burma. With so much experience, he could easily establish his credibility as a "guide," as soon as he overcomes his transient infirmities.

"Too bad about this little health setback," Luo clucks, sympathetically. "Nothing serious, I hope?" His bland inquiry triggers a flurry of denials.

"Oh, nothing but a little weight loss," Red Ox guardedly allows.

"Just a temporary slump in energy," Xiao Niu mumbles.

"Occasional chills, is all," his wife interjects from the *kang*.

Prompted by their overeager disclaimers, I catch myself scanning Xiao Niu's ashen face for traces of jaundice or telltale sarcoma blotches. Is that spittoon of his a seething cauldron of tuberculosis? Is the beading on his brow the clammy sweat of cholera?

"Hmmm," Luo nods. "Doesn't sound like fun. A lot of that going around?"

"Oh, what I've got is *nothing*," Xiao Niu hastens to assure us. "Road life's great, but a lot of Wolf Fang people just can't keep up with it for long. They burn out. Some settle elsewhere and simply stop coming back. We never even find out what's become of them."

"Not that staying home is any guarantee of health," his wife chimes in. "For one thing, you can't eat decently here, not like on the road. It's not every day that we can sit down to a 'Foundation' banquet, you know. Most of the time it's nothing but *mantou* and radish. On a diet like that, children stay scrawny. Mothers can't even nurse their babies properly."

Just to keep themselves fed, she adds, some Wolf Fang women take to hanging out at the truck stops we passed on the way here along the Taihang highway. But after a few months of "going to the highway," they, too, start wasting away with health problems of their own.

And every festal season, a few Wolf Fang migrants come straggling home and don't set out again after the holiday. They just lie down on the *kang* and stay there, slowly fading away.

"But *I'm* still on my feet," Xiao Niu concludes brightly, "and, well before Chinese New Year, I'll be on my way again, for sure. Can't afford not to be. In this *mang-liu* game, if you stop moving, there's always somebody right behind you, waiting to take your place."

The pan-Chinese *mang-liu* flows have a replenishing effect, he explains; one migrant wave triggers another. "For instance, I know I can always find work in the button factories in Wenzhou. How come? Because the Wenzhou families who first set up that button center have now all migrated to the United States and Europe. You run into the same story, more or less, all along the coast. Wherever the locals have made a little money, they use it to move on to someplace where the opportunities are even richer, leaving their old jobs to people like us."

"It seems like our Taihang is just about the only place left where you *don't* see new *mang-liu* coming in to replace the original migrants who've left," Red Ox sighs.

"Maybe that's because before we started hitting the road, we hardly even *had* jobs for anyone to take over," Xiao Niu tartly rejoins. "But it might liven things up here if we could skip a few rungs on the *mang-liu* ladder and get *ourselves* to the places these coastal types are going to."

"Remember Blinky Shih from up in Ax Head village across the lake? The pimply kid that used to sell us eel traps," Red Ox prompts. "Hear tell he's made it all the way to America."

"*That* little turtle-shit? Who'd have imagined," Xiao Niu shakes his head in awed incredulity. "How'd he manage a thing like that? I've seen lines wrapped around the block in front of the American visa offices in Canton. And, for all their patience and their application fees, most of those poor curb-warmers in the queue get nothing but the brush-off.

"In Wenzhou and Fujian, you hear about 'backdoor' entry to the U.S. But it costs more than you could ever earn here in a lifetime of factory wages. And, even so, there's no guarantee of success. Besides, those coastal immigration 'brokers' only want to deal with their own kind. They won't even talk to outsiders like us.

"Of course, if you had some kind of *sponsor* in America, it might be a different story . . ." He lets his speculation hang in the air while he pauses for a rhetorical hock into the spittoon. Then he goes on to sound us out about the American reality on the ground, as reported on the *mang-liu* grapevine.

Is it true that the farms over there are all run by machines and everyone lives in cities? That Chinatowns are all over the place, and nobody's put off by Asian faces or speech? That every street corner has a computerized cash-dispensing robot that can transfer money for you, instantly and anonymously, to anyplace on earth? That you may walk any street you like at any hour of the day or night and no police-man can touch you just for *being* there?

WHAT TO SAY? Should we try to qualify his premises or leave intact the brightly daubed vision of America? Not that he's exactly wrong in his particulars, but any *mang-liu* who actually gets as far as the U.S. had better be braced for far stiffer challenges than merely finding an ATM. Still, who needs *us* to tell him that? Nuance and balance are not what he's after; encouragement, rather, for his heroic climb out of his sickbed and back to the road. He'd doubtless welcome our more mate-rial support, too, judging from his broad hints about "sponsorship."

In Chinese, the United States is called *Mei Guo*, the "beautiful country." It's not necessarily an expression of admiration. These days, the phrase can just as readily carry overtones of irony, resentment, or, at best, covetous envy. Many would-be migrants hardly care to join the ongoing American pageant for keeps. They just want a quick piece of the action—preferably a detachable piece that they can carry home as a trophy, like a fat New Year's carp.

In grade school we were taught about the twelve thousand Chinese laborers who built the western leg—by far the most challenging part—of America's transcontinental railway in the mid-nineteenth century. They faced blizzards, rock-falls, vertiginous heights, dyna-mite blasts, wage-gouging, loneliness, and scorn with undeniably heroic endurance. And yet when, in my high school history text, I fi-nally came upon a picture of the "Golden Spike" ceremony that marked the link-up of the railway's western and eastern sections, the photo showed only top-hatted Anglo politicians and burly, be-whiskered Irish harriers; not a "Celestial" in view.

Where had they all gone? Were the coolies kept out of sight, an embarrassment to the assembled dignitaries? Or did the "Chinamen" simply not care about the momentous occasion, the spanning of a con-tinent from sea to shining sea? It wasn't *their* continent, after all, and they were in no way invited to care. Few enough of them would ever get a chance to ride that railroad to the opposite coast, anyway.

Within a year of the Golden Spike ceremony, brave California work-ingmen would launch the first of the anti-Chinese pogroms that eventually led to America's Oriental exclusion laws.

Yet those early Chinese railroad-builders were lineal precursors of today's "blind river" of migrants. Then, as now, the ones who made it as far as the United States would be only the outermost fringe of China's *mang-liu* tide. How many of Wolf Fang's wanderers, even today, know or care about the "economic miracles" wrought by their far-flung toil?

Xiao Niu prods me out of my reverie with an interrogative little cough; he's still waiting for an answer to his queries. He's got the American scene broadly right, I try to reassure him; I trust he won't be disappointed. Red Ox urges us again to enjoy the banquet, but with all the hocking and the gritty road tales, we're not feeling too hungry. We dabble ceremoniously at the array of dishes, stretching out a bowlful apiece of gruel as best we can. As soon as etiquette allows, we excuse ourselves to go take a look at the reservoir. Before we're even out the door, a dozen women from the kitchen surround the table and, without even bothering to sit down, fall upon what's left of the Foundation feast.

Red Ox guides us down to the lake along a shortcut between the backs of the courtyards. We have to string out single file to fit through the muddy, shoulder-width passage. The closer we get to the lake-front, the deeper the houses nestle in the gullies. After a while we start to catch intermittent glimpses of the bare slopes rising over the compound walls.

We've regained at least part of our retinue, I notice: the same silent children who tagged after us on the way to Comrade Secretary's house. Now they scuttle alongside us on the bluffs overhead, still cagey and wordless as ever. Anytime they spot me looking at them, they avert their eyes and scamper out of sight.

Our narrow passageway gradually steepens until we're practically forced to jog along at a half-trot, like livestock in a cattle chute. We continue our blinkered stampede until we come to the last dwelling in the village, a shack too mean to even surround itself with a compound wall.

More of a lean-to than a proper house, it's really only a haphazard collection of loose planks, broken oar-staves, and styrofoam floats, all approximately held together with festoons of netting and dried pondweed. There's no door, as such, for Red Ox to knock on, so he just rattles the whole ramshackle assemblage a few shakes, calling out, "Hey, Duck Egg."

The nickname fits the person who comes out to meet us: a hulk of a man, as big as Red Ox himself, and perfectly hairless. Nearly neckless, too, with his unbuttoned Mao tunic draped as loosely about his sunburnt shoulders as a Humpty Dumpty frock coat. His black pantaloons, gathered at the waist with a twist of rope, end at midcalf to expose a pair of feet so splayed and calloused they almost look like scaly duck webs—the result, presumably, of long, barefoot years treading the undulant decks of fishing rafts.

"Get out the boat," Comrade Secretary orders. "Our guests want to see Coxcomb Hill."

The boatman waddles off to the shore, tying a gray bandana onto his gleaming pate. He wades waist-deep into the marsh grass and hauls out a flat-bottomed sampan. Unlimbering the stowed sweeps, he lashes them into the oarlocks aft. Red Ox scrambles aboard and sets to bailing the craft with a half-sectioned plastic bleach bottle.

These preparations give the rest of us a moment to admire the view from the boatman's hovel. This little promontory may be prime lakefront real estate, but it still feels to me like a tenuous toehold on a steep and scraggly slope. The flooding of the valley lopped the surrounding mountains in half so arbitrarily that the landscape elements still don't quite harmonize. The shoreline's a little too busy, full of spits, hooks, and inlets. The rootless mountains rear abruptly to a jagged ridge. Fitful cat's-paws of wind ravel the water's surface. A narrow fringe of startlingly green marshland rings the entire lake except for the bank directly opposite us, where the tree-clad palisade of Coxcomb Hill anchors the entire panorama.

Red Ox offers his great slab of a hand to steady us as we scramble on board and settle into the bamboo benches amidships. He himself squats on his haunches in the squared-off prow. On a narrow deck behind us, the boatman, Duck Egg, works the oars with crossed arms. As we pull away from shore, the widening expanse of lake behind us serves to amplify the web of village sounds: buckets clanging, woks sizzling, women's voices. We can make out the grunts, barks, and cackles of domestic animals, but—unsettlingly—no laughter or shouting of children.

Despite Duck Egg's brisk rowing, we hardly seem to make headway. Our sampan feels becalmed, as though somehow trapped in the bubble of a carpenter's level. So smooth is the water surface that it looks almost concave. Light reflects back from the edges of the lake with a heightened, rainbow intensity. Yet, here at the center, sunbeams penetrate the amber water to illumine the dizzy swirl of pondweed just inches below our keel.

Each dip of our oar stirs the fingers of pondweed anew, so we always seem to hover right over the vortex of a clutching vegetative frenzy. I can't see how anyone could distinguish one part of this lake bed from any other, but at a certain point about twenty minutes out from shore, Red Ox suddenly announces, matter-of-factly, "I was born here."

"Where?" I ask, staring from ridgecrest to shoreline to pondweed.

"I mean right here, where we sit," he insists, trailing his huge hand over a gunwale. "Straight down under us is the house I grew up in."

Peering overboard, I see nothing but the same teeming tendrils as anyplace else in Lake Solidarity. But Comrade Secretary's already nostalgically detailing for us the drowned town below: the lively High Street with its two-story shop houses, the turnpike out to Yi county, the fairground meadow with its weekly livestock market, the crossroads banyan tree where old men would play chess and gossip. And all around the town stretched level fields.

"They may have been dry and stony, but at least our fields were flat. Nothing to get rich on, of course. When it came time for land reform, after Liberation, we found we didn't even have anybody here to "struggle against"—none of us had ever prospered enough to count as a Landlord or even a Middle Peasant. But we *did* have little fields of our own; we weren't landless day laborers.

"And then came the Great Leap Forward, to show us what we could really make of our land." As far as Comrade Secretary is concerned, this mass mobilization of the early 1960s was Wolf Fang's finest hour and his own zenith as a Communist "vanguard."

"In the first year of the campaign, we finished the dam—ahead of schedule, no less." The next year, as the waters started to accumulate in the reservoir, the village collectivized its farming according to Chairman Mao's dictates. By consolidating the fields and using the newly available irrigation waters, Wolf Fang achieved record harvests of both rice and winter wheat. "The year after that, we were able to grow watermelons here. *Watermelons*—can you imagine?"

"And then?" Luo prompts.

"And then," Red Ox sighs, "the very next year the reservoir waters covered everything—houses, fields, roads, trees, everything. No crop has really grown here since. The government sent us relief grain and helped us rebuild our homes on higher ground. But after a few years, the grain just stopped coming; Lixuan saw to that.

"And twenty years later, by the time you got our relief payments going again, Old Luo, the dole had already switched from grain to cash. Except the stipend they offer is way too small to save us now. We still have to roam all over the place in search of work. We supply *mang-liu* labor to any sweatshop, mine, or construction site that will have us.

"So now," he spits once overboard for emphasis, "*we're* the crop."

HIS METAPHOR DEFIES rejoinder, a real conversation-stopper. We all stare glumly into the water, where Comrade Secretary's expectoration unfurls on the surface over a backdrop of beckoning pondweed fronds. As the lacy spit-flower dissolves in our wake, the shadow of a cliff overtakes our bow.

The mirrored reflection of Coxcomb Hill looks even more romantic than the actual wooded bluff looming above us. The tea-colored lake mellows the image. Trees stand out in meticulous outline—pine, maple, willow, bamboo. Each species layers its own signature leaf form to cumulatively add up to a hypnotic moiré of forest canopy. Rock outcrops lead the eye to the summit, where the upturned eaves of a roof, glimpsed through foliage, hint at a lonely pavilion.

But, before we can quite lose ourselves in the floating, ethereally reflected landscape, our daydream is cut short by the bump of our prow against a very concrete bank. Coxcomb Hill looms straight overhead, a sheer escarpment choked with dense undergrowth. Red Ox loops a hawser around an overhanging willow and we disembark onto a convenient stepping stone—the first of many thoughtful footfalls and handholds provided.

Using roots as stairs and vines as banisters, our trail reduces the seemingly forbidding ascent to a series of easy stages. Where no other step presents itself, niches are chiseled directly into the rock. Passing through a cleft between boulders, the path tunnels a few feet down to allow for extra headroom. As though planned for scenic variety, every switchback presents a fresh vista—a lakeshore inlet, a backlit poplar, a writhing cedar. Each overlook offers some sort of bench or ledge from which to enjoy the view.

Who, I ask Red Ox, has invested so much thought and effort in this trail?

"Pilgrims, I guess," he shrugs. "There used to be a temple up there, though nobody knows how long it's been since it's housed any monks. Even when I was a kid, we still did an occasional *bai-bai* [ceremonial sacrifice] here. Kept it up right until the Japs invaded.

"After Liberation, though, we more or less forgot about this place. Oh, the Red Guards came up once or twice and made a great show of smashing a few idols. But after that, nobody really had any business up here—not of a respectable sort, anyway. Who'd come to such a lonely place unless they had something to hide?

"Which is maybe why Shih Liguo decided to retire here, now that I think of it. Real-world life probably just got to be too much for him. In his fight against modern times he must have piled up more than his share of enemies. Whatever it was he was fleeing, his hideout here became a rallying point for all the rest of us who didn't like the way things were going in town.

"Even before the election, though, Liguo's family caught up with him and dragged him off to Yi county. Hasn't been back here since. Health problems, I hear. But even from his sickbed down there, he still stirs up fresh gossip to plague us. What he *can't* do anymore, is anything useful, such as maintaining this path. Since he left here, Coxcomb Hill's gone to seed."

A thick growth of underbrush confirms the neglect. Wherever the path levels out, we find ourselves wading through waist-high grasses. Brambles flourish in the sunny patches, clutching at our cuffs. Despite the thoughtful layout of the trail, it still takes some bushwhacking to reach the top. "A pity, isn't it?" Comrade Secretary frets, reverting to his investment-promotion mode. "Properly looked after, what a vacation resort this place would make! Honeymoon heaven."

Nor is he the first to dream up such a use for the hill, evidently; broken glass and condom-wrappers attest to recent trysts. Trampling down a stand of nettles, we crash our way through to the ruin whose upturned roof we'd seen from the lake. It's not exactly the contemplative pavilion we'd imagined, nor even recognizably much of a temple anymore. More like a dilapidated bus-stop shelter incongruously transplanted to the middle of a hilltop briar patch. Tin cans glint dully amid the dead ashes of a campfire in the middle of the floor. On what's left of the altar, someone's used a cinder to draw a huge priapic scrawl.

Red Ox, ever the booster, coughs delicately and murmurs his embarrassed reminder that "We can modify anything or rebuild as required. Including Liguo's house," he adds briskly, directing our attention away from the ruined altar. "Come have a look."

Through a gap in the back wall, he ushers us out of the temple. The modest rise we stand on is covered with bamboos, as prescribed by the canons of *feng shui*. From here we can sight across an orchard of young persimmon trees to Shih's abandoned cottage. The whitewash still shines, although the thatched roof sags a little and the fenceposts loll askew. A ripple of wind doffs the coppery persimmon leaves. Shih's front gate flaps desultorily on its hinges, but its clatter is drowned out by the groan of the bamboos that surround us here on the temple knoll.

"Liguo planted these persimmons himself," Red Ox points out. "That's how he got his land deed and building permit—a special perk for ex-army cadres who retire to take up farming. Not that he ever actually raised any fruit here; kind of a token farmer, he was. More of a thinker, I'd say. Even after his knees gave out and he stopped coming into town, he'd still hobble through his orchard and sit at his lookout point there, thinking. From way across the lake, we'd spot him on that log, not budging for hours on end."

"Then why'd he build his house over on the other side?" Zeng wonders.

"That's where the well is. And, besides, he could keep an eye on his persimmons. But of course, if you redevelop the place as a resort, you can resite your buildings wherever you like."

Red Ox and Lawyer Zeng then launch into a learned discussion of pipelines, gradients, and windbreaks, presumably for our benefit as potential resort developers. I opt out of considering this hypothetical spa, and instead drift off through the bamboos to sample Shih's view from the lookout in front of the temple.

Here, on his own turf, I try to conjure up the gravitas of Liguo, the crusty zealot who carved out this hilltop aerie and fanned the flames of the Wolf Fang election fracas. I envision him pacing his orchard with a deliberation born of more than just arthritis. In my mind's eye, he's the very picture of an intellectual in the grandly oxymoronic Chinese tradition: a communitarian anchorite, a canonically hidebound improviser, a reclusive agitator.

Such have been the scholar-generals, poet-revolutionaries, and painter-bureaucrats who've cumulatively written the panoramic scroll of Chinese civilization. The indrawn figure of the activist *auteur* recurs from the earliest semimythic culture heroes right through the assassin-errant Jing Ke and on down to Mao or Deng. Even in the flux of action, such intellectuals never mentally quit the hermitage; they're autistically answerable only to their own inner promptings.

For them, history making, like calligraphy or landscape painting, is a studio art, best practiced in contemplative seclusion. Their right of historic authorship stems solely from their own intrinsic balance and integrity, without reference to such unseemly externals as mere empirical reality, let alone public acceptance or material accomplishment. As far as they're concerned, noble failure can be the highest form of success. They wear mass opprobrium or royal disfavor as badges of honor. In exile, they make sublime eccentrics; but, given a crack at power, they can just as easily turn into unchecked tyrants. Either way, they brook no outside challenge to their self-assured mastery of all they survey.

So now, spread before me, is all that Shih surveyed. I slouch against the temple wall and scan the wraparound vista, left to right—270 degrees of fluted slopes, glassy water, and cloudless skies. In the late afternoon glare, the clangor of contrasting colors and textures is almost dizzying: the tawny hillsides scored with purple crevasses, the gnashing skyline, and fathomless heart of the lake. I shield my eyes and sink down onto what must have been Shih's sunset-viewing log.

No choice here but to sit stiffly erect; the perch is fitted out with a footstool rock, but no backrest. Shih's roost has a curiously settling effect. I rescan the panorama in reverse, slowly, frame by frame, as though unfurling a silken scroll with the right hand while the left hand simultaneously rolls it back up on a cherrywood "take-up" dowel. The scene naturally composes itself into a horizontal landscape in the classic literati style. The scallop of marshland at the water's edge draws the eye upward through deep rock clefts to the undulant ridgecrests. Where the grass-furred mountain flanks give way to bare stone, canted sunbeams pick out every dent and ridge for a dense crosshatch of shadows, like brushwork stippling.

Viewed through this scrim of painterly mannerism, the overwhelming landscape becomes manageable—even portable, something a decorous literatus can carry off to his mental "studio." There,

composedly, at leisure, he "writes his heart," as the Chinese verb for painting has it. With power like that, no wonder these conventions have, over centuries, been so well worked out that they were even codified (in the mid-Qing) into a painter's manual, *The Mustard Seed Garden.*

This is no dumbed-down, paint-by-numbers crib sheet. More like a typographer's sampler—a dazzling array of "alphabets" in which you can spell out, stylishly, any conceivable scene. Virtually every Chinese intellectual owns a copy, or at least has seen one—page after woodcut page of prototypes. *Here's* how to make a plane tree. Here's a definitive pine, a willow, a poplar. Dozens of different exemplars in each species. Scores of bamboos, maybe hundreds of different rocks and hills. Rivers, rills, ocean waves; clouds and brumes; cranes, swallows, and chickens; deer and even donkeys—all rendered with an elegant economy of brushstrokes. Who but the heirs of an ideographic language could ever dream to taxonomize the world so?

Nor does the *Mustard Seed* stop at taxonomy. In the latter chapters, the author, Wang An-jie, discourses (with examples) on how to compose a landscape. Sitting here on Shih's roost, I find myself automatically "editing" the scene before me according to Wang's canons—let's transpose this cedar to that crag instead of here; trim out a redundant mile or two of cordillera; how about we posit a swirling mist on that marsh to smooth things over?

And there, just a little off-center on my mental "scroll," to anchor the composition, sits Wolf Fang. Miniaturized like this, the dusty, threadbare village looks quaint—an aesthetic patchwork of tile roofs and gray stone walls and half-timbered mud-and-wattle. Hardly any people in sight: just a half-dozen children playing some game—jacks?—on the bluff nearest the lakeshore. If they're making any sound (which I somehow doubt), we anyway can't hear them from here. Compositionally, there's just a tad too much of the village, sprawling on either side of its little bay. Suppose we lop off the northern ward? Yes. Better.

In the colophon on his page about how to render houses, Wang An-jie writes: "A landscape has doors and windows, just as a person has eyebrows and eyes. Without eyebrows and eyes, one is blind. But they must be properly apportioned—neither too many nor too few . . . Place them aright, in the appropriate 'sockets' of the landscape . . . They bring the scene to life." Houses and villages are to be mere scaling factors, in other words; just bits of ballast to keep the immensity of the Chinese tableau from carrying off the scholar-painter in a swoon. People and their habitations, Wang An-jie writes, should be rendered "not finely, like a cockleshell, but playfully, like a child's mud pies."

Painters aren't the only ones to use such models as scaling factors. It's endemic to all the scholarly studio arts. Statecraft, for example. Mao, unfurling the grand sweep of the Cultural Revolution, had his model villages: "In agriculture, learn from Da Zhai; in industry from Da Qing," a collective farm and state-run oilfield, respectively. His propagandists cooked up broad-brush images and heartwarming fables of these paragons. Resources were pumped in from all over China to Potemkinize them as pilgrimage shrines. Statistics were fudged with abandon.

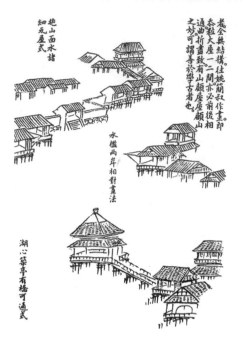

But the life cycles of these models can be as ephemeral as a child's mud pies, too. After the Dengist restoration, Da Zhai and Da Qing abruptly found themselves scrapped, like abortive album-leaves from a studio sketchbook. They weren't just forgotten, but actively, even vituperatively, debunked in the official press. The new order had other models to promote, embodying its own "to-get-rich-is-glorious" ethos. Baigoudian, for instance, enjoyed a brief currency. So did Daqiuzhuang, in neighboring Tianjin, at least until its Party secretary murdered his accountant for embezzlement and then held off a battalion of police in a week-long siege.

And Wolf Fang, the paradigm for rule of law and free elections, may have been the shortest-lived model of all; an album-leaf scrapped before the ink was even dry in the sketchbook.

BUT BEFORE I, too, can retreat too far into my own mental "studio," Zeng comes to interrupt my meditation and fetch me off the lookout log. No time for sunset-gazing here; we've got to get back

over to Wolf Fang before dark. At the bottom of the cliff, we find
Duck Egg already at his oars, waiting for us. No sooner do we settle
amidships than Red Ox unties the hawser and we're off, rowing
briskly. The reason for the rush soon becomes clear: in such a cloudless
sky this far north, night falls fast. The blue zenith deepens to a bur-
gundy that rapidly blots out all but the westernmost horizon. Before
us, the waters blaze with reflected glory, but directly underneath, the
lake depths already register a bottomless black.

The only sound is the creak of the oarlocks and the slap of the
boatman's feet upon the deck, at least until the night winds kick in.
Then the village sounds come back in a jumbled rush over the waters:
doors slamming, pots clanging, barks of laughter, water splashed in
pails. And frogs, lots of frogs, a sudden raucous chorus of them. As we
pull up to shore, lights are starting to wink on in the windows of Wolf
Fang, and we have to button up against the chill. Red Ox says his
goodbyes and heads for home, leaving it to Duck Egg to guide us to
Bai Yimin's house.

By the time we reach the northern ward (the neighborhood I'd
mentally edited out of Wolf Fang from my lookout perch on Coxcomb
Hill), only a last jugular pulse of sunset still throbs in the cyanotic
sky. The wind is picking up. Duck Egg raps on the gate and announces
our arrival. We file gratefully into the shelter of the one-room cottage.
Zeng enters last, after lingering a moment out in the courtyard to finish a cell-phone call.

From the fitful bluster of an autumn night, we're abruptly plunged
into the clammy torpor of a sickroom. Madame Bai, the matriarch
we'd met earlier near the roadhead, now sits huddled over a packed-
earth stove, tending a clay pot of the sort used to simmer Chinese
herbal medicines. Acrid vapors permeate the room. "Come in, come
in," she sighs without rising from her stoveside squat. "Yimin's just
getting up."

He hardly looks it, bundled under a quilt on the *kang*, staring at
the ceiling with his mouth agape. Even in the ruddy stove-glow, his
sweat-slickened brow glints with greenish highlights, like a face from
van Gogh's *Potato Eaters*. But when he hears us clump in, he manages

to rise to his elbows and cast us a wan smile. "They told me you'd come," he murmurs in a voice that's no more than a hoarse vestige of the ringing tenor we'd heard on the videotape. "Welcome, all." He motions us over to the square wooden table in the middle of the room. "Ma, can we have some tea?"

He sits up with an audible creaking of joints and hunches himself over to the edge of the *kang* nearest the table, keeping his quilt wrapped around him. We pull up some benches and sit down. He tweaks on the light, a naked, low-wattage bulb dangling on a wire from the rafters. Under a thin, transparent sheet of yellowing vinyl, the tabletop is covered with hand-drawn, overlapping charts: output of pondweed and peppercorns; classroom hours logged in the village school; menstrual timings of all the local women (for family-planning oversight); infrastructural outlays; relief-grain payments. All laboriously penciled, with many erasures. Tucked in a corner, half-smothered by overlapping charts, a faded New Year's card shows the Wealth God affably chatting on a cell phone while juggling bundles of U.S. dollars and Chinese renminbi.

To make room for the tea, Bai moves a hefty, phonebook-sized abacus off the tabletop. "This," he confides to Luo, giving the beads a shake, "has become my constant companion. And I've hated the damn thing since I was eight." His main childhood recollection of the abacus, he tells us, was as a punishment when he'd misbehaved: he'd have to kneel on it, facing the family altar, with the hard, wooden knobs digging into his bare knees. "And whenever our schoolmarm gave us a pop quiz on the abacus, I'd always draw a blank.

"But now, I feel like I'm forever facing an abacus exam. Trick questions, too, posed by people who don't wish me well. The very same people I've fought with all my life: the Old Party Secretary's faction and the county bureaucrats. They're just waiting to trip me up."

"Well, at least you've got the village behind you," Luo condoles.

"Sometimes I wonder," Bai sighs. "When it comes to a showdown, our Wolf Fang people are the world's best scrappers to have standing at your side. But in between battles, they each have their own little needs, which are not always strictly by the book. Red Ox helps out as best he can but, aside from turning a blind eye now and then, what more can he do?

"And then there's Shih Liguo. It was a sorry day, Old Luo, that you ever let him know about the election weapon. As far as he's concerned, it's just another kind of purge. He still hasn't figured out that it's meant as a way for people to bring in *new* representatives, not just to kick out the old ones. Can't you speak to him, Old Luo?"

The lawyer shrugs, helplessly.

"Remember our Peach Garden Oath the night we got so drunk? How Liguo called me his loyal, stouthearted right-hand man, his Guan Yu? Well, I'm growing into the role. I'm really starting to feel like Guan Yu," Bai laughs, rucfully. "Like Guan Yu at Jing Zhou."

The mention of Jing Zhou is chilling to anyone who knows *The Romance of the Three Kingdoms*. It's the place where Guan Yu was brought to bay by a rival faction in the three-way struggle to establish a new pan-Chinese dynasty on the rubble of the fallen Han empire. Besieged in an isolated castle, Guan Yu tried to slip the noose, but lost most of his remaining followers in the escape. Alone, with just a few retainers, he fled into a mountain defile that tapered upward to a trap: he found himself caught in a field of tufted sedge between sheer cliffs.

His enemies lay in wait. With snares hidden in the windswept grasses, it was easy to capture the hero alive. Dragged in fetters to the camp of his rival general, Lu Su, Guan Yu hurled imprecations at his captor. Lu, unfazed, calmly ordered Guan Yu beheaded. He had the head sent as a peace offering to yet another rival in the three-way power game, the better to cement an alliance against Guan Yu's faction.

"I'm caught, Old Luo, between a rock and a snare," Bai sighs, "just like Guan Yu. Except for me, there won't even be any fine, defiant speech before they hand over my head to my enemies."

Luo has nothing to say. It's left to Ah-loong to break the awkward silence. "Do you know how Guan Yu became a god?" Since nobody stops her, she goes on to tell the story of a Buddhist hermit in deep meditation who's visited by Guan Yu's ghost. The hero appears as a thundering horseman with nothing but cloud atop his neck. He flashes his halberd and keens endlessly, "Give me back my head." The monk

admonishes him, "What's past is no longer present. Every effect has a cause. So now you want your head back. But what of your many followers? To whom shall they appeal for the return of their heads?" Whereupon Guan Yu, in a sudden burst of enlightenment, dismounts and begs to "take refuge" as a Buddhist, that he may serve ever after as a temple guardian.

If this is supposed to be comforting, Bai seems at a loss just how to take it. He shifts uneasily and then, changing the subject, calls out to the kitchen: "Ma, can we get some dinner for our guests?" Turning back to us: "You'll stay the night, won't you? The *kang*'s nice and hot. Plenty of room."

I'm a little squeamish about imposing on an invalid's hospitality (not to mention sharing the sickbed of a man so obviously ill). But we're still keen to continue our foray into Wolf Fang. Ah-loong's already nodding enthusiastically, but Luo wavers. He glances over to Zeng, our chaperone, who curtly announces, "I'm expected home. Besides, I didn't even bring a toothbrush."

Madame Bai, grateful enough to be spared a *kang*-ful of complicated houseguests, ushers us through the courtyard and points out our path over the ridge.

WE MAKE OUR WAY to the road under a sky of cold, high, overbearing stars. We blot their gimlet stares soon enough, though, with the dust we kick up in our efforts to turn our car around. No easy business, making a three-point turn on this narrow, rutted track. The Toyota bucks skittishly, like an old nag wedged in a tight stall.

Zeng pores over his map by the wan light of the dashboard while Luo hangs his head out the rear window, squinting forlornly for any trace of a roadside landmark. Even after we successfully find our way back to the macadam Provincial Highway, the drive around the lake and down through the ramparts of the Taihang remains nerve-wracking.

The bends and hollows that struck us as so charmingly intimate on the drive up this morning now seem crabbed and tortuous. Each twist of the steering wheel brings some new stile or haystack looming in our headlights. Where, now that we need them, are the noodle-stall rest stops with their welcoming highway-nymphs? I gingerly "walk" the car down through the switchbacks—at least until a truck bears down behind me, high beams ablaze.

Then I've no choice but to plunge headlong through a half-dozen curves to the first scintilla of shoulder that presents itself. I dive into the breach, praying there's enough margin to bring the car to a halt. The truck hurtles past, clearing us with just inches to spare. Whereupon it vanishes without a trace, obliterated from our sight by the next black bend in the highway. It takes me a minute to unclench my fingers, one at a time, from the steering wheel and resume our terrorized flight out of Sleepy Hollow.

Straggling into the outskirts of the Yi county seat feels like a resurrection. Never before has a provincial night market looked so good to me, with its bright lights, smoky street stalls, and loud, beery babble. We stop to buy some flatbreads and mung bean soup, just to soothe our knotted stomachs. At the next stall, Luo spots a rotund little man gnawing on a kebab.

"Why, it's Constable Cai," he announces, delightedly. "The very man we need."

I look closer and recognize a character from the TV film: Shih Liguo's relative, the florid policeman who got hounded out of Wolf Fang. I turn to Luo in puzzlement. "But wasn't he . . . ?"

"Oh, he turned out to be all right in the end. A liaison channel to the county administration. Very helpful." Luo bustles over and backslaps the hapless little constable, who almost chokes on his kebab. "Long time no see!"

Cai is considerably less effusive in his greeting. He turns to the lawyer and declares, neutrally, "Lawyer Luo. You're back."

"Well, just for a day trip, actually," Luo allows, as though a disclaimer were called for. "Brought some friends up from the city to see the lake." The policeman briefly eyeballs the rest of us; we're duly logged and entered, if not exactly welcomed. Luo presses on. "So we thought we'd look in on Liguo on our way back to town. Can you show us where he stays?"

"He's just a couple of lanes over from here. I'll bring you to his door, but I won't go in with you, if you don't mind. Liguo grows no easier to get along with these days."

Cai unhurriedly finishes his kebab, gets up from his stool, and threads his way between the street stalls. Our little platoon falls in obediently behind him. He strides right out of the brightly lit ambit of the night market and into a dim maze of alleys, offering no chitchat as we march. The directions couldn't be more straightforward—just turn left, then right, then left again—but I wonder if Luo, of all people, could have found this place without a guide. The brick row houses are all identical, the numbering system arcane, and the lanes abut in arbitrary T-junctions. Every household seems to have the same weepy CCTV soap opera playing at top volume.

Shih's house is no exception. Through the narrow front window, the only light that shows is the pallid flicker of the television. Cai raps sharply on the glass and then goes his way with just a cursory nod. We're left huddling in the lane long enough for me to start wondering if there's anybody awake inside, but presently we hear the fumbling of a chain latch. The door creaks open to reveal a stubby matron in a half-buttoned tunic of padded cotton.

Even the feeble light of the lone streetlamp is enough to set her blinking as she scans us up and down. She nibbles her lip in evident consternation and, without asking our errand, calls out over her shoulder, "Old Mister Big? People here to see you."

In the blacked-out interior behind her, there's no making out the person so addressed. All we can discern is a hunched shadow that lurches across the orb of the TV. We hear, rather than see, his hobbling, flat-footed, agonizingly deliberate progress up the hallway. Only when he's practically abreast of her can we glimpse the face. It's Shih Liguo all right, of video fame, he of the unkempt eyebrows and trim little Sun Yat-sen mustache. But different, too—stooped over his cane, sunken and ashen, minus his dentures.

At the sight of us, though, he straightens up and his eye regains a spark, at least, of its former fire. "Wine," he orders his wife. "Get us some wine. And some dishes to help it down."

"But you know what they told you about drinking," she starts to protest.

"Ayah, doctors!" he grumps. "What could *they* understand about pledging a friendship? Go on in," he urges us. "Take a seat in the, uh, parlor."

He waves his cane with such affable abandon that we have no choice but to tag along smartly behind his wife as she scurries down the hallway, flicking on light switches. She deposits us on a sagging couch in front of the TV. The only other furniture in the room is an even more dilapidated armchair and an overloaded bookcase. Most of the volumes seem to be anthologized Communist classics, including several 1960s editions of Mao in their characteristic red vinyl covers. The bottom three shelves are heaped to bursting with dog-eared periodicals.

Madame Shih goes off to busy herself in the kitchen, leaving us to stare at each other and listen to Shih's measured shuffle as he makes his painful way back down the hall. By the time he scrapes into the room, he's already recouped his dentures somewhere en route. He lowers himself heavily into the armchair and turns to us with a smile that somehow displays a few too many teeth.

"Old Luo, you're just in time," he announces in his commanding tenor. "We've got to go to court again, to get another election."

The lawyer looks like he's about to move a point of order. Shih heads him off, dropping into a more tentative voice. "But tell me, first, who . . . ?" He manages to indicate the three of us without recourse to any pronoun or hand gesture, merely by pointing (impressively) in our general direction with his eyebrows.

"Oh, don't worry about them," Luo reassures him. "They already know all about what we did in Wolf Fang." He introduces us. "This is Zeng, a legal colleague from my office; Mei-lang, a Taiwan compatriot; and that's Lin-Ken, your fellow author."

"Indeed?" he turns to me with collegial interest. "So what sort of things do you write?"

"Oh, just travelogues," I ad-lib self-consciously. "You know, descriptive stuff for foreigners. Old Luo told me about the Lake Solidarity scenery, so we had to go see it for ourselves."

Shih nods politely, clearly unimpressed by my lightweight choice of genre. With some relief, I invite him to turn the conversation to the more consequential realms of literature. "And what about you? What do *you* write?"

"Satires, diatribes," he beams, showing even more teeth.

"Let's hear some," Luo urges. No need to ask twice.

"Oh, it's nothing lofty," Shih offers with a great show of diffidence aimed at me. "Just everyday 'trip-off-the-tongue' rhymes, of the sort you can hear on any street corner. You know the style?"

I've heard a few of these barbed political doggerels in my time. As an irreverent alternative to the stultifying official media, a really wicked trip-off-the-tongue can attain widespread word-of-mouth circulation virtually overnight. Such ditties have far too much opinion-shaping power to be left to chance. At times of factional purges and mass mobilization campaigns, rival propaganda teams vie to cook up and circulate their own supposedly spontaneous street rhymes.

But this is the first time I've ever met an avowed fabricator of trip-off-the-tongues. I guess it's just another variety of studio auteurship, although hardly in the rarified, hyperintellectual mode that I'd attributed to Shih in my Coxcomb Hill reverie a few hours ago.

"Here's one I call 'The People's Choice,' " he begins. He scans the tetrameters in the air with his left hand, occasionally adding an extra finger wag for emphasis. His voice takes on a jaunty lilt, as if steadying a wayward tumbrel on its brisk course down cobbled lanes. A free translation, preserving rhyme scheme and tempo:

> When I was but a communard,
> To take a bath was never hard.
> Each Friday, when I changed my duds,
> I'd line up for a tub of suds.
> The soap was rank and gray and drab
> But sure did purge my crotch of crabs.
>
> But now we've joined the WTO.
> The commune bathhouse has to go.
> These days, I spend my renminbi
> At the foreign joint-venture *parfumerie*,
> Where dazzling choices, rows on rows,
> Beguile my eyes, enchant my nose.
> A bar of puce or pink or green?
> With citron scent or tangerine?
> We'll sell you any soap you seek
> As long as it's from *our* boutique.
>
> I mount a bar (Cashmere Bouquet)
> Upon my soap dish, for display.
> It's far too fragrant, pink, and nice
> To waste upon my body lice,
> And much too dear to *ever* use,

But I've enjoyed my Right-to-Choose.
I smell like fish-meal. Never mind;
As long as I don't fall behind
My neighbors.

                 Comes Election Day,
The candidates, in fine array,
Present themselves to win my vote
With fancy packaging. But note
The fine print: all these brands galore
Come from the same joint-venture store.
They promise much. I can't afford
The price tags. Still, they may rest assured
Their blandishments I can't refuse,
For I've no option *not* to choose.
So count the votes and, with one voice,
All hail the sacred People's Choice.

Author to author, I feel I ought to say something encouraging. "It's a classic in its genre," I assure him.

"*Ayah*," Shih sighs. "Time was, such polemics mattered. Those days are gone. Words still wield power, all right, but now it's the ad-man's jingle, the politician's hot air, and the bland, bloodless prose of the legal brief.

"Not to dismiss legal briefs, as such," he adds, hastening to mollify the two lawyers. "You *know* how we appreciate the blow you struck for us, Old Luo. You 'stormed the citadel,' you 'took Tiger Mountain by strategy,' " he pronounces, rattling off a string of Maoist slogans. "But a committed vanguard fighter can't rest on bygone victories. We must make Perpetual Revolution! Otherwise, our past gains only turn into present quagmires. Like Wolf Fang."

SO NOW, at last, it's out in the open between them, the issue these two have been skirting since we arrived. Luo sputters in pent-up frustration: "What's such a quagmire about Wolf Fang? How can you deny what we achieved there? Spare me your sophistries; a victory's a victory."

"Not when you give away so much ground before the battle's even joined," Shih snaps back. "Look at the conditions you had to concede before they'd even allow the election at all: amnesty for the ex-secretary, no collection of back dues on the relief grain. And, worst of all, the limits they set on eligible candidates."

"What limits?" Luo protests. "The nominations were wide open to everybody."

"Everybody except *me*," Shih shrills. "They wouldn't let me anywhere near the place. Tried to keep me in the dark even about when the election was to be held. For 'health' reasons, they claimed. Hah!"

"But you know, Old Shih, that your condition would never . . ."

"And *you* know perfectly well that keeping me out of there was the only way they'd let the election to go forward. Which was an outright betrayal. The people of Wolf Fang wanted fundamental change. They were waiting for something dramatic. They're waiting still."

"Drama," Luo draws out the word, ironically. "Who promised a drama? That's not the point of an election, nor of a legal action. It's all about incremental, orderly improvement—to allow social change, for once, without a bloodbath."

Shih borrows a sneer from his idol, Mao: "A revolution is not a tea party."

"Maybe not," Luo rejoins, "but after the turmoil we've all been through in our time, just having a quiet tea party almost seems a revolution of sorts."

"Well, then, let's get *really* revolutionary with a full-blown dinner party," Shih laughs, abruptly changing tone to defuse a debate that he sees will get him nowhere. He reverts to his role as our genial host. "Come to the table!"

The table in question is a Formica, folding-legged affair that Madame Shih has set up in the hallway. It's spread with what we've come to recognize by now as standard Taihang guest fare, a truncated version of the Foundation banquet we had in Wolf Fang: string beans, sauerkraut, julienned potatoes, and the ubiquitous Spam. Pride of place on the table is reserved for two new bottles of *erh guo tou*, still shrink-wrapped in cellophane.

They don't stay wrapped for long. The first bottle sustains us through two more trip-off-the-tongue recitations. By the second round of *erh guo tou*, Shih is toasting Ah-loong and me with flowery protestations of China-Taiwan amity and the international brotherhood of man.

"Forget about race or creed," he exhorts us. "What care we for differences of political system? These things are made up, imaginary! The real world is nothing but good people versus bad people," he pronounces in ringing tones that leave no doubt where, in this schema, he'd place the present company. "Good versus bad. That's all that matters." He raises his glass in yet another toast and drops his voice reverently, turning his fervent gaze straight on Luo. "*That's* why we've got to redo the Wolf Fang election. We've got to keep at it until the Triumph of the Good. Isn't that what we swore the night of our Peach Garden Oath, when we drank so much good wine? Let's do it again, Old Luo. Let's bring another suit."

"On what grounds?" the lawyer protests. "You can't sue to void an election just because you don't like the result. You've got to show *some* kind of cause—voting irregularities or something. Otherwise, no judge would even hear the case."

"No judge ever *did* hear your case the last time, either," Shih reminds him bitterly. "It was all decided out of court. And the election was already riddled with irregularities before anyone ever got to cast a vote—from the time that you let them limit the nominating rolls. This was no real election; it was a television play. Except it never even got a fair airing on TV."

"What difference does *that* make?" Luo explodes. "Even if we weren't seen all over China, the Wolf Fang election was real—it *did* happen. The voting was free and fair and we changed the leadership. We achieved pretty much everything we set out to do that drunken night in Beijing. *You're* the one that needs to remember our Peach Garden Oath. What we swore then was loyalty and mutual support. Give Bai Yimin a chance."

"He's had his chance and failed," Shih pronounces levelly, like a sentencing judge. "Now it's time for someone else's chance."

Luo rolls his eyes and sighs a Chinese proverb: "A maker of nothing is a wrecker of all."

The rest of us stare glumly at the remains of the dinner—the last shreds of sauerkraut adrift in ponds of Taihang vinegar, the brown sauce curdling on what's left of the Spam.

PORK MINCE ON wafer-thin cucumber slices embedded in nests of purple basil. Translucent vermicelli in a clear broth, served in a whimsically carved melon rind. Grilled bass wrapped in pandanus leaves. Mincing, token portions, too pretty to eat, each marooned on its own atoll of bone china.

White-gloved waiters bring on dish after dish with a deferential flourish, the sort of service you'd expect in the private room of a five-star Thai restaurant around the corner from the CCTV studios. And some of the deference on display here may be truly unfeigned, for we're in the company of genuine celebrities whose faces would be recognized all over China, the same faces—an anchorman and a field correspondent—that featured in our samizdat copy of *The Wolf Fang File*. Less famous, but with a glamour all their own, are the cameramen and the film editor.

I'm delighted—and, to tell the truth, a little flattered—that such luminaries should take time out to lunch with a pair of frumpy print fogeys like us. Not that I'm automatically star-struck by television personalities. One meets one's share of video journalists in the course of things. Some are crack reporters by any reckoning, but there's also a fair share of vacuous, blow-dried talking heads. None of those in *this* lot, however, as is evident within minutes of meeting them.

For one thing, there's their obvious engagement with their story. The mere mention on the telephone that we'd just come back from

Wolf Fang was enough to get us a same-day lunch appointment. All four CCTV men are avid for news of the place. Nor will they settle for a general rundown of latest developments, either. They want updates on particular Wolf Fang personalities—far more detail than we'd had a chance to glean, alas, on our whirlwind visit to the village.

Wolf Fang aside, they're keen on journalistic "shop talk" and eminently informed about what's happening in world media. They keep abreast of daily newscasts from Hong Kong, Taiwan, and Japan and chat knowingly about TV features from Europe and America. The cameraman seems to be a particular fan of certain Iranian videographers I've never heard of, while the editor has developed a connoisseurish interest in Russian MTV.

They liberally intersperse their talk with English-language trade terms like "voice-over," "sound bite," and "setup." By the dessert course (coconut flan) the conversation's already turned to the staple themes of press-corps bonding rites everywhere: the deadline from hell, the gloriously serendipitous interview, the perfidy of desk-bound news executives.

Presuming on our newly established camaraderie, and pandering to their weakness for English-language newsroom jargon, I gingerly probe, "So how did it feel to get 'spiked' on the Wolf Fang story?"

My question draws a blank. "Spiked?" the anchorman blandly inquires.

Their incomprehension leaves me feeling churlish, with my classically crass disaster-scene query—"How did it feel?" And to fellow newsmen, no less. No backing out now, though, so I lamely try to explain to these videogenic Gen X-ers what it was like way back in the Linotype era of print journalism.

There was this newsroom god, you see, the city editor, and he had on his desk an inverted nail-type thing—the Spike—such as a pawnbroker might use for lapsed pawn tickets. And it would sometimes happen that a reporter's story, no matter how advanced its stage of completion, might get yanked out of the paper for whatever reason even as the pages were going to print. Then your opus would wind up impaled on this Spike. Your copy was still live and writhing, but doomed. Oh, it *could* be revived, theoretically, for a later edition, but we all knew . . .

"So even over there you run into that?" the anchorman murmurs.

It's been known to occur, I allow.

"Then you know how we felt. We'd lived and breathed that story for a month. It was our first effort together as a news team. We were going to change the world. Already our sheer presence in Wolf Fang had made a difference on the ground, and the people there were counting on us. In our office, to this day, we still hang a red flock banner they gave us proclaiming us 'Honorary Citizens of Wolf Fang.' But what can you do?"

"What *can* you do?" I echo.

"Well, we've got our backers and we carry on," he shrugs. "We win more battles than we lose. We get to film actualities pretty much as we see fit, even when we can't publicly air what we shoot. Sometimes we make programs for internal Party circulation that are a little bolder than what we're able to publicly broadcast."

"And at least we're amassing footage," the cameraman adds with manifest pride. "The video record of this time is there for future generations to see, even if present audiences can't.

"Someday, when the time comes, we'll be able to link up with you. We're all set to close that final gap and get on track [*jie gui*] with the rest of the world."

FOR OUR FAREWELL BRUNCH, Luo—ever the sentimentalist— chooses the same noodle stall where he'd pledged his Peach Garden Oath with Bai and Shih.

The cramped, dingy joint is a kind of anti-McDonald's. No decor to speak of, just three tables separated from the kitchen by a grease-stained curtain. Over the doorway hangs a hooded cage from which an unseen bird cuts loose with a continuous stream of clucks, whirrs, and titters.

Instead of a bewildering array of Combination Meals, the noodle-stall menu offers just a few (extremely good) selections: razor-shaved pasta, mustard-marinated celery hearts, cold pork in a Sichuan pepper sauce, and "bean curd brains" (a kind of savory pudding). We order one of each dish—more than enough to feed the three of us, and all for about the cost of a single Big Mac.

In a neighborhood of two- and three-room tenements, the noodle stall becomes a much-needed adjunct to every family's kitchen. The place hardly feels like a public space at all. No anonymity here, and no impersonal McCourtesies. Master Chen, our one-man host, waiter, and chef, wades like a nosey uncle right into his customers' personal affairs without qualm.

"What, no *erh guo tou*?" he reproaches Luo as he takes down our order. "Remember the last time you brought in some strangers," he adds, eyeing the two of us hopefully.

"Well, it *is* the middle of the morning," the lawyer reminds him.

"Too early for you to be at home," Chen nods. "Business is slow, then? What are you up to these days, anyway?"

"Oh, a tenants' rights case in Tianjin," Luo launches enthusiastically into his latest crusade. "Some land developer wants to evict over three hundred households without fair compensation . . ."

"You mean just like your brother would love to do to all of us here?" Chen tartly inquires as he fires up his wok back in the kitchen.

Luo drops the topic fast, smoothly shifting gears. "And I was just back in Wolf Fang, too. You know, that Taihang place where those two drinking buddies of mine came from?"

"I've *seen* one of those two, the old guy, hanging around here once or twice within the past couple of months, by the way," Chen offers. "He comes stumping right up to the door and stands there awhile, thirsty-like, leaning on his cane. And just when I think he's about to come in for a drink, he turns around and hobbles away."

"Just like Liguo, isn't it?" Luo asks us over the stir-fry sizzle of Chen's wok. "Always outside peering in. No way he'll ever sit down to anyone's table except on his own terms."

Maybe so, I point out, but Shih's hardly the only one with a grievance about Wolf Fang. I can't think of anyone, except maybe the Yi county cadres, who'd be quite satisfied with the way things have worked out there.

"But those are just *outcomes*," Luo admonishes. "When you're talking about law or elections or even news reporting, it's the *process* that matters most. As long as you diligently keep at it, there's always still hope."

The kitchen clatter has subsided enough by now that we can once again make out the unbroken stream of birdsong. "Do you know that creature?" Luo asks, casting his eyes upward to the cage above the door. "It's called a 'Hundred Cleverness Bird.' Pretty expensive. Master Chen's most prized possession, no doubt.

"Its value is in its versatility. It imitates the calls of other birds—crows, mynahs, sparrows, larks, any bird it hears. Every morning, Chen and the other bird hobbyists carry their birds to the parks. They hang these hooded cages up in the trees so the birds can learn their repertoire from nature and from each other. On his way to and from the park, Chen tells me, he always makes a point of swinging the cage really hard. That way, even shut in and hooded, the bird enjoys the illusion of free flight. Keeps him healthy and tuneful, Chen says.

"I always fancy that, if you shook the cage long and hard enough, the 'Hundred Cleverness'—if it didn't die first—might someday finally find a song that didn't imitate anyone else's, but was all his own. And *that* might be something worth hearing . . ."

Under the Skin

AS ALWAYS, Ah-loong starts with the essentials in her account of the Taiwan Gang luncheon—a detailed menu: "Pickled jellyfish, smoked squid, and steamed chicken claws for openers. Quite a respectable braised carp. Cashew prawns and a red-cooked bean curd. Ham hocks simmered with black mushroom and bamboo shoots. The kale may have been a bit overcooked, but the garlic sprouts were perfect. Three desserts: almond gelatin, steamed sponge cake, and a fruit plate."

Not bad, the twenty-odd ladies of the Gang agreed, especially for just RMB 180 ($21.95) a head. The Le Foo Hunan Restaurant could be considered again for future feasts. A far better banquet than last month's venue, a downtown seafood palace, had managed to serve at half again the price.

The Gang's monthly meetings have been a Beijing institution for nearly a decade now, ever since "reform and opening" started bringing in squads of corporate, journalistic, and diplomatic expatriates with Taiwanese wives. I've always enjoyed Ah-loong's monthly account of the luncheon, not only for the vicarious gastronomy, but also for the nuggets of quirky information to be gleaned; the Taiwan women, thanks to their appearance and language facility, enjoy far wider horizons in China than most expatriate dependents.

They can travel and shop without getting bilked. They blend into a crowd and insinuate themselves into the gossip circuit. They know how to read the fine print and the body language, and they can cater a soiree to charm any Mandarin. Altogether dangerous people, a fifth column whose mobility unnerves Chinese officialdom and mainstream Western expats alike.

Yet the Taiwanese wives hardly feel at home here. Attuned as they are to its nuances, Beijing sometimes can overwhelm them. Local acquaintances—staff, friends, kin—press them with hard-luck stories and implicit obligations. To buffer themselves from the grimness of China, the women of the Gang need to club together and draw a sharp distinction between "us" and "them." The monthly luncheons help them to shore up the bulwark.

So does a certain studied hauteur, which, handily, many in the Gang had already cultivated long before they ever came to Beijing. Marrying a foreigner, in Taiwan's conservative society, meant facing down a social stigma that would leave them all the more prickly about standing on their dignity. They grow into the role of "Taitai" (an honorific for a married woman that, in Taiwan, means no more than "Missus" but in the mainland context sounds more hoity-toity, like "Madame").

Queenliness, to many of the Taiwan wives, translates into conspicuous consumption, for the Gang has more than its share of nouveaux riches. For instance, at today's luncheon, Ah-loong relates, Yu-mei wears her Armani sundress, Wei-ch'ing sports a Sassoon coiffure, and Heng-ch'iao shows off her Phuket suntan.

Talk drifts from the perfidy of servants to the price of Ming snuff bottles at the weekend "ghost market." Ch'iao-wen and Tsai-yun gloat over the pairing of their offspring at the Beijing International School's homecoming dance. Meng-li one-ups them with snapshots of her daughter, in jodhpurs and riding hat, straddling her pet pony at boarding school in Surrey.

Hsin-chen tells how a geomancer from Taiwan exposed a battery of hexes that the Communists had slyly built into the floor plan of her deluxe diplomatic flat. Yi-ling, a recent arrival, wants to gush on about her new wall-sized TV with surround-sound karaoke, but nobody cares to listen. Nor is there much interest in talk of politics, whether the free-for-all melee of Taiwan's democracy or the recondite skullduggery of Beijing's palace intrigue. After all, why risk offending anyone?

Once the last dessert dish is cleared, the Gang settles down to a sale of cultured pearls. The vendor, a fawning peddler that Yu-mei discovered on Wangfu Jing (the Champs-Élysées of Beijing), flips open the hasp of a battered attaché case to reveal a nacreous trove of pendants and chokers and brooches and great looping strands. The baubles pass from hand to hand. Many never make their way back to the attaché case but wind up sold on the spot, at prices up to 40 percent less than the government's Friendship Store would charge. The peddler racks up sales of over RMB 5,200 at the luncheon table, Ah-loong estimates. Everyone congratulates Yu-mei on such a worthwhile find. These bargains are even better than last month's sale of silk brocade; incomparably better than the previous month's gauche offer of herbal slimming soap.

Merchandising in general, most of the Taiwan wives agree, makes for a more satisfying after-lunch program than any of the earlier attempts to enliven the meetings with more "cultural" entertainments. Through Ah-loong's wry retelling, I've kept track of some of the Taitais' past postprandial misadventures. Who could forget the butter-fingered conjuror? Or the soporific book-reviewer? Or the diminutive hypnotist whose mesmeric gaze always seemed to settle on his subject's décolletage? And then there was the time, a couple of years ago, that the Gang got caught up in the Great Foundling Flap.

Edwina, a vice-consul's wife, had visited a certain local orphanage in the course of her search for an adoptable child. Although red tape ultimately foiled her quest, she was impressed enough with the foundling home to tell the rest of the Gang about it—the sweet, scrubbed, docile children, the spartan facilities, the sincerity of the director, the bureaucratic obstructionism he faced.

The women were so moved they resolved to help the orphanage and sent Edwina back to ask the director what they could do. He suggested a modest donation to buy new uniforms for the children. The Gang took up a collection right at the luncheon table: problem solved. But the next month, when the director called for new cookware to upgrade the sanitation of the kitchen, the sum outstripped the pocket change around the table and required a follow-up phone-a-thon.

The following month he was back with a detailed scheme for a new playground, complete with trampoline and wading pool. The Gang decided to send a delegation out to the foundling home to inspect the site. But just before the scheduled visit, it was countermanded by the Health Ministry. No foreigners allowed in Chinese orphanages, they said.

"Who are they calling foreigners?" some of the wives wanted to ask. Hadn't they all heard years of Chinese paeans to "Taiwan compatriots"? But why press the matter? After all, with husbands in corporate or diplomatic circles, there were careers to be considered. No point in needlessly crossing the powers that be.

It was only a year or so later, when Edwina paid a discreet farewell visit to the foundling home at the end of her Beijing stint, that the Taiwanese wives heard an update. The director was long gone, no one could say where. The kids' uniforms looked as threadbare and the kitchen as grimy as ever. The new director had ambitious plans for a vocational school. Donations most welcome. The Gang tacitly resolved then and there to stick to merchandise sales in future luncheons.

The wisdom of this decision is confirmed anew in the happy, satisfied bustle of the group each time it wraps up its meeting. Ah-loong describes how, after this month's pearl sale, the women emerge blinking into the Indian-summer sunshine of Chang An Road, fingering their new chokers and trading last-minute tidbits of gossip. Newcomers to Beijing swap phone numbers with the Gang's established doyennes. The Le Foo doorman shoos away the usual klatch of boulevard beggars—an amputee on crutches, a mother cradling a listless baby, a smudged granny with glittering, half-mad eyes. One by one, the chauffeurs pull up at curbside in their Audis and Volvos to ferry the Taitais home in time to meet the afternoon school buses, supervise dinner preparations, mix cocktails, and dress for the evening.

"SO THAT LEFT just Keiko and me standing in front of the restaurant," Ah-loong relates. Keiko is stranded without a car, since her computer-executive husband has commandeered the company limousine for the day. She lives all the way out by the airport, a twenty-minute drive on the newly completed expressway. Ah-loong offers to ferry her home, and the two of them troop off to our battered Toyota.

Keiko's a Beijing neophyte, and Ah-loong has kept an eye on her throughout the luncheon. The two of them were the only ones at the table who didn't buy pearls. But, unlike my wife (who, in the context of the Gang, stands out as a bit of a bohemian), Keiko evidently has no problem with jewelry per se. As described by Ah-loong, she's slung with gold chains and earrings, rings and bangles. Impeccably coifed, manicured, and perfumed, she presents the very picture of a cosseted Taitai with money to spend.

"So why would she hang back at today's pearl sale?" Ah-loong wonders. "And, just as strange, Keiko hardly touched the lunch. She only dabbled at the bean curd and the greens, bypassing all the meat and seafood and even the garlic sprouts." Such reticence seems disturbingly un-Taiwanese, especially in a svelte thirty-year-old like Keiko, unshadowed by any weight problem. Unless, of course, there's an ideology behind it. Nosing the Toyota through the gridlock on the Third Ring Road, Ah-loong gingerly broaches the subject: "How long have you been a vegetarian?"

Only a few months, as it turns out. But what months they've been, Keiko relates in the squeaky, baby-doll lisp of a Taiwanese trophy wife. There she was, less than a year ago, the consummate Taipei yuppie: right clothes, right clubs, right school for the children, an impeccably correct arranged marriage. She'd been the envy of all her classmates from the Japanese department of Taiwan's premiere finishing college for ladies.

"Yet it all seemed somehow lifeless. And then I met the most *alive* person I've ever known: Prioress Cheng Yan, the guiding light of Tz'u-chi Abbey in Hualien. She brought me back to life, taught me how to value and serve life, my own and others'. When you revere life, you naturally don't want to *take* life just in order to feed yourself or to dress up. Going vegetarian was the easy part. It was a lot harder to clean out my wardrobe. But now it's no pearls for me, no silk or leather. I feel a lot better for it."

They're on the airport freeway by now. Ah-loong keeps her eyes straight on the road to avoid having to react to Keiko's religious testimonial. We'd visited Tz'u-chi Abbey the previous year out of curiosity, since the place had become so famous in the international Chinese-language press. The Buddhist nunnery was known for its worldwide charitable works. Its prioress was touted as the "Mother Teresa of Taiwan."

More like the General William Booth of Taiwan, as far as we could see. Like Booth's Salvation Army, the Tz'u-chi mission bases its global outreach on the positivist premise that for faith to move mountains, it must be properly organized. In its tight hierarchies, its "can-do" rhetoric, its sing-along litany, and even its lay members' blue uniforms with red piping, Tz'u-chi recalls the Salvation Army.

No coincidence, perhaps. Like General Booth, Sister Cheng Yan rode the wavecrest of an industrial revolution. At the peak of the East Asian economic boom, when Tz'u-chi took off, the economic metamorphosis of Taiwan was no less profound than that of nineteenth-century Britain. Such a sea change attests, on the one hand, to the transformative power of modern organizational methods. At the same time, it underscores the moral need to renovate a sordid world. Why would a confident new industrial power like Taiwan shrink from the task any more than did Victorian England?

Especially when salvation is at stake. For Cheng Yan, like Booth, motivates followers with the prospect of bliss after death. The particular style of bliss may differ—a Buddhist escape from lowly reincarnation, rather than a heaven of harps and haloes. But the basic mechanism remains the same: accumulation of merit by good deeds. Somewhere a ledger is kept, and the object is to amass as large a positive balance as possible—a kind of spiritual mercantilism.

Reserving any of her own theological doubts about the Roll Call Up Yonder, Ah-loong's delighted to stumble upon a Cheng Yan devotee in Beijing. The two women exchange phone numbers in the driveway of Keiko's split-level garden apartment. This is somebody to keep in touch with, Ah-loong muses on the homebound freeway. After all, accumulating merit is probably a more worthwhile hobby than accumulating pearls.

A COUPLE OF WEEKS later, a hot merit-garnering opportunity crops up in the *Beijing Youth Daily*: a piece about Xi-yuan Hospice, purportedly China's first hospital expressly devoted to care for the dying. Ah-loong clips the article for our files and then digs out Keiko's phone number to alert her.

The tabloid spreads the story over a two-page layout garnished with a picture of an apple-cheeked young nurse tenderly cradling the wispy gray locks of a wheelchair-bound ninety-four-year-old. The accompanying text dwells on the dedication of the staff and the student volunteers who come in from time to time to cheer up the lonely, forsaken inmates. As a nongovernmental hospital—a fairly recent innovation in China—Xi-yuan has had to buck more than its share of bureaucratic opposition, the story adds. Many of its patients are charity cases, so cash flow is chronically precarious.

Showing me the clipping, Ah-loong admits that, much as her sympathies are roused, the story also leaves her a little queasy. Mortality is a fact she'd always managed to squirm away from in her life so far. When her teenage sister was dying of cancer, Ah-loong was packed off to an aunt's house, ostensibly to cram for high school entrance exams. When her father abruptly died of a heart attack, she happened to be in Japan as an exchange student. Even when our house cat would drag in freshly killed mice, birds, or lizards, Ah-loong's first instinct would always be to call for somebody else to get a dust pan, quick. Her immediate next instinct, though, would be to blush at her own qualms. She knows, intellectually, that death is simply a datum that has to be confronted, and she's ashamed of her own squeamishness.

"Yet here they're talking about whole wards of patients confronting their own mortality," she marvels. "And even more amazing, there's a battery of staff and volunteer care-givers, all sworn to ease the final passage of strangers." Such altruism and bravery verge on the saintly, she feels. If only she could help in some way. The prospect both fascinates and repels her. She knows she can't face the hospice alone, and to show up with her foreign-journalist husband would unduly complicate her first approach. So she turns to Keiko for moral support.

Xi-yuan sounds like a case worth looking into, Keiko agrees. The two of them decide to go out there for a visit the following day. Recalling Edwina's orphanage experience, Ah-loong suggests they not come on as grandly philanthropic Taiwan Taitais. Better dress down a little and announce themselves simply as newspaper readers intrigued by the *Youth Daily* story.

The next morning Keiko's company limousine, a Lexus, pulls up at our door and she emerges in a simple white cotton blouse and blue slacks. No jewelry, no makeup. Only the manicure and the unmussable razor-cut hairdo suggest she might be anything other than a local shop clerk or a factory worker. All the way into town, she gleefully relates, the chauffeur kept eyeing her curiously in the rearview mirror. He must have been even more mystified when she sent him off to amuse himself for the rest of the day.

Planning their foray, Ah-loong and Keiko settle into a sofa next to our livingroom divan, where I'm lying prone for an early-morning massage from Dr. Guan, our own local version of Figaro, the *facto-*

tum della città. By day, Dr. Guan presides over one of the city health board's one-room neighborhood street clinics. But she is also a government-certified accupressurist, and before and after working hours she supplements her income by making house calls.

We sought her out at a friend's suggestion in our first week in Beijing, when we were all charley-horsed from moving furniture into our new apartment. Since then, she's been ironing out our muscular kinks three times a week. At the same time, like the Barber of Seville, she fills our ears with anecdotes. Over the years, we've heard all about her clinic, her wide-ranging house-call rounds, and her far-flung family. We've come to rely on her as a conduit of street wisdom on the news of the day.

Why not try her out on the Xi-yuan story? The reaction proves more than I had bargained for. At the mere mention of a private hospital, I feel the masseuse's fingers tighten on my shoulder. "Pill mills," Dr. Guan snorts. "The hottest racket going in health care. That's what you get when you drag medicine into the marketplace."

Abruptly weaned from their decades-long addiction to direct government subsidies, China's hospitals and pharmaceutical companies nowadays suffer harrowing withdrawal symptoms. They face wholesale personnel reductions and deep cuts in staff benefits. The only glimmer of relief comes from indirect subsidies—the medical benefits that some other government units still guarantee to their serving and retired employees.

So pharmaceutical salesmen fall over each other trying to sell overpriced new formulations, big-ticket imported drugs and hi-tech, capital intensive procedures. Doctors are wined and dined and lavishly bribed. And hospitals, when they get a rare patient from a work unit still solvent enough to honor its medical-care obligations, go out of their way to administer the costliest medicines, treatments, and diagnostic tests. So lucrative is the prescription racket that some doctors set up their own clinics just to garner drug-company kickbacks for themselves without having to share them.

"You want to know if a clinic's honest?" Dr. Guan advises. "Ask what they give for something basic like migraine or constipation or insomnia or heat rash. If it's a China-made generic medicine sold for just a few renminbi, the clinic might be okay. But if they're going in for foreign name-brand drugs, you'd better watch out."

ARMED WITH THESE CAUTIONS, the two undercover Taitais set out for Xi-yuan by public transport. Nobody even looks up from the pavement as they line up at the bus stop. Keiko and Ah-loong exchange a glance of complicity; the disguises are working. The outing takes on a tinge of Girl Scout titillation.

The number 15 pulls up and the orderly queue dissolves into a scrimmage of frantic jostlers trying to cram five abreast through the narrow door of the bus. Keiko gets elbowed from behind and Ah-loong's unsure whether or not she's been goosed.

Somehow they both make it aboard. Five stops later, at the East Fourth subway station, they're squeezed back out of the bus along with a dribble of fellow passengers. They cross the sidewalk under the bland glare of shiny-new, mirrored skyscrapers and head for the stairway down to the trains.

The stairs plunge straight down into the earth, without a bend or a landing. The unswerving shaft bores through successive archaeological strata—six Chinese dynasties and three nomad encampments—buried just beyond the grimy tile walls of the stairwell. Halfway down, the oblivious commuters have already plumbed beyond the primordial forest plains roamed by the early hominid Beijing Man a quarter of a million years ago. Everyone jogs briskly and impassively down the steps. Nobody so much as glances at the equally stone-faced passengers clanking up toward the daylight on the rickety escalators alongside.

Ah-loong is no stranger to subways. She's a seasoned veteran of many a commute in America, Europe, and Japan. "But I've never been in a rush hour like this," she tells me, recounting her adventure the following morning. "The silence is positively eerie." Where are the collegial greetings, she wonders, the schoolboy high jinks, the last-minute parental admonitions, the hand-holding lovers? Where are the

beggars and buskers and hustlers—the familiar fauna of subway platforms worldwide? Nearing the bottom of the stairway, she catches her
first concentrated whiff of the real subterranean Beijing on the cool
updraft from the tunnels below.

Each city has its signature smell, and nowhere is it more distilled
than in the metro. It's compounded of soil chemistry, groundwater
seepage, and the fetor of crowds fed on the local diet and wearing
the local garb. New York's subway smell mixes a neon crackle of
stale ozone with faint overlays of engine oil and cologne. The London
tube wheezes wet wool, tobacco, bog mud, and fried fish. Tokyo's
Yamanote-sen is redolent of scented soap and *sake*-barf.

But the underground essence of Beijing outdoes them all in com-
plexity. To a basic substratum of sour loess clay add the daily exhala-
tions of nearly a million garlic-loving commuters. Garnish with a few
millennia of accumulated night soil; dash in a hint of eucalyptus oil
from mentholated muscle liniments and bronchial vapor-rubs.

And marinate in sweat, lots of sweat. Colossal labor gangs completed the subway network in just a couple of years. It was part of the
same building boom that flattened the old neighborhoods in Beijing's
core and replaced them with the ponderous banalities of Tiananmen
Square and the Great Hall of the People. Such prodigies, according to
Mao, would demonstrate the power of Collective Action and the in-
vincibility of Socialist New Humanity.

Old-timers blame the 1960s construction frenzy for destroying
the city's *feng shui*—the interplay of "force lines" inside the earth that
balance the energies of a geographic site just as acupunctural meridians do for a living body. Traditional Chinese architecture and city
planning carefully incorporated these force lines into features like the
old city wall that used to surround Beijing. But the wall came down to
make way for the metro and the Second Ring Road. When you block
or breach the *feng shui* of a locality, the theory goes, the place sickens
and harms its denizens. Superstitious twaddle, as far as Communist
city fathers were concerned. Nevertheless, they carefully laid out
their subway and freeway to follow the contours of the original wall.

"Watching the streams of commuters crisscross the platforms,"

Ah-loong relates, "you could almost believe that the alignment of the ancient wall really *did* intersect mysterious energy currents which still drive Beijingers, even down there, even today"—long after the fortifications have been razed. The crowds scarcely interpenetrate, but dart en bloc from stile to stairwell and train to train. Rushed and cramped as they are, none of the commuters betray a sense of private urgency. Rather, they swarm like schools of fish, teeming and eddying collectively in response to unseen, impersonal forces.

"Zombies, I think to myself. The living dead," Ah-loong admits. "But then I catch myself and remember where we're headed."

THE TWO TAITAIS EXIT the subway at West Fourth station, the opposite end of the city from where they'd boarded the Circle Line, and a world away in atmosphere from the glitzy new spires of eastern Beijing. No mirrored glass out here but scabrous concrete apartment blocks, their coffin-sized balconies bricked in with cabbage stashes for tiding over the coming winter. Strung between the balcony railings, laundry-laden clotheslines brave the smog that belches from the smokestacks to the west. Keiko and Ah-loong board a bus headed yet deeper into the industrial suburbs.

Just a few minutes' bus ride beyond the subway station, the city peters out to no more than a sparse scattering of low-rise shop rows, warehouses, and factory dormitories. The squat, featureless buildings blur past the dusty windows of the careening bus, block after block. There's nothing to distinguish the hospice building from any of the unprepossessing brick heaps around it.

"Sheer luck, finding the hospital at all," Ah-loong recounts. Between the crush of strap-hangers, Keiko just barely manages to glimpse through the window the characters "Xi-yuan" daubed in red on a whitewashed wall. She rings to get off the bus and heads for the door. But by the time the bus crowd can peristaltically squeeze the two women down the jam-packed aisle to the rear exit, they've already overshot their stop.

Dumped on the roadside, Keiko instinctively pats down her pockets. Ah-loong reties her hair bun and rams a pencil through her slap-dash *chignon* to hold it in place. Their long bus and subway trek has left them feeling thoroughly pawed over, though not exactly violated. Such an impersonal press of humanity hardly even counts as touch. The commute has taken the starch out of their cottons, making their disguises all the more convincing.

As if to add one last fillip of authenticity, they accrue a thin film of road dust scuffed up on the long trudge back to the previous bus stop. No sidewalks out here, just a dirt shoulder stained in spots with mo-tor oil. The hospital's on a long-distance traffic artery, so heavy trucks incessantly thump past on their way to Hebei. Windblown scraps of plastic fleck the bare and stunted trunks of abandoned orchards.

At Xi-yuan's painted gatepost, they turn left into the hospital courtyard. A scrawny chicken scurries out of their path, but the gate-house rooster carries on his preening, unperturbed. A battered old ambulance emblazoned with a red cross dozes under a plane tree off to one corner. Its black and yellow bunting proclaims that it has lately doubled as a hearse.

Nobody challenges Keiko and Ah-loong as they cross the courtyard and stroll right into the hospital. They pass the front office. Through the open door, they glimpse a pair of lab-coated doctors huddled over a chess board, smoking, too engrossed in their game even to look up. "By now we're starting to feel a little spooked," Ah-loong admits, "as if our makeshift costumes made us not just anonymous but actually invisible."

They pad down the empty, silent corridors, barely stirring the dust motes that hang in becalmed noontime air. Flat Beijing sun-shine—the world's most matter-of-fact light—streams over the dingy whitewash, the concrete floors, and the blank, closed doors. A nurse pushes a pill cart down the hallway. She glances incuriously at the in-truders and mumbles, "Who're *you* here for?"

Ah-loong, startled at the abruptly broken spell of invisibility, can only mutter, "Oh, we're just looking." As soon as the words were out of her mouth, Ah-loong confesses, "I felt so inane, addressing her as though she were a salesclerk at Bloomingdale's." Her reply, however, elicits no more than a perfunctory shrug and the pill cart clatters on its way, leaving the two visitors to wander on alone.

They turn a corner and stumble onto a frieze of silent tension. A rangy, simian giant of a man straddles a stool, teeth clamped intently on the spoon with which his teenage nurse is trying to feed him gruel. Splotches of rice porridge dot the floor like atolls in the puddle of piss that spreads out from his left pajama leg. He glints wickedly at the nurse from beneath brows fused together in dogged determination. She peers blandly back at him, just waiting for the jaws to unclench enough to retrieve her spoon.

The frozen violence of the scene stops the Taitais in their tracks, Ah-loong relates. Just then, one of the chess-playing doctors from the front office (alerted by the pill-cart nurse?) scurries around the corner, buttoning up his white lab coat. He introduces himself as Qian Wei, the hospice director, and smilingly leads the two visitors back down to his office. They tag along behind him in meek relief.

But by the time they settle into Qian Wei's rickety armchairs, the women manage to recompose their features into seemlier masks of unflappability. Keiko does the talking, trying to regain the initiative. "We saw your write-up in the paper and thought we'd come out for a look."

In a nasal, singsong tenor, the director thanks them for their interest. He inquires gently where the two of them come from. "Oh, the South," Keiko airily offers, and then quickly shifts the subject with a volley of questions. How many beds in the hospital? About fifty just now. Occupancy rate? It fluctuates between 75 and 85 percent as a rule. How old are the patients? We've had them from age two to 102, but they average in their sixties and seventies. Fees? Basic bed charges run to RMB 550 per month, which includes round-the-clock nursing. Meals and medicines are extra.

While Keiko's quizzing him, Ah-loong has plenty of time to survey the spartan office. "Not that there's much to see in there," she notes, and itemizes: a pine study desk and a metal folding chair; a chipped tea mug overflowing with cigarette butts; a battered Naugahyde couch with a gimpy hind leg that lists perilously in one corner; a bat-

tered guitar hanging by its shoulder strap beside a brass-plated cruci-
fix, an embroidered Buddha, and a soap-ad calendar. The whole room
smells like an ashtray. Dust coats everything.

"Most common diagnoses?" Keiko asks. "Strokes, rheumatoid
arthritis, dementia, various cancers," Qian Wei ticks off on blanched,
attenuated, nicotine-stained fingers that look somehow more like a
jazz bassist's than a doctor's. Then he gives up the enumeration with a
shrug. More commonly, he says, we simply admit patients for general
decrepitude, lassitude, and despair.

Some come here only because their relatives see that the end is
near. The paperwork of dying (what with police reports and funeral
arrangements) is just too onerous in China for most families to handle
by themselves. Some patients have no family at all and are brought in
by their neighbors. Some just wander in on their own. Some are literally dumped on the doorstep. Plenty of destitute cases, taken on for
charity.

A sad enough catalogue, but Keiko's not rising to the bait quite
yet. First she's determined to try out the touchstone question Dr.
Guan suggested. "So with such a wide range of problems, what kind of
treatment can the hospital offer?" Mostly palliative care, some pain
pills and sedatives. "And what do you charge for drugs?" Qian Wei
runs down a menu of common, China-made pharmaceuticals, all
priced well within Guan's guidelines for probity.

As Keiko presses on with her inquisition, Ah-loong turns her attention to assessing the director himself. A long, shiny, clean-shaven
face framed in thickly pomaded hair. An attentive, even quizzical expression. But the eyes seem animated by more than just the statistics
he's reeling off.

"You can practically *see* the calculations flit across his mind as he
sizes up the two of us," she laughs. "Our accents, word choice, grooming, dress." It doesn't take him long to figure out that these are no
simple day-trippers up from Fujian. Nor to guess what his visitors are
getting at with all these questions about prices and occupancy rates.
He's heard it all before.

"Funny you should ask that," he sighs. "We get one or two gov-

ernment inspectors a week in here with pretty much the same check-
list." He's well aware of the drug-pricing and prescription rackets
that go on in the turbulent free-for-all of China's newly marketized
economy. Alas for him, he's in no position to cash in, he explains. He's
got his hands full with old people. They're too poor to fleece, most of
them, and too desperate to ignore.

"Ever since I opened the hospice three years ago, I've had more patients than I could handle," he says. "I knew there was a need for a
hospital like this. But who ever dreamt how much?" Surely not the
quasi-governmental organization, the Chinese Geriatric Association,
with whom he'd had to go into a nominal partnership at the outset to
get a license. When the Geriatric Association's Party bosses saw the
unexpectedly high volume of business, they demanded a bigger stake.
They couldn't be persuaded that, despite its impressive occupancy
rate, the hospital was in fact running at a loss.

Even harder to convince were the government inspectors who
started cropping up every few days for unannounced reviews of the facilities and the dispensary accounts. Then there was Xi-yuan's original landlord, an army unit that initially rented Qian Wei an unused
twenty-five-room sanatorium out by the Fragrant Hills. Noting the
rapid "turnover" of "guests," the commandant concluded that his location might be worth more than he had thought after all. Within the
year, he gave Xi-yuan its walking papers.

"So then I found this place—an abandoned office block—just days
before I had to get out of there. No time even to repaint. Just had to
load our equipment onto trucks and ferry our patients as best we
could." He describes his exodus with a busload of very mixed-up old
people. More patients arriving in hourly relays by ambulance. Wheel-
chairs lined up on the curb, stretchers, intravenous drips, oxygen
tanks—the works.

"And then the neighbors wouldn't let us in," he relates. "A group
showed up from the factory dorm next door, plus people from the
garage and the noodle stall across the road. They staked out our
courtyard and barred the door. 'A jinx,' they said. 'A bunch of terminal old people? A special hospital for the dying? Why, it'll simply *de-*

stroy the luck of the neighborhood,' they said." It was all Qian Wei could do to talk—to beg—his way into his own legally leased and fully paid-for premises.

The neighbors weren't the only ones who balked at the "inauspicious" hospice. As his work consumed more and more of his time, even his own wife (a minor TV actress) finally left him. She decamped to her parents' house in Tianjin, taking their three-year-old son with her. And now he's been served another eviction notice by the current landlord. Beijing's Fourth Ring Road is slated to plow right through this district, making the land too valuable to use for something as unremunerative as a hospice. Xi-yuan might have to move all over again.

The accelerating saga of his woes comes in shorter and shorter sentence fragments. His brow furrows at the recollection. He massages his temples as if to dispel his manifold headaches. And then, astonishingly, he cries. His shoulders hunch up and his eyes slam shut against the onset of tears.

"Keiko and I have *no* idea what to say at this point," Ah-loong shrugs, still amazed at the recollection fully a day later. "Here's a grown man, a stranger—a *doctor*, no less—openly weeping right in front of us." It's a severe breach of face, a degree of self-revelation and vulnerability way out of line with everyday Chinese norms. Even if his recital may have been pitched partly for effect, Qian Wei's grief is plainly real.

The two women are completely disarmed. The silence of the room sponges up the awkwardness of the moment. Keiko, unable to stand it any more, blurts at last, "How can we help? What can we do?" Qian Wei's brows clench all the tighter, but he steadies his breathing. When his eyes snap open again, they're quite unclouded.

"Your concern alone is help enough," he declaims with a decorum all the more unnerving on the heels of his previous outburst. And then, even more incongruously, he breaks into a sunny smile. "But just come and have a look. Time for afternoon rounds. You can see for yourselves."

Without waiting for an answer, he's out of his chair and off down the hall, the white lab coat flapping behind him. Keiko and Ah-loong have no choice but to launch themselves into his wake, hurrying to keep up with him. He takes the stairwell two steps at a time. Without a knock on the door or a backward glance at his gasping tagalongs, Qian Wei barges right into room 10-A, the first door on the corridor. Once inside, though, the abrupt burst of velocity squelches itself in a tableau of torpor.

On one of the two beds, a diminutive body stretches barely half the length of the cot, wound like a papoose in white bedclothes. On the pillow, surrounded by a wispy gray frizz of hair, the tight black chevron of the open mouth dilates rhythmically—the only sign of breath. Ah-loong feels a first involuntary gag of revulsion at the spectacle of imminent death, as she later confesses. She quickly turns to the opposite bed.

There sits the very picture of a rosy grandma—plump, soap-scented, and smiling vacuously. The slanting afternoon sunlight from the window suffuses her vellum complexion. Her legs, in black silk pantaloons, dangle over the edge of the bed without quite reaching the floor.

It takes the two Taitais a split-second to register that the legs end in three-inch "golden lotuses." Back in Imperial China, rich households used to bind their daughters' feet to achieve these stunted little hooflets. The resultant mincing gait once inspired poetic ecstasies among Qing dynasty connoisseurs of womanhood. A luxuriant crop of sex fetishes grew up around the tiny embroidered slippers, the silken bandages, and all the paraphernalia of bound feet.

So it's all the more shocking—almost obscene—to abruptly confront these "golden lotuses" sheathed in nothing more than white cotton schoolgirl socks. The toe-bones curl visibly under the soles of the feet and the little hooves taper to horny points. This woman must be well into her eighties, at least, to have suffered such mutilation before law and fashion ended the practice. Not only did the foot-binding leave her crippled for life, it must also have visibly branded her a "class enemy" throughout the decades of Maoist frenzy, the daughter of a household rich and decadent enough to afford purely ornamental women.

Yet whatever her lifelong suffering on this account, old age has left her with a smooth, unlined baby face. A nurse slowly plaits a ribbon into her long, silver braid, but the woman just stares blankly into space without reaction. Qian Wei rocks on his heels in the doorway for a minute, taking in the scene. Then he squats down on his haunches squarely in front of her.

Her eyes remain vacant as ever, but her smile rounds into an "O" of surprise, like a fish yanked gasping into the air. He raises an admonitory finger and recites, without preamble, "Forty-four stone lions." This is a well-known tongue-twister in Chinese—"*Sishi sige shitou zuode shizi.*" Not much of a conversational gambit, though, it seems; no response.

Qian Wei repeats it again twice, each time louder than the last. Finally, like a long-disused clock suddenly striking the hour, the old lady starts trying, sketchily, to echo his recital. "Forty . . . four forty . . . four stone . . . lions." She keeps at it even after Qian Wei stands up to leave.

"You've got to give them something to do," he explains. "Anything. Doesn't much matter what. Just to keep them alive. Up here, you know," he adds, tapping his forehead lightly.

These confidences are delivered in over-the-shoulder snatches, for Qian Wei's already charging out the door and down the hall, en route to the next room, 12-A. He wades right in, again without prelude, rubbing his hands like a banquet host. "Look what we have here," he enthuses. "*Visitors!* Foreign guests that your daughter sent over from the United States."

"He caught us so off guard," Ah-loong laughs, "that we instinctively glanced back, half-expecting to find some Americans standing behind us. But he's talking about *me*, as it turns out." Qian Wei unhesitatingly takes Ah-loong by the elbow and squires her, with dinner-party suavity, up to the bedside. He introduces the pallid occupant of the bed not by name, but by attribute: "She speaks beautiful English. She's been to Cow-Crossing University," as Oxford is called in Chinese. "Try her out," he urges.

The doctor's sudden shot in the dark leaves Ah-loong reeling. She gropes in vain to remember anything she's said so far that could have offered the remotest inkling she speaks a word of English. But before she has a chance to collect her wits, the diminutive patient extends a birdlike claw over the bedrail and inquires, in impeccable Oxonian tones, "Howd'ye dew?"

The old lady shrugs herself an inch higher on her bolster and attempts to smooth her nightdress—as near to a curtsey as she can manage, given her failing strength. The plummy English phonemes modulate a reedy whisper of a voice. Ah-loong leans over the bedrail, the better to hear. And how *is* my daughter, the old lady wants to know. Keeping up with her studies? Finding anything edible out there? Any plans to come home soon? Speaking Chinese, Ah-loong admits in all honesty that she's none too sure on any of these points.

"Never mind," sighs the faience figure in the bed, reverting to Canton-accented Mandarin. "Might all be for the best, anyway, if she stays there for good. When I came back from Cow-Crossing, anything seemed possible for an educated lady. Who was to know that within a few years . . . ?"

Keiko, at the foot of the bed, reads the woman's age from her medical chart: eighty-four. It must have been the mid-1930s when she came back to China, a member of a vanishingly small elite of female university graduates. How much easier it would have been to remain abroad, free of traditional Chinese strictures upon women and safe from the gathering military menace of Japan. Only filial piety or patriotism could have prompted her return. Yet odds are she never got a chance to put her education to use. Coming from a household that could presume to send a daughter to Oxford, she'd have been stigmatized in New China for her family background.

Even now, after the 1980s reforms reopened the option of foreign study, scions of such families fare better in academic meritocracies abroad than in the Party-dominated hierarchies of Chinese universities. And once overseas, they now know better than to fall into the trap of sentimental or patriotic homecomings. So China's brain drain turns into a heart drain, leaving many parents to face old age on their own, far from their expatriated offspring.

Xi-yuan's Oxonian won't be drawn out on any of this, however. When it comes to her post-university life, she maintains a very British stiff upper lip. On the other hand, she's happy enough to reminisce about her English years: the coronation of Edward VIII, Masters' Tea at Newnham, punting on the Cherwell. Do they have punts in her daughter's college in Idaho? Probably not, Ah-loong concedes, casting a pleading glance over to Qian Wei for help.

But the doctor is absorbed in teaching the Oxonian's even older roommate how to fold paper cranes, another of his make-work projects. They've already produced four origami cranes together, strung on a thread. "So it's agreed," Qian Wei beams, taking in the length of the bed with a hand wave. "You'll make me a whole strand of them from here to there, right?" The elderly patient is already too concentrated on her folding even to nod assent. The half-finished crane in her hand trembles like a newborn nestling.

Qian Wei leaves the room with no more ceremony than he entered. Ah-loong and Keiko hastily excuse themselves to the Oxonian, who pronounces herself (in English) "delighted to have made your acquaintance." By the time the visitors finish their parting pleasantries and make it out to the corridor, the doctor's nowhere to be seen. They exchange a nervous glance, not sure which door to try or what they might find behind it without anybody to steer them through this labyrinth. They opt for the next in the row, 14-A.

Sure enough, Qian Wei is inside. He sits becalmed in the Sargasso half-light of a green-curtained room. The patient he's visiting glows with a subaqueous pallor against the pillow, his wasted limbs trailing off among the bedclothes like boneless fins. Qian Wei, head bowed and eyes shut, presses one languid hand between his palms. The patient's eyes, under a widow's peak of black stubble, remain wide open, moist and motile, the only part of him that betrays any sign of life.

Keiko steps into the room and gently closes the door behind them so as to shut the hall light out of this green gloom. But the two women still hover by the threshold, uneasy about entering this apparently exclusive space the doctor and patient share. No words are spoken. Hard to tell just what it is that passes between them—empathy? Faith healing? Or is it just that Qian Wei feels himself momentarily stymied by the hopelessness of this case?

If that's it, then he gets over his funk before long. Presently, he lets go the hand, which the patient retracts with the fluidity of a sea anemone tendril. The man turns his face to the wall, eyes still wide. The doctor stands up from the bed and rejoins Keiko and Ah-loong unhurriedly, like a diver wary of the bends, surfacing in stages.

"Cancer," he explains, as they turn the corner into a new ward. "Pancreatic. Thirty-two years old. We thought he'd be gone months ago. Some hang on against all odds; some surrender without even a fight."

"AND SOME," he adds, pushing open the next door, "fight by surrendering." He stands aside to usher the ladies into room 10-B, a curator proudly showing off one of the jewels of his collection. "Meet Comrade Qiao Jing-yuan, suicide."

The subject of this introduction nods genially, quite unruffled by Qian Wei's description, like a dignitary on a dais basking in an after-dinner tribute. She sits squarely at stage center in the cramped room, a small and twitchy figure perched on the edge of an overstuffed Morris chair. Before her, on a low stool, a teenage nurse patiently unreels a toilet roll. With birdlike pecks, the little lady tears off the paper, square-by-square, and pleats it into neat triangles, which she stacks on the arm of her chair.

"God knows what they were up to," Ah-loong muses. "Just caught in that timeless afternoon light, running intently through the same mysterious motions again and again, like bewitched prisoners in some fairy-tale castle." Finally, the woman in the armchair breaks the spell with a sustained, throaty eructation, like a Beijing Opera drum roll. She spits daintily into one of the wads of paper and adds it to the soggy mound overflowing the plastic spittoon under her bed.

With this fanfare, Qian Wei continues with his introduction: "Before her stroke, Comrade Qiao was Party secretary of the Liang Qi-xuan Museum. She came here a month ago, after trying to gas herself at home. She nearly blew up the Ministry of Culture's Drama Section dorm in the process."

No wonder he's so proud of this trophy patient. Any Work Unit Party secretary is a big shot of sorts. All the more so, one in charge of so important an ideological "property" as Liang Qi-xuan, a Beijing Opera actor famous in the 1930s for his transvestite roles. Unlike many of his thespian colleagues, Liang chose to stay on in China after the Communist Liberation. During its initial "Red honeymoon" years, the new regime sought to co-opt his prestige by inducting him into the Party and the show legislature.

Liang was lucky enough to die peacefully in 1957, just before the onset of mass purges that wiped out most Chinese artists and intellectuals of his generation. After the death of Mao and the fall of his arts-czarina widow, Jiang Qing, China's classical culture enjoyed a transient reprieve from official vandalism. To signal this restoration, the Communists needed a traditional arts hero they could lionize without reopening the wounds of the Party's Cultural Revolution excesses. Liang filled the bill: a collaborationist artist who had conveniently died in his bed before the regime could get around to killing him.

So what could have driven the keeper of Liang's legacy to attempt suicide? No further clues from Qian Wei. Full of curatorial solicitude, the hospice director discreetly bows out of the room, leaving his guests to their own leisurely appreciation of this choice exhibit.

"Why don't you two stay here and chat a while with Comrade Qiao?" he suggests to Keiko and Ah-loong. "It might help you get a better feel for what Xi-yuan's all about. I'll go finish my rounds." He's out the door without waiting for a reply, leaving the two Taitais to grope for an appropriate conversation-starter after such an introduction.

Unsure of her etiquette, Ah-loong assumes a disarming cocktail-party smile and picks up on the most innocuous topic she can find in Qian Wei's spiel: "So how did you become involved with Liang Qi-xuan?" Comrade Qiao smiles back just as brightly and replies: "Well, I began by shooting my aunt. That's how I became a Communist."

IT WAS DURING the land reform right after Liberation, she goes on to explain. The aunt was matriarch of the largest landowning family in the village. Comrade Qiao, daughter of an adjunct wife to the same landlord, worked as a charwoman in the extended household. When she was just fifteen, the Communists marched into her hometown. Comrade Qiao lost no time in squaring accounts with the old back-stairs tyrant of her family. She personally blew her aunt's brains out with a revolver at point-blank range when the old lady was declared a class enemy after a brief but boisterous trial-by-harangue in the courtyard of the ancestral home.

"Very exciting," she recalls. "First time I had ever touched a gun."

This show of zeal paved her way into the Party. In fact, she modestly avers, she hardly deserved so much credit. Like most everything else she's achieved as a Communist, Comrade Qiao was just doing what came naturally.

"Shooting my aunt was a revolution, *my* revolution. I'd dreamt of it for long, mentally rehearsed it in great detail. I'd hardly dared to hope it was really possible, though, until Chairman Mao opened a way. But when the chance came, I was ready to play my role without even a trace of stage fright. An actress, I was, a regular trouper, even back then," she laughs. "After all, what's the People's Revolution but the sum total of a thousand million personal revolts? You push yours and I push mine and it all adds up to history. That's all there really is to the dialectic, isn't it?"

After whetting her appetite for vengeance, the revolution offered plenty of scope to gratify her next nascent appetite: sleeping with soldiers. She had no family—she'd seen to that. No home except the Party, which was a rolling roadshow. In her green fatigues and shoulder-length hair, she had only to turn up at any train station to get herself carried steadily closer to the frontline of revolution: Korea.

In those days, you could substitute slogans for rail tickets. The Red Army surge across the Yalu, as Comrade Qiao recalls it, was Maoist "People's War" in the purest sense, drawing on China's boundless demographic reserves to sling bodies into the breach. Her own body, young and willing, moved in easy stages up through Manchuria and on down toward the 38th parallel.

She never actually saw combat, though. Through the intercession of a sergeant she had met in the army's political wing, she morphed into a camp follower of a seemlier sort as a member of a troopentertainment propaganda team. The troupe's productions were pretty rough-hewn, she admits, but she became addicted to the attention of crowds. "You can sway them this way and that, change moods and minds. What power!"

She came back from Korea married to her sergeant, six months pregnant, but stagestruck as ever. Stuck in a Manchurian garrison town, away from the aphrodisiac tang of danger, the marriage palled. "He beat me. I 'struggled against' him," Communist parlance for denunciation through Party channels. The standoff continued right through the birth of their son. They named the child Zi Qiang ("Self-Strength") after one of the patriotic slogans of the day. He had a little clenched face, Qiao recalls, "and he always wanted to suck me dry, all the time, day and night."

The boy turned out to be autistic from infancy. The sergeant's beatings continued, and so did Comrade Qiao's "struggles" against her husband. She won in the end: the sergeant wound up divorced, demobilized from the army, and stuck with the baby.

Comrade Qiao was on her way to something grander than motherhood. Her old Production Unit, the Red Army Propaganda Team, sponsored her to attend the Central Drama Academy in Beijing. This famous old institution still retained so much of its pre-Liberation flavor that she found it daunting at first.

"Everybody jabbering on about Ibsen and Chekhov and Shakespeare—what did I know about any of that?" A classmate, Xiao Zhou, son of a Beijing merchant, tried to help her. "He spoke five languages, translated scripts for us. An Ibsen specialist. It was all way over my head, though," she laughs. Nor could she make much sense out of Stanislavskian "method acting," which was then in vogue.

"They kept telling me to emote. Every character was supposed to have her own past going back way before she even stepped onstage. I should 'find my feelings' and inject them into my role. I didn't know where to *begin* to look. My only experience of 'finding feelings' was at the Party's 'speak bitterness' sessions, when we were 'struggling against' somebody."

A true Communist, she explains, has no personal past; it's all subsumed into class identity. Luckily for her, Stanislavsky was soon to be flushed out of the Central Drama Academy when Mao's "Hundred Flowers" experiment with cultural pluralism gave way in the late-1950s to an "Anti-Rightist" backlash. Those who had flirted with foreign ideas now became purge targets. For instance, her friend Xiao Zhou, the Ibsen expert, dropped into the oubliette of internal exile. Chinese theaters became the exclusive preserve of didactic revolutionary melodrama.

By that time, though, Comrade Qiao had already cast herself as a rising star on the broader stage of politics. "I lacked the talent to ever become a really first-rate actress," she admits. "I was always more Red than expert," an allusion to the ongoing tug-of-war between political correctness versus technical accomplishment in Communist administration.

Rather than seek glory in front of the footlights, she maximized her power behind the scenes as Party secretary of a series of drama troupes. "At least you'd never go hungry that way," she recalls.

Even in the nationwide famine after the debacle of Mao's headlong "Great Leap" into grassroots industrialization, traveling theater companies were among the few production units that could still count on steady work. So it remained right through the vagaries of the Cultural Revolution. The less bread there was to go around, the more the Party had to rely on "circuses" of every kind. Drama troupes crisscrossed the countryside like guerrilla detachments, frontline shock forces of agitprop.

But to steer clear of trouble in those treacherous decades, a drama company's Party secretary needed to be the subtlest actress in her troupe. Every script, every polemic, had to be framed with such multilayered ambiguity that it could never retroactively backfire, no matter which way the factional struggle might turn. And no sector of public life was more politically charged than the theater.

After all, hadn't the whole Cultural Revolution started with a piece of tendentious drama criticism? And wasn't the movement led by an ex-actress, Madame Mao?

Thanks to her bravura performance as Party secretary, Comrade Qiao survived the decade unscathed. She showed just enough revolutionary fervor during the leftist ascendancy without ever mortally affronting any rightist luminary who might come back to haunt her.

"It's not hard to play revolutionary drama," she says. "Only remember, you're always part of a tableau, even if you're the star. Never stand out. Just look *this* way when all eyes turn so, and *that* way when they all swivel around." She demonstrates with stagy glowers left and right. "The crowd will cheer you. They'll all say, 'Wah! What fire, what zeal.'"

So adroit was Comrade Qiao's Cultural Revolution balancing act that she won the coveted Liang Qi-xuan assignment and even found herself on a panel of arbiters to "rehabilitate" purged Culture Ministry cadres after the trauma. There she once again came across Xiao Zhou, the Ibsen expert. His file was the first news she'd had of him in nearly twenty years. It related how, early in his exile, he'd been left paraplegic when he was denied medical treatment after a tractor accident.

The Xiao Zhou who appeared before the Culture Ministry panel was a far cry from the bourgeois stripling she'd known back at the Academy so long ago. By now, he'd developed a barrel chest and calloused hands from shouldering his way on crutches all these years. His face was ashen, as if ingrained with Gobi dust. Comrade Qiao personally signed the "rehabilitation" order that reassigned him to the ministry's Beijing compound to resume his translation work. He moved into a ground-floor room directly opposite her own in the Drama Section apartment block.

So when she had her stroke, a decade later, it was to Xiao Zhou's door that she managed to crawl for help. He ferried her to the doctor on his hand-pedaled tricycle cart. Afterward, he nursed her until she regained full motor function. In gratitude, she married him—"the most sentimental step I've ever taken in my life," she laughs. Still, the marriage had its practical side for each of them. Lifted out of the tenuous limbo of a rehabilitated rightist, Xiao Zhou got to share the perks and status of a long-standing Party member like Comrade Qiao. And she, for her part, got a full-time nurse and watchdog. She hadn't reckoned, however, on how much his disability would restrict his capacity to fetch and carry.

Nor could she have foreseen the sudden vogue for foreign plays that presently propelled her husband's career to overtake her own. In the prolonged cultural crackdown after the 1989 Tiananmen massacre, the only way for directors to stage even veiled social commentary was through translated scripts. That way, any heterodoxies could be retroactively blamed on the likes of Ibsen, Dürrenmatt, or Goethe. Xiao Zhou soon had more translation work than he could handle.

Meanwhile, Comrade Qiao wound up being squeezed out of the Liang Qi-xuan Museum. With the restoration of inheritance rights in post-Mao China, Liang's children could now press claims to his papers and heirlooms. For nearly a decade, the museum had been working on an annotated and illustrated hagiography of Liang. Now direction of the project passed to the family, and with it effective control of the museum's staff and resources.

For the first time since shooting her aunt, Comrade Qiao was at a loss for a role. "Casting used to be so straightforward," she sighs. "You never had to wonder if you were a hero or a villain, a star or an extra. No soul-searching involved; it was all done by committee. But now, the world has suddenly gotten so complicated. Nobody's even sure what's the script, so we have to make up our own lines as we go along. It's like Stanislavsky all over again. Not my style."

Never one to be upstaged, she decided to go out with a bang. "Any actress knows, when your scene is over, it's time to get off the stage," Comrade Qiao shrugs. Hence the bid to gas herself. As it turned out,

Xiao Zhou lurched into the flat and knocked open the windows just in time. Otherwise, any passing smoker might have ignited the grand finale she'd scripted.

And now she finds herself playing an unexpected epilogue in Xiyuan. She could wish for a bit more of an audience. Xiao Zhou rarely manages to hand-pedal himself all the way out to the hospice. And she finds herself thinking back surprisingly often upon her sergeant and her son, even though she's had no word from them in decades.

Still, her current invalid role is not such a bad part, on the whole. She enjoys plenty of attention from Qian Wei, who keeps trying to diagnose new ailments for which he can prescribe costly imported tonics. She's well aware that he pads her bill since, unlike most of his patients, she has a solvent work unit to cover her expenses. Never mind. If it helps fund the hospice, no harm done. She could hardly be more comfortable, after all. Round-the-clock nurses, color TV, meat or fish every second day. "Even the occasional visitor—like you two," she smiles.

HEARING THEMSELVES ADDRESSED directly for the first time in Comrade Qiao's hour-long monologue, Keiko and Ah-loong snap out of their trance. The teenage room nurse has long since nodded off on her stool with the toilet roll still in her hands. The window has gone purple with twilight shadows, the Taiwan Taitais' first inkling of how late it's become.

"The *children*," Keiko gasps with a start. They must already be back from school. The cook no doubt has dinner well in hand, but Keiko had better reach home and change out of this get-up well before her husband returns from work. She leaps up from her stool in a flurry and starts edging to the door, all the while profusely thanking Comrade Qiao for sharing her story. Ah-loong follows suit. As far as the old actress is concerned, it's a standing ovation, and she graciously accepts it as her due.

The women find the hospital corridors as empty as when they first came in. Encountering nobody all the way to the door, Keiko and Ah-loong let themselves out with no farewells and make their way across the front courtyard.

Beijing's lens of smog swells the setting sun into a fat, orange pumpkin hanging just beyond reach over the Xi-yuan gatehouse. Backlit plastic tatters flutter crimson in the thornbushes across the road, turning a bleak patch of bracken into a fleeting vision of a bougainvillea bower. To round out the bucolic mood, a pair of rustics roost silhouetted on the streetside gate. They take turns hocking gobs of phlegm into the courtyard dust. The straw-hatted silhouette concentrates on his spitting, but the bare-headed one catches sight of the two women and rises to meet them. Only then do they recognize Qian Wei. Seems they're not to escape without exit ceremonies after all.

"Ah, *here* she is at last," the doctor bustles up to the two women. "The Japanese Emperor's Plenipotentiary Undersecretary for Apologetics" (a mere ten syllables in Chinese). He ushers Keiko obsequiously back to the gatehouse. "Mr. Chen has been waiting for you, madam. For fifty years."

At Qian Wei's noisy homage, the gatehouse occupants—a stone-faced old lady in a gray cotton tunic, a ginger cat, a burly rooster, and two adolescent chickens—all drift out to the courtyard to inspect the newly arrived dignitary. The old man on the gate remains seated. He pushes back his straw hat and peremptorily waves away any blandishments Keiko might try to offer. "Keep your reparations," he grumbles. "Don't *want* your mother-jumping money."

"Mr. and Mrs. Chen here are simple people," Qian Wei explains, as though to smooth Keiko's presumably ruffled feathers. "Farmers, you see. Cash can't buy the kind of peace they require."

"At this point, Keiko's completely confused," Ah-loong relates. "What's this doctor up to now? And why announce her as some kind of Japanese functionary?" Her bewilderment must be plainly visible to Qian Wei standing beside her. But Chen can't see her face in the gathering dusk, so the doctor presses on with his charade.

He briefs Keiko on how the Chens have been faring since their son brought them into Xi-yuan. Back home on their farmstead in Hebei, it seems, the elderly couple had always lived in a one-story hut. In the hospital, they just couldn't get used to an upstairs room. Too drafty, they said. Too many people-sounds, not enough earth-sounds. So Qian Wei moved them into the free-standing, one-story gatehouse. Here, he explains, they can be "on their own with just a few of their pets." Keiko nods politely, wondering what comes next.

Chen, throughout this preamble, has been working himself up to a tirade. Now he cuts loose with a shrapnel of gravel-voiced imprecations. "All I want is for your dog-fart emperor to say he's sorry. Son of a bitch. Let him be sorry for the eight years of mine he wasted. Sorry for the sweat and pain and fear. Sorry for my boy growing up without a father, my wife without a man, begging for handouts."

The story comes pouring out of him. How, as a yokel newlywed in Japanese-occupied Hebei, he was grabbed at random by a local secret-police agent with a monthly arrest quota to meet. How he was baselessly accused of membership in the Communist underground. How he was dunked upside-down in a cistern until he "confessed."

How he was packed off to Kyushu in what amounted to a slave ship and put to work in a Mitsubishi coal mine. How he was starved and beaten and worked on back-to-back shifts. How his lungs clotted and his skin broke out in suppurating sores from malnutrition, coal gas, and exposure to the dank, raw, maritime weather. How fellow prisoners died in droves all around him, so that he wound up digging more graves than coal.

How even after the Japanese surrendered, the prisoners remained penned up in their mining camp with no food at all, eating grass and tree bark for a fortnight until the American occupation troops arrived. How more of the prisoners died on the troop ship back to Canton. How he straggled home through the alarums of the raging Chinese civil war. How he found his wife and his by-now teenage son in the servants' quarters of the local landlord's house. How, when reunited, they could hardly even recognize each other in the haggard strangers they had become.

The well-rehearsed cadences quicken as he gathers momentum. In the waning light, the voice loses its gruffness and takes on an abstracted, almost disembodied tone. It's as though the tale is telling itself, independent of the speaker. All the intervening triumphs and miseries, the Great Leaps and juddering halts of Chinese communism, seem to evanesce. Old Chen is back there in the 1940s, alone with the single enormity of his life, the great wrong that gives him meaning.

And at last, after all these years of mere perfunctory sympathy from everybody around him, his story finally reaches the only ear that matters: that of the "turtle-cunt emperor of Japan"—or at least his plenipotentiary.

"The old man's inconsolable grievance left me feeling genuinely ashamed—though of just *what* I couldn't begin to say," Ah-loong admits. But she feels her own face flush in the darkness as Keiko, tears streaming, bows stiffly and steeply again and again, the very picture of Japanese abjection.

But no plenipotentiary grovel can slake Chen's grief. He stares blankly as though stunned by the utter inadequacy of this long-awaited apology. He rams his hat brim down over his eyes, outraged anew, and stomps off to the gatehouse with his wife in tow. The screen door slams shut behind them, leaving Keiko to bow her apologies to the cat and the rooster.

Qian Wei hails a taxi-van from the road and squires the two women aboard with a toothy smile. "So you see how it is here. You had a good 'speak bitterness' session with Comrade Qiao? Interesting? Do come again. Soon."

AH-LOONG SLEEPS IN late the next day and treats herself to a long bath. She looks a lot fresher than when she'd straggled home in the taxi-van last night. She sighs contentedly—"I feel like I've died and gone to heaven"—then, remembering yesterday's expedition, catches herself and amends the pronouncement: "Well, maybe not *died*, exactly . . ." She launches into the detailed account of her hospice visit, which she'd been too tired to relate immediately upon her return.

I'm flipping omelettes when she sits down to her brunch of croissants and coffee at the kitchen table. Nowadays, thanks to Deng's "reform and opening," dozens of Beijing shopping malls offer such amenities—for a price. The per-capita cost of this morning's brunch exceeds that of a full day's die-in at Xi-yuan.

It's a Wednesday, the morning after my weekly copy deadline— always my most relaxed day of the week. I've got plenty of time to hear Ah-loong detail her experience and sort out her impressions. "The stench," she wrinkles her nose at the recollection: piss and puke and tears that no amount of disinfectant can override. The stagnant smell of human bodies that aren't going anywhere anymore, that have reached the end of the line. But what dismayed her even more, she adds, was the complete lack of privacy.

"There they lie in their beds, these patients, poked full of tubes and needles. People barge in and out of the ward rooms all the time. Total strangers suffer their death agonies in adjacent beds. It's as though they had no identity of their own anymore. Like they were already dead and cremated. Just ash, already, blown at random by any passing breeze."

Sounds pretty grim to me. But perhaps not all that different, I suggest, from hospitals in general anywhere in the world. Nor, for that matter, from a lot of other places besides hospitals in contemporary China, I suppose. I peer out the kitchen window at the unconcealed spy camera on the compound wall, a pointed reminder to all the diplomatic enclave denizens. No privacy and an end-of-the-line smell; so what else is new?

Ah-loong rolls her eyes at my obtuseness. "Well, what's *new* is that it's all laid out before you. Of course the hospice feels a lot like the rest of China. What else *could* it be but a concentrated version of the surrounding milieu? You go from room to room and each case opens up a little window onto some corner of Chinese life."

But at least in Xi-yuan, she feels, there's less hypocrisy because the inmates have no place left to hide. "They may have spent a lifetime trying not to look at themselves, but now the game is up. And they're ready to talk about it, many of them, because they're lonely or scared." She draws up short, startled at her own confessed voyeurism.

"But there's something else there, too," she adds, reflectively. "Maybe it's the hospice director himself." Qian Wei, as she describes him, sounds like the least typical "unit chief" in all of China. Normally, anyone with any kind of official title can't bestir himself from his office, as a matter of face. But Qian Wei's just the opposite.

"You can't keep him in a chair," Ah-loong relates, admiringly. "He's got to be all over the place all the time, mixing into everything. Completely wrapped up in each of his cases, at least as long as he's with them. Nonstop, zany improvisation. Well, plain *lying*, in fact. To pathetic, dying people at that. And he *makes* you play along with him, like it or not."

She cites yesterday's encounters with the Oxonian and the gate-house crew to show how Qian Wei can seize upon anything—any prop, any passerby, any scrap of bio-data, any quirk or credo—to humor his patients into the beyond. "As Deng Xiaoping said, 'It doesn't matter whether the cat is black or white, as long as it catches mice,' " she sums up, alluding to the most celebrated aphorism of China's "Reform and Opening."

So you've found him at last, I congratulate her; that seeming oxymoron, the true-believing, ideological Dengist. Ah-loong shrugs. "Whatever works, works. Reality is the only test that counts, and there's nothing realer than dying. 'Seek truth from facts,' " she reminds me, citing an even more famous maxim, attributed to Chairman Mao himself. Call it truth, fact, or solace—whatever it is that's to be found at Xi-yuan, she's determined to seek out more of it. Why don't I go along with her next time and see for myself, she suggests. The Mid-Autumn Moon Festival comes up in a week. We can go then.

SUCH A PLAN IS roughly equivalent to visiting skid row on Thanksgiving Day. In the whole year, the Mid-Autumn Festival is the one occasion when Chinese will go to any length to rejoin their families back home. To spend the day alone, like these Xi-yuan inmates, must be the saddest nadir of homelessness. Their depression would only be heightened by the mounting holiday frenzy in the outside world beyond the hospice walls.

For weeks before and after the holiday, all public transport is choked, as migrant workers make their tortuous way back home. Ticket lines back up at every depot, filling the sidewalks for miles around with transient street-sleeper encampments. Tramps who can't get a berth simply trudge home with their bundles, sometimes trekking the span of several provinces.

The feast at the end of the road justifies the weary journey—if not gastronomically, at least ritualistically. The festival falls around harvest time, on the evening of what is thought to be the roundest and brightest full moon of the year. The whole clan gathers at a round table, a symbol of completeness. Whoever can't make it is conspicuous in his absence; an empty chair is left for him. Everything on the table is round: mounds of dumplings, plump chickens, silver discs of pomfret fish, soup tureens, and great globular pomelo fruits—for those who can afford such dainties.

But rich or poor, no household is without the one indispensable centerpiece of the feast: the mooncake, a filled pastry about the size (and density) of a hockey puck. Stamped with auspicious ideograms, the cake can contain dates, raisins, lotus or poppy seeds, red beans, preserved egg yolks—anything as long as it's sweet and precious. Prosperity has brought gourmet mooncakes to Chinese cities. Some now even come embossed with edible gold leaf. They're elaborately packaged in fancy paper and gaudy tins. On the way to Xi-yuan, we stop at the giant Guangming Shopping Plaza on the Third Ring Road to pick up mooncakes for the hospice inmates.

The whole ground floor has been given over to Moon Festival paraphernalia. Overexcited children in their Sunday best carom about the aisles or press their faces against the display cases, leaving nose-prints on the glass. Their parents purchase mooncakes in job lots. Sales clerks in white smocks and caps, like surgeons, bustle about the floor, packing up orders and replenishing stocks.

The entire shopping mall is decked in red, the color of choice for any auspicious occasion. Red bunting proclaims holiday greetings, crepe autumn foliage festoons the ceiling. Mythological figures—the Star of Longevity, the Moon Maiden, the Money God, and his inseparable sidekick, the God of Bureaucratic Preferment—disport themselves on crimson cake boxes and biscuit tins. Cardinal rule of Chinese retailing: the redder the package, the hotter it sells, as Communist iconographers well know.

We press our way through the holiday crush and buy three dozen assorted mooncakes, all nicely swaddled in ruby cellophane. Amply provisioned, we roll on out to the hospice. We pass the director's office in the entry corridor, but Qian Wei is closeted with visitors, too busy to receive us. He spots us through the open door and waves us on directly to the wards.

We head upstairs and start at the far end of the corridor with 14-A. Ah-loong reminds me about her last visit to this room, describing the cancer-wracked wraith she'd seen there. "Couldn't speak, couldn't move," she relates. "All he could do was stare at you out of those big, unblinking eyes in the greenish light of the curtained windows."

But there's no trace of that underwater gloom this time when we nudge open the door. The knotted curtains dangle off to one side of the casement. Light and sound fill the room: the midmorning glare from the window and the bombastic bluster of *Bao Gong*, a popular serial drama, from the radio. As detailed in the script, Bao is an upright Qing dynasty magistrate who sleuths out the iniquities of corrupt officials and rapacious landlords. Just now it seems that he's shrilly interrogating some wellborn miscreant about a rape case.

A short-fused firecracker of a man in a blue Mao jacket squats on the edge of a bed, a transistor radio pressed to his ear. From the way he's cranked up the volume, I guess his hearing is faded. His crew-cut stubble bristles with indignation as he follows the courtroom action.

Each time Bao entangles the lisping defendant in some fresh contradiction, the man on the bed growls "*hao*"—"good"—like a fan at a prizefight. On the opposite bed lies the cancer patient of Ah-loong's previous visit, limp as a beached whitefish, his eyes staring straight at the wall.

"What are you listening to, Uncle?" Ah-loong asks the room's new occupant. "Who's yer Uncle?" the man shoots back at her. "Call me Comrade—a Party man still, even if they've ditched me here to die.

And you *know* damn well that I'm listening to the *Bao Gong* show. Best thing on the air anymore. At least *somebody* still knows how to nail the fascist bourgeoisie."

At this point, Qian Wei sidles into the room, excusing himself for not being able to receive us downstairs. "Another newspaper interview—*Health Care Weekly*," he sighs with a trace of incipient celebrity ennui. "I see you've already met Old Chua. Happy Moon Festival, Comrade," the doctor shouts cordially to the man with the radio.

"Poisonous little turd, isn't he?" Qian Wei adds in a more conversational tone, well under Chua's audible range, while still smiling straight at the old man. "He used to be night watchman for some spring foundry. Been there since the sixties. One of those stolid sloganeers you'll find in any factory. A Party man, as he's no doubt already told you. You can imagine how keen the plant was to retire him once he became too lame and deaf to work. He's got no family, so his unit dumps him here. That was a couple of months ago. Not one bill of his have they paid yet.

"He's already been through practically every room in the ward. He fights with any roommate I give him. Calls them reactionaries and running dogs. Accuses them of stealing things and spying on him. Stands on his rank as a Party member. Insults my staff. Finally, I had no place to put him but here with *this* one," he nods toward the pallid figure across the room. "At least *he* can't provoke or complain."

Qian Wei smiles unflaggingly throughout this recital, his voice still inaudible to Chua. Then, helping himself to one of our mooncakes, he resumes his hearty boom. "Look what our visitors have brought you, Comrade. Season's Greetings!" The old man sputters something about "feudal superstition," but snatches the pastry briskly enough and stashes it in the drawer of his bedside table. This whole maneuver he accomplishes with one hand, like an organ grinder's monkey catching a tossed coin. With the other hand, he keeps the radio pressed to his ear.

Without waiting for thanks from Old Chua, the doctor steers us over to the opposite bed. He wordlessly props a wrapped mooncake against the wall that the emaciated youth is staring at. The wasted body doesn't stir. Only the huge eyes open wider still, as though reading the ornate characters *ming yue*—bright moon—stamped on the pastry. Then the man speaks. His thin whisper sounds like it comes from afar, a rustle of wind over grass.

He's taken the ideograms from the mooncake and expanded them into a five-character poetic strophe: "*Bright moonlight shines in at my window.*" Ah-loong supplies the next line: "*Could it be fresh ground-frost?*" Qian Wei picks up the quote: "*I raise my head to spot the full moon . . .*" The cancer patient concludes the quatrain: "*I lower my head and think back upon my homeland.*"

Nothing terribly original about the citation; it's probably the best-known verse in Chinese: Tang dynasty poet Li Bai's minimalist evocation of exile. Almost any schoolchild would have memorized it. But in the whisper of this dying wraith, the hackneyed lines take on new resonance. What exile is this aged youth facing? What "homeland" does he dream of?

Qian Wei lays a hand briefly on the sallow shoulder. Then we file out of the room without a further word. The cancer patient never turns away from the wall. "I hardly imagined he still had a voice," Ah-loong admits once we're outside.

"He practically doesn't," Qian Wei says. "What you heard in there was closer to thought than speech. No place like a hospice to bring out whatever culture a person does or doesn't have. Let me show you a case in point."

HE GUIDES US THROUGH two wards and down a staircase. We cross an inner courtyard and pass the grimy furnace of the hospital's heating plant, disused since last winter. We're headed for the northwest end of the Xi-yuan compound, the sunset quadrant. Such geomantic niceties are lost on me, but Ah-loong immediately knows where we're going: the dying room, which, by the canons of *feng shui*, must sit in this corner of every hospital in China.

We hear the deathwatch across the courtyard long before we see any of the celebrants. A six-syllable mantra, *Namu Amituofuo*—in the name of the Buddha of Light—threads its way between the brisk, repeated tock of a wooden clapper and the more leisurely ring of a bronze bell. The chant, in a minor key, is anything but upbeat. But it's been going on long enough to take on a momentum of its own, which makes it sound oddly jaunty. The voices fit snugly together, like a well-disciplined choir.

Which makes our first glimpse of these chanters all the more incongruous. They're hardly a picture of drill-team precision. A dozen of them shamble about the courtyard outside the dying room, so revved up from their singing that most of them have unbuttoned their black Buddhist vestments to cool down.

They present a curious grab bag of Beijing street people: middle-aged matrons and fresh-faced teenagers, stoop-shouldered clerks and strapping stevedores, trim office tea girls and dowdy bag ladies. They clump together in shifting conversational constellations of two or three, smiling and nodding to each other.

Except instead of exchanging pleasantries, their only utterance is "*Namu Amituofuo.*" Perhaps they're out here in the courtyard because they can't fit into the jam-packed dying room itself, where twenty more celebrants are chanting full bore. Qian Wei wriggles his way gingerly into the back of the crowd like a burglar picking a lock. Ah-loong and I are left outside for a moment with the peripatetic chanters.

"Are you relatives of the patient, then?" I ask a portly old gentleman fanning himself with a plaid handkerchief. He shakes his head, no. Perhaps from the same work unit? Not even that, he explains. "I'm from Capital Steel." He points out others in the crowd: "She works in an aircraft factory, he runs a barber shop and that one's a schoolteacher. All of us live out here in the west end of town. We only get together for the chanting." He offers me a red-bean dumpling from the ample provisions they've laid in for their vigil.

But I have no time to eat since by now Qian Wei's insinuated himself into the room. A puff of incense belches out from the doorway, as though displaced by the intrusion of his mass. He reaches back and yanks Ah-loong in behind him. She, in turn, grabs my hand and we all inch through the press of bodies to the bedside.

Propped on pillows at the center of all this attention, a smiling little woman floats like a lotus on the swelling sound and the billows of incense. She herself doesn't sing, only mouths the words. Her face glistens with sweat from the heat of the crowded room, and maybe from the agony of her terminal bone cancer.

But this woman is not one to make concessions to mere physical pain, Qian Wei informs us, shouting to be heard over the din of the clapper and gong; she refuses all anesthetics. She checked in the day before yesterday with this whole retinue in tow. Batches of chanters have been arriving in relays ever since then to relieve each other and maintain the mantra round-the-clock. The woman announced at the outset that she'd take three days to die. She paid up front for three days precisely.

By that reckoning, she must now be coming down the homestretch. He leans over the bedstead, still tugging Ah-loong in his wake, and announces, "Elder Sister, I've brought you a Buddhist from Taiwan."

Is this another of his inspired improvisations? Maybe he could figure out from Ah-loong's accent and body language that she was a Taiwanese. But how was he to know that she was raised in a Buddhist nunnery there? The youngest of six children, she'd been too much of a handful as a toddler for her busy shopkeeper mother to manage while minding the family bookstore. So Ah-loong was parked with her two aunties, who had taken religious orders. Growing up in such a milieu, the little girl saw, early on, more than her share of Buddhist last rites. By age five, she'd already imbibed her notions of eschatology.

The nuns had told her how, in the end, the onrush of delusions, doubts, and demons comes at you like a river rapid, full of hidden snags and whirlpools. Only Buddhist concentration could pilot you through these treacherous shoals to escape endless rounds of dross incarnation. You must keep your mind clear in the few days before and after your clinical demise. Convent life was a protracted dress rehearsal for that one crucial deathbed scene.

Yet even as a preschooler, Ah-loong had qualms about this worldview. On the one hand, she took comfort in the simple daily routines of the nuns, who adored and pampered her. But sometimes, when her isolation sank in—being the sole child in a world of spinsters—the tireless chant of Buddhist litany struck her as one of the loneliest sounds on earth, like the tinny little thrum of a ship's engine breasting the infinite surge of a night ocean. Her squeamishness about the whole subject of mortality dates from those days, she suspects.

With typical aplomb, though, Qian Wei has left no time right now for Ah-loong's misgivings. The woman in bed never opens her eyes but gropes the air in front of her for the promised Taiwanese Buddhist. Ah-loong takes her hand and murmurs, with the queasy shyness of agnosticism, "Stay steadfast and clear, Elder Sister. Sakyamuni Buddha awaits you."

The woman's face glows all the brighter. "Is he waiting?" she whispers. "Never doubt it, Elder Sister," Ah-loong pronounces, more firmly this time, bolstered by the blissful reaction she's induced. "Just take it step by step. You'll get there." The woman's brow sets in concentration and her legs twitch a little under the coverlet.

First the doctor, then Ah-loong and I merge our voices into the ongoing *Namu Amituofuo*. Under the cover of the general chant, we slip away from the bedside and out of the room. "See what I mean?" Qian Wei sums up. "Culture, as I was saying. Whatever you value or believe comes out in the Chamber of Great Peace," the customary Chinese euphemism for a hospital's dying room. "Culture is all you've got in the end."

ROUNDING THE COAL PILE on our way back into the main hospital block, we skirt a wheelchair that's been rolled out into the afternoon sun. Its occupant seems fused in place like a taper melted into a candlestick. He gazes right through us, incuriously, until he catches sight of my distinctly un-Chinese mustache. Then he starts waving expansively and declaims, in broad American, "Hello, my dear friend."

This seems to call for a reply, so I shake the proffered hand and inquire, "Where, my dear friend, did you learn such good English?" He smiles and nods enthusiastically but makes no response. I ask the same question again in Chinese; still no answer. I offer him a mooncake. His smile fades a little as he repeats, "Hello? My dear friend?"

Qian Wei, looking on, suggests, "Perhaps that's all he remembers, that one phrase. Maybe that, for him, is 'culture.' This man was a doctor, a famous osteopath at Beijing Union Hospital. Missionary-educated. I don't know who he takes you for, maybe someone he knew half a century ago. Nowadays we can't get him out of that chair. Stays in it day and night. It's all we can do to bathe him and dress the sores that cover his back and legs. He refuses even to lie down. He's convinced that the moment he does so he'll die."

A first hint of autumnal chill already crisps the afternoon air, so we urge the old osteopath to come with us back indoors. He doesn't object (or comment at all). At the turnoff into the wards we find an orderly to take him over. We part with a vigorous handshake. "Goodbye, my dear friend," I offer. "You rest now." He nods happily.

Qian Wei escorts us to his office and fills three tea mugs from an electric kettle. He plants himself in his desk chair and motions us to the couch. He lights a cigarette and offers us the pack. He shows no curiosity about how Ah-loong, his visitor of last week, has suddenly transformed herself from an apparent Fujianese day-tripper into an expatriate wife complete with foreign husband. Asking questions is not Qian Wei's style. He'd just as soon draw his own inferences.

I'm sizing him up at the same time that he's taking my measure. So far, I'm impressed with what I see, as Ah-loong had predicted. The man is smart and quick, if just a tad too mercurial for comfort. But even his slipperiness stands in ebullient contrast to the inert stoicism of so many Chinese. And here in a hospice, of all places. Since I don't share Qian Wei's reticence about questions, I ask the obvious: "How'd you get into this line, anyway?"

"Well, we're living in the era of 'socialist market economics,' aren't we?" he smiles. "I'm just reading the market and seizing the initiative. I think I've latched onto the hottest growth sector around."

"How so? Where's the 'growth' in death?"

"Just look at the census numbers. China's on the verge of a death boom such as the world has never seen before."

Back around the turn of the century, he explains, Sun Yat-sen, Father of the Country, was still exhorting Chinese to breed more people to build up national strength. Through all the wars and famines of the early 1900s, population still managed to grow by a third. After Liberation, China had a postwar fertility spurt just like everyplace else in the world. And people started living longer. It wasn't until the fifties and sixties that the Party suddenly hit the brakes and proclaimed its "One Child" policy. The result, Qian Wei claims, could have been predicted by any shopkeeper: a huge inventory problem, a backlog of dated stock.

"A third of our work force," he sums up, "is already over forty-six—none too early to start thinking about dying. And we'd *better* think about it, because nobody else will be in a position to think on our behalf. Not our own offspring, surely."

Qian Wei sees the under-thirties—the young, productive mainstays of the economy—outnumbered by ever more hopeless margins. In a one-child family, with current life spans and retirement ages, odds are each child will eventually have to support six pensioners—his own parents plus four grandparents. That means each married couple will have thirteen dependents: a dozen seniors, plus its own precious one and only child.

"Is that so unprecedented?" I wonder. "With their famous filial piety, haven't Chinese always cared for their own family elders?"

"But not single-handedly. Nor so many elders at a time and for so long a retirement. And that, too, at a time when the whole ideal of filial piety, like all our Chinese ideals, has been completely trashed by decades of communism." He lets this sink in for a moment while he stubs out his cigarette in his teacup.

Unsure how to react, I just stare at him blankly. The smoke from his ashtray curls in a lazy question mark over his head. He lights up again and raises the ante with a purportedly autobiographical reminiscence about growing up under Mao. Qian Wei's proud to have been born in the same month as People's China, October 1949. Of impeccable pedigree, too: his grandfather was a minor Manchurian warlord who fought alongside Mao's Eighth Route Army in the anti-Japanese war.

This revolutionary background earned him entry to a series of elite Beijing boarding schools where, in those days, inspired teachers could still impart the main lineaments of a Chinese classical education. So, while he grew up a fervent Maoist, he also knew his Four Books and Five Treatises, and he venerated the preceptors who taught them.

He remembers the Moon Festival of 1965 as the high point in this chapter of his life. His school celebrated with a moonlit boating expedition to the Summer Palace lake. Teachers and students shared mooncakes. They vied with each other, composing impromptu couplets on the moon according to the canons of classical Chinese poetics. "Those were the sorts of games we played in those days, can you imagine?" he sighs at the remembrance of lost innocence. It was the week of Qian Wei's sixteenth birthday. He had a girlfriend who made much of him that night.

Within a month of this idyll, Madame Mao and her leftists had launched the opening diatribe of the Cultural Revolution in Canton's *Liberation Daily*. By winter, some of Qian Wei's classmates started sporting Red Guard armbands, and by spring they were already lynching the faculty. In the anarchy that ensued, Qian Wei claims he used to ambush the Red Guard leaders in the *hutongs* around the school and drub them for affronting their teachers. A few such escapades were enough to make it dangerous for him to remain in Beijing.

Getting out was easy enough. Patriotic vagabondage was all the rage at the time, with seemingly every youth in China jumping trains in search of revolutionary adventure. Qian Wei followed his girlfriend back to her home in Henan, where her father was Party boss of a large commune.

Far from offering a safe haven, though, his Henan connection got him arrested. Like Party functionaries all over China, the girlfriend's father was battling for his political life in the infighting of that summer. The last thing he needed was a dubious outside "in-law" to defend. He simply arranged to have his daughter's lover picked up in an ongoing Purify Class Ranks campaign. Qian Wei was packed off to Inner Mongolia for "labor reform."

Hunger is what he mainly remembers from his prison days. "The place was semidesert. Nothing would grow there, no matter how we scratched in the dirt. It was the talk of the camp when somebody once *did* manage to tease a radish out of the ground. We never found out who. Maybe the poor chump meant to hide it away and eat it bit by bit. But a camp inspection must have caught him off guard; the radish wound up chucked in the latrine."

The image of that radish still mesmerizes Qian Wei. It floated for days in the communal slop pit, bloating up most enticingly—"Just there for the taking, if you could get over the stink. We all wondered when one or another of us would break down and fish it out." That's how he recalls the Moon Festival of 1966; watching the radish by moonlight bobbing away in a sea of diarrhea. Next morning it was gone.

He spent nine more Moon Festivals in Inner Mongolia, but at least they were not all behind barbed wire. "Barefoot doctoring" provided his ticket out of internment. One of Qian Wei's duties in the labor reform camp was to assist the visiting paramedic sent down monthly from the local "production brigade" (Cultural Revolution parlance for a village).

This "doctor's" job amounted to cooking up records of checkups and treatments supposedly provided to the inmates. "It was all nonsense, of course," Qian Wei relates. "The man had neither knowledge nor medicine to dispense." In the end, the brigade "physician" proved no better at healing himself than others: he succumbed to gastroenteritis.

To avoid a hiatus in its medical paperwork, the production brigade requisitioned the paramedic's "apprentice," to take over the job. So Qian Wei found himself abruptly "promoted" from labor camp internee to "educated youth." This was a catch-all label for urban students internally exiled to remote backwaters of China during the Cultural Revolution to damp down the factional street-fighting in the cities.

One of the lonelier moments of his life, he recalls, was when he took over the previous paramedic's kit. All that he had was about two meters of gauze, half a bottle of aspirin, an unlabeled vial of some bitter white powder—quinine, perhaps?—and a dozen rusty acupuncture needles. With this, he was supposed to doctor some 30,000 souls spread over an area half the size of Beijing.

He also inherited a red vinyl-bound copy of Mao's famous "June 26th Directive" on health care. In it the Chairman had pronounced (and Qian Wei's predecessor had underlined) that "Doctors of the type we need in villages don't require much skill. Even without, they'll always be better than witch doctors. Besides, this is the only type of doctor the villages can afford."

This, presumably, was meant to be inspirational. But Qian Wei found it less and less convincing as the years went on and he was called upon to treat everything from burns to dysentery to nervous breakdowns with virtually no medicine. He wound up increasingly emulating the witch doctors that Mao decried. He embraced what amounted to sympathetic magic.

Whatever the complaint, it seemed a patient could always be persuaded to feel a little better at the margin if you tied a round of gauze on him. Qian Wei even devised his own version of acupuncture: simply jab in a couple of needles just deep enough to hurt and divert attention from chronic aches. Especially effective was the mysterious bitter powder. A mere dab of it on the tongue was enough to cure many an ill. It tasted so foul that the villagers felt positive it must be doing *some* good.

It was the brigade's schoolteacher who best confirmed Qian Wei's evolving therapeutic style. The old man had been banished to Inner Mongolia long before the current crop of "educated youth"—as early as the "anti-rightist campaign" of 1958. Instead of sulking in exile, he'd thrown himself into the work of the village school. It was thanks to him that many of the brigade's current leaders could spell out their quotations from the Chairman or churn out the endless written "self-criticisms" that the Cultural Revolution required. The man was an inspiring and attentive teacher, widely revered in the village. Now he was dying of stomach cancer and Qian Wei had nothing but aspirin to ease his pain.

But even more than the gnawing at his entrails, what tormented the old teacher was the "rightist" stigma he still bore. He'd dedicated all his adult career to educating children, nearly two decades of it out here on the frontier. Unmarried, he'd made a family of his students and his production brigade. And still he was branded a "class enemy." It negated the clear and hard-fought facts of his life.

Qian Wei was at a loss how to ease such anguish. Even acupuncture needles couldn't touch it. All he could do was to lamely promise to bring up the case with the brigade's Party secretary. But then the doctor got busy again with his barefoot rounds. And, besides, the Party official in question was an aloof and doctrinaire Red bigot with no tolerance for such appeals. Qian Wei let the matter slide.

The next time he saw the teacher, it was clear that his cancer had run its course. The man no longer wished to speak of his pains, only about his "case" with the Party. Desperate, Qian Wei could only blurt, "Good news—I took it up with the secretary, and you've been 'rectified.' " The teacher promptly died, Qian Wei swears, with a smile on his lips.

"Well, what else was I to do?" the doctor asks, still defensive about it after all these years. "And, anyway, who was to know or care just *what* I told him, at that stage?" Surely the old schoolteacher himself wasn't complaining, and whom else did it concern? Qian Wei wound up convincing himself that what he'd said was hardly even a lie. If that secretary had really been a "vanguard of the proletariat" and the Communists truly a party of the people, that man *would* have been "rectified" long ago.

"Everybody needs something—anything—to believe in at the moment of death. And everybody *deserves* that much at least. But that's exactly what's been stripped away from us these last several generations in China. I knew then and there that this was the only effective medicine I could give my patients; to help them find their belief, whatever it may be, and die at peace in it. I'm not out to save everybody at a whack, like Mao or Jesus. I just hope to comfort the handful of people that come my way, as a conscientious 'barefoot doctor' should."

Even this modest mission, however, posed daunting odds. Finding something to believe in has been far from easy for half a century now in China. Religion is reeling under sustained, systematic attack. The snitch culture of a police state undermines faith in any human relationship, even family ties. Patriotism, Party loyalty, hero worship, and ideology have all been strained beyond the breaking point by the wild vagaries of official line.

If Maoism knocked out the spiritual props, market-oriented reforms effectively demolished the material support system that many once relied on for a decent death. Food, housing, and medical care—however rudimentary—used to be guaranteed to anyone who belonged to a work unit. Not anymore. With state enterprises and agrarian cooperatives going bust all over China, everybody's now left to shift for himself.

"Under the circumstances, no wonder we've turned into a tribe of such consummate survivors," Qian Wei sums up. Come famine, come war, come market economics or mass mobilization, your modern Chinese is primed to wriggle out of any scrape and live to write another self-criticism. The one thing Chinese are *not* programmed for is non-survival.

"Why do you think our old people cling so tenaciously to perks and power," he asks, "whether in their own little households or the national leadership? Yet statistics show that more and more of us will soon have to face the one thing that nobody survives: our own mortality." Far from depressing him, though, this grim prediction seems to visibly brighten his mood.

"What a business opportunity," he smiles, lighting up another smoke. "Let's franchise out a nationwide chain of hospices. Or how about retailing a line of geriatric-care products?"

Surely we must know of some companies back in our home countries that have experience in these fields, he coaxes. Here's a chance to tap into the biggest death market in human history. Could we introduce him to some likely joint-venture partners?

"Because otherwise, this work becomes very difficult to sustain," he adds, smoothly shifting gears from entrepreneurial boosterism to the wheedle of a charity fund-raiser. "Half the patients here can't afford to pay. And my expenses mount steadily. Especially on personnel, with the high turnover we get in this type of work. My grandfather's fortune is all that keeps us afloat right now."

It turns out the old warlord left a substantial stash of bric-a-brac in the family mansion. Some of the lesser pieces were returned to Qian Wei after the restoration of private property in the wake of the Cultural Revolution. To make ends meet, the doctor's been selling off this trove bit by bit in the antiques markets. He's down to the last few pieces by now, he claims.

He opens a desk drawer to reveal a couple of inkstones, some snuff bottles, and a jade cigarette holder. He buffs each item on his sleeve as he lays it out on the desk. He dotes on these gewgaws with a hint of the same curatorial avidity that he brings to the choice assortment of terminal cases assembled here in the hospice. Seems connoisseurship goes back for generations in his family. Would we be interested in any of these items?

"Whatever you can do to help . . ."

WE TAKE A PASS on his antiques, but promise to undertake for Xi-yuan such small, improving measures as we can. For one thing, we schedule regular visits for every Thursday afternoon. That way, the hospice inmates—those who survive the interlude—can count on a recurrent weekly benchmark. (Keiko, for her part, has committed to come on Mondays, so the patients have at least two visits a week to look forward to.)

Then, too, we undertake some modest building renovations. Flouting the Taiwan Gang's Great Foundling precedent, Keiko and Ah-loong solicit funds from the Taitais to buy a coat of paint for the wards and some fresh tiles for the communal shower-room. We hit up our friends for old discard furniture to create ad hoc sitting rooms in odd corners of the building so ambulatory patients won't have to languish all day in their beds.

As more newspapers and even a local TV station pick up on the hospice story, other volunteers get in on the act. On several visits there we run into posses of fresh-faced college students scrubbing the windows, sweeping the courtyard, or chatting with the patients. The Hacienda Hotel Group even offers to renovate one of the rooms as a VIP dying chamber. The result is a typically antiseptic five-star suite, complete with bland still-life wall art and flouncy floral curtains.

These little attentions add up over a few months. By Christmas, parts of Xi-yuan are starting to look downright respectable. A few fresh panes of glass, for instance, transform the passageway between the A and B wards from a bleak wind tunnel into a sunny dayroom. Sprawled on a mismatched assortment of throwaway furniture, an equally eclectic gaggle of Xi-yuan inmates gather there for an impromptu afternoon karaoke.

We stumble upon them when we visit the hospice with our youngest daughter, Melati. She's in her second week of winter break from Fang Cao Di People's Grade School and she's already bored enough around the house to seize upon even a visit to an old folks' home as a welcome diversion. Any qualms she might have had about the morbidity of the outing vanish as she wanders into the "day room" to find a florid fat man warbling a falsetto rendition of a Taiwanese torch song.

Perched on a hassock opposite the pudgy crooner, the silvery granny of room 10-A swings her bound feet in waltz time and smiles vacuously as ever. The music seems to soothe even the brain-dead simian giant that Ah-loong had seen tussling with his nurse over a spoon on her first Xi-yuan visit. His head lolls back and forth rhythmically on his neck while a mousy little man in green pajamas nods encouragement beside him.

At the freshly glazed window, a wispy albino peers through the frost-flowers on the glass. Although his back is turned to the group, he hums along with the music. His nasal monotone sounds sardonic, an effect underscored by his clever, pinkish eyes. A Muslim, evidently; his crocheted white hajj cap matches his blanched complexion.

The song ends—". . . and all I want is your looooove." The voice breaks, whether from the strain of the falsetto or an excess of bathos.

"Only love," the fat man sighs. "Is that so much to ask? They never visit anymore, my children. And all because I want to marry again."

The hajji at the window swivels around to fix him with an albino squint. "Quit complaining," he advises. "Look at me. I remarried last year, a young girl in her fifties. And what did it get me? A regular civil war at home. My new wife and my old skinflint of a son bicker over my property before I'm even dead. And *I* wind up stuck in *here* while they fight it out.

"Why talk about home or family? Once you're here, there's no place else for you. *This* is your home now." He traces a tight perimeter around his chair with the toe of his Chinese cloth shoe. "Welcome to my home, little miss," he salutes Melati. "Your turn to give us a song."

All eyes turn to her, which is pretty much her idea of group dynamics at its best. She rises to the occasion, primed by recent mega-doses of Christmas TV, and offers a sort of rumba version of "We Three Kings of Orient Are." Some in the group smile politely; most just stare, slack-jawed.

In hopes of getting a rise out of them, Melati switches over to more familiar ground. Without missing a syncopated beat, she rumbas right on into the best known of Chinese Communist anthems, "The East Is Red." No use; still no reaction. Mildly miffed, she gives up on the crowd, opting instead to strike up an individual conversation.

She pulls up a stool in front of the albino hajji and asks about the "olden days." He starts out with terse, straightforward answers. But soon the earnest, wide-eyed child brings out the Munchausen in him and his tales get more and more extravagant.

"Did you have ice cream in your time, Uncle?"

"Not the fancy kind on a stick. In winter we'd freeze mushy persimmons on the windowsill and then spoon them out for dessert."

"What about airplanes, Uncle?"

"Nah, just really big kites. We'd paint them with tigers to scare off Japanese bombers."

"And TV? Did you have TV?"

"Never heard of it. For entertainment, we'd sit up nights, charting production statistics and Great Leaps Forward. Or else we'd swap stories about model workers and soldiers."

His ironies are lost on Melati. This day-room history lesson strikes her as no less plausible than the heroic, strength-to-strength progress of New China that she's taught every day at the government grade school. We leave her in the solarium, since she's getting on so well with the hajji, and set off on our weekly round of the wards.

WE'VE BROUGHT our Oxonian a dish of narcissus bulbs, a customary gift at this time of year. Left on a windowsill at midwinter, the bulbs sprout blue-green shoots that grow nearly an inch per fortnight. By Chinese New Year, a couple of months later, they'll put forth star-shaped blossoms with white petals and fragrant yellow centers. The Oxford-educated lady in 12-A was nostalgic for these flowers—said they reminded her of Wordsworth's daffodils—so we picked up some bulbs for her at our corner market.

Halfway down the hall, though, we realize with a pang that our Oxonian must have already "graduated" from Xi-yuan. Instead of her modulated tones, there now issues from her door a nonstop din of contrapuntally anguished voices. We nervously peek in to see who's taken over room 12-A.

Lathered in a sweat of grief, a woman thrashes back and forth in her bed inconsolably sobbing "*Erh-ah, erh-ah*"—"My child, my child." Xiu-ying, the room nurse, has to wrestle her down, pinning her arms to the mattress to keep her from dashing her head against the bedrails. The room's other inmate needs no restraint; she's already paralyzed with rage. Her back arched against the wall in a rictus of hate, she glares across the aisle at the moaner and sputters imprecations in some dialect unknown to anyone else in the room. Spittle flecks her lips in a froth of indignation.

"What's she saying?" I ask Xiu-ying. "No clue," the fraught nurse gasps without loosening her grip. "It's been like this in here ever since the two of them moved in on Monday." I edge up to the bed. The moaner breaks stride just long enough to register my presence and realize it's not the one-and-only face she has eyes for. The nurse seizes upon the lull to pluck a battered Raggedy Ann doll from the foot of the bed and thrust it into the old lady's arms.

"She brought this from home," Xiu-ying explains. "It sometimes works." Not this time, though; the moaner simply resumes her pitch and yaw, wailing "*Erh-ah*" louder than ever.

Ah-loong, her flower bulbs still in hand, tries her luck on the other side of the room. But there, too, she draws a blank. She meets only narrowed eyes and an unbroken stream of incomprehensible invective. Everything about Xi-yuan affronts this patient—the moans, the bedpans, the well-wishing strangers. "Nothing you can do in *this* room," Xiu-ying advises us. "Better back off."

We retreat, defeated. The sheer loneliness of the hospice beats us down. All afternoon, scrambled signals have jammed every human connection we've attempted, from Melati's rumba to the hajji's "historical" malarkey. And now this pair in 12-A, each driven into unbroachable solitude by the other one's death throes. The endgame of life turns everyone autistic. More than ever we sense what odds Qian Wei faces and how frail is his ad hoc arsenal of techniques. You can only get so far by lying to the dying. We slouch dejectedly downstairs to the B block.

But on the ground-floor ward, we find we're not as alone as we feel. A solitary figure approaches from the far end of the hallway—just a wriggling black cipher against the sunlight that streams in from the courtyard windows. Where the full glare hits the linoleum and ricochets off the whitewashed walls, the silhouette seems suspended in space, as though emerging from a shimmering heat mirage. Only in the shadow between windowframes does the figure resolve into an earth-bound form clad in loose black pajamas. And even then, he maintains only the barest contact with the ground, just one cloth-shod foot rooted in place. His other limbs seem to poise effortlessly on mere sunbeams.

Ah-loong recognizes him as Zhou Da Yeh (Great-Uncle Zhou), one of her favorites at Xi-yuan. For him, at least, the Communist revolution has brought true "Liberation," though not perhaps as Chairman Mao might have planned. Over the course of many Thursday afternoon installments, he's filled her in on his serialized life story, which she's relayed to me at home (although I've never before met the man in person).

Orphaned by the great famine of 1942, he'd been dragooned as a teenager into a warlord legion in his native Shaanxi. When his unit defected to join Mao's Eighth Route Army, Zhou embarked on a decade of triumphant civil war soldiering. He marched from the steppes of Manchuria to the jungles of Yunnan to the boulevards of Shanghai.

After the Communist victory, as a reward for military service, he won a coveted urban job assignment instead of being sent back to his dirt-poor hometown. He joined a Beijing construction brigade that helped build the subway, the Great Hall of the People, and other showcase projects. He was well into his forties before his brigade finally allotted him housing of his own—a benchmark that changed his life in two respects: he got married and he got religion.

As soon as he landed his two-room apartment, he was able to wed (through the matchmaking service of his local street committee) a widow fifteen years his junior. She came ready-equipped with a young daughter. Both the women in his life are educated far beyond Zhou's own bare literacy. His wife teaches school and his stepdaughter is now a lab technician. He's proud of their successful careers, although they're so busy with their work they hardly ever have a chance to come see him in Xi-yuan—one reason why the old man so looks forward to Ah-loong's Thursday visits.

Zhou's government flat overlooked the shambling wreck of Bai Yun Guan, the White Cloud Temple, Beijing's main Taoist sanctuary. Grounded in the wry philosophical texts of a pair of quietist nature-worshipers, Taoism evolved over three thousand years into a hodge-podge of shamanism and folk cults. So its temples, right up through

the 1940s, boasted more life and color than those of the stately Confucians or the contemplative Buddhists.

Bai Yun Guan once supported thousands of black-robed, long-
haired Taoist monks. Specialist gods crammed every niche and chapel.
Fortune-tellers, herbalists, exorcists, and scribes lined every arcade.
But by the mid-1960s, when Zhou moved in next door, all this bustle
was gone. Most of the temple stood empty, its red lacquer faded, its
roof-tiles sagging, its gods neglected, its ponds choked with weeds.
Without city residence permits or ration tickets, monks had no choice
but to disperse to their ancestral villages. Denied licenses, mounte-
banks decamped.

Still, the derelict temple presented the largest open space in the
neighborhood, a respite from the encroaching gray apartment blocks.
So Zhou got in the habit of morning walks there. On one of them, in
an inner courtyard, he met the old Taoist who was to become his
master in *qi gong*, the art of marshaling and controlling the body's
life force.

As an Eighth Router, Zhou had been indoctrinated against all
forms of "superstition." But, as he told Ah-loong, "There was no
claptrap about my Bai Yun Guan master. Whatever he taught me was
down to earth: how to breathe, how to balance, how to feel—I mean
really *feel*—your own body and the ground under your feet."

Just a couple of years after Zhou moved into the neighborhood,
Red Guards destroyed what was left of Bai Yun Guan and hounded the
qi gong master out of Beijing. But by that time, Zhou had already absorbed enough Taoist technique to practice on his own. He still
haunted the shattered temple to tap into its incomparable *qi chang*, or
force field.

"No place like it for *qi gong* or meditation. I must take you there
when I get better," he keeps promising Ah-loong on every visit. She
hasn't the heart to tell him that while he's languished in Xi-yuan, Bai
Yun Guan has been "restored" by Beijing municipality into a more
raucous honky-tonk than ever. Not that Zhou's one to be flapped by
such changes, anyway. As Ah-loong describes him, his *qi gong* is self-
contained, untouched by external circumstance—an autism of an-

other, far more benevolent, sort than the crusted loneliness and mis-communication that's been oppressing us all day at the hospice.

This balanced homeostasis of his now guides Zhou's solitary shadow-boxing drill in the Xi-yuan corridor. He advances, oblivious to his surroundings, with reference only to his own center of gravity. His movements are so slow as to be almost imperceptible. No steps, as such—no pause between strides—yet he shifts from foot to foot, flu-idly adjusting his weight to maintain uninterrupted poise. His eyes follow his fingertips so intently that it isn't until he's practically in front of us that I can tell, from the dull glaze of his pupils, that this man is blind.

Even so, he somehow seems to sense the two of us here gaping, transfixed, in the middle of the corridor. With no visible change of course or pace, he manages to glide between us and the window, touching neither. Ah-loong opens her mouth as though to address him, then stops herself short as the opaque eyes sweep unhurriedly across us and the fingertips point on down the hall. Better not to encroach upon his concentration. Still, she's frustrated to miss out this time around on her usual meeting with Zhou, a regular weekly high point.

Clutching her narcissus bulbs in front of her, Ah-loong leads me down the corridor in Zhou's wake. The hallway seems all the emptier now minus the dense, deliberate figure that so powerfully filled this space only moments ago. The whitewash and linoleum sheen, the zebra patches of window light and shadow, the blank, shut doors all make the vista that much more disorienting. So, when Qian Wei appears from a side corridor with his typical White Rabbit bustle, Ah-loong is so startled she almost drops her bowl of flower bulbs.

The doctor, unfazed by the near-collision, steadies the bowl in her hands just in time to save it. "Who's *this* for, then?" he laughs. "For me?" Ah-loong admits she'd brought it for 12-A.

"Ah, her," he nods. "She 'checked out' over the weekend. *That'll* teach you to plan ahead. In a place like this, it may *look* like everyone sits all day with nothing but time on their hands. But in fact nobody can ever count on enough time to see a bulb sprout into a flower. The trick is to put things to use as and when they come up. Catch-as-catch-can. Never bet on the future here. Doesn't pay."

He hoists the bowl up to eye level and squints over the green little narcissus shoots as though aiming a rifle. "Let me have this, okay?" he proposes. "I might be able to turn it to good account. Come see." Still sighting across the flower bulbs, he advances warily down the corridor like a ranger on patrol. We hang behind him for cover. Without glancing back at us, he briefs us on his quarry:

"Old Mother Yang could be lurking anywhere. She gets around. I've trouble enough coaxing most patients out of bed, but *this* one just can't sit still. More nervous energy than she knows what to do with."

The old lady turned up at the hospice a couple of weeks ago from Manchuria, Qian Wei explains. She'd been a paramedic at a railroad hospital up there, at least until her work unit shut down last year. Devoutly Protestant. Widowed, with a stepchild in Japan who doesn't even know she's here.

"She read about us in the *Health Care Daily*," Qian Wei relates, "and bought a one-way train ticket from Shenyang. Arrived at our door with two changes of clothes, an enameled lunch pail, a hand-stitched Christian burial cloth, and the exact amount of cash for two months' ward fees."

That, he explains, was how long the doctors gave her to live when they diagnosed her with intestinal cancer. No use just lying around in the meantime, though, as far as Mother Yang is concerned. She still walks pretty well with her cane, despite arthritis. Refuses to wear a hospital gown. Nor will she eat hospital food—can't afford it, she claims. She'd rather stump across the highway, dodging truck traffic, to take a couple of steamer buns a day at the roadside stalls.

For Qian Wei she's a perplexing guest. "Pokes her nose into everything—the office, the laundry, the dispensary, other patients' rooms. Once she flushed a rumpled nurse and a kitchen boy out of a mop closet."

Still, intrusive though she may be, she *does* know all about hospital management—how to keep things clean, maintain medication schedules, prepare for emergencies. Full of useful suggestions and not shy about offering them. On the whole a real help to Qian Wei, although his staff doesn't have a lot of patience for her just popping up without warning wherever she likes.

"But *that's* not what she came here for. Sometimes I wonder how and when she'll ever get down to the real business at hand."

As he recounts Mother Yang's story, he's still probing along the hallway with the flower bulbs at eye level. Now and then he veers his gaze off into a side corridor, a closet, or a window, still sighting across the narcissus sprouts, hoping to draw a bead on his prey. He emerges at last, with the two of us in tow, into the tiny back courtyard where Xi-yuan's laundry hangs on serried clotheslines.

There, among the half-frozen bedsheets and nightshirts, he comes upon a stocky figure barely five feet high. A steel-gray pageboy bob frames her jut-jawed face. Big, mannish hands, arthritis-gnarled, gangle out of the sleeves of her black Mao tunic. Qian Wei strides right up to her and aims his narcissi point-blank at her chest.

"Bang! You're dead," he announces.

"Not quite yet, Doctor," Mother Yang calmly retorts. "Forty-four days to go."

"Then maybe you can spare some time to help me sprout these," Qian Wei suggests, offering her the narcissus bulbs. "Why don't you take them back to your room? They'll match that handsome blue-and-white shroud you've got draped over your armchair."

She receives the bowl from him at arms' length and peers into it as though taking stock of a spittoon. "*For all the glory of man is as the flowers of grass. The grass withereth, and the flowers thereof falleth away,*" she observes, dyspeptically.

"If you say so," Qian Wei allows equitably. "But who cares if flowers don't last forever? They're pretty when they bloom and they smell nice." He doesn't give her the opportunity to trump him with another biblical quotation but hastens to change the subject, blithely introducing us as "Mr. and Mrs. Kaye from America, charter members of the Xi-yuan Benevolent Association."

This is the first we've ever heard of any such body, but Mother Yang's clearly impressed. She brushes aside a damp nightshirt, the better to take us in through her glinting, rimless bifocals. Then she nods approvingly to Ah-loong: "It's very important, what you're doing."

"You mean the 'Benevolent Association'?"

"No, the marriage. Treat him well," she earnestly advises my wife, with an offhand wave of her cane in my general direction. "That's the best way to promote China's International Friendship." It seems this conversation may not be meant for my ears, so I do my best to withdraw behind a hanging bedsheet. I wonder what's coming next from Mother Yang—a geopolitical analysis or a round of connubial counseling? Neither, as it turns out; rather a recap of the old lady's own marital history.

Growing up a good Methodist girl in Mukden, the capital of the wartime puppet state of Manchukuo, she was lucky to find work as a nurse's aide in the Japanese railroad hospital. At least it was better than getting drafted into service as a "comfort woman" to entertain Emperor Hirohito's troops. Yet as it turned out, after the victorious Red Army marched in, she wound up comforting the Japanese after all.

The hospital's new Party secretary, a Henan farmboy-turned-soldier, called her in and gravely explained that the new leadership simply could not run the establishment without the help of Japanese expertise. The existing medics, all Japanese draftees, would have to be persuaded to stay on here even after their countrymen withdrew. Would she kindly volunteer to marry Kato Sensei, the head of Internal Medicine?

"The man was thirteen years my senior. Grim, unsmiling, and bristling with whiskers. Spoke no Chinese at all in the beginning. Not that it really mattered, since he didn't like to talk much in any language. Hardly the husband I'd have chosen.

"But what could I do? The Party and the country needed me. Besides, Kato was a good man, a serious man who lived for his work. He taught me a lot about how to handle patients. And, in the end, we got along. I let him have his way in everything." Her gaze shifts down to her gnarled hands folded on her cane. "Except I never could give him children."

Instead, they adopted one of the runtier half-Japanese war orphans abandoned in the pediatric ward. The boy had a heart murmur, allergies, and a slight club foot. Without home nurturing, he might not have survived. But before their adopted son could even reach his teens, Kato fell victim to overwork and died of a stroke. That left Mother Yang to raise the child alone during the Cultural Revolution.

The task was all the harder due to the stigma upon the household for its Japanese and Christian connections. So in the early 1970s, as Maoist fervor waned and Beijing-Tokyo relations normalized, both mother and son gladly seized upon the diplomatic thaw to "repatriate" the boy to Japan—a country that neither of them had ever seen before.

She hasn't laid eyes on her son since, and in the intervening years exchanged only a few cards. She didn't want to complicate his adjustment to Nagoya or his relations with Kato's sister, his sponsor. He sent some money a decade ago after he'd found work as an apprentice in a tire factory. But now he's married and Mother Yang has scrupulously avoided letting him know about her economic difficulties in the declining rust-belt of China's industrial northeast. Nor would she apprise him of her present illness.

"I never asked any of the Katos for anything," she declares with pride. "That shows them how civilized and self-reliant China is. It's hard, but that's our duty when we marry a foreigner. Isn't it?"

Ah-loong, who has never before considered her marriage from the standpoint of national face, prefers to shift the conversation over to Mother Yang's more recent duties. She effusively thanks the old lady for her wonderful support of Xi-yuan.

"They're a good work unit," Old Mother Yang replies, self-deprecatingly. "They fill an important need. If they weren't here, I wouldn't have known where to turn at this stage." Yes, but you've made yourself so helpful, Ah-loong persists, such a mainstay of the hospice.

"It's work," the old lady shrugs, "and I *need* work. *As long as it is day, we must do the work of Him who sent me. Night is coming, when no one can work,*' saith our Lord." Her voice drops from the ringing declamation of the pulpit to the ruminative murmur of the confessional. "I don't know how *not* to work. Back in Shenyang, I had nothing to do."

And down here so *much* to do, Ah-loong nods, so many friends . . .

"Ah, *that*, no," Old Mother Yang interrupts. "It would be plain silly, if you think about it. In a place like this, who has time for friendship?"

WELL, MAYBE NOT FRIENDSHIP, exactly, but the hospice *does* foster a rare degree of openness and trust. With little left to lose, inmates have no reason to hold back their opinions, emotions, or autobiographies. Reminiscence is the standard mode of discourse at Xi-yuan.

Just about anywhere else in China, a twinge of nervous circumspection—a reflexive over-the-shoulder glance—chills human relationships. It's not just self-preservation. For the sake of others, too, best not to burden anyone with needless confidences. The punch line of the turbulent past century in China: play it safe, for you never know how things may turn out.

After a while, these truncated contacts become so automatic that we hardly even notice them anymore, at least until we leave China for a breather. Flying out to India for our Chinese New Year break, it seems perfectly natural to run the hour-long gauntlet of exit formalities without once making eye contact with anyone. It's only upon stepping off the plane in Bombay that the contrast hits us as forcefully as a welcoming blast of cow-dung-scented humidity.

A cleanup crew of happily gabbing sweepers swarms up the gangway even as the passengers climb down. Our shuttle bus idles on the tarmac while the driver leans out the window to finish a voluble chat with his ground dispatcher. In the terminal, machine-gun-toting security guards smile and nod to us like strolling *mariachis*. Passengers back up to fill the cavernous entry hall as half the immigration counters are closed (it's two A.M.). Families run through sleepy head counts. Strangers, who may have sat taciturn right through their incoming flights, now strike up casual conversations in the long, shuffling lines. The immigration officer leafs page-by-page through my passport as though skimming a novella: "So how'd you like Burma? Mongolia, how?"

Even after we get through the gamut of baggage handlers, customs agents, redcaps, and cabbies, we still face a crush of shyly smiling airport urchins at curbside, demanding ballpoint pens and candies. No sign of our Bombay hosts, who were to have met us—some mix-up in dates. Never mind. We can share a cab into town with our newfound friends from the passport line, as long as we don't mind a sleeping infant across our laps. It all works out, somehow.

Things continue to work out, somehow, right through this reconnaissance trip to sort out details for our next year's posting to India. Through friends-of-friends-of-friends, we line up a home base to work from and the perfect school for our children. We reconnect with old cronies and seamlessly resume grandiloquent dialogues from a decade before. We gorge on *dahi poori* and catch up on the latest *drupad* tapes. We relish the richly detailed Indian panorama, unfolding like a Mughlai miniature painting: all jewel-clear hues, intricate textures, and sharp-etched faces.

China, by contrast, strikes us, upon our return, as a subtle, ink-brushed landscape scroll—all gray shadows and swirling mists and half-glimpsed silhouettes. To anchor the composition, we need some more substantial foreground figures. So, as soon as we can, we gravitate out to Xi-yuan, where we know that staff and inmates—perched as they are at the very edge of the void—all stand out in starker relief.

But on our first visit back to the hospice, nobody's in any position to sit still for fine-brushed portraiture. We're hardly through the front door when we're practically bowled over by Qian Wei as he comes shooting out from his office door like a fresh-sprung pinball. He spots us in passing, but he's too frantic to stop. "You're back," he notes. "Hello. Come *on*."

We fall in behind him at a jog, ricocheting through the corridors with no clue as to what sort of emergency we're dashing off to. A right turn heads us toward the Hacienda-refurbished VIP suite. But the carpeted, five-star calm is now shattered by a volley of abuse from the bedroom.

"Not *there*, you clod," roars a hoarse baritone inside. "How many times must I tell you? It goes *that* way. No, *this* way. Right *here*. Now the other side . . ."

Qian Wei briefs us sotto voce in the anteroom. "Commandant Kang here has 'Served the People' for many years in the area of penology. He's headed some of our most respected institutes of correctional education—a highly distinguished cadre from a very solvent work unit."

He nudges open the Formica-paneled door. The suite's solitary inmate, a neckless torpedo of a man, looks physically overbearing even in his present condition. A plastic splint stiffens the stroke-palsied fingers of his left hand. One leg, bolstered on pillows, aims skyward like a howitzer. Amid a mush of slack facial muscles, the left eye

bugs maniacally wide. The other orb beetles at Qian Wei from under
a clenched brow. In the isolation of the VIP suite the man practically buzzes with impotent frustration, like a horsefly trapped under
a bell jar.

"*Charge* her with something, *anything*, Director Qian," he orders.
"She's a slacker, a saboteur, a counterrevolutionary, a petty thief,
a bad element. No *end* of charges you could bring, Comrade. I'll offer
all the evidence you need. Charge her with something so I can
reform her."

The little nurse under discussion keeps fumbling with the array of
cranks and levers at the foot of the fancy, mechanical hospital bed.
She's been trying to fulfill the commandant's rapid-fire series of con-
tradictory orders about how to adjust his position. But Kang's last
outburst is the final straw. She bolts from the room in tears.

"*Catch* her! She's getting *away!*" the commandant shrills as though
sounding an alarm siren. Then he shouts after the hapless nurse,
"Don't think you can run off so easily. It takes more than a show of
tears to escape *me*." He turns to Qian Wei for reassurance. "She won't
go far, *will* she, Comrade Director?"

"I certainly hope not," the doctor murmurs worriedly as he stares
at the door the nurse just exited. Her footsteps still echo down the
corridor, the slap-slap of rubber sandals receding at a brisk trot. With
an effort, Qian Wei wrenches his attention back to the bedside and
tries to soothe the patient.

"Never mind, Comrade. We'll get you another nurse, a better one.
Maybe somebody a bit more experienced? Or perhaps a younger one?
More energetic, you know, and easier on the eyes . . ."

He's visibly nonplussed, casting about for some sort of pacifier to
quell this tantrum. It's the first time I've seen Qian Wei at a loss for a
placebo to offer. He scans the room for something to fling into the
breach. His eyes rove over the heaped floral tributes, the get-well
cards, the remains of a three-course lunch, the overflowing ashtray,
the medicine cart with its pricey painkillers and tranquilizers, the
bedpan, the walker, the TV. No inspiration in any of them. He glances
imploringly at us, but then quickly looks away. Clearly this is one case

where the old "foreign visitor" gambit won't work. In the end, he's reduced to staring disconsolately out the window onto the airshaft.

Whereupon the answer to Qian Wei's quandary comes stumping in on black sneakers, brandishing a cane. "What's all this? What *is* the matter here?" Old Mother Yang demands, barreling up to the bedside in high dudgeon and hooking her cane on the bed-rail. The runaway room nurse, still sniffling, now lurks in the doorway. The old lady tucks her chin into her chest like a prizefighter and stares down at the VIP patient over glinting spectacles.

"She makes the bed all wrong, Elder Sister," the commandant whines, pointing at the little nurse. "She props me up this way and that until I'm all tied in knots. She, she . . . steals my things. I can't find my cigarettes or my paper or my glasses. She spills food on me at mealtimes and rubs me the wrong way when she bathes me and . . ."

"Poor *dear*," Mother Yang lisps in mock sympathy. She reaches over the bed-rail—a stretch for one so short—to punch up the pillows briskly. "There," she snaps. "And *there*. Comfy now?" The commandant nods meekly.

"And here, by the way, are your cigarettes." She hands him a pack of Marlboros that had surfaced when she was smoothing the bedding. "Little Cai," she calls out to the doorway, "why don't you fetch him the newspaper and his spectacles from the nightstand, where he left them?"

The nurse retrieves the *Liberation Daily* and helps the commandant on with his reading glasses. "Cai's our best, you know," Old Yang informs him in a chattier, more confidential tone. "She's seasoned and attentive. That's why she's here instead of out on the wards. It's not her fault you need so much help. *Is* it, now?"

"No, Elder Sister," he admits, abashed.

"You're lucky to have her," she presses on. "I'll bet in your time you've seen some *real* helplessness. You know what happens—don't you?—to people left to rot on their own, completely forgotten, with nobody to care about them. You're a lot better off than that. You'll try to be more careful, now. Right?" He bows his head, defenseless under her onslaught.

"And you, too, Little Cai. Who should know better than you how to keep up with a patient? How can you let it come to this?" The nurse swabs the commandant's brow and neck with a washcloth, smoothes the newspaper on his lap, hands him a cigarette, and strikes a match for him. Kang, mollified, grunts and smokes.

"That's it, then," the old lady nods. "I'll be back to look in on you. And meanwhile," she adds, arching her brows, first to the commandant and then to the nurse, "you know where to find me, don't you?"

Then, turning to Qian Wei, Ah-loong, and me: "Shall we?" She waves her cane like a shepherd's crook and bundles the three of us out the door, down the hall, and into the hospital's front courtyard.

THE YARD'S BEEN GUSSIED UP with picnic tables—one of Keiko's many innovations over the last couple of months, Qian Wei informs us. Beer-ad-emblazoned umbrellas (donated by a Taiwan Gang husband in the beverage business) flutter in the fitful spring breeze, lending an incongruously festive air. Club Ded. Mother Yang pulls up a stool for herself and motions us to the plastic deck chairs. Only then do we get a chance to catch our breath and register the changes in her.

For one thing, she's swapped her Mao suit for a set of hospital pajamas—a transformation as telling as if she'd given up military fatigues for a monastic cassock. Against a backdrop of rumpled blue-and-white pinstripes, instead of the austere black tunic, the lines of her face and the set of her jaw seem softer. All the more so since her hair has grown, filling out the crisp-cut pageboy bob and highlighting how long she's already been here; well beyond her self-allotted two months.

We congratulate her on her undiminished vigor, but that just sets her sighing. "Ayah! As Job said: '*If only You would hide me in the grave and conceal me till Your anger has passed! If only You would set me an hour and then remember me!*' I'm on borrowed time, here. And borrowed money."

"Let's not start on *that* again," Qian Wei admonishes. "You know you're on staff now. No borrowing involved. This is your work unit. We need you, and we'll care for you for as long as you can stay here."

Sounds like a pretty fair deal to us. We inquire after the details of Mother Yang's new job. "Public relations," she grandly styles it; hearing complaints, mediating disputes, keeping an eye on staff, guiding visitors, distributing donated books and magazines and holiday treats.

In any normal neighborhood of urban China, tasks like these would be discharged by the little old grannies of the Party's street committee. As outsiders from the liberal West, we'd always dismissed these busybodies as petty curbside spies. They *are* every bit of that, but also much more, we've gradually come to realize.

They're professional neighbors, collective responsibility incarnate, their brothers' ineluctable keepers. At least that's the ideal. They observe and facilitate grassroots life at eye level, rather than from on high. In the Xi-yuan context, Mother Yang's switch to hospital clothes signals her new status as a career patient who is occupied full-time with the business of dying, her own and everybody else's.

"Before, when I'd given myself a two-month time limit, it set me apart," she explains. "I was too wrapped up in myself to notice that everybody else around here was in the same position. To my mind, I was special, a big shot, with an important appointment—my own death—writ large on my calendar."

That way, she could continue to play her lifelong role of the Good Soldier marching to orders from above. "Nobody could fault me," she explains, "as long as I was just doing my duty on somebody else's behalf instead of my own—for my parents, my emperor, my revolution, my work unit, my husband, my son, my in-laws, my Church."

Conveniently enough, in her time there's been no shortage of calls to duty—so much so that self-abnegation now passes for the cardinal Asian value. "Looking back on it, even my Jesus seems a bit dictatorial, with 'thought problems' of His own," Mother Yang confides. "*'No man cometh to the Father but by Me.'* As far as I could tell, that simply meant as long as I'd stitched a cross onto my shroud, *He'd* take care of everything and I could die easy without having to worry much about it myself."

She became a master at the paradoxical knack of drawing her self-importance from her self-denial. "You know," she recalls, dreamily, "in all my seventy years, I've only once been in a restaurant. I mean a *real* restaurant, with napkins and menus, not just some roadside noodle stall. It was after I'd helped deliver a baby at the hospital. The family took us out for dinner. We ordered Squirrel Fried Fish. Best meal I ever had. But would I ever just go into a restaurant and order myself a Squirrel Fried Fish? Impossible. Too indulgent. Not dutiful enough for me."

It took Xi-yuan finally to demobilize the Good Soldier in her. Chinese New Year came and went and still she's alive, still herself. And at last it dawns on her that dying is not a dischargeable duty, not something to *do*. It's just part of who we *are* all along, inseparable from the rest of life; a condition, not an event.

"Why go on denying your*self*, then, when there's no way to deny your death? And that lets me put on the same pajamas as all the rest and really work *with* others for the first time, instead of just *for* them. For we're all in the same condition, you know. *You're* dying just as much as I am. Even the doctor, here, is dying . . ."

"A million deaths, every day," Qian Wei laughs, a little nervously. "And I guess I'd better get on with them," he adds, then cocks a glance in our direction. "Coming along?"

Mother Yang waves us on our way, but stays put on her stool, luxuriating in the spring sunshine. It's too early yet for buds on the plane trees. But she cranes forward, chin almost touching the pommel of her cane, to observe the commotion of sparrows bathing themselves in the warm courtyard dust.

WE FOLLOW QIAN WEI THROUGH the front door and back to his newly spiffed-up office. He's now decked out his room with all sorts of Buddhist paraphernalia. Rotogravured Bodhisatvas peer down from his walls. A plaster cast of an austere Sung dynasty Sakyamuni sits cross-legged atop his file cabinet, lightly dusted with incense ash. Tz'u-chi pamphlets in ornate Taiwan-style characters litter his desktop. A corner of a saffron shroud, blazoned with sutras, peeps out of his desk drawer.

We tease him about the new decor and he admits that Keiko had a hand in it. Most of the Buddhist trappings she either hung here herself or gave to patients who then donated them to the hospice upon "checkout."

Under Keiko's aegis, a subset of the Taiwan Gang has launched a weekly Tz'u-chi support group. The members take turns visiting the hospice. They discreetly fund things like Mother Yang's upkeep, which (unbeknown to the old lady herself) allows Qian Wei to maintain the face-saving fiction of her staff job at Xi-yuan. Putting up with a bit of religious kitsch seems a small price to pay for the support of such patrons.

"And besides, this Buddhist stuff kind of grows on you," Qian Wei admits, with a reflective drag on his cigarette. "Maybe the Buddha was something of a barefoot doctor, himself. At least he seems to have grasped how everything changes when considered in the light of sickness, old age, and death. And there's no length to which he wouldn't go in the name of compassion. Very creative that way."

So, I ask, do you now train your staff in Buddhist doctrine? The sheer notion of preaching sutras to that motley gaggle of teenage yokels amuses him. "We can't all be Bodhisatvas," he laughs. "I'm doing well if I can just get them to wash their hands before feeding patients. All they can think about, most of them, is what they can filch from the closets or how to steer each other into bed."

By day, at least, the nursing supervisors are there to keep an eye on them. But at night, Qian Wei is left all alone in the hospice with three dozen hormonally frothy employees to proctor. "They fall into and out of love affairs with amazing speed, and I lose a lot of staff in the process. One of these nurses once even accused *me* of trying to get fresh with her," he adds, scandalized. "And all I'd done was to go up one night and shut her window screen on account of the mosquitoes."

Personnel issues take up more and more of his time, he sighs. Staff turnover is a constant problem. It gets harder by the month to find, hire, and keep people to do this kind of unprepossessing work for the low wage that Xi-yuan can afford. In the beginning he could count on local high school dropouts. But nowadays, you just can't *get* a Beijinger to carry a bedpan. Qian Wei has to recruit among the migrant workers that flood the city. And they seem to come from farther and farther afield all the time: the scrub hills of Anhui, the steamy jungles of Guangxi, the Ningxia badlands. Xi-yuan's become a Babel of regional dialects. Half his staffers can't even understand each other anymore.

But at least, Qian Wei beams, he himself now has someone at hand round-the-clock to understand him and cheer him on. He punches a three-digit intercom number into his desk phone and coos into the receiver, "Are you okay? There's someone here I'd like you to meet. We'll be right over." Smugly savoring the suspense he's built up, he leads us across the back courtyard to a two-room suite he's carved out in Xi-yuan's utility shed, adjacent to the laundry room. "My home, at least for the present," he proudly announces. "My wife and my boy."

Even framed in the dust-caked screen door of Xi-yuan's back shed, Madame Qian seems somehow on-camera, projecting an image of ice-queen allure. Her lacquered hair offsets a flat moonface and fragile features. A faint blush of rouge highlights the eggshell-white complexion so prized in traditional Chinese ideals of femininity. As we enter the suite, she presents her best profile—the side with the dimple—and welcomes us in the stilted warble of a film celebrity. Only the motile, coal-black eyes belie her preternatural composure.

Yet classic as her image may be, it's not a face we recognize from our four-year exposure to Chinese mass media. Evidently, her hopes of screen fame remain unfulfilled. Yet with looks like hers, how could she be expected to bury herself in this mortuary with Qian Wei? Who could have guessed that, of the two of them, he'd be the one to wind up with all the print and broadcast exposure, while her own career would languish?

But now she's back from Tianjin, and here to stay, Qian Wei gushes. And already she's making herself indispensable. He's placed her in charge of Xi-yuan's accounts and government liaison work. I'll bet she's a star in both roles, too. Those darting eyes don't look as though they'd miss much in a ledger. And her charm could beguile even the sourpuss inspectors of the Health, Labor, and Pricing boards.

Hard to conceive of such a cool customer as anyone's mother, but traces of a child are all over the suite. Light filters through colored-paper stickers of pandas and parakeets on the windows. A pint-sized People's Liberation Army cap hangs on a bedpost, beside a yellow plastic water gun and a rubble of strewn toy trucks. Wobbly first efforts at calligraphy flutter on the walls, interspersed with bold watercolors of multihued sunbursts and lollypop trees. Not content with these efforts, the budding artist has crayoned great loops and whorls directly onto the plaster around the doorjamb.

A white puppy careens in from the next room with a toddler in hot pursuit. The two zigzag through the jumbled, overcrowded furniture—under the table, across the bed, rebounding off the dresser. But when the beribboned mutt darts out the screen door into the courtyard, the child hauls up short in front of Qian Wei and hugs his father around the knees. The doctor cups the little cheeks in both hands and introduces us. "Qian Chuan-yi, say hello to our guests."

The boy buries his face in Qian Wei's lap and dutifully parrots, "Hello, Auntie. Hello Uncle," in a muffled little voice. But he doesn't stay shy for long. He's soon at my side, tugging experimentally at my sleeve and fingers. I crouch down to offer him a better look at my mustache, his principle object of interest at the moment. I ask him about one of his watercolor efforts, a boxy truck coasting down a steep slope with a tiny stick figure on the roof.

He laughs at the stream of misinflected Chinese pouring out of such a grotesquely foreign face—even funnier, no doubt, than the dubbed edition of *Sesame Street*. But he answers me readily enough: "Oh, that's the car I go to school in every day." I look closer and note the red cross, the black-and-yellow bunting: it's Xi-yuan's hearse-cum-ambulance, ferrying a solitary child into some unseen abyss.

"Doesn't he get lonely, the only child in a place like this?" Ahloong asks Qian Wei sotto voce, thinking back on her own solitary girlhood in the Buddhist convent.

"Oh, he's the darling of the wards," Qian Wei assures us brightly, not bothering to whisper. "He's got fifty doting grannies to spoil him."

"But wouldn't that only make it all the harder?" I protest. "What about all the . . . ah . . . checking-in and checking-out?"

"You mean the sickness and the dying?" Qian Wei asks, brushing aside my euphemisms. "But that's the whole point of raising him here. Chuan-yi may already be more at ease with these facts than you or I. He's learning how to take death personally, to let it get under his skin."

That doesn't sound to me like child's play, but the boy looks none the worse for the experience. Bored with our adult talk, he's already out the door, chasing his puppy between the coal piles. Still, Ah-loong's unconvinced. We're talking about a four-year-old here, she reminds Qian Wei (pleading as much for herself, forty-five years ago in the Buddhist nunnery, as she is for little Chuan-yi here in the hospice). What could possibly be the mental-health benefits of confronting your own mortality at that age?

"Same as at any age," the doctor replies, a little taken aback by Ah-loong's intensity. "It reminds you that you're finite and imperfect."

Of course, nobody would claim otherwise if directly asked, he admits. But how many, in their deepest hearts, truly realize their own limits?

"Because once you grasp that," he admonishes, "then everything changes. You've got to pay constant attention, trim up your life, be ready to draw a line under your accounts from one minute to the next. You can't let things slide. Whatever needs doing, you've got to get down to it now, while you can. You're always engaged in the world, though never attached to it."

He delivers this litany slowly, pausing between versicles to test his words. It seems neither a rehearsed rap nor one of his manic, heedless extemporizations. He speaks quietly, for once, as though to himself, and sounds almost surprised at what he hears himself saying. Has he pitched his ventriloquism to a whole new artistic plane? Or are we hearing for the first time his own true voice, not modulated for effect?

PRESENTLY HE CATCHES HIMSELF and switches over to a brisker, newsier voice as he briefs us for our evening round of the wards. On the way across the courtyard, Qian Wei warns us whom *not* to expect. The albino hajji has told his last tall tale. Bao Gong's aficionado has gone to face a sterner Magistrate. My dear friend the missionary-educated doctor at last relinquished his wheelchair and lay down to sleep. The brain-dead simian's still here, but he's lost his mousy sidekick. An attack of ischemia rang down the curtain on Comrade Qiao's last bow.

So we meet new faces in practically every room. But from patient after patient we get the same reception: as soon as they figure out Ah-loong's Taiwan connection, they start soliciting her for Buddhist trinkets. Keiko and her group have already left their mark. Rosaries dangle from the bed-rails. End tables sport plastic laminated icons, microfiche sutras, tin vials full of Ganges River sand. Inmates, whether avid for status within the hospice or in the hereafter, vie with each other collecting such treasures. One man pleads for Ah-loong to bring him a vial of sand "because somebody swiped the one I used to have."

After so many encounters with acquisitive strangers, it's a relief to come upon a pair of familiar figures: the moaner of 12-A and her testy roommate. This time, at least, the scene here is a lot quieter. Xiuying, the room nurse, crochets in a corner. Instead of sputtering invective, the hellcat roommate stares, glassy-eyed, at the ceiling, her jaws visibly clenched as she grinds away at her molars. The moaner snores, propped on pillows, cradling her Raggedy Ann.

A thirty-ish woman perches on a stool at the bedside, her back turned to the door as we enter—the old lady's daughter, Qian Wei informs us. This, presumably, is the child she was moaning for the last time we saw her. The taffeta blouse, pinstriped skirt, and telephone pager brand the daughter as an up-and-coming executive type, perhaps with one of the multinational branch offices in Beijing.

Just now, though, she's fumbling her way through the unbusinesslike task of mixing powdered milk with hot water in an enamel mug. When she's achieved the right temperature and consistency, she tries to spoon the mixture into her mother's open, snoring mouth. It's a moment of poignant role reversal between two women who, in a lifetime together, will have each nursed the other in turn. "Ma . . . ," the daughter ventures softly, dribbling one spoonful down her mother's chin. "Try to eat now, Ma . . ."

At that point, the pager trills and the old lady stirs convulsively. She spits up the milk that's already been poured down her, then goes on snorting and gagging more and more violently. After a couple of dry heaves, she starts bringing up bile—burbling at first and then spewing until her shirtfront is soaked and her quivering ribs show through the hospital gown.

The room nurse springs to her bedside, dabbing her face with towels and catching what she can of the black liquid in any container that comes to hand. She fills up a bedpan and then a plastic washbasin, and still the flood keeps coming, now tinged with red.

The paroxysm stretches out nightmarishly. The eyes open wide, but unseeing. How can a form so depleted dredge up so much? She's turning herself inside out; it can't go on much longer, yet it just won't stop. The roommate starts muttering fervently, whether prayers or curses there's no way to tell. What to do? Qian Wei, Ah-loong, and I scramble about, hunting up more towels and basins for the nurse.

But when we turn back to the bedside, we find the way blocked by the daughter. She's thrown herself on the bed-rail, beating her chest with a fist and clenching her brows so hard she squeezes tears from the corners of her eyes. "Ma, don't leave me," she sobs. "You *can't* go away, Ma . . ."

The grief is so pat that it momentarily freezes the frantic action in the room. The four of us stand gaping with our towels and buckets in hand. The roommate's grumbling grinds to a halt. Even the convulsed patient gags silently for a moment between heaves.

I've *seen* this tableau before; it's a cliché, I catch myself thinking (ashamed, at the same time, of my gratuitous cynicism). In the months that the old lady's been here, has the daughter mentally rehearsed this deathbed scene to cinematic perfection? The lines, gestures, and inflections all fit the mold of a classic filial-piety soap opera. Medium shot of kneeling child; over-the-shoulder pan of mother's death throes; zoom in on daughter's anguished profile; music up and under.

Except in Xi-yuan, there's no cameraman to cut to the next scene, so the daughter goes right on howling louder and louder. Finally Qian Wei has to haul her to her feet and spin her around. He grabs her by the shoulders and shakes her sharply twice before she halts in midwail.

"Look," he chides, "your mother's going through a rough passage. Things are happening fast. She needs calm, so she can keep her wits about her."

His tone is steady and conversational, but urgent. He clutches the young woman by the elbow and steers her across the room, talking nonstop to preempt any further outbursts. "Imagine your mother was running over stony ground in the dark. You wouldn't shout at her then, or do anything to distract or scare her, would you? You'd . . ."

By now, he's maneuvered her out the door. We hear his muffled voice in the corridor, interspersed with numb "uh-huhs" from the junior executive and occasional trills from the beeper. I feel wretched about the way the daughter's been sidelined. Where do we get off, dismissing her grief as gauche or inconvenient? Yet as soon as she's gone, the crisis ebbs.

Ah-loong clutches the dying woman's hand to steady her. Raggedy Ann, flung to a corner at the onset of the seizure, lies on the floor in a bile-sodden heap. I resume swabbing the old lady's chin and throat—without much effect, since my towel is already drenched. Xiu-ying dashes out in search of a mop and new linens. Gradually, the gagging and the bilious flood subside. As the commotion recedes, we first register the background whir of the roommate griping vehemently away in her bed.

The nurse comes back within minutes. We help her sponge down and towel-dry the patient, replace the soggy sheets, and change the hospital gown. Even so, tension hangs in the air. The old lady's eyes still gape in unfocused horror. Her breath comes in spasmodic gasps and her limbs are so stiff it's hard to dress her. She responds to neither word nor touch. The roommate hisses on, unabated, behind us.

At a loss for what else to try, Ah-loong takes up the *Namu Amituo-fuo* refrain we'd heard on our first visit to the Chamber of Great Peace last year. She starts it softly, like a cradle song to lull a troubled child. Slowly she builds up timbre. I add my voice, and soon Xiu-ying joins in. Somehow, this stopgap seems to work. As we gain momentum, the exhausted figure subsides into her pillows. The breath steadies, the eyes close, the features relax, and she sleeps. Even the roommate pipes down.

After such a storm, the sudden calm is unnerving. I think back on the mortuary where I last saw my father nearly a year ago. He'd been an invalid for twenty years in the aftermath of a stroke, but it was phlebitis that finished him in the end. Its final onset came so fast that he died while I was still in the air en route back to America, in response to my sister's summons. The long flight from China gave me time enough to conjure up half a dozen alternative scenarios—tense medical vigil, tender farewell, grim siege, miraculous remission, violent agony, radiant transfiguration.

The one thing I was *not* prepared for was the fait accompli of his death. But there he lay, already cold in this vapid, teal-carpeted mortuary room with somber Muzak seeping from the wall speakers. My sister waited outside while I stumbled in, jet-lagged, for my last moment with my father. No coffin; he'd chosen cremation. So he waited, draped in a sheet on a gurney as if ready to be wheeled off for yet one more medical procedure in the long series he'd endured.

I didn't know how to react, where to stand, what to do with my hands. They'd taken out his dentures, so he looked gaunt and drawn. His jaw hung slightly open. He was overdue for a haircut, I noted automatically. Gray strands spread out on the pillow behind him. He'd have hated that, if he'd had any say. He'd been a dapper, finicky, fidgety man—all the more unnatural, his present stillness.

And yet the slack jowls, the streaming hair, the cotton-swaddled torpedo shape of the body all combined to convey a feeling of frozen velocity, like a supine luge racer poised momentarily at the top of his last and wildest plunge. I took my place behind the gurney and bent over to press my forehead against his.

The chill of that touch caught me up short, as burningly cold as a winter windowpane with a blizzard raging just the other side of the glass. That shock was the hook I needed to catch the grief I'd been fishing for ever since I'd entered the mortuary.

Alone with the corpse, I yanked up wave after wave of great, wrenching, indecorous sobs from someplace so deep my knees went weak. It must have been fully half an hour before I managed to wobble back out of the funeral parlor. My head felt all swollen as though from a bout of grippe, but I'd reached the catharsis I sought and bonded with my father one last time.

And now I glean from Qian Wei that I'd been no more than a noisy heckler on the sidelines as my father struggled to surf the shoals of his own mortality. So here I stand, barely a year later, solemnly intoning alien prayers to damp down the turbulence of some stranger's passage. I mentally divert a few *Namu Amituofuo*'s my father's way, chastened.

Hearing our chant, Qian Wei nudges open the hall door. At first the daughter hangs back, but when she sees the nurse checking the pulse she ventures closer to the bedside. She seems a little surprised to find her mother calmly sleeping again. She opens an end-table drawer and pulls out a shopping bag. "You know, Doctor, I brought along her long life vestment," the Chinese euphemism for traditional grave clothes: a blue silk, ankle-length robe. "Should we start getting her ready . . . ?"

WRUNG OUT AS we are after the scene in 12-A, Ah-loong still can't leave the hospice without a call on Zhou Da Yeh. He somehow recognizes her before she's even in the room, although she's barely uttered a word or two on our way down the hall. "*Gu niang*"—my girl-child— "you've returned!" he sings out from his bed. "How long has it been? I'd thought I'd never see you again!"

Ah-loong practically skips to the bedside, propelled by a daughterly combination of delight at the warm reception and guilt for her long absence. The old man has draped his black pajama top over his bare back, although the early spring weather retains more than a hint of winter chill. She lays a hand on his shoulder (thinner, she notes), and laughs, "Uncle Zhou, how did you know it was me?"

"Third eye," he pronounces with an owlish nod, solemnly winking one of the other two.

"Then maybe you can see who's here with me?" she teases. "Meet my husband."

He pans across the room with blank cataracts and waves tentatively in front of him. I sit down on the bed and take the proffered hand.

"Long have I aspired to meet you," I pronounce in a stock two-syllable phrase of Chinese politesse.

"Ayah!" he beams as though at a particularly rich joke. "You never told me your old man was an Outland Comrade," adding the honorific to soften the dismissive Chinese expression for a foreigner. Was it my bad accent, my stilted diction, or my smell that gave me away? But before I have a chance to ask, Zhou starts squirming on the bed. It's not with sheer pleasure at encountering us, as I self-flatteringly suppose at first. As soon as he shrugs off the pajama top, we see the angry red rash that's set his skin on fire even in this raw mid-March air.

"Hai-yai," he cries. "They're swallowing me whole!" His hands claw the sheets in reflexive scratching motions, but he restrains himself from tearing at his own flesh. Instead, he pleads, "Bring me that stuff on the table there, would you?"

Ah-loong finds a tube of mentholated itch cream and starts smearing it on his back. She passes it to me so I can work on the other shoulder. Old Zhou can only rock gingerly back and forth in bed, sucking his few stumpy remaining teeth in anguish and self-pity.

"Poor Uncle," Ah-loong clucks. "What's got into you?"

"Spring," he tartly replies. "Life stirs anew. Cooties on the march all over this hospital." I offer Ah-loong my handkerchief to wipe off her ointment-slicked fingers.

Zhou's writhing subsides enough for him to remember his obligations as a host. "Have a cookie," he grandly offers. "They're in the top drawer of the table. You'll find the key under the thermos. My daughter, my other *gu niang*, brought them on her last visit," he proudly confides as Ah-loong fumbles with the lock to liberate a cellophane sack half-full of sandwich cremes.

The chalky biscuits taste as if they've been there for at least a month, but we munch them dutifully in honor of their importance to him. Ah-loong passes the sack to Zhou, but he declines, preferring to husband his hoard. We reverently scoop the crumbs back into the bag.

"So when do we go to Bai Yun Guan, Uncle?" Ah-loong gaily inquires.

"Ayah, it's no use, *gu niang*," he sighs. "I can't make it. Don't walk too well anymore. But I can still tap into the *qi chang*, you know," he adds brightly, "without even leaving this room."

He rolls upright, back straight, legs folded under him, palms spread open on his knees. No need to close his eyes as the cataract-frosted lenses turn his gaze inward anyway. Spring sunlight fills his lap and glistens on his ointment-lathered chest. He manages two deep breaths before the rash renews its attack. "Aiee-yoh," he whimpers, wriggling against the bedclothes.

"TAKE YOUR MORTALITY personally," Qian Wei had preached. "Let it get under your skin." It's one thing to consider these notions abstractly; quite another to live by them literally, we discover. Within a few days of our visit to Xi-yuan, we come down with Zhou Da Yeh's rash—a merciless, unremitting, subcutaneous reminder of our own bodily corruptibility.

It starts in the webbing between the fingers. In a matter of hours, it's racing up the arms like the frantic red spiral of a barber pole. It luxuriates in the armpits for a day or two, then lashes across the back and chest to find a congenial home in our most intimate clefts and nooks. Within a week, it's spread all the way down to the backs of our knees and our ankles.

The rash spares no cranny and gives no respite. In the midst of a press briefing, I find myself grinding my shoulder blades against the

chair back. Soaking in the bath, I burst flailing out of the tub to attack my hide with a loofah. Snoring abed, I snap awake to discover the
taint invading my navel. Scratching only renews the itch. We feel like
suppurating corpses already, on fire before we're even cremated,
worm-eaten before we're even buried.

Dr. Guan comes around for our weekly massage, takes one look at
the red-and-white tracery between our fingers and refuses to touch us.
We've got scabies, she informs us—infinitesimal, chiggerlike skin par-
asites. They're common in Chinese hospitals, lurking in the bedding
all winter, ready to attack patients and staffers alike come spring. You
can prevent them by boiling the sheets, avoiding contact with carri-
ers, and scrubbing yourself obsessively with disinfectant soap. Too
late for any of that now. At this stage our only answer is to poison the
invaders. She writes us a prescription for a sulfur-impregnated oint-
ment to be larded liberally onto the affected areas.

We buy this brimstone-reeking concoction and follow her directions, but our chemical warfare shows little visible effect. After their
initial onrush, the red welts mobilize into platoons, squadrons, and
brigades. They're ubiquitous, yet intensely local and always on the
move, like Mao's guerrilla armies. And they only grow more aggres-
sive as the weather warms up. Ah-loong and I pore grimly over each
other's bodies, smearing on the salve and tracing each new foray of the
rash as though trying to puzzle out some cryptically menacing campaign map.

After a while, though, the tide of war turns our way. We carpet-
bomb the enemy with megadoses of fetid petroleum jelly. The
red pustules grudgingly retreat to a few last-ditch guerrilla redoubts
in the thickets of groin and armpit. We press on toward a showdown, troweling on the sulfurous gunk so thickly that we exude a perpetual reek of hellfire wherever we go. Friends avoid us like Beelzebub
incarnate.

With the onset of summer, our signature stink gets gamier than
ever. The besieged scabies mount their final, desperate suicide attacks,
keening and howling in their death agonies. We itch all the more vehe-

mently, but never mind; we exult in the hecatomb of their mass-asphyxiation. At last, a glimmer of light at the end of this tunnel.

AS PART OF our final leave-taking from China we drive out for one last visit to Xi-yuan. No ceremonial farewells, we resolve. One lesson we've learned from the hospice is how to take departures in stride—including our own. Only Qian Wei and Mother Yang know that we're getting ready to shift. To the rest of the inmates, we don't even mention that we're moving out of the country. Why upset them pointlessly?

We need not have worried, as it turns out. The day of our Last Tango at Xi-yuan, nobody has time to care whether we're around or not. When we get to the director's office, the place is abuzz with excitement about a new arrival—a nameless baby who's just been abandoned in the hospital. Half the patients, at least the ambulatory ones, are hanging around the office, craning for a glimpse of the child where he sits enthroned on the Naugahyde couch. Nurses bustle in and out on gratuitous pretexts, just for a chance to coo at the impassive infant.

The baby came this morning in the arms of a nondescript middle-aged lady who'd ostensibly dropped by to ask about interning her elderly father. Before filling out the paperwork, the woman excused herself to use the bathroom. That's the last anyone at the hospice ever saw of her. She left the baby propped on the couch and there he sits still, placidly alert, three hours later.

"I don't know what to make of it," Qian Wei shakes his head. Madame Qian, in her government-liaison function, calls the police. But the beat cop who turns up sees scant hope of ever tracing back the origin of this child.

In the cities, where the one-child policy is strictly enforced, so heavy are the penalties for extra offspring that only the richest urbanites can afford the fines for outsized families. The rest have every incentive to jettison any inconvenient progeny wherever they can get away with it. Daughters are doubly disposable since they can't carry on the family name, the core duty of filial piety. "We get a half-dozen cases like this a day just here in West Beijing alone," the policeman says. "Mostly girls."

This one's plainly an exception to *that* rule. He sits foursquare on the couch, his male identity proudly displayed through the split cotton shorts that Chinese tots wear in lieu of diapers. "You'd expect him to at least cry, or pee, or *something*," Qian Wei frets. "Isn't that what's normal for a baby his age?"

Just what *is* his age seems far from obvious. We're already well into Beijing's muggy summer, so the child wears only shorts. Well-nourished and scrubbed, round and buttery, he actually looks like a pretty solid beach ball of an infant. From his size alone, you'd guess he was a year old or more, the very picture of a bouncing baby boy.

Except he *doesn't* bounce—or babble, or whine, or smile, or wiggle, or do any of the things you'd expect of a robust pre-toddler. He can't even sit upright for long without a pillow to prop him. He only stares at us gravely with limpid eyes as black and deep as millponds. The perfectly round head, with just a light down of hair, accents the sheer size of those steady eyes.

"Why would anyone abandon such a sturdy, healthy-looking child?" Qian Wei wonders. "And a boy, to boot. What could be wrong? Do you think he's half-witted? Or a deaf-mute?"

Madame Qian sings a few bars of Canto-pop at the baby. No reaction. I flutter a hand over his face. The eyes follow my gesture without a flinch. Ah-loong ventures a tentative tickle. The child doesn't laugh or squirm, but tracks her fingers intently as they ripple across his belly. His gaze, though, has none of the listlessness of idiocy nor the bridling recoil of autism. The calm, dark eyes absorb all the attention showered upon them.

Qian Wei has every reason to worry. A patient like this poses an open-ended lifelong drain on Xi-yuan. But the baby's so disarming that he seems a blessing rather than a curse. "Nothing else for it," the director sighs. "We're a 'facing-the-end hospital,' after all," he says, spelling out the full Chinese term for a hospice, *ling-zong yi-yuan*. "And who *isn't* 'facing the end,' when you come down to it." He gathers the baby up to his chest. "Come along, my little man."

The child shows no resistance to the unfamiliar embrace. He rides in the doctor's arms with the unaffected grace of a born-to-be-served prince, as though this lofty perch were his accustomed way of getting around in the world. He splays one pudgy hand upon the white lab coat and raises the other just slightly for balance. He sits erect, back straight and head held high so that the enormous eyes ride on a level with Qian Wei's.

We fall in behind the director. So do Madame Qian and a couple of nurses. Our group shapes up into a reverent flock, like some Catholic processional with the icon of the Blessed Infant held aloft in front. As we step out of the office, the baby calmly scans the hallway, left and right. The crowd parts before him, as though on cue.

A few biddies can't restrain themselves from offering grandmotherly advice: "Support his head." "Get him a blanket." "Feed him something." Most of the patients, though, just beam at the new young presence among them. One old man reaches out with trembling hands as though to caress the dimpled baby shoulders but then falls back to rejoin the hushed crowd. Our little processional mounts unhurriedly to the ward.

We head for 14-A, where the cancer-wracked stripling sits alone again in the green shade of drawn curtains, having outlasted a catalogue of roommates. Qian Wei explains to him the new arrival while we install the child in the vacant bed, propping him between pillows. In all of Xi-yuan, only this wasted youth can muster a gaze almost as wide-eyed and steady as the baby's. We leave the two of them to commune, silent and unblinking as a pair of groupers in the seabed gloom.

THE YOUNG CANCER PATIENT IS one of the few Xi-yuan inmates we recognize anymore. The brain-dead simian's still there, and so is the scrubbed granny with the "golden lotuses." Old Uncle Zhou has already merged his life force back into the greater *qi chang*.

Unfamiliar faces fill the rest of the rooms; men in sweat-soaked singlets, women fluttering palmetto fans against the enervating August heat. We've brought a sack of peaches to pass around. Scanning the walls and bedsteads, it looks as if Keiko's Buddhist gewgaws are making still further inroads. So are the scabies, judging from the ubiquitous welts. We finish up our rounds in 12-A. No trace of the moaner or her Raggedy Ann doll. The new inmate there is an enormous whale of a woman so overcome with the heat that she can only loll naked and gasping on the bed—a spectacle that stuns even her spitfire roommate into silence.

We scrub obsessively with disinfectant anti-scabies soap before presenting ourselves at Qian Wei's office to set out on our lunch date. He's upgraded the decor, we note: the plaster Sakyamuni has been traded in for an array of quite presentable antique bronze icons, all ranged around an elegant lion-shaped ceramic incense burner of Ming five-color ware. Gone is the teacup-ashtray, replaced by a handsome celadon bowl in a lotus motif (although still heaped with butts).

Qian Wei and Mother Yang face off across the little desk, sharing a Coke. I pull out my pocket watch (a nickel-plated Soviet railroad chronometer) to remind him of the time. The collector in him seems more interested in my affected timepiece than in the hour. Nevertheless, he gulps down his soda and urges Mother Yang to finish hers.

True to his word, he's kept her in the dark as to why he's summoned her or where we're all going. So she teeters between puzzled amusement and brusque annoyance as we shepherd her out the hospice gate and down the Hebei trunk route.

We make an odd quartet for any passing trucker to ponder: the doctor flapping in his lab coat, Ah-loong and me scuffing through the dust in Bermuda shorts, the mystified old lady in pajamas stumping along with her cane, alternately chuckling and grumbling. A few doors down, we steer her into the North Star Palace, the queen of truck stops (at least for this stretch of highway).

By prior arrangement, a table has been laid for us in a private alcove. Nothing fancy, but at least it's got napkins—the classy touch that Mother Yang seems to remember best from her only prior experience of high-toned restaurant dining. We've prearranged the menu, so almost as soon as we arrive Old Cui, the North Star proprietor, emerges from the kitchen in jerkin and thong sandals with the first dish. He plunks a steaming platter squarely in front of Mother Yang and announces, with a flourish, "Squirrel Fried Fish."

She's left speechless, as though she'd been unexpectedly reunited with a long-lost friend she'd given up for dead. She cocks her head slightly, first to one side and then the other, as though trying to reassure herself that this apparition is really what Cui says it is. She tentatively nudges the platter to survey the carp lengthwise rather than head-on. She inhales blissfully—and then stops short with a gasp. "My teeth!" she cries. "I left them in my room."

Everybody laughs, and Cui dispatches a busboy to the hospice to collect the dentures from the room nurse. More and more dishes land while we await the busboy's return: scallions and sausage, a veritable haystack of sauerkraut, julienned potatoes with pork. Hardly high cuisine, but specialties of Manchuria, Mother Yang's home. By the time she's got her teeth installed, she's ready to dig in with a will. Three liters of beer help us dispatch the meal.

"To Mother Yang," the doctor offers a toast. "Xi-yuan's Minister of the Interior."

"To Director Qian," she replies. "Our Great Helmsman."

"How about I just settle for Minister of Agitprop?" he modestly proposes.

"Oh, sure," she teases him, "along with Minister of Sports, Youth, and Culture."

Buoyed by beer, we go on allotting each other a gaudy range of cabinet portfolios in the People's Republic of Xi-yuan. Ah-loong's named Foreign Minister, principally for being able to put up with the likes of me. I get to be Central Bank Governor and Economic Czar, since I'm picking up the RMB 136 lunch tab. Qian Wei wants additional charge of the Planning Commission, the better to implement the PRX's sacred manifest destiny. And just what great national mission might *that* be? I ask.

"Why, to annex territory, of course," Qian Wei grandly proclaims. "We'll set up a whole chain of colonies, an archipelago of hospices the length and breadth of China."

"You mean like the Greater East Asian Co-Prosperity Sphere?"

Mother Yang asks warily, alluding to Japan's wartime euphemism for its conquered empire.

"Actually, I was thinking more of the Magic Kingdoms of Disneyland," Qian Wei reassures her.

It takes us fully two hours to drain the bottles and demolish the carp. After Old Cui has cleared away the bedraggled skeleton, I discreetly ask Mother Yang what she thought of the Squirrel Fried Fish. "Pretty good," she admits judiciously. "But, you know, it somehow doesn't quite compare with the first time. Maybe you just can't enjoy a once-in-a-lifetime experience twice in a lifetime."

WITH OUR BELLIES FULL and the sun at its zenith, the trudge back to the hospice seems a lot longer than our outbound stroll. Mother Yang leans on Ah-loong's arm and imparts some last-minute counsel on the care and feeding of foreign husbands. I plod ahead with Qian Wei. Cottonwood fluff floats in the gray smog. Ambient tufts of it catch in the bracken or founder in the roadside puddles of motor oil. The drifting white floss lends an extra muzziness to the sun-stroked landscape, like the feather-flecked aftermath of some cosmic pillow fight.

We're jolted out of this sleepy daze, though, when Qian Wei spots the Xi-yuan ambulance edging its way back to the hospice across the oncoming traffic lanes. "Oh my god, he's finally come!" the doctor gasps. "I'd all but given up on him. I've phoned him all week, trying to persuade him. Sent the car around daily to collect him, but he always stood me up. Today I gave it one last shot. And now he's here!"

"*Who's* here?" I ask, completely bewildered.

"Why, it's Gu Qiang, the writer. What a coup for Xi-yuan! If only we could help him."

Gu is indeed a name to conjure with, the fiery polemicist of the left. A Long March veteran, he was already pamphleteering back when Mao was holed up in Yenan. At the onset of Deng Xiaoping's "reform and opening" in the 1980s, Gu and a handful of fellow ideologues stood alone in Party conclaves against the tide of economic liberalization. After the Tiananmen massacre and ensuing crackdown, Gu's hard-line stance served as a rallying point for resurgent conservatism. The old zealot was lionized by young neo-authoritarians who came to dominate China's business and intellectual elite. His acid aphorisms were widely quoted. Then he mysteriously dropped from sight about a year ago. Now I see why.

The man who emerges from the ambulance is a walking corpse. It takes half a dozen people just to extract him from the van. The driver flings wide the double doors and Gu gropes for the ground with his cane and one cloth shoe. His wife hovers behind, shouting encouragement into his ear. Qian Wei races up to support his elbow.

Two nurses come on the run, alerted by the hullabaloo. An orderly clatters after them with a wheelchair. Gu apparently neither sees nor hears any of this. His eyes, behind opaque black glasses, aim unwaveringly over the heads of the gathering crowd. But somehow he seems to sense himself hemmed in and starts laying about him with the cane.

"Get back!" he orders. "I can stand on my own." He draws himself up to his full five feet four inches, the tendons of his emaciated neck straining from the tight collar of his blue tunic. In ninety-degree heat, his long-sleeved jacket is buttoned to the top, as though to ward off an encroaching chill.

"He can stand on his own," his wife shrilly reiterates to the courtyard at large, then turns back to Gu. "There. I told them," she bellows straight into his ear. "Now you sit down here."

She edges him into the wheelchair and arranges a damp yellow washcloth atop his white crew-cut stubble. The nurses trot ahead to clear a path. An orderly wheels him, on the double, straight into the director's office.

"Who's in charge?" Gu demands as soon as he's installed on Qian Wei's couch. The director comes forward, pouring tea for his visitors and gushing on about what an honor it is to meet such a venerable fighter. "Give him the papers," Gu commands, cutting short the introductions as though he'd heard not a word. His wife hands over a slim manila dossier.

"My medical history," Gu announces. "And my credo."

Qian Wei skims page one, nodding to himself as he confirms facts he'd already ascertained by phone. "Diagnosed with nose and throat cancer a year ago," he reads out. "Metastasized early this year. Cancer now lodged in brain. Radiation treatments discontinued due to side effects. Ninety-eight percent hearing loss; ninety-five percent sight loss."

The dry medical recital casts a new light on the peremptory little man before us. His very testiness takes on a dimension of heroic defiance. Braving all odds, Gu's determined to stand fast against the yammering riot of rogue cells in his skull that jam all thought and sensory signals. Even beyond the excruciating physical pain, his loneliness and frustration beggar the imagination.

He peels off the dark glasses and massages the bridge of his nose. With his broad brow and deep-set eyes, he must have been dashing once, after an ectomorphic fashion. He tugs at the yellow washcloth and hands it wordlessly to his wife. She automatically freshens the towel with a splash from her tea mug and drapes it again over his skull. Her haggard face, plain as a steamer bun, could blend seamlessly into any Beijing street crowd. Who could guess the private hell she lives in, bound by her heartstrings to this tortured cadaver?

Qian Wei turns to the next page in the manila dossier. It's a poem, of sorts, scrawled with a soft lead pencil in bold, jagged characters. The doctor reads it silently to himself, his head bent deeper with each line. When he's done, he hands the smudged notebook sheet across to Ah-loong. I peer over her shoulder. The doggerel rambles on for forty lines in the seven-syllable didactic strophes beloved of Chinese grade school texts. With cancer drilling through his skull and tintinabulating in his ears, Gu still maintains a strict rhyme scheme and plodding meter.

He's titled the page with the three-character Chinese phrase for "euthanasia," literally calm-joy-death. First, Gu recaps his medical history in detail. Then he homes in on his theme:

> Long since have I spent down my life's worth,
> The joy of life now amounts to nil.

Calm-joy-death, calm-joy-death,
Now is the very day and hour to die.
My wife and daughter don't object,
I beg my Leaders to back me, too,
And break tradition to do a mercy.
Fervently I'd thank my Great Healer.
It's inhumane to block my path
And leave me drowning in a bitter sea.
In my youth, I pursued a life of revolution,
Now, pursuing death is also revolutionary.
Freedom of livelihood is a sacred right,
Freedom to die is sacred too.
From the Death God's hand I wrest my rights,
Life or Death are mine to choose.
No one else has any say,
Responsibility rests with me.

Hardly immortal verse, but it makes its point. Gu squares off against the room at large, as though he'd just nailed his ninety-five theses to the cathedral door. "So that's where I stand," he announces. "Now, how is it going to be? Pills? An injection?"

Qian Wei and Madame Gu exchange a glance of hopelessness. They'd been back and forth on the phone to each other all week, both knowing that this impasse must inevitably come. No way to give the old warhorse what he wants, yet no way to deny the urgency of his anguish.

The doctor rolls his shoulders uneasily, as though trying to shift a weight on his back. "Ah, you know, Comrade Gu, our country at present has no law . . ."

Gu rakes the room expectantly with glittering, sightless eyes. He tugs at his wife's arm like a pestering child. "So? Well? What did he say?"

"He says he can't," she shouts. "Against the law."

"What?" Gu shrieks, clutching her chin right against his ear. "What's his answer?"

"He says no," she yells even louder. "The law."

Qian Wei can't stand the stark minimalism of this husband-and-wife telegraphy. For him, there's always got to be another word or two to say, some mitigating turn of phrase, some verbal jujitsu that can even the odds and reconcile all irreconcilables.

"Let me try," he begs Madame Gu, planting himself on the couch alongside the old man's other ear. "Comrade, this is Dr. Qian," he bellows.

"Who?" the head swivels on its taut chicken-neck, startled at this new voice from an unexpected quarter.

"The hospice director," Qian Wei reiterates. "We can help you, Comrade."

"Then you *will* see me through?" Gu asks eagerly.

"We'll bring you calm-joy-death. It's what we're here for."

The blind eyes narrow. "How?"

"By sheer staying power. We'll stand by you to the end."

Not one to be stopped by a blank stare of incomprehension, Qian Wei rushes headlong into a catalogue of how many patients have made the one-way journey through Xi-yuan and how case after case has ended in a peaceful, dignified, and timely death. He's talking fast, improvising, his preferred solution to any awkward situation. Gu's wife, stationed at the other ear, struggles to reduce the doctor's spiel into shoutable snippets. Qian Wei winds up his peroration with a description of the three-day blissed-out Buddhist die-in at last year's Moon Festival.

"You mean you're going to *pray* for me?" Gu roars, incredulous. He bangs his cane on the floor and squares his shoulders under the Mao tunic. "But I'm a dialectical *materialist*."

"No prayers, no prayers," Qian Wei shouts in exasperation. "Not unless you want them. We're here to give you what you *want* . . . What-*ever* you want."

"I want a needle," the old man says, flatly, but Qian Wei just brushes past this point-blank demand.

"Look," the doctor promises, "we'll keep you comfortable. If there's pain, we treat pain. If you can't sleep, we'll help you sleep. If

you don't want to eat, you don't eat. We don't prolong things, don't waste your time."

Then he adds, as though as a casual afterthought, "If you're sleeping, you know, you don't even *feel* the hunger pains."

The proposition hangs in the air. The room falls quiet for the first time since Gu and his high-decibel retinue stormed in. After a pause, the old man recapitulates in a voice far too small for himself to hear, "You mean you'll starve me to death in my sleep?"

The doctor nods. "Calmly. Joyfully."

"How long does it take?"

Qian Wei squirms at the direct question, but chokes out "A week, ten days."

"Starting when?"

"Anytime."

Gu silently hands his towel to his wife for a fresh splash of tea-water. He doesn't say no, but neither does he commit to end his days at Xi-yuan. Nobody stirs for an instant. Then the old revolutionary thumps his cane again on the floor and orders, "Let's go!" He waves aside the wheelchair and stumps out the room and down the hall under his own steam, his wife steering him at the elbow. "We'll call you," she tosses over her shoulder to the doctor.

WHETHER THEY DO OR NOT, we never find out. After our last hospice visit, we only catch one more fleeting glimpse of Qian Wei—in the incongruous context of our send-off cocktail party.

Autumn is already upon us and the Moon Festival is nearing again, jamming up social calendars. Rounding up colleagues and contacts won't be easy. Luckily for us, our friends who run a downtown bookstore-cum-teahouse agree to host the occasion for us. At such a central and public venue, at least we can greet all our invitees at one go, instead of having to break down our farewells into a drawn-out series of mini-fêtes.

So on the night of our Great Goodbye Gala, all we have to do is anchor down one end of the bar and greet a series of fellow journalists, diplomats, policy wonks, academics, officials, literati, punk-rockers, multinational executives, priests (Buddhist and Catholic), actors, techno-geeks, dissidents, and spooks. It seems everybody we ever knew in Beijing passes before our eyes.

Drowning people are said to experience something of the kind, though minus the accompanying cocktails and chitchat. So we're just about down for the count already when Qian Wei crops up on the receiving line with his wife in tow. We'd mailed them an invitation but hardly expected them to actually come. We almost don't recognize them at first, him in his faun-silk bombardier jacket and her in black tights and stiletto heels. It's the first time we've ever seen Qian Wei in anything but a white lab coat. Masterful as he may be in Xi-yuan, he seems to feel a bit out of place amid the self-consciously Great and Good of Beijing.

"*So* glad you could make it," I pronounce for the nth time this evening. "What will you drink? Let me introduce you to some friends of ours." But Qian Wei won't stay. "We just stopped in on our way through the neighborhood," he says. "I wanted to give you this."

He fumbles something out of his jacket pocket and presses it into my hand—a glass and metal disc, delightfully palm-sized, with a stolid, gratifying "tock." I open my fingers to find a handsome old pocketwatch with a steam locomotive engraved on the back.

"It's my grandfather's," Qian Wei explains. "Swiss-made, I think. A railroadman's special. Beats your Soviet version any day. Take it back to the West with you to ease *all* your arrivals and departures."

"Qian Wei, I can't accept this from you," I protest. But he's already merging back into the cocktail crowd and edging toward the stairs.

"May your sails fill with a prospering wind," he declaims in a stock Chinese valediction.

BY SPRING our prospering wind has blown us to Taiwan to cover an election. Once again, Ah-loong feels as though she'd died and gone to heaven. To enhance the impression, we've taken a sublet on Yangmingshan, the mist-shrouded, bamboo-clad, rainbow-wreathed mountain that looms above Taipei. The moist air soothes our smog-ravaged lungs. After years of dutifully parsing China's state-run press, we revel in the free-for-all cacophony of Taiwan's lively media. And, just to round out our bliss, we get to soak every day in hot-spring baths nestled among forest groves.

In the midst of this idyll, we get a call from Keiko. She's at her mother's house in Taipei, back on a brief home leave from Beijing. We set a time to meet and I motorcycle downhill to pick her up at a designated corner near the Carrefour hypermarket. Gone is her simple Xiyuan mufti of blouse and slacks. Now she's tricked out in a trim tartan pantsuit that would warm any Taiwanese mother's heart. She perches delicately sidesaddle on my Honda and we ascend the ladder of hairpin turns back up to Yangmingshan.

Driving in Taiwan only confirms the illusion that we're already in heaven: people here clearly take their own immortality for granted, judging from the way they dart and weave and blithely overtake each other on blind curves. Somehow, Keiko and I survive this out-of-body experience and arrive at our rented bungalow intact.

Ah-loong's laid out high tea on our patio under a giant oak festooned with dew-spangled spiderwebs. Far above the urban snarl of Taipei, we survey the tumbling clouds. With the camaraderie of war survivors, we swap Gang gossip and impudent jokes about the crudities of China. We nibble on seaweed-wrapped rice crackers washed down with green tea—Taiwanese treats not to the mainland taste. Beijing seems far away.

But Keiko wants to update us on Qian Wei. She's completely sworn him off after a couple of disappointments. The Gang had stumped up a few thousand renminbi to refurbish the shower-room on ward B. But after three months with no visible improvement, Keiko asked Qian Wei what was going on. It was just a matter of fitting the job into the contractor's busy schedule, he assured her. An advance had already been paid and the rest of the money was held in reserve, pending completion.

Puzzled, Keiko asked to see the hospice accounts, or at least a contractor's receipt for the advance. Qian Wei repeatedly evaded the request. Finally, after weeks of nagging, Madame Qian came up with a set of sketchy ledgers that looked suspiciously ex post facto. And even those hokey books failed to reflect any sums clearly identifiable as the shower-room advance or other Gang outlays.

At the same time, Mother Yang confided in Keiko, Xi-yuan was rocked by sex scandals. Qian Wei was caught a couple of times disporting himself with nubile nurses in empty ward rooms. It got so bad, reportedly, that Madame Qian once even lost her usual frosty composure and chased a half-dressed vixen right out the hospice door and onto the Hebei road.

"I didn't want to make a scene about it, but we decided as a group to just drop Qian Wei cold. We moved Mother Yang out of there and set her up in a small apartment of her own over in East Beijing. And I haven't been back to Xi-yuan since."

Better to cut her losses cleanly, she figured, lest the whole exercise turn counterproductive. Far from gaining any merit, she risked plunging herself ever deeper into *samsara*, the world of illusory attachments that bar the path to enlightenment.

But the episode left a bad taste in her mouth, "a sense of letdown," as she puts it. "All our efforts wasted on such a sleaze."

I know I should be appalled, but somehow Keiko's revelations only raise my sympathy for Qian Wei. Maybe embezzlement and adultery are just the job hazards of his business, like dope addiction for a jazzman. After all, he *is* a professional improviser upon other people's tunes, embroidering slapdash self-narratives for strangers. And he's always playing 'round about midnight, when people most need to cut themselves a little slack.

Summing up our own botched lives, all any of us can hope is an A for effort. But it takes a funky, compromised soul to *really* fathom the mortal urgency of that unearned A. Mercifully, Qian Wei is corrupt enough to give the rest of us the benefit of the doubt.

And doesn't he deserve an A for his *own* efforts? Hear how tirelessly he jives to bring his patients in for an easy landing. What makes him work like that? The chance to scam some more donations or jump another nurse? Or is it that, having done all those things, he's driven by his own need for absolution? For he's dying, too, as he knows better than anyone. And he's riffing his own self-narrative as he goes along.

"If the Buddha really tallies merit somewhere," I venture, "might not Qian Wei still squeak through with a positive balance? After all, we're talking here about *samsara*. How do you weigh one phantasm against another?"

Both women hear me out with growing horror. "That's ridiculous," Keiko explodes. "It's one thing to tell cheery white lies to the poor dying patients. But fudging the accounts is quite another matter. Not to even mention his harassing the staff! If you can't tell the difference, you have no moral compass at all."

IN THE BOY SCOUTS they taught me that if you don't have a compass, you can still orient yourself with a watch, as long as the sun is out. And a watch I've got—Qian Wei's old railroad timepiece. But in the sulfurous mists of Yangmingshan, it suddenly stops ticking.

Fearing the worst, I take it to a jeweler for an autopsy. He opens the back, only to find the clockwork unscathed. The problem, he tells me, is that the watch-hands can no longer clear the face. Upon closer inspection, we see why: it seems the enamel of the original numerals had chipped a little at some stage and someone (Qian Wei's grandfather?) had added an extra oaktag watch face. In the unusual humidity of Yangmingshan the oaktag swelled up, blocking the passage of the hour hand.

As soon as I remove the false face, Qian Wei's watch runs just fine.

Cousin Felix Meets the Buddha

BY THE TIME I get back from work, Cousin Felix is already nestled into the sofa, well along in his second gin-and-tonic. He looks right at home in my living room; I've never seen him before in my life.

Par for the course. Such are the ways of *guanxi*, the far-flung net of interlocking acquaintanceships that drive so much of Chinese social and professional life. Ah-loong had warned me earlier, when I phoned home in the afternoon, to expect an unknown guest this evening. A few hours before, Felix had rung her up out of the blue. He got our number, he explained, from his Auntie Mei in Texas, who turns out to be the stepmother of Ah-loong's sister's husband's niece.

On the strength of such a fragile link, this in-law of an in-law has now invited himself over for dinner tonight. No way out of it for us; the claims of *guanxi* will not be denied. To do so might offend not only the immediate claimant, but also the whole chain of associates that connects him to you. Besides, you never know what benefits—what tidbits of information or timely assistance—might flow from even the most tenuous *guanxi* bond.

A *guanxi* artist like Felix cultivates his affiliations with almost religious zeal. On our very first meeting, he name-drops his way through the cocktail chat like a voodoo shaman invoking protective spells: General This and Secretary That and Section Chief Such-and-such. For him, the *guanxi* network has talismanic power as the concrete, worldly manifestation of a spiritual concept: his *yuan* (or karma), his fated lot. *Guanxi* is the hand he's happened to draw in the mahjong game of life. Every tile he's dealt must be played with utmost care.

All the more so in Felix's line of work. *Guanxi* is his entire stock-in-trade, judging from his account of the business that's brought him to Beijing. As far as I can tell, he's some kind of middleman between American engineering consultants and Chinese military units. But as to precisely what products he's pushing, all I get out of him is a flurry of vague buzzwords as he shifts from Chinese into English: "Aw, you know, control systems. CAD/CAM. Artificial intelligence sort of thing. Fuzzy logic. Super hi-tech. Cutting-edge *stuff*, man."

And with that he tosses me a deliberate, owlish wink from behind his thick (but fashionably rimless) eyeglasses. He must reserve this air of knowing joviality specially for Americans. He's long since figured out how to deal with the likes of us, having lived in the U.S. (Texas and Atlanta) since the age of twelve. Before that, he'd grown up in the Chinatowns of Borneo. His accent, in English, presents a peculiar mix of Dixie drawl and clipped Malaysian creole.

Just as I'm struck by the oddness of his speech, so he's intrigued by our eccentric home decor. As we shift from sofa to dining table, he peers through his specs in round-eyed perplexity at our clutter of Indian and Indonesian knickknacks. "Wow," he murmurs. "And I thought *I* was the family weirdo."

He collects Tibetan *tangka* paintings and such, he tells us, but nothing like this "wild" South Asian stuff. As though clutching for some familiar flotsam amid a heaving swell of alien trinkets, he homes in on a walnut-sized bronze statue of some multiarmed deity we'd picked up some time ago in Katmandu.

"You guys do Tantra?" he ventures (stretching out the first syllable of the Sanskrit word into a nasal American triphthong). We have to admit we don't know much about mysticism. Our little Nepali bronze serves us only as a paperweight.

"Oh, then you're really missing something. Tantra's where it's *at*. I been into it for ten years already."

Like a lot of Borneo Chinese, Felix was raised a Catholic, he relates. At Georgia Tech, his American roommate turned him on to charismatic, born-again Protestantism. But then one day, in an airport bookshop on one of his business trips, Felix stumbled upon a tract by a certain Venerable Cloud Forest, a Taiwanese Tantric adept.

"That book changed my life," Felix claims. "It taught me how, simply by concentrating your mind, you can just reach out and grab a hold of whatever you need." Since then, he credits Tantra with bringing his business back twice from the brink of bankruptcy. When he was hospitalized for liver failure, Tantra alone pulled him through that life-or-death crisis. "Man, Tantra's even helped me score with girls," he confides while Ah-loong's off to the pantry for a second bottle of China-made table wine.

"Well, American girls, anyway, and overseas Chinese," he adds, as a dyspeptic afterthought. "I've got a ways to go yet before I figure out how to deal with these mainland babes. They're all permanently on the rag. Same goes for pretty much everyone else here, too—customers, partners, bureaucrats, even my landlord. High-strung, slippery people, all of them. What a load of goddam *foreplay*! When do they ever finally climb into the sack and get down to business?"

Ah-loong's back now with another round of Dragon Seal cabernet, so Felix has to mute his locker-room tone. But he's not through yet expounding on how China, flighty and womanish, balks him at every turn. Cultures, like people, have their *yin* and *yang* traits, Felix is convinced. The West, he says, is forthright, progressive, linear: *yang*. China, on the other hand, is pure *yin*, feminine. It keeps its treasures hidden, internal, *nei bu*—literally "inner realm," Communist bureaucratese for "official secret." True to China's *yin* nature, Felix adds, its history runs in cycles, like menstruation. Every generation or two, the whole country seizes up, convulses. There is a gut-wrenching purgation, a great letting of blood, a wholesale flushing out of the old to ready the ground for the new. And then the so-called "new order" turns out to be just another round of hope belied by oppression, culminating in revolt all over again. Dynasty after dynasty repeats this pattern. The current People's Republic is no exception, as witness the long trauma of the Cultural Revolution—a spasm whose aftershocks reverberate still.

Maybe we'll never see the end of these cycles, Felix sighs. "And if we ever *do*, imagine the hot flashes when an ancient Dragon Lady like China goes into menopause!"

This vinous reflection puts a damper on table talk, and not long afterward Felix calls it a night. But the next morning, he's on the phone again. He reports, with great alarm, how on his cab ride home he was overcome with a mysterious chill. Perhaps he's not used to Chinese cabernet? No, nothing so mundane. It's his psychic sensitivity. Our in-law, it turns out, is a finely tuned barometer of karmic vibrations; last night he felt a steady cold draft emanating from a pair of Indonesian puppets at his back. Maybe we should have our living room exorcised.

POPPYCOCK, OF COURSE. Nevertheless, that same afternoon we somehow coincidentally find ourselves dialing up the nearest approximation we know of an exorcist: our friend Norbu, the Tibetan lama.

He's a relatively new-fledged lama. Barely a year ago, he was well-known about the foreigners' enclaves of Beijing as a reliably presentable bachelor to round out a dinner party or a Sunday picnic. He had all the hallmarks of a diplomatic compound habitué:

- good English (reflecting his upbringing and education in the Tibetan diaspora communities of India in the 1970s)

- serviceable Mandarin (acquired since his family's 1986 return to the ancestral homeland in Qinghai province)

- a fine-tuned sense of protocol (cultivated as a sometime translator for visiting diplomats and Buddhist clergy)
- lots of free time (thanks to his undemanding desk job at the semiofficial Minorities Cultural Association)
- a penchant for silk shirts and fashionably shaggy hair; a taste for Carlsberg beer
- his own quietly bilious take on official policy; helpful with occasional news tips about repression in Tibet
- a flair for storytelling and ingenious metaphor
- broad (if quirky) general knowledge gleaned from his eclectic circle of friends
- a talent for clowning, mimicry, and puns; good with kids

Altogether these attributes add up to an interesting, genial, and mannerly guest, but none too conspicuously different in kind from a few dozen other hangers-on—academics, artists, some of the tamer dissidents—who frequent the gated compounds where the Chinese government herds foreign diplomats and journalists.

But then a year ago, Norbu broke out of this mold; upon our return from a summer home leave in America, we learned that he had decided to take Buddhist monastic orders. The next time we met him was at the touristy Jie Tai Temple in Beijing. We rented a courtyard there and invited him to join us for moon viewing at the Mid-Autumn Moon Festival.

Norbu came decked out in solemn maroon and yellow robes, but he was still effusive as ever in his greeting. I ventured a tentative, wondering hand-pass across the stubble of his shaven pate, and we both laughed as though he'd thought up a particularly clever costume for a theme party. He had a new name, Nyima Tenpel, given by His Holiness the Dalai Lama himself, no less—"but you can still call me Norbu."

Yet despite all his reassurances of continuity, he'd clearly undergone a profound transformation. He declined beer at dinner and retired early to drone an hour's worth of sutras in his room. The next morning, he told fortunes for the kids with his prayer beads. A few hours later, his new acolyte, Mr. Kung the BMW dealer, showed up to whisk him away in a teal-blue limousine.

After his ordination, we somehow got to see more of Norbu than ever. Not that we'd exactly seek him out. But he has a knack for showing up at moments when a more religiously inclined family than ours might think to call a clergyman: right after my father's death, for instance, or when we founder in troughs of career funk, or interludes of amorphous malaise.

He phones up in Hindi—"*Namasteji*"—and we invariably wind up inviting him over that very night. Sometimes he's in full monastic robes, sometimes in shirt and jeans (although, even in civvies, he maintains the same ochre and maroon color scheme). We feed him curries and listen together to our Indian music tapes. His taste runs to flashy instrumentals and romantic ballads.

Part of our house is tatami-covered, so we remove shoes upon entry and stack them in a pigeon-hole cubby by the door. Once, on his way out, Norbu inadvertently grabbed the wrong pair and discovered that he and I have the same foot size. After that, he'd routinely swap shoes with me on his visits—whether as a joke or a lesson in Buddhist detachment I was never quite sure.

Another time, he showed up with a hyperkinetic poodle, "Hui Hui," that a neighbor had given him when the dog spontaneously started tagging along after Norbu rather than its original master. Such a donation is no small matter in China, where a pedigreed pet is still an emblem of conspicuous consumption that can command a five-figure price in a land of four-figure incomes.

Hui Hui, too, became our regular houseguest, treeing our long-suffering cat atop the refrigerator and messing the tatamis. We should feel honored by these attentions, Norbu reminds us. He cites tales of sainted lamas who managed to meditate even as Tibetan Lhasa Apso dogs tunneled through the voluminous sleeves of their robes. Norbu is convinced that Hui Hui is karmically bonded to him from past lives and has valuable lessons to teach us all about the guru-disciple relationship.

As far as we can see, the only tricks the poodle has mastered in a year of discipleship are the manic pursuit of tennis balls and how to beg with his front paws waggling in the air. Nevertheless, as we banish our cat to the front porch and mince hotdogs for poodle food, we find ourselves learning from Hui Hui such deep truths as the Law of Transitivity of gurudom: the disciple of your guru is *also* your guru, willy-nilly.

Norbu often likes to treat himself to a bath in our home; there's no hot water at his work-unit housing in a slapdash new high-rise out beyond Beijing's Fourth Ring Road. If his visit stretches into the evening, he sleeps over with us since elevator service to his seventeenth-floor apartment shuts down after eleven P.M. He always arrives with overnight kit. Not toothbrush and pajamas; those we provide. More crucial for him is the set of sutras he brings for evening chants.

IN THE SAME YELLOW SHOULDER BAG as the sutras, he also carries a plastic album of photos from western China's Qinghai province, home both to his genetic and his monastic families. It doesn't take much prodding to get him to leaf through the album with us.

The first few pages feature formal votive portraits of his late uncle and his teenage nephew—both of them Living Buddhas, like Norbu. Evidently, Buddhahood runs in the family. Our friend himself was recognized as an incarnate lama before he was two years old. But in the diaspora milieu of India, his parents chose not to raise him in the strict monastic setting traditionally reserved for high lamas. Anyway, he admits, as a boy he showed no innate predilection for monkish life.

Even after the family's return to Qinghai, Norbu still shrank from assuming the priestly role charted out for him. His father, scion of an aristocratic family, felt "a call" to come back and help fellow Tibetans recover from the anti-Buddhist pogroms of the Cultural Revolution. But Norbu, as a product of twentieth-century English-language education in India, found a literal belief in reincarnation a bit hard to swallow.

Nor was he convinced enough of the post-Mao "reform and opening" to accord China the propaganda coup of luring a young, hip lama out of the diaspora and into a government-approved monastery. To those Tibetans, like his father, who'd witnessed the initial Red Army onslaught, the incremental improvement in China's treatment of their homeland may seem impressive. But to Norbu, a child of exile, Chinese-occupied Tibet still looked a lot grimmer than the diaspora milieu. As long as the Communists remained utterly unapologetic about their past depredations, he owed them no thanks and no fealty.

Besides, he was having too much fun in Beijing to even think of moving. Like many another deracinated thirty-something, he was enjoying café society in the Chinese capital. Norbu never found himself at a loss for a sinecure position or a casual dalliance with some Chinese or foreign coed. Those of us who knew him in the early 1990s hardly dreamt we had a Living Buddha for a beer-drinking buddy.

Yet all that while, he'd never lost touch with the forty thousand souls back in Qinghai who still revered him as "their" lama. In his photo album, after the stiff hieratic portraits of his uncle and nephew, Norbu himself debuts in a seemingly casual snapshot. It shows him silk-shirted and smartly barbered—just as we first knew him—sprawled, grinning, amid a dozen robed and shaven monks in a flower-strewn meadow.

For all its relaxed mood, the picture conveys an underlying tension. Against the greensward background, gleaming tonsures and monochrome crimson drapery dominate the composition. Only Norbu, in paisley silk at the center of the frame, provides a piebald exception. All faces are turned toward him. What must it have cost him to go on denying the expectation implicit in all those eyes? And what, then, made him suddenly turn around and embrace the ordained identity he'd resisted for so long?

A clue comes from the next leaf in the photo album: an eight-by-ten color glossy of Norbu's "root guru," Samudra Rinpoche. Even in humdrum Fujicolor, the eyes of the portrait exert a mesmeric pull. They're pure black, with no trace of highlight—a soft, welling black, like springtide sea swells in the dark of the moon. (The name Samudra means "ocean" in Sanskrit.) The eyes peer out from a dense web of wrinkles—more lines, it would seem, than a human face could possibly accumulate in a single lifetime. This is no fanciful conceit, Norbu insists: Rinpoche has already lived through twenty-seven attested incarnations in the two and a half millennia since his initial enlightenment as one of the original disciples of Gautama, the historic Buddha.

But in just the eighty years of his present incarnation, Samudra's seen enough to etch a face full of character. Born to a noble Tibetan family in Sichuan, he was recognized at age six as an incarnate lama and spiritual head of a major temple in Inner Mongolia. He studied his fourteen-year *geyshe* (doctor of divinity) course in Lhasa, where he was an elder classmate of the current Dalai Lama. In the 1930s, when Mao's troops passed through Sichuan on the Long March, Samudra's family helped the Red Army with food and guides. This pre-Liberation track record exempted Rinpoche from the full brunt of persecution after the Communists came to power. His temple was never sacked, nor was he forced (like so many others) to abandon monastic robes to take up a job and a wife. He shuttled freely between Sichuan, Mongolia, and the international left-wing ecumenical conference circuit—a poster boy for China's alleged ethnic and religious tolerance.

Yet for all his special perks, Samudra has remained true to his Buddhist tenets, Norbu assures us. At the height of the pogroms, Rinpoche used his privileged position to shield as many victims as he could. And he's kept up contact with his old classmate, the Dalai Lama, providing a "backdoor" liaison channel between Beijing and the Tibetan diaspora leadership.

But it wasn't only on the strength of Samudra's biography that Norbu recognized him as a root guru. After all, through his family upbringing, our friend had already heard plenty of lama stories and had seen more than his share of Living Buddhas. Samudra's charisma, though, was of a different order. It convinced Norbu as nothing had before that an incarnate lama can tap into levels of reality beyond mundane experience.

"It was as though I had grown up in a harbor town but never really knew there was an ocean out there," Norbu explains. "Of course I had heard it and smelled it all my life, and I had an idea there must be *something* out past the jetties. But I never quite grasped that these intuitions of mine all came from a single source: the same endless, ever-present, ever-changing ocean."

When he first saw Samudra Rinpoche, Norbu recalls, it was like meeting an Ancient Mariner, an old veteran with the sea in his eyes and his voice: "I just knew—I can't even say how—that he had actually tamed this ocean that we call inner space. He'd *been* there, sailed all the seas. And so had I, I realized as I heard out his sea stories. We had been shipmates, he and I, forever—many lifetimes—long enough to trust each other completely." So Samudra alone could guide our playboy friend to rediscover his buried Buddha nature. That's the essence of a root guru, Norbu explains: a steadying, trusted presence amid the flux of self-discovery.

That flux, as he describes it, sounds pretty disorienting: "The very ground I stood on no longer felt solid to me; I realized I was still way out at sea." That's when he knew he'd been nothing but a foolish, drunken sailor, dreaming himself so snug in port that he'd forgotten all about the ocean. So now he's got back his sea legs and dedicated himself to "steering a safe course home for myself and all my shipmates. To the *real* shore, not just some dream harbor."

When he comes to this part of the story, he has Ah-loong enthralled, but for a spiritual landlubber like me, this paradigm shift of Norbu's sounds like a perfect recipe for psychic seasickness. Still, I keep my queasiness to myself. After all, the whole process seems to have brought him a new peace and energy. And I must admit, Norbu does look transfigured in the remainder of the photo album, which chronicles his ordination as a priest.

Most of the pictures are indoor shots, temple scenes: long, crimson rows of seated monks; prayer flags receding off into the incense-shrouded depths of shadowy cloisters. In these rhythmic compositions, you can almost hear the stately chants and feel the mea-sured pace of monastic life. Norbu, freshly tonsured, takes his place among the monks, his face radiant in meditation. Samudra, enthroned on a dais, beams compassion over the entire congregation.

Alongside the muted temple interiors in the album, a few outdoor shots blaze with the ozone blue of Qinghai's high desert sky. Here's Norbu in full priestly regalia astride a white stallion that he'd been given by some devotees. The horse, still half-wild, reportedly won't let anyone but Norbu ride him.

Another shot shows Norbu on the crest of a hill against a rolling panorama of clouds. He's framed by a double rainbow—an unbeliev-ably good omen. Equally auspicious is the last picture in the book: a pair of eagles circling above the temple where he took his monastic orders. At the very moment he was ordained, Norbu swears, the birds swooped down to the temple as though in prostration. Then they soared back up to the heavens.

THE PHOTO ALBUM PRESENTS a Karma Komix version of Norbu's metamorphosis, with all the smooth momentum of a fable: rising from doubt and degeneracy, our friend finally lives up to his or-dained destiny. A saintly mentor guides him. He's supported by a chorus of true-believing, picturesquely costumed coreligionists. Signs and portents prosper him on his way.

For all I know, things may actually be that simple back in the Shangri-La of Norbu's ancestral home. But here in Beijing, Living Buddhahood looks a good deal more perplexing. We get a glimpse of his high-wire balancing act when he invites us for a group excursion to the Yong He Gong, the "Palace of Peace and Harmony," Beijing's most prominent Lama Temple.

On the appointed date we arrive to find our friend resplendent in brocade robes. Still more impressive than his costume is his eclectic retinue of followers, whose only common denominator may be their devotion to Norbu. A few of the faces are already familiar to us from the expat ghettoes—the usual array of diplomatic spouses, earnest young exchange students, and "foreign experts." Smartly tailored Hong Kong and Taiwan *commerçants* squire their svelte trophy wives. But most of the entourage is made up of miscellaneous Beijingers who would be unlikely to meet each other, much less any foreigners, under normal circumstances.

A frumpy housewife arrives fresh from market, her shopping bag bulging with vegetables. Unctuous Mr. Kung, the car dealer, rolls up in his BMW. A pair of miniskirted high school girls join the group, suppressing their titters and solemnly chomping their gum. A uniformed army officer tags silently and respectfully behind. Flanking Norbu in the temple forecourt are a pair of leather-jacketed, crew-cut, manicured, and pomaded toughs—the sort of street-smart, newly rich *getihu*, or privateers, that have flourished under post-Mao "reform and opening." Norbu instructs us to turn off all our pagers and cell phones. Then we move *en bloc* along the aisle of schlock stalls leading up to the temple gate, accompanied by the electronic cackle of "Laughing Buddha" souvenir dolls.

The Lama Temple is a "must" on any Beijing tourist itinerary—not just for the splendor of its courtyards and pavilions, but also for its historical import. It used to be an imperial palace before it was turned over to a predecessor of the present Dalai Lama by the eighteenth-century emperor Qianlong. In accepting the gift, official guidebooks stress, the Dalai Lama implicitly conceded Chinese sovereignty over Tibet and Mongolia.

Norbu's guided tour of the Yong He Gong, however, differs subtly from the conventional account. Here, he points out, is the hall where Qianlong came to be ordained as an ordinary monk. Here sat the emperor. Here, above him, sat the abbot. Here's an inscription in Qianlong's own calligraphy: "Seeking refuge"—that is, surrendering himself to the Buddha, the law of *dharma*, and the monastic congregation. The tutelary relationship between the lamas and the Qing emperors was a two-way street, Norbu emphasizes. If the Dalai Lama put Tibet under imperial protection, it was only because the emperor had embraced the Law. It was a contingent relationship, not some kind of immutable international treaty. To a regime that flouts *dharma*, what kind of allegiance can a Buddhist people owe?

Luckily for Norbu, no temple officials overhear his heterodoxy. The officially recognized monks of the Yong He Gong eye him narrowly from across the courtyards, but they leave us alone as long as nobody in our group takes unauthorized snapshots. Why bestir themselves? For all their imposing crimson robes, these so-called monastics amount to no more than an underemployed gaggle of salaried ticket collectors, proctors, and janitors. Their lackadaisicality reflects their status as state employees. They infuse the temple, despite its innate splendor, with the threadbare futility of any other public-sector work unit.

Even so, the Yong He Gong regularly draws scores of ordinary Beijingers who might well be avid for Buddhist spiritual guidance, if any were on offer. So we infer, anyway, from the crowd of random temple visitors who swarm around Norbu by the time he reaches the rearmost sanctuary of the Yong He Gong, the pavilion with the five-story-tall Maitreya, the "Buddha-Yet-to-Come." Old grannies, factory girls, off-duty cops, shopkeepers, young brides—all bring their incense, prayers, and vows here in pursuit of narrowly focused goals: a business license, a winning lottery number, a high exam grade, a healthy son.

Designed to overwhelm, the looming gilt icon barely fits into its lofty chamber. The massive shoulders scrape the fragile loggias high above us. The ringletted pate bumps up against the painted ceiling. From no point in the room can the whole statue be taken in all at once. Instead, we only see details—an eye, a nostril, a sweep of drapery, a raised hand—all jumbled and foreshortened so as to bear down upon the lowly onlookers huddled around the house-high feet of the idol.

No wonder the cowed worshipers turn for comfort to the authoritative figure of Norbu when he happens into the room. They press our friend with detailed, practical queries. How to set up a household altar? Which way should it face? Where to get beads? How to pronounce the Sanskrit words of the sutras? Norbu answers simply, sensibly, reassuringly. Never mind pronunciation, just think of what the sutras mean. If you only have one room, put the altar wherever it won't get in the way but will cheer you in your daily life. Don't worry about mixing and matching different icons on the altar—"They won't fight."

The crowd swells rapidly to spill out into the adjacent courtyard. One of Norbu's leather-jacketed sidekicks shoulders his way to the front and yanks the lama off to the chapel of the Medicine Buddha to perform a promised prayer—a timely exit, since Chinese law expressly forbids any form of "religious proselytization." Who knows how this sort of spontaneous give-and-take might be construed if it came to official notice?

Yet even without any overt "proselytizing," Norbu's Beijing circle grows apace. In the next few months, he finds himself increasingly in the thrall of his acolytes. One of them gives him a phone-paging beeper, so that devotees can reach him quickly in moments of spiritual need. His hotline response is almost instantaneous, at least the few times we try it out.

But when he comes to our house for a bath and urban retreat, he sometimes unhooks the pager from the yellow sash of his robe and leaves it to beep, unanswered, alongside the sutras by his pillow. And, with the onset of spring, he talks more and more of a retreat beyond the beck of the telephone, back to his putative home in Qinghai.

So he's in the midst of his farewell rounds in Beijing when we beep him to exorcise whatever it was that Felix had sensed in our living room. Norbu's happy enough to drop by. He'd been meaning to look in on us anyway. He shows up that very night, with Hui Hui in tow. We're more than a little abashed about reacting to anything so corny, not to say downright benighted, as somebody's bad vibes from a piece of our household bric-a-brac. We've left a string of messages on Felix's answering machine in hopes of luring him over to explain his presentiments himself, rather than leaving the awkward job to us. So far, no response from him.

Nothing to be embarrassed about, though, as far as Norbu's concerned; demoniac possession strikes him as a perfectly legitimate anxiety. The first thing he wants to know from us is who it was that sounded the spook alarm. We start to describe Felix, and it turns out that our exorcist has already met our in-law.

It was at the downtown Wanguo Hotel a couple of weeks ago, where Samudra Rinpoche was lunching with Norbu during a stopover en route to resume his duties in Mongolia after a few months of winter leave back home in Sichuan. The lamas were waiting on a buffet line when they were hailed from an adjacent table by an English-speaking overseas Chinese matching Felix's description—thick specs, blow-dried mane, weird cracker-cum-baba phonemes.

"You guys staying here?" he asked, jabbing an inquisitive fork in the direction of the robed clerics and taking in the whole hotel with a sweep of his butter knife. Samudra's secretary, Tensing Tsangpo, deftly interposed himself between the Rinpoche and the threatening flatware to deflect Felix's urgent requests for a private audience. Throughout the meal, our in-law kept sending over the waiter with notes in English and Chinese announcing that, as a serious student of Tantra, Felix wondered which sect the holy men might belong to. Finally, Tensing went over to talk with him and demurred again about setting up a meeting. Maybe next time.

At this point in his tale of their earlier encounter, Norbu abruptly reels off a cell-phone number where we might try to reach Felix. The number just came to him out of the blue, he claims—something that happens to him quite a lot, evidently. Such an explanation seems hardly less likely than letter-perfect recall of a business card he may have seen a fortnight ago. Either way, the number works; we arrange for Felix to drop by the next morning.

He arrives on schedule bearing gifts for Norbu: Taiwan-printed sutras, laminated Buddhist icons, and, oddly enough, a battery-powered massage vibrator. He's far more circumspect this time than he'd been at the Wanguo. No more talk of "you guys." Now Felix humbly addresses Norbu as a Rinpoche and entreats him to inspect his jadeite prayer beads (which Norbu duly blesses). Our in-law even pays respects to Hui Hui, discreetly offering the poodle crumbs from our brunch croissants.

Norbu asks Felix to recount his forebodings about our living room. After hearing him out with the chin-stroking gravity of a medical diagnostician, the lama directs us all to settle into a lotus position on the tatami. He pulls out his bundle of sutras and selects the appropriate texts. Hui Hui, who must have seen these preparations before, subsides into a reverent crouch with his paws neatly splayed in front of him. Norbu riffles through a stack of plastic-laminated icons until he finds a suitable image, which he props up against his sutras for us all to meditate upon.

Not the most reassuring of pictures: a great, blue, horned, leering head with three bugged-out bloodshot eyes. A cluster of eight other multicolored heads surround this visage, the whole ensemble framed in an aureole of lurid stylized flames. What looks like a sinister bat-cape behind him turns out to be, on closer inspection, a fan of thirty-two arms. Each arm terminates in a hand that brandishes either a different item of murderous-looking cutlery or some bit of severed anatomy. With his remaining two hands, the deity clutches to his breast a sky-blue woman who snorts into his bovine nostrils as she impales herself upon his straining member. His scrotum dangles beneath her snub, blue rump—a neat counterpoint to the clusters of gouged eyeballs that swing about his knees like white, slimy grapes. The god and consort toast each other in blood quaffed from neatly sectioned skulls. They wear diadems of mini-skulls and garlands of shrunken heads. They're draped in flayed and dripping skins—human? Under his sixteen feet, the deity tramples assorted persons and animals (who seem to take it all with unnerving equanimity).

"Think of him as a kind of guardian," Norbu invites us cheerily. "Just visualize his strength and energy. Make it your own. Let it protect you." He will not be drawn out, however, on just who or what the figures represent, or why the horrific details. "That you can only learn when you're ready. And then, too, only from your root guru, the teacher who is right for you."

When I ask him how come, he replies with a stream of cyber-babble that he must have picked up surfing the Web on his work-unit computers. It's a matter of intellectual property protection, he warns.

If you try to pirate any item of Tantric software without a proper copyright, you might wind up with a virus that could crash your mainframe for aeons—countless rebirths. In other words, leave the iconography to the priesthood.

But after chanting his exorcism, after a lunch and a round of auto-biographical chatter from Felix, Norbu shows himself less reticent about sharing some mysteries with us. Our in-law has been relating how, in a freak ice-storm on the Atlanta Beltway, he pulled his car out of a potentially fatal skid only by frantically reciting the *Om Mani Padme Hum* mantra.

"That mantra has saved me again and again," Felix admits. "In tax audits, in stockmarket plays, even at the card table. And yet, you know, I just picked it up from reading Venerable Cloud Forest. I never had any real guru to pass on the proper lineage."

"Perhaps I can help you there," Norbu allows. As it turns out, he has received the "patent" on that mantra from the Dalai Lama himself. As a small child, Norbu was singled out by His Holiness at a mass prayer meeting in India and personally initiated into *Om Mani Padme Hum*. Back in Qinghai, Norbu reveals, he is known as "Maniwa," bearer of the *Mani* mantra.

This, for us, is a staggering revelation. Not only is it a sudden breach of his long-standing taboo against revealing his own lineage and incarnation name to any of his Beijing contacts. Even more stunning is the ubiquity of the franchise he claims. *Om Mani Padme Hum* is the most commonplace, staple prayer of Tibetan Buddhism. It's as though some Chinese were to assert that he had a patent on chopsticks. The *Mani* mantra spins in prayer wheels, flaps on banners, and keeps prayer beads clacking all over the Lamaist world.

"But as to what it *means*, ah now, *that* takes some teaching. Well, you could call it compassion, a kind of fellow-feeling for all beings. That may sound vague and airy," Norbu continues, "but in fact, *Mani* is hard, like a jewel. And hot, like a flame.

"Like a candle flame, blazing upward right here," he traces the line of the mystic Third Eye in the middle of his brow. "A flame that makes these other two eyes pour tears of compassion, like a candle melting.

"Come to Qinghai with me next week and see for yourself," he invites Felix. "Maybe that's the place for your *Mani* initiation." And to us, as an afterthought: "You come, too."

A WEEK LATER, Mr. Kung the car dealer whisks us to the airport. The limousine is crammed with duffel bags full of presents for Norbu's various relatives and acolytes. Gliding noiselessly down the landscaped autobahn we could be in any modern capital in the world.

But as soon as the BMW pulls away from the curb at the departure terminal, we begin to feel the onset of China's Wild West. There's a frontier eclecticism about the line of passengers at the check-in counter for Xining, the Qinghai capital: Moslem traders with burly beards; old-style cadres in outdated Mao suits; leggy, big-boned Qinghai beauties in slinky dresses, heading home to show off the finery they've earned (never mind how) in the Special Economic Zones of the coast.

A trio of American hunters rolls up to the counter with five baggage trolleys full of hi-tech rifles and fancy camping gear. They're on their way to bag the rare Blue Sheep, found only in the Qinghai hills, I learn from one of them, a Detroit accountant. He's been saving up for this trip for three years, he confides.

Standing behind us, a young Tibetan mother carries her son in a sling on her back. Although too young to walk, the baby's already ordained as a monk, judging from his pointy yellow hat and diminutive crimson vestment. He smiles and coos happily, all the while fixing us with a steady, unblinking Buddha gaze. The tiny lama claps at the sight of Norbu's robes and presses his hands together as in greeting. Our friend rattles his prayer beads in reply, which elicits a gurgling stream of baby talk.

I'm listening to babble of another sort from a team of Australian development experts lined up at the next counter. This is already their fifth aid mission to Qinghai, I'm told, but I'm at a loss to figure out just what it is they do there. Something about "appropriate technology" and "empowerment." Sensing my muddle, one safari-suited woman helpfully explains that she's a "gender consultant."

Before I have time to find out just who in Qinghai consults her about what, we're all bundled into a bus and rattled across the tarmac to the wheezy turbo-prop that's reserved for the Xining run. Norbu and Felix take opposing aisle seats, the better to continue their Tantric chat. So Ah-loong and I each get a window.

We judder aloft and head due west. Within less than an hour, we're already clear of the flat, lush agrarian plains of Hebei. Below us stretch the loess hills of the Ordos Loop; green enough along the terraced hillcrests, but scored with eroded gullies between the ridges. Then even those scabrous hills disappear, erased by the rhythmic blank scales of overlapping sand dunes. Eventually, the desert gives way to gray, rocky crags daubed here and there with the red blush of ferrous outcrops. The sun swings due west, right in front of us, diced into stroboscopic slivers by our propellers. The slanting, late-afternoon light brings out the finespun filigree of stream courses below—just a faint, barely perceptible tracery of valleys etched green upon the wrinkled rock massif.

But the perspective turns itself inside out when the plane finally bears down on its runway in the agrarian outskirts of Xining. Now the green valley becomes the foreground, dwarfing the faraway cliffs. We taxi to a halt amid a world of budding poplars, freshly seeded wheat fields, white apricot blossoms, and glinting rivulets—all highlighted against a distant backdrop of purple rock buttresses.

The foreground-for-background swap is so abrupt it's almost hard to fully absorb. Even when we're safely deplaned and waiting by the baggage carousel, I can't quite shake the sense that the smiling, green prospect outside the airport window is only a thin, illusory scrim drawn across the overwhelming reality of grim, rocky crags.

Group by group, our fellow passengers disperse. Beardless boys in hajj caps arrive by motorscooter to whisk off the Muslim traders. The Mao-suited cadres disappear into a chauffeured Volga sedan. A tractor-van full of relatives shows up to receive the baby lama and his mother. The American hunting party and the Australian aid delegation each get a China-made Cherokee of their own.

We're the last ones out of the airport, by the time we pluck all of Norbu's duffel bags off the carousel. The Provincial People's Political Consultative Committee (PPCC, a figurehead appointive "legislature" of which Norbu's father is an honorary member) has arranged a jeep for us—our first indication of the kind of clout our friend and his family can wield on their home turf. Not that the mud-spattered vehicle per se is particularly grand. But yellow silks stream from its side mirrors, denoting "Lama aboard."

This proves even more effective than a siren or a rooftop beacon; our little Buddhamobile commands right-of-way all along the route into town, scattering buses and tractors in our wake. We cruise past the gatepost of the official Xining Guest House, hardly slowing down. The sentries snap us a smart salute. Desk clerks, bellhops—everyone we meet in the concrete cavern of the Guest House—receive us with the same cowed circumspection, a far cry from the cursory norms of Chinese state hospitality. We have an entire wing of this Stalin-era palazzo to ourselves.

After installing us in our rooms, Norbu takes off with the driver to visit Xining friends and relatives and distribute some of the loot in his duffels. We're left on our own to explore the town, such as it is—an assemblage of gray, cheerless apartment buildings and dingy little street markets. Crumbling remnants of the original city wall melt into the surrounding tenement blocks. A few spindly, tile-covered minarets dominate the squat skyline.

Still, even Xining is making a stab at post-Maoist urbanity. At the main intersection of town, welders work in round-the-clock shifts to complete a pedestrian overpass, although there's hardly enough foot or vehicular traffic to justify it. Inside a Hong Kong joint-venture restaurant, sleek cadres and uniformed army officers dig into such pricey delicacies as camel's hoof and abalone, unabashed by the passersby staring in through the fancy plate-glass windows.

Citizens might as well feast their eyes, at least, on these publicly funded banquets, since there's not much else on offer in Xining by way of evening entertainment. A few strollers stop to admire the shower of sparks from the welders overhead. At the corner, a couple of "privateers" with ghetto-blaster stereo tape decks run impromptu, outdoor karaokes. Street hawkers sell fried bread and steamed snails. We stop in a Muslim noodle shop for tea and dumplings.

Felix twits the slow-witted waiter for gaping at us. "Don't worry. We're just foreign reporters—you know, media celebrities. Let me take your picture. Pose there, against the meat hooks, that's right. Tomorrow you'll be in all the international papers. Now top up our soup, like a good fellow, with a little more broth." This patter leaves Ahloong and me writhing with embarrassment, but our host just blushes and smiles and takes it all in good fun.

Still woozy from the elevation (we're a mile and a half above sea level), we turn in early and treat ourselves to what we know will be our last hot shower for a week. Next morning, Norbu and the jeep await us promptly at eight A.M.

OUR FRIEND IS in high spirits, sporting a pointy yellow lama cap with jaunty purple wings. He gaily sings out the roadside auguries. We pass a leaky water main: "Look, it's flowing our way—very auspicious." A flower-decked funeral van parked across the road: "They're headed in the opposite direction from us, a good sign." A dozen farmers walk ahead of us, shouldering their spades: "They're going to dig, to probe the ground, to make it ready for new seeds."

We try to get into the spirit of things, but only manage to note indelicacies like night soil collectors or country families trundling invalids into town on barrows. Norbu scolds us: "You won't get anywhere if you keep looking for negativities." That's when we realize how seriously he takes these omens. He perches on the edge of the front seat, alert and erect as a deer in a morning meadow, scanning attentively through the windshield so as not to miss any symbols or portents.

Only when we're well under way, more than an hour out of town, does he relax a little and point out the sights in a more conventionally touristic sense. We're following the Tsong River valley, he tells us, birthplace and namesake of Tsongkappa, the reformist monastic who founded the Yellow Hat sect that has dominated Tibetan political and religious life since the fourteenth century. There, up that valley, is the birthplace of the current Dalai Lama, the 1989 Nobel Peace Laureate who is now exiled in India. The house has been converted to a "Red Star School" for training Communist cadres, Norbu relates, but pilgrims still come to furtively venerate the site.

We cruise through villages of tamped-earth courtyard houses. Trim and tidy as they are, their mud construction lends them an endearing lopsidedness: no angle is quite plumb. Edges are rounded, walls are buttressed, columns and pilasters bulge at the midriff. Round, white riverbed rocks ballast the corners of the courtyards, as though the builders feared the walls might otherwise fly away. Except for the Chinese latticework windows and tiled gates, we could be looking at mud architecture from anyplace on earth, a Hopi pueblo or a warren in Timbuktu. Flowering peach and almond trees leap over the walls, transfiguring the courtyards.

The jeep churns over a high, barren mountain pass marked with a pile of pilgrim stones, each invested with pious iterations of the *Mani* mantra. As we sputter on down into the valley on the other side, we realize that we've crossed into Tibetan territory. Not that there's any marked change in the geology, architecture, or the methods and patterns of cultivation. But the fluttering prayer flags introduce strong vertical accents and primary colors into the flat, pastel mudscape of the villages. Human figures silhouetted in the fields look denser, more rooted, in their quilted brown robes, with only a glint of jewelry or a red bandanna to relieve the sobriety of the costume. White, ninepin-shaped stupas punctuate the rolling countryside.

Then, swooping up to the top of a rise, we come upon a town that feels unlike any of the rest. Instead of nestling among fields, this settlement stretches along the spine of the hill in a single street. All the shops and eateries stand cheek-by-jowl, facing the road, backs turned to the surrounding landscape. No evidence of separate living quarters;

the merchants must sleep on their business premises. There's a transient and beleaguered feel to the place, like a frontline battle trench.
Judging by the shop signs and the star-and-crescent pennants, it's a
Muslim town, although the most prominent building in the row isn't
a mosque but a birth-control clinic.

Parked combines and trailers dwarf the huddled stalls and storefronts. This town, Norbu explains, is an important truck stop on the
national highway linking Qinghai to Sichuan. We pull over to scout a
place for lunch. "You can eat a Muslim's food, but don't heed his
words," our Living Buddha quotes a Tibetan proverb, matter-of-factly.
Our young Tibetan driver nods his judicious assent.

We choose a dive with some pretensions of gentility: concrete
walls adorned with smoky, faded posters of palm-fringed swimming
pools—odd motif for these parts. This could be our last chance for a
while to eat vegetables, Norbu advises, so we order up spinach and
fried peppers. We find a table and sink into what appears to be a bus
seat. Evidently our host has furnished his establishment with salvage
from wrecks in the surrounding mountain passes—a thought that
does little to improve the dining ambiance. No use dwelling on it,
though. Our fellow patrons all seem quite at ease in similar seating.

Off in one corner, a trucker plies a plump local wench with
sorghum wine. Oblivious to this courtship-in-progress, the Tibetan
farmer across the table from them fastidiously whittles away at a
steaming plate of ribs with his brass-handled bowie knife. A pair of
cops loll in the next booth, sipping bowls of sugared date-and-lychee
tea. Three monks drift in through the outdoor kitchen—a grizzled
dotard leaning on the arm of a middle-aged man, trailed by a teenager
laden with bundles. Must be mountain nomads on a long pilgrimage,
Norbu guesses, judging from their wiry physiques and patina of
grime. They're a good omen, he adds: three monks together add up to
one Bodhisatva in spiritual force. Hearing our voices, the old monk sidles up for a closer gander at us through cataract-frosted eyes. The
flash of Norbu's yellow lama robes seems to have impressed him, but
he can't quite make out the rest of us.

While he's puzzling it over, his two companions drift across to the next cubicle to banter in Tibetan with a grinning, bearded farmer in a blue Chinese tunic and white skullcap. This must be a Tibetan Muslim, Norbu suggests: a more-or-less coerced convert. "Cut off from his people in a place like this, how could you expect him to hold out?" Norbu asks. "No wonder the Chinese promote these roads. A truck stop like this can be as effective as a whole army garrison in trampling our culture."

This strikes me as an uncharitable view of a harmless community that's only trying to make an honest living through useful service. But I presently get a brief inkling of the kind of cultural squeeze that Norbu has in mind. After lunch, I reach the jeep ahead of the others, who've detoured through the bazaar to buy sweets. Climbing aboard to wait, I find myself immediately surrounded by a crowd of three dozen young men in skullcaps, the biggest spontaneous audience I've ever drawn in China. They stare unwaveringly through the vehicle's windows, neither smiling nor menacing. I'm relieved when Norbu and the rest show up a few minutes later. We stow the sacks of candy they've bought, rev up the jeep, and roar unceremoniously out of town.

Coming down the ridge, we leave the Tsong valley and run alongside the broad main stream of the Yellow River. We're close enough to the source that the flow is swift and turbulent and glacially cold. But even this high up in the watercourse, the river is already yellow—a vernal, forsythia yellow, as it bears its burden of silt to the plains of Gansu and Ningxia. Here in Amdo, Norbu reminds us, are the headwaters of both the Yellow River and the Yangtze, the two main watercourses that have nurtured China for thousands of years "like a mother's breasts." He squints across the sun-flecked rapids to the brooding massif that rises on the opposite bank. "Wait until you see how the Chinese have treated this land, their Mother."

We cross a high concrete bridge and leave the Yellow River to follow a canyon up through the ramparts of the massif. Scraggly brown bluffs hem our road on either side. Our jeep churns up toward a V of blindingly blue sky. At the top of the notch, we break into a broad plateau. Up here the surrounding mountains bear down on us harder than in the plains below. Colors are more vivid, shadows crisper, the highlights more dazzling. Spring is not so far advanced at this altitude, scarcely more than a green mist hovering over the fields or snagged in poplar branches.

We see our first yaks, shaggy, shambling bovines, but with a rooted dignity all their own. Norbu laughs at the sight of them. He twaddles his forefinger and pinkie in the air to mime a pair of horns, hailing the yaks as "Yamantaka." That elicits only blank stares from the rest of us: Yama-who? He reminds us about the horned deity he pulled out of his deck of icon cards back at the "exorcism" at our house. *That* was Yamantaka.

I peer out the window, a bit at a loss to link up that fearsome image with these sad-eyed Dr. Seuss animals. They seem so at home against the backdrop of this pastoral idyll of stupa-studded greenery. Our friend himself, in his winged lama cap, fits right in, too, with this idealized Buddhist landscape. So it sounds somehow natural when he offhandedly informs us that "up ahead is Menya, one of my villages." But before we have a chance to ask him just what he means by "his" village, we round a bend to find a couple of thousand devotees lining the road.

NO TELLING HOW LONG these people have been waiting. Long enough, apparently, to arrange themselves in neat ranks, five or six rows deep, on the steep embankment. There's an air of quiet expectancy about them, robed figures each canted at a slight incline to the road, eyes straining in the direction of Xining. As soon as our jeep heaves into sight, the whole crowd shudders as if catching its collective breath. The women, with a nasal, unearthly wail, take up the drawn-out chant of the sacred syllables "*Mani*." The sound rises in pitch and intensity as the jeep rolls up to the crowd and parks in the middle of an elaborate lotus design chalked on the asphalt.

Faces press in at the window like a breaking wave, sunburnt faces, some weeping, some beaming. Children's faces, shy and curious. Old women with the toothless smiles of newborns. Young matrons, their brows furrowed with the intensity of their chant. Teenagers with laughing eyes. Husbandmen, frankly staring. Village elders, grave and fierce as cigar-store Indians. Norbu steps down from the jeep and the human wave parts for him. We scramble in his wake, gasping, as the elders escort him down the "main street" of Menya, a rutted dirt track between packed-mud walls. People prostrate themselves in the dust before him, weeping with joy. Chalk lotus *mandala*s have been carefully laid down in his path every few yards.

Over his shoulder, Norbu tosses us the information that "They've got a phone here"—explanation enough, as far as he's concerned, for the mass epiphany. He reminds us to snap as many photos as we can, the better to show his Beijing followers the reconstruction work he's sponsoring here in Amdo. Ah-loong clicks doggedly away with her venerable Nikon, while Felix and I try our best with our cheap point-and-shoots.

At the end of the street, cypress branches smolder on an altar atop the gateway to the village temple. A dozen young men perch on the flat roof of the gateway, blowing sostenuto tenor blasts on conch shells. On the tide of the *Mani* chant, we're swept into the temple building itself, a large, colonnaded room of unfinished pine so fresh-hewn that it still smells of resin. The village temple was wiped out during the Cultural Revolution and has only just been rebuilt, Norbu explains. Over time, the wooden wall panels and columns will be filled with painted icons. But for now, the room is unadorned—except for the back wall, which is crammed with painted deities, vivid floral and geometric *mandala* designs, gilt statues in glass cases, and portraits of distinguished lamas. Among the photos I can recognize the Dalai Lama (whose picture is technically illegal but widely displayed), the late Panchen, and Norbu's late uncle.

Norbu takes his place on an elevated throne, framed in red and yellow brocades. We're motioned to a seat facing him on an ornate carpet below his perch. All four of us receive a formal welcome offering: a brick of dried and compacted tea leaves, wrapped in brocade and draped with a filmy silk *khatag* scarf. A score of elders crouch in the corner of the room behind Norbu. Everybody else waits quietly in the courtyard. Not a peep even from the dozens of little boys peering in at the door or the latticework windows, although they elbow each other furiously and roll their eyes at each new gaffe of ours as we struggle to slurp and whittle our way through our first multicourse Tibetan banquet.

The meal starts with greasy, salted butter-tea. Then comes a plate of steamed mutton dumplings, precariously stacked in a slithery pyramid and prone to squirt at the first chomp. Next, a mound of rice smothered with yak fat, "Tibetan ginseng" (a kind of tuber), plus red beans and sugar. After that, a plate of boiled mutton served along with the requisite bowie-knife equivalent. The meal finishes up with a bowl of yogurt and more salty tea. A heavy diet, bereft of greenery, that leaves you with a gut like a sour-mash still.

Yet Norbu smiles beatifically as each new course lands. At first we take this as a sign of nostalgia for a cuisine he must seldom taste in Beijing. But in the course of our stay in Amdo, everywhere we go we find ourselves served the same banquet set—grease tea, ravioli, yak fat, mutton, and yogurt (hereafter abbreviated as GRYMY). After a week of such feasts, we realize that Norbu's apparent gusto about GRYMY is an act of pure Buddhist grace on the part of a curry devotee born and bred in India. We also get an inkling of how his late uncle might have attained his impressive girth.

As we're rounding on our third bowl of yogurt, the village headman begins his peroration. He's a hulking, stoop-shouldered man with a crinkly smile. His long braid wraps twice around his balding pate. The Amdo dialect seems to go in for a lot of tongue-clucking and tooth-sucking phonemes that lend a rueful and hesitant tone to the headman's whole speech. Norbu translates, sporadically, for our benefit. On behalf of Menya's 300-odd families, the headman hails the lama and welcomes the foreign guests. He's gratified to report that the crops have been good, the rains timely, and the taxes manageable. The village men have been lucky to find off-season work on building crews in towns and tailoring for the rich nomads of the uplands. The children are healthy and in school.

Norbu takes it all in, smiling and nodding and tossing off little asides that make the whole group murmur with laughter. After a while the talk turns numerate, with the lama doing elaborate sums on his prayer beads. We suppose he's reckoning village finances, but when I ask about it, Norbu sets us straight: he's actually fixing a quota of *Mani* mantras for the village to recite in the coming months. "You see, we're still on the planned economy here," he jokes.

These mantras, he adds, will make up for the ones destroyed in the Cultural Revolution. He laughs at my bafflement about how mantras, once spoken, could ever be unsaid by a turn of history. It seems Menya is trying to rebuild a stupa to replace one that was wrecked by Red Guards. But it's not just a matter of bricks and mortar. The accumulated mantras are the "active ingredient," Norbu explains, and you can't just siphon them from the old stupa to the new. You've got to say them all over again for the stupa to have force. Norbu issues the village a target of three million *Mani*s for this year.

That settled, the lama shifts his "throne" to a brocade-draped bridge chair in the front courtyard. It seems the entire village has lined up out there to receive him. They've ranked themselves in hierarchical orders. First come the elders, then the sturdy young farmers, followed by the old grannies. Middle-aged women carry babes-in-arms. After them come teenage girls, their hair done up primly in braids. A disorderly gaggle of children bring up the rear.

The line coils all around the courtyard and stretches out the temple gate into the "street." No shoving or jostling; everybody seems to fall automatically into place, a Great Chain of Being as unassailable as any that ever linked a medieval manor in Europe. One by one, the devotees file up to Norbu. Each bows and presents him a *khatag*, a tea brick, and a loaf of bread. The lama blesses each villager, who then shuffles on down the line to receive from an elder a specially consecrated candy (the same sort we bought just a couple of hours ago at our lunch stop). Behind the "throne," the temple gradually fills up with a wall of bread loaves and tea bricks. Over a thousand people receive benediction in this way, a real assembly-line operation.

Yet Norbu somehow seems to home in on each one of them with laser intensity, at least for the split second they're face-to-face. For one thing, there's eye contact, the lama repeatedly ducking to peer under the brows of the bowed faces. Then there are the custom-tailored gestures of blessing—gently swiping his beads across an old lady's brow, cupping a toddler's cheek, splaying a full palm with mock-machismo on some swaggering teenager's crew-cut pate. Our friend's glad-handing, baby-kissing instincts are as finely honed as any Chicago alderman's. And like a seasoned ward-heeler, he moves along briskly through the crowd.

Nor do the villagers, for their part, like to hang around the temple after their fleeting "audience." By the time the last little boy has been duly blessed, the courtyard's almost deserted. Just where everybody's gone is a mystery to us. The whole village seems eerily empty as we tag along behind Norbu for a turn about the grounds.

Not much street life here. Most human activity goes on inside family compounds, leaving the alleys in between as the province of a few dogs lazing in the shade. We dive into a warren of dirt tracks that thread their way between high mud walls. No trace of a grid pattern; the narrow, airless lanes are full of quirky twists and intersections at odd angles. The few passersby we encounter seem taken by surprise when our little procession heaves suddenly into sight as we round a bend. An old lady hurriedly pitches herself prone into the dust in a full-length prostration. Three little girls demurely withdraw into a recessed doorway.

A six-year-old boy leads Norbu by the hand through the maze of lanes. He chats affably and precociously with the lama, in marked contrast to the awe shown by almost everyone else in the village. When I ask how come, I'm told that this boy is the reincarnation of a distinguished old monk who had been Norbu's attendant in a previous life. This pint-sized ancient leads us past the stupa restoration project (no more than a brick pediment, so far). A few more twists and turns through the deserted streets and we emerge onto the main blacktop road.

Suddenly we find out what became of the temple crowds that melted away so mysteriously after Norbu's mass blessing. They've all rematerialized here. The villagers line up back at the roadside in hierarchical ranks, as before. We board the jeep and drive slowly off to the otherworldly strains of the *Mani* chant.

As SOON AS we're rolling, the three of us in the backseat burst out with all the reactions we'd been stifling ever since the sudden appearance of the Menya crowd had caught us off guard. "Did you see those statues in the temple? Must be worth a few hundred thousand, at least!" Felix estimates. "And that *Mani* singing!" Ah-loong enthuses. "Every time they launched into their chant, it brought tears to my eyes." As for me, I wonder how Norbu came to be lord of this particular village in the first place.

But our friend's too wrung out just now to deal with our comments and queries. He sinks back into his seat, smiles, and shrugs, mumbling a promise to talk it all over with us later tonight—our first inkling of how draining all this adoration must be, how spent it must leave him. And yet his face seems eased, rather than furrowed, in its tiredness, worn smooth like a river-polished rock.

He's already fast asleep by the time we swoop across the river and into Rui-an town, the county seat for this part of Amdo. The highway bridge terminates in a traffic circle with a clumsy, equestrian statue of some Long March commander who might have passed through these parts in civil war times. Convened around this plaza are the main public utilities and administrative buildings: post and telegraph office, courthouse, bus depot, birth-control clinic, gas pump, Party headquarters, police station, "hundred products" general store.

From the grandeur of the traffic circle, you'd expect a regular sunburst of boulevards to radiate off in all directions. But Rui-an's topography permits no such Place de l'Étoile. Just beyond the bridgehead, the riverside bluff tapers off into a narrow ridge, barely wide enough for a single, congested main street.

At the speed bump for this turnoff, Norbu jolts awake and peers grumpily through the windshield. Muslim stalls line this stretch of road—bicycle mechanic, portrait photographer, tobacconist, stationer. The road shoulder shears off steeply on one side, plunging into

a jumble of squat, utilitarian Chinese-style houses along the waterfront. Across the river, the smoking arc furnace of a mini–steel mill
glowers atop a low butte.

None of this should be here, as far as Norbu's concerned. It's all
an unwelcome add-on, a vitiation of the great Choeling Lamasery,
the town's original raison d'être as a place of human habitation. In
its time, Norbu proudly informs us, Choeling as a seat of learning
far outshone Labrang, the refurbished monastery that now diverts
tourists to nearby Gansu province. At Choeling, he relates, eighteen of Amdo's highest Living Buddhas each kept an "embassy."
Temple colleges here taught sutra exegesis, religious dialectic, Tantric meditation—even astronomy and medicine. Scores of farming
districts and nomad tribes maintained residential courtyards here
for their brightest sons to live in while they studied for monastic
orders.

The monastery occupies a separate ridge, which doesn't intersect
our route until we've driven a good half-mile inland from the river. To
Rui-an's main street, Choeling presents only its back walls and side
doors. The monastery, Norbu explains, has its own layout on an axis
quite apart from the town's.

Once, Choeling housed more than five thousand monks. Now there are barely four hundred—already a heartening comeback from the total devastation of the Cultural Revolution. In those days, the monks were forcibly "secularized"—married off and relegated to menial jobs. The derelict buildings bivouacked (successively) Red Guards, PLA troops, sheep, and yaks. Our first glimpse of the monastery recalls the devastation of the 1960s and seventies. At the far end of Rui-an, the main drag obliquely approaches Choeling's shattered outer wall. Through the crumbling masonry, we spot what's left of a couple of outlying "embassy" buildings—pillars and balustrades sagging awry, bleached like driftwood.

But once we leave the Rui-an highway, the monastery shows its more presentable face: fresh-packed mud walls, lavishly carved balconies, and lacquered wooden portals. We take a sharp turnoff and drive right through Choeling's main entrance. Norbu explains that the three-tiered gatehouse is, itself, a *mandala*. As we pass through the entryway, he points out the powerful Tantric diagram embedded in the ceiling to distinguish the sacred monastic precinct from the mundane town. From the eaves of the pagoda-style gatehouse roof a fringe of hanging prayer flags flutter like cilia, peristaltically waving us in.

We don't get far down the gullet of Choeling, though; Norbu's is the first door past the gatehouse. As soon as we broach the courtyard of his "embassy," we're met by a reception committee of a dozen monks. Only one of them looks a day less than sixty years old: a smiley, undersized person of ambiguous age. Judging by his height and unlined face, he could be a particularly scrawny preteen, yet he carries himself with the assurance of a grown-up. The others deferentially line up behind him in a row.

Tired as he is, Norbu immediately snaps to attention at the sight of this group. The elder monks, he explains, are abbots of individual temple colleges in the monastic "university." The boy-man is fourteen-year-old Tsultrim Drakpa, Choeling's only other recognized Living Buddha. As the monks one-by-one present their *khatag*s and tea offerings, Norbu bows deeply to each. The old men have to catch him by the elbows to keep him from prostrating himself flat on the ground. Little Tsultrim Drakpa scurries back a pace to brace himself against Norbu's headlong homage.

This is a far more complex exchange of greetings than the straight-forward swap of oblations for blessings at Menya village. Here Norbu faces a reception committee of revered elders and teachers who are yet his nominal disciples. And who knows what rarified protocols obtain when Buddha meets Buddha? Much of the nuance is lost on us, since it depends more on ritualized gesture—bows and blessings and who stands where—than on translatable speeches.

The whole reception is over within a quarter hour, but the ceremonial aura lingers long after the Choeling delegation takes its leave. As we settle into the snug little courtyard that's to be our temporary home for the coming week, even the basic domestic arrangements take on an air of ritual significance.

NORBU'S PLACE LENDS itself to this hieratic mood, thanks largely to the two full-time acolytes, a father-and-son team, who look after the house as devotedly as priests tending a shrine. An earnest young monk, Pema, shadows Norbu as a sort of butler, tending to the lama's personal errands. Chogyal, a bandy-legged old peasant as smiley as his son is grave, serves as general coolie and handyman. Between them, they create an atmosphere of order and dignity befitting a far more substantial lamasery.

In fact, this little courtyard is the last remnant of what used to be a much larger establishment. The three-room cottage is all that's left of the sprawling "embassy" complex maintained here at Choeling by Norbu's prior incarnations. The original compound was leveled in the Cultural Revolution. This lone surviving building, we're told, was once a porter's lodge; nobody ever dreamt at the time that it would someday house the next Living Buddha in the lineage. But, even in the present straitened circumstances, Pema and Chogyal do their best to keep it up to embassy standards.

From the cottage's tiny entry foyer, a kitchen branches off to the left. To the right of the foyer, Norbu's so-called audience chamber is barely large enough to accommodate two low tables and a stool. The lama keeps court on a narrow raised platform at one end of this room. At night, this space doubles as his bed, but by day he sits in state on a brocade cushion in front of the room's sole window. His throne faces a little lacquered altar table half-buried in religious flotsam—silk-covered sutras, brass bells, bronze icons, smoking incense-burners, laminated Dalai Lama portraits, offering bowls full of water, a potted plant with exuberant yellow flowers.

Norbu settles onto his cushion and bids us "Welcome to my *mandala*."

This strikes me as a strange usage of the term. Maybe I'm still not grasping his concept of a *mandala*. I mentally review the things he's already referred to today as *mandala*s. What, I ask him, is the common denominator between this cottage, the fearsome deity he showed us on the day of our exorcism, the Choeling gatehouse, the chalk designs on the asphalt back in Menya village, the geometric patterns on the temple wall, and the yak-butter sculptures we saw on our luncheon table?

"Nothing mysterious about it," he reassures me. "A *mandala* is just a kind of order that you put things in. It helps you keep track of what's where."

He indicates the jumble of trinkets on his altar. "For instance, this little table of mine is a *mandala*. Visitors come and bring me these offerings. Later on I pass along the same things to other visitors. Import-export. And in the meantime, for the short while it's with me, each of these items finds its proper, orderly place here." My face must register my doubts; all that heaped altar clutter hardly strikes me as a paradigm of order. So Norbu hastens to offer another example.

"The same goes for your job. *Any* job. It's a kind of *mandala*, a temporary order that you bring to things. At least that is how it ought to be when you are doing your job properly, as a devotion. You can just *feel* it, can't you? How all aspects of the job—your tools, your materials, your colleagues, your public—fall naturally into place in an order all their own. No matter what kind of work it is: your writing, Pema's housekeeping, Felix's deal-making. For every job, there is a Way of it, an order, something an expert worker knows, instinctively, by long experience."

"So what's *your* job?" I ask. "What's the work for which this Choeling *mandala*'s created?"

"Simple enough," Norbu laughs. "You and I—we're here to become Buddhas."

Sounds like a pretty tall order to me. Surely he must mean to study the Buddha, to appreciate Him, even to imitate Him, perhaps. But to *become* Buddha?

"Well, why not?" Norbu challenges. "All we mean by 'Buddha' is one who is enlightened, who sees things clearly, free from subjective distortions. And *that* is just a matter of perspective and proportion, isn't it? Of order, in other words. A *mandala*."

If Buddhahood is the task we've set ourselves, I protest, then I for one can hardly lay claim to "an instinctive sense of the Way of it through long experience." But Norbu's quite unfazed at having his own words thrown back at him. "Then you can simply *borrow* experience from a guru," he suggests. "Watching an expert, you just naturally sense the rightness of his every move. The guru himself is a *mandala*, an order. If you follow him closely, you become just like the guru, already well along on the path of enlightenment."

For many are the paths to Buddhahood, he assures us. Every Buddhist deity we've encountered—the bull-headed Yamantaka ("Slayer of Death") icon at our exorcism, the five-story-high Maitreya ("Future Buddha") at Beijing's Lama Temple, the Compassionate Tara this morning at Menya village—each represents, in its own way, an enlightened state of mind. We can become any one of these beings, he promises, if only we can attain that deity's characteristic state of mental equilibrium and clarity. This isn't a matter of autohypnosis or a delusion of grandeur, he adds. But it *does* require great concentration to hold simultaneously in mind all the many facets of a highly evolved consciousness. "So pay attention and keep an open mind," he bids us. "Look beyond the surface of things."

Thus admonished, I make a closer inspection of the scene before me, starting with the scroll painting hung behind Norbu's altar. It depicts two Living Buddhas, sitting back-to-back, surrounded by assorted spirits, acolytes, and devotees. Alien as the iconography is to me, the two main figures in the painting look somehow familiar. A round-faced, beaming lama dominates the foreground. His widow's-peak tonsure makes him look a little like Norbu himself. Behind him, peering into the background (Sichuan? Mongolia?), sits a sad-eyed, swarthier lama with a bulbous brow—could it be Samudra Rinpoche?

I ask Norbu about these identifications and he guffaws at my over-reading of these likenesses. "Sure. Right. You guessed it. What an eye!" he teases. "And that's not all: see this funny creature here?" (Some sort of vaguely leonine heraldic beastie rampant, pawing the air.) "That, believe it or not, is Hui Hui. And this fat little barbarian?" (A flame-haired midget squatting in the bottom-left corner with a pained expression on his face.) "That's you."

Hearing myself likened to this crabbed troll, I decide it's time to go out and stretch my legs. I step into the courtyard for a breather. After so many hours cramped in the back of a jeep or squatting cross-legged on prayer rugs, it's a relief to finally unlimber. In the shadow of the *mandala*-emblazoned gatehouse, Norbu's little compound centers on a brick altar for burning cypress branches. Against the whitewash-spattered mud wall, a flowering walnut tree scatters petals over the rusted hulk of a parked tractor. I wind up my tour of the grounds with a visit to the outhouse. The toilet is just a pit bridged by a couple of pine planks for squatting. Behind the trench is a pile of ash and a spade to use in lieu of flush. A six-inch gap between the thatch roof and the mud walls lets in plenty of light and air.

Basic as these sanitary arrangements may be, the Tibetan outhouse is still a lot cleaner and less of an ordeal than the dingy, crusty public toilets of the Han people who dominate China's heartland. Perhaps it's the ventilation that does it, or the spadeful of ash: at least each user takes responsibility for his own leavings.

BUT IF AMDO TIBETANS manage to resist Chinese toilet culture, they're evidently more susceptible to other Han domestic amenities.

So we conclude, anyway, from a visit later that evening to Norbu's "sister," Rinchen Tsering, and her policeman husband, Thubten Namgyal. To reach their house, we have to leave the monastic precinct and hike back to the secular end of town. The farther we get down the Rui-an high street, the more the architecture borrows from the ad hoc vernacular of Chinese urban squatter settlements. Packed mud construction gives way to cinderblock. Instead of wooden latticework, the windows sport iron grilles. TV antennae outnumber prayer flags.

Halfway down the road, Norbu spots a Tibetan about his own age in a conspicuously outlandish getup: billowy silk shirt, blue jeans, silver pendant, hair gathered back in a ponytail. We've seen plenty of more gaudily costumed people in Rui-an, but for them the heavy ornaments and elaborate coiffures are all badges of tribe or sect. This man's foppery, on the other hand, would pass for a flamboyantly individualistic fashion statement in the coffeehouses of L.A., Milan, or Calcutta.

Norbu hauls up short at the sight of him: *"Waah!"* The other man seems even more surprised and eyes Norbu up and down, taking in the lama's monastic habit before he ventures an incredulous *"Wah! Yaar?"* They fall to animated chatter in Hindi, catching up on what seems like a news backlog of many years. And, sure enough, when Norbu pauses long enough to introduce his friend, it turns out that the two of them haven't seen each other since they were dormitory mates in the Tibetan boarding school in Mussourie, India.

The man presents us with his business card, which announces him as Tashi, dealer in curios. Although still based in Nepal, he says, he travels more and more in China these days because that's where the best antique hunting is to be found now. Also, increasingly, the best market, as Chinese acquire both the cash and the taste for bric-a-brac. Are we collectors? Whatever our pleasure, he can find it: Tibetan, Nepali, Indian, or Chinese. His card lists a pair of contact numbers: one in Katmandu and another in Chengdu, Sichuan. Or else, he suggests, we can reach him care of a wire-service reporter of our acquaintance, whom he describes as his Beijing girlfriend.

Watching the two old school chums catch up, I find myself wondering how much external conditioning (versus innate spirituality) separates our stately lama from this fantastic harlequin. Were it not for the Living Buddha status that has hovered over Norbu, acknowledged or not, since childhood, might our friend have wound up a will-o'-the-wisp like Tashi?

Felix looks all set to get down to business with the curio-monger, but we have no time to linger as we're expected for dinner. Our driver has already gone ahead of us to unload all the duffel bags stuffed with family presents that Norbu brought with him. We find our jeep parked in front of Rinchen and Thubten's trim, new concrete house. To alleviate the starkness of the unpainted, bunkerlike structure, the outer gates sport woodblock Chinese door gods and gold-brushed good-luck calligraphy. A tasseled red silk lantern glows over the entryway.

Inside, an eclectic hodgepodge of posters fills up most of the wall space. In the parlor, a red-faced Guan Gong, the Chinese god of military and commercial success, squares off against a livid Medicine Buddha *tangka* calendar. The hallway is lined with mawkish animal photos and giant blowups of "Hello Kitty" cartoons.

Since women cannot stay in the monastery, Rinchen and Thubten have offered their own bed to Ah-loong for the duration—a sumptuous queen-sized spring mattress, all done up in purple velour, throw pillows, and lace flounces. Like chubby cupids, a pair of twin baby boys preside over this connubial couch in a framed rotogravure. This picture is more than just decorative, Norbu points out. It has a talismanic function, too, since Rinchen and Thubten are "trying for twins." They've already got a two-year-old daughter who stays with a childless aunt back in Thubten's home village, in line with Amdo Tibetan custom.

Under Beijing's birth-control policy, a couple from China's dominant ethnic group, the Han, would have to stop at only one child. But as a member of a minority, Rinchen's entitled to another pregnancy. "So that's one extra privilege, at least, that we get from the government just for being Tibetan," Norbu tartly concedes. "Little do they know they're helping us establish a dynasty." The irony, he adds, is that Rinchen's particular branch of the dynasty owes its very existence to Chinese persecution in the first place.

She's not actually his biological sister, Norbu explains, but rather a cousin; the daughter of his late uncle, the portly Living Buddha whose revered portrait we encounter on altars all over Amdo. Celibate all his life, the uncle was dragged from his monastery at the onset of the Cultural Revolution and forced to marry. When it came to ex-lamas, China's family-planning cadres—armed with inquisitorial powers and comprehensive medical records for everyone—proved that they could promote, as readily as prevent, fertility. Rinchen is the result of this forced union.

Even after marriage, though, the uncle didn't get to live long with his new family. As anti-Buddhist pogroms intensified, he was interned in a "Reform Through Labor" camp, where he ended his days hand-transcribing quotations from Chairman Mao in crude Chinese characters. Rinchen still keeps these smudged copybooks of his, which were turned over to the family by prison authorities after his death—a poignant legacy from a Tibetan-language poet once renowned for his devotional verses.

The tragic circumstance of her birth continues to haunt Rinchen's life. Such a person, the daughter of a high lama, shouldn't even *exist* in a well-ordered Buddhist society. So Rinchen poses a quandary for post–Cultural Revolution Tibetans: How to treat the lineal descendant of a Living Buddha? Should she be seen as a respected blue-blood or as an affront to the faith and the community? Shadowed by such questions, no wonder she tries to lead as uncontroversial a life as she can manage in a Qinghai context. Rather than plunging into the traditional Tibetan village world of Amdo, she retreats to the limbo of the county town's bilingual civil service. She lives in the Chinese end of Rui-an and holds a low-profile job as a clerk in the electric utility office.

When it came time for her to marry, Rinchen sought a mate within the same "sandwich class" of bilingual middle managers. Thubten, a smiley sergeant in the local constabulary, filled the bill admirably. Their marriage was the toast of Rui-an's junior bureaucracy. "Go ahead, show off the wedding pictures," Norbu urges, so Rinchen obliges with a whirlwind tour of their satin-covered family photo album:

Shy high school mug shots of each of them. Formal bridal tableau, she in her organdy gown and he in a tux. Honeymoon in Beijing, the two of them beaming in front of the Great Wall, Tiananmen, and such. Some boulevard photographer snapped a Polaroid of them at a sidewalk café on Chang An Road, downing beers with an as-yet-untonsured Norbu. Next we see Rinchen back home cuddling their firstborn. There's Thubten in his office, resplendent in his olive-green uniform behind a large and cluttered desk.

Ah-loong congratulates them on their handsome home and family and on Thubten's promising career. So the force (i.e., the police force) has been good to you? Well, yes, but . . .

But what? Well . . . the bosses. Much of his work is pure transla-tion, he admits, just mediating between his Han superiors and his Amdo countrymen. Ironic, considering that most of the Chinese cops were born, raised, and recruited right here in Amdo. But they're ab-solutely clueless when it comes to Tibetan language and culture—too obtuse even to catch the curses that are hurled at them. So a go-between like Thubten winds up bearing the full brunt of popular resentments.

And the tasks get more and more thankless every year—rooting out pamphleteers and firebrand preachers, "following up" on failed escapees who have been caught on the Nepal border, and such. Even ostensibly straightforward criminal cases—smuggling, feuding, theft—take on a political edge when you get into them. They show how the consumerism and the payola culture of the Han heartland subverts and fragments the Tibetan community, a far cry from the high hopes that Thubten had pinned upon "reform and opening" in his student days at Xining's Minorities Institute in the early 1980s.

Still, the ebb of Maoist fanaticism *has*, at least, transformed his own personal life into a picture of provincial bourgeois respectability. Thubten and Rinchen's upstairs parlor proudly exhibits a panoply of coveted consumer durables. Half the room is devoted to their "entertainment center"—a twenty-four-inch color TV, complete with VCR and karaoke amplifier. Three separate remote controls loll on the over-stuffed cushions of their leatherette sofa. At the other end of the parlor, behind the Formica dining room set, a glass-front cabinet shows off their collection of porcelain ornaments and trophy bottles (unopened) of Johnnie Walker Red and Rémy Martin.

THE BOTTLES REMAIN unopened, alas, throughout our welcome-to-Rui-an dinner. But at least we're spared another round of GRYMY tonight. Instead, we're served a lavish spread of boiled vegetables, mayonnaise salad, and tinned ham. After dessert (lemon custard, no less), the author of this feast emerges from the kitchen to accept our plaudits: Tenzing, an affable ex-monk who spent twenty-two of his sixty-odd years in a Chinese reform-through-labor camp. That's where he learned to cook the exotic delicacies we've just savored, he tells us with pride; for his "good attitude" he was named personal chef to the camp commandants.

While we're left to digest this bit of news along with our dinner, our hosts turn to the pleasant task of unpacking Norbu's duffel bags. There are presents for everybody. Rinchen gets some frilly blouses and a snappy Jane Fonda warm-up suit; for Tenzing, there's a nylon windbreaker. Thubten, notorious dandy that he is, gets a pullover sweater and a tweed sports coat—"to wear on duty when you're assigned to the 'plainclothes' detail," Norbu kids him.

The holiday mood is interrupted by the arrival of a couple of petitioners: a ponderous young monk and a wiry, compact, middle-aged nomad with staccato gestures and twitchy eyes. Both prostrate themselves full-length before the lama right there on the parlor floor. Then the nomad nudges the monk forward to do the talking.

He doesn't take long to get himself totally entangled in his convoluted story. Only a few sentences into the saga and already Norbu has to interject questions just to keep the pronouns straight. Behind the monk, practically hopping with frustration, the nomad can't restrain himself from tossing in details, clarifications, and emphasis, which only add to the confusion. Finally Norbu waves the monk aside and tells the nomad to speak for himself. Then the tale pours out in a froth of fear and rage, sentences treading on each other in jumbled cadence. The nomad slaps his chest, recoils from imaginary blows, darts glances over his shoulder as though pursued. His gestures are amplified by the flapping sleeves of his robe. A dagger glints in his sash, ready to hand—no mere showpiece but a vital part of his personal accoutrement, judging from the tenor of his tale.

Even with all the histrionics, however, the whole story leaves the lama as mixed up as ever about who did what to whom. Something involving the wastrel son of a local Party secretary in one of the nomad districts. Someone's daughter was affronted, people were beaten up, retaliatory shots fired, someone wounded in the head, someone else knifed, Norbu translates for us as near as he can figure it all out. And, evidently, the imbroglio is still escalating. Norbu orders the monk to collect full information from all parties and bring back a coherent, objective summary as soon as possible. Then he dismisses the pair. With another round of prostrations, they take their leave, the nomad still tossing off philippics over his shoulder as he's bundled down the stairs.

What a mess, Norbu sighs. Although he's only hearing one side of the story, the situation has him worried. It takes on overtones of ethnic conflict, Han versus Tibetans, as well as intra-Tibetan clan and sect rivalries among the nomads themselves—a no-win situation. Our visitors wanted Norbu to weigh in with the prestige of his Living Buddhahood. But before he can do so, the lama needs more facts. If it really turns out to be a case of administrative malfeasance, Norbu says, he'd have to refer it to his father in Xining, who could take it up with the People's Political Consultative Committee, of which he is a member.

Would that actually do any good? I ask, skeptically. More than you'd suppose, Norbu assures me. China's boomtown climate makes for increasingly high-handed officialdom all across the country, and in outlying minority areas the cadres show even less restraint than in the Han metropole. A countervailing voice back in the provincial capital can serve as a crucial check on local satraps. Don't be too quick to dismiss a ceremonial conclave like the Qinghai PPCC, Norbu warns us. Used sparingly, it may be a bit like the dagger that nomad was wearing just now: not so purely ornamental as it looks.

THE NOMAD'S SOBERING STORY puts us on alert as we thread our way, silently, in single file, back up the main drag of town to Norbu's house. It's not exactly a free-fire zone, but an implicit tension marks this empty, windblown highway as a front line between clashing cultures.

Techno-pop pours out of the neighboring houses as we say goodnight to Ah-loong in Rinchen's doorway. Snatches of movie dialogue blare from a TV somewhere among the bracken of antennae in the huddled Chinese shanties below the high street. A gibbous moon, newly risen, japes over the steel mill across the valley. Hardly any signs of life up at the Tibetan end of town; just the occasional glimpse of some lonely robed figure scuttling across the road ahead of us, silent and fleet as a tumbleweed.

We veer off the main highway and pass through the *mandala* gatehouse arch into the monastery. Along Choeling's central thoroughfare, all doors are shut; the inward-looking, self-absorbed courtyard houses present only their outer walls to us. In the lone streetlight, wind-tossed tree shadows plunge crazily across the blank masonry and the packed-mud street. Warily picking our way between wheel-ruts, we don't let our guard down until we're safely inside the snug little box of Norbu's audience chamber.

The tidy, thought-out order of our sleeping arrangements enhances the coziness of the little room. Pema and Chogyal have cleared away all furniture and laid down quilts for us on the carpets. For Norbu, they've stowed the "throne" cushion and spread a sumptuous eiderdown. In the flattering half-light of an overhead 40-watt bulb, Norbu's raised platform takes on the glamour of a deluxe railway couchette: glints of polished wood and brass, billows of snowy linen before a pitch-black window. The lama uncinches the pleats of his

waistband and gathers his robes up around his shoulders before settling down in his first-class berth with his head nestled against the
altar. Felix and I, still in our jeans, settle in for a night of ordinary
"hard-sleeper" curled up on the carpets below. Norbu admonishes us
to remember our dreams.

In this, I fail him. The night passes in an eyeblink of deep, refresh-
ing sleep; if I dreamt at all, I certainly don't remember it. But my
awakening could hardly be more dreamlike. My eyes snap open to see
Norbu, already sitting cross-legged, silhouetted against the backdrop
of the window, with Felix kneeling reverently before him. The moon
is setting over the *mandala* gatehouse and the sun has yet to rise. Color
filters into the cloudless sky. In the window behind Norbu, the gilt
cupola on the gatehouse roof gleams without dazzle in the predawn
gloaming. Nothing yet casts a shadow. The darting swallows, the rip-
pling prayer flags, the ghostly almond tree against the courtyard
wall—all glow in flat, omnidirectional, unsourced light; the timeless
twilight of a *tangka*.

Except no *tangka* could convey the audio track that accompanies
this scene: the low thrum of chanting from every courtyard in the
monastery. It's a close-weave web of sound punctuated with bells
and trumpets. The bass line—a surging, spondaic, basso profundo
growl—serves as a foil for singsong anapestic tenor flights. The chant
is relentless, like the engine of a ship churning through dark, rough
seas.

Against this backdrop, Norbu sits with his robe draped over his
head, a rooted black pyramid centered in the *tangka* frame of the window. Out of this featureless, motionless silhouette, the voice rises,
barely audibly in a steady, low-keyed stream of Hindi-accented English. He must have been speaking with Felix for some time already. I
tune in on the discourse in midsentence: ". . . just a crib sheet, really,
like what you'd carry into an exam back in school. Something to help
you remember a lot of details and keep them all properly sorted out."

He's back on the subject of *mandala*s, I guess. Perhaps Felix voiced
some bewilderment at all the exotic details of iconography that constantly surround us in a place like Choeling. "It can get pretty confus-

ing, can't it?" Norbu allows. "All those icons with so many heads and arms and tools and emblems. Some even seem to be—pardon the expression—*fucking*." Here he breaks into a pretty convincing imitation of a Beijing gangster and drawls in Chinese: "Mother-jump! What kind of a God is *that*?" He resumes in English: "Well, there *is* a meaning, rest assured—every element in every *tangka* is there for some reason."

The same goes for the more abstract types of *mandala*, too, he adds. These can be anything from a yak-butter sculpture to an unbelievably intricate design that monks spend weeks assembling with colored grains of sand. Some are no more than chalk squiggles on the ground. The famous sage Marpo once even sketched a *mandala* for his disciple Milarepa by pissing in the dust. Whatever the medium, these geometric *mandala*s are meant as blueprints to help you find your way through the abodes of the deities, Norbu explains. Just as the details of each deity's physique denote aspects of his consciousness, so do the features of his dwelling. "If you can find your way around his house and learn to be at home there," he suggests, "it can make it easier for you to *become* the deity."

But don't try this on your own, he warns. "Better not get into the practice of any deity without a guru and an initiation. After all, these are pretty high-powered states of mind we're talking about. If you get it wrong or mix up any part of the 'crib sheet,' it can be very dangerous."

To hear him tell it, a Buddhist practitioner can't do much without priestly permission. Even the most basic mantra, like *Om Mani Padme Hum*, by rights should come from a guru. "After all, isn't a mantra just a way of putting things in order, kind of a *mandala* in sound? And, you know, there's a mantra, a protocol, for everything."

SOMETIMES, a ticklish protocol problem can leave even a Living Buddha stumped for an appropriate mantra, as we discover later that morning when a well-to-do shopkeeper hosts a breakfast for us and assorted Tibetan worthies of the town. Aside from Norbu, the chief guest is Rui-an's county magistrate, who has promised to supply us jeep transport over the next couple of days for our expeditions up to outlying monasteries.

Mixing dignitaries from the Communist and the Buddhist hierarchies presents awkward questions of precedence. The magistrate pointedly arrives later than we do. He offers a tea brick with *khatag* and he bows his head for a pass of Norbu's beads, but he omits the full prostration. He's seated down below the "throne," but in a privileged place, directly facing the lama. The two guests of honor seem at a loss for how to address each other, and both appear relieved when I exercise my barbarian's prerogative to ask naïve, direct questions. Yes, the magistrate is the first ethnic Tibetan to head the county administration. No, the local Party secretary is still a Han. The magistrate, a shrewd-faced man in his fifties, has been in government ever since he graduated from the Minorities Institute in Xining in 1969.

Those must have been trying times for an ethnic Tibetan to launch a bureaucratic career, I reflect. How might this man have had to show his Maoist fervor during the ethnic cleansing and iconoclastic frenzy of the Cultural Revolution? And what flip-flops has he been through in the decades since then to survive the ensuing swings in Party line? Not surprisingly, the magistrate won't be drawn out on these subjects, despite my daintiest efforts to probe. Suffice it to say that things are looking up nowadays for Amdo's Tibetans—as indeed for all of China, under the Party's "enlightened line of reform and opening in pursuit of a Socialist market economy," he adds in a breathless burst of stock piety.

Nevertheless, he points out, Rui-an remains one of Qinghai's officially designated "poor counties." This status has its consolations: it lightens the tax burden appreciably. Among Tibetans, nomad areas of the county are better off than the agrarian villages, and the market economy allows for some transfer of wealth between the two. Still, he admits, when I ask about it, that most commerce remains in the hands of non-Tibetans: Han and Hui, who migrate here in increasing numbers.

That's about as far as he cares to go, however, on the delicate subjects of ethnicity and the distribution of wealth in Rui-an. The magistrate hurriedly retreats into his bureaucratic shell, reeling off a protective smokescreen of statistics—grain production, animal husbandry, electrification rates, kilometers of paved road. At last, we've found our way back into the realm of mantras—the steadying quantitative incantations of Communist officialdom all over China.

Nobody else in the room seems to care much about his numbers. Attention drifts, eyes glaze, and people strike up whispered conversations. Norbu motions a late-arriving monk to come sit beside him on the dais. The two bow their heads together in low chuckles over some private joke. When the lama moves into the courtyard to bless the assembled neighbors, the magistrate uses the opportunity to excuse himself. His departure stirs no fanfare. People are too intent on lining up for Norbu's blessings. After passing out a sack of candies, our friend resumes his throne and seemingly picks up his joke with the same monk right where they left off.

The monk is taller than Norbu, rangy, loose-jointed. The sun has bleached his robes and burnt his skin until both are nearly the same oaken shade. Out of his dark face, the eyes flash all the whiter because of his characteristic posture: head slightly bowed, chin tucked into his leathery neck, he peers from beneath brows as bristly as the stubble of his tonsure. Even when he laughs, which he does a lot, the glance never wavers and the eyes never squint. There's a density about him that sets him apart.

This is Jigshed, Norbu introduces, "a very sincere practitioner." In the worst of times, when many fell away, Jigshed remained steadfast to his vows, defying torments and temptations. Norbu adds, as an afterthought, that Jigshed is a devotee of Yamantaka, the bull-headed deity of our exorcism. His Yamantaka initiation process lasted for eighteen totally sleepless months.

But surely, I object, he must have had to recharge himself somehow in all that time. Norbu relays my question and the monk nods a one-word reply. "Meditation," Norbu translates. "The body takes care of itself; it's beside the point." Did he never rest? I press. No time; can't afford to break concentration. But didn't he dream? Meditation,

Jigshed nods again. By this time, Norbu's openly chuckling at how my every question draws a blank. "How about letting him interview you, instead," he suggests. Why, sure, if there's anything he'd like to . . .

Jigshed swivels his beetle-browed gaze full onto me for the first time. He says something curt and cool, like Lewis Carroll's caterpillar: "*Who*," Norbu translates, "are *you*?" Well, I stammer, I'm a middle-aged American, a writer, a father of three . . .

"Yes, but who *are* you?" Well . . . a seeker, a student, an evolving soul, I sanctimoniously aver. "Sure, but where do you seek, O Seeker, when you're trying to find *you*, your*self*? In your head? In your heart? In your pants?"

All I can do for a moment is gulp speechlessly. Then I try again, just mumbling, with no idea of what I'm getting at. I recall how, as a child, I'd try now and then—just experimentally, you know—to actually *feel* myself thinking. And how once or twice I even convinced myself I could trace the flicker of thought about the orb of my mind, like summer lightning.

Or how my sister and I, bored with the grown-up talk over the weekly family brunch at my Aunt Betty's in Brooklyn, used to while away Sunday afternoons drawing mechanistic diagrams of the human psyche. Our pictures featured cutaway views of a compartmentalized human head crammed full of demons and demiurges, dynamos and dump trucks. It was all linked up by chutes and ladders, and run by white-coated technicians from a Central Control Room.

Norbu struggles hard with the translation of this one. Jigshed's interest visibly flags in my plodding, Western approach; evidently I'm getting "cold," drifting further afield from whatever he's getting at with his unnerving question. I look to Felix, but he just blinks blandly back at me through his specs. Ah-loong keeps fumbling with her camera to avoid my mute appeal. No help from either of them. I'm on my own and on the spot.

Look, I blurt, I'm not as up on this stuff as I once was. I mean, about finding myself and all that. Maybe I don't care so much anymore. You know what I like best now, sometimes? When I'm bicycling in Beijing at, say, rush hour in the winter, and the road's overcrowded and everybody's too busy and too happy going home to even bother gaping at a foreigner like me. And someone in the crowd stops for a *jian bing* (fried bread) on the street, really enjoying it. And somebody else is playing with a baby in a roadside doorway. And the smog makes for a pretty sunset. And if I watch quietly enough, I almost convince myself that I can taste the *jian bing* or smell the baby's hair. And nobody sees me, nobody even looks my way. Because I'm nobody then. I'm not even there. I'm them."

"Ah, then, you've *got* it," Jigshed pronounces. But he beetles me a look as though he somehow doubts I've got much of anything. And I have to admit I feel a long way from a state of Buddhist self-detachment as I squirm under the laser-beam of those eyes of his. It's a relief to escape from the room and go for a walking tour of the monastery.

IT'S EARLY AFTERNOON ALREADY, and the slanting light brings out the russet walls and gilt spires of Choeling. The murals shine like new—no wonder, since hardly any of them are more than a decade old, having been repainted from scratch after their total obliteration during the Cultural Revolution. Inside the temples, dust motes and incense smoke laze upward among the *tangka*s and banners and gaudily painted rafters. We mount successive terraces until we're near the roofline of the central refectory. Norbu and our two monastic guides do what they can to explain the functions of the assorted colleges and the iconography of the images.

What brings us up short, though, is the last and tallest of the temple halls, the analogue of the Maitreya sanctuary that we'd seen in Beijing's Lama Temple. Unlike the overstuffed chamber in the Yong He Gong, here the Maitreya tower is completely empty: five stories high, with nothing in it but bat droppings and sagging beams. Even the walls have been scraped to a featureless gray. No romantic, eloquent Piranesian ruin, this—nothing at all to suggest that it was ever even conceived as a room for human occupation. Just as blank as a sealed elevator shaft.

We peer in through a vent near the roofline. In the updraft of dead air, we catch a whiff of an annihilation more complete than the corruption of a grave or the encroachment of a desert. The fanaticism that wrought this destruction aimed to snuff the Maitreya all at once like a candle flame, leaving no trace.

And yet the hope of the Maitreya, the "Buddha-Yet-to-Come," burns on undimmed for the dozen old men who run the monastery, the abbots of the Choeling colleges. A glow of faith illumines the sexagenarian faces lined up in two facing rows across the long table of the abbots' refectory above the main courtyard of the Dialectic College. Norbu presides over the luncheon on a high throne. Our friend is the only one alive right now who can fill that throne, he tells us. Norbu and little Tsultrim Drakpa are the only known current incarnations of any of the eighteen high lamas whose "embassies" comprise Choeling. And the boy lama, as a junior student in the monastery, can hardly preside over its council of abbots.

Given the urgency of their need for him, Norbu's hard-pressed to explain to these old men why he must remain, for the present, in the outside world rather than taking day-to-day charge of Choeling. Intellectually, they may recognize that only away from Amdo can he best pursue the fund-raising and public-relations missions so vital to Buddhist reconstruction. But just how he operates "out there," and in what sort of milieu, remains to them a mystery. At the same time, they long to have their refectory throne filled full-time. "And someday soon," he promises—quietly, as though more to himself than to the room at large—"I'll come back here and fill it for them."

Upon Ah-loong, Felix, and me the abbots place far more modest demands. They merely want to know from us how soon to expect the wholesale Buddhist conversion of the countries we come from. We gently hint that the U.S. and even Taiwan—let alone mainland China—might have a way to go yet. They greet this news with a good deal of head-shaking and tongue-clucking, whether out of skepticism or disappointment at our prognosis, I can't quite tell.

What most interests them, though, are the half-frame reading glasses hanging on a lanyard around my neck, much thinner and lighter than the googly-eyed hornrims these abbots are used to. I hand my glasses for inspection to the venerable cleric on my right. They're passed down one side of the table and back up the other. One by one, each old man holds the specs in front of his face and squints across the room. They can't seem to grasp, despite my attempts to explain, and Norbu's dutiful translation, that these glasses are meant for close-up vision, for reading. Nor will any of them be persuaded to actually try on the eyewear and see for themselves—arms'-length inspection is both more respectful of me and less polluting to them. No wonder they come to the consensus that my glasses may be stylish but not worth much for seeing.

As the GRYMY comes around to its inevitable yogurt course, the yard below fills with the yammer of dialectic practice. We press onto the refectory balcony to watch. Maybe a hundred monks are splayed about the heavy cobbles of the courtyard, like garnet-and-ochre stars on a slate-gray firmament. They gather in constellations of two or three or four debaters. One monk in each set acts as the Challenger. From up here on the balcony, he's a whirligig of flailing robes. He rocks back on his heels to recite his premise, then lunges forward to score his debating point with as much hubbub—hand-clapping, finger-waggling, bead-rattling—as he can muster. The Defender sits before him, rooted in a lotus position, rebutting every assault with an apt citation of Immutable Law.

The point of the exercise is to cultivate unflappability, Norbu explains. A true dialectician should be equally adept as either Challenger or Defender. Most of the jousts are one-on-one, but here and there an elder debater might solo against a row of junior Defenders. Or a senior monk might maintain stolid composure bedeviled by a gang of high-pitched preteen hectorers. In one klatsch of debaters, when rhetoric fails him a little monk resorts to a cannonball charge and everybody in his group collapses, laughing, to the cobbles. Spirits run high. This is the intellectual gallop of the day, the afternoon romp around the paddock of monastic discipline.

But descending from the refectory we cross the courtyard and get

an eye-level look at the debaters. Only then do we grasp how truly unnerving can be the onrush of the Challenger, the rhetorical head of steam he builds up, the violence of his body language, the zeal of his doubt. At the same time, we sense the maddening deadpan, the sheer, hunkered-down dogmatism of the Defenders. How their impassivity must goad their opponents to paroxysms of nay-saying. I can imagine such training coming in handy for monks during the mass denunciations of the Cultural Revolution. This game is played for keeps, I realize, like a bullfight. I offer the comparison to Norbu and he just flashes me the two-finger Yamantaka sign, grinning.

RETURNING TO HIS OWN COURTYARD, Norbu finds an entire village full of people waiting for him—grannies and toddlers and plowmen and farm wives, maybe fifty devotees altogether. As soon as they heard that Norbu was back in Amdo, they all trekked across from deep in the mountains over Gansu way, their headman explains. They've waited most of the afternoon for a brief audience, after which they'll make the six-hour hike home, returning well after dark.

Norbu repeats his usual blessing ceremony for them, distributing candies. But what really makes a hit with this crowd is when the lama produces a stack of pictures of himself to give out. Just ordinary Fujicolor snapshots—taken, as it happens, in our Beijing living room. We thought it odd, perhaps even a touch vain, when he asked us to reprint a few dozen copies. But now in this courtyard we can see first-hand how much these icons mean to Norbu's devotees. Anyone lucky enough to receive a picture kowtows with gratitude and sheds tears of joy. Ah-loong climbs up on a stool beyond the back row for an over-the-shoulder shot of all those hands reverently cupping the little snapshots and all those heads bent in devotion. She finds the scene so moving that she starts sniffling herself.

And she feels even weepier when she finishes what should be the last picture on the roll and then feels no tug on the spool as she tries to rewind. Her heart freezes: could it be that the film has snapped? She's so worried about it that, as soon as the courtyard has emptied and Norbu's withdrawn to his "embassy" for a rest, she drags me off to town to find a photo shop. She wants to open up the camera in a proper darkroom so we can find out what's going on without exposing the entire roll.

Midway down the Rui-an high street, we come upon the House of Yuan Portrait Salon. A signboard displays samples of Yuan's art. Formal wedding pictures posed before a painted pastoral landscape. Unsmiling baby portraits. Hand-tinted icons of Buddhist lamas, including Norbu's late uncle and the nominally forbidden portrait of the Dalai Lama. We duck in under the door flap (which turns out to be the vaguely Italianate painted pastoral canvas backdrop for the wedding pictures), and there sits Yuan himself, amid spotlights and bridal veils and PLA caps. His goatee makes him look rather bohemian and artistic, a breed apart from your run-of-the-mill high street shopkeeper.

Can he process black-and-white film? Sure. Make contact sheets?

No problem. When can we pick them up? Later tonight. How much? Three RMB a sheet. In Beijing, black-and-white proof sheets take a week and cost RMB 80 a sheet, so we delightedly leave four rolls with him. Then we ask him to check out our camera. He disappears into his closet darkroom and emerges a moment later to announce that there was no film on the spool at all: Ah-loong had been "shooting blanks" ever since yesterday.

I try to comfort her with the thought that we had two other Instamatics going at the same time that she was shooting with the empty Nikon, so at least the day's photography has not been a total loss. She's unconsoled. As soon as we get back to the embassy, she blurts out her disaster to Norbu. He, too, seems pretty crestfallen, especially considering how keen he was to document Menya and Choeling. I hasten to reassure him that we still have two-thirds of the pictures we shot. And anyway, I add, isn't there something appealingly Buddhist, in a Zen sort of way, about shooting with an empty camera? Maybe those are the "truest" pictures of all.

Norbu's not amused. Nothing Buddhist about incompetence, he says. Good thing we've still got some pictures left. But in that case, why even mention the gaffe with the Nikon at all? In what way is it helpful, and to whom? Just because you have worries or doubts or misadventures is no reason to dwell on them. Not unless you can do something about them. Otherwise, you might as well keep them to yourself. Or, better yet, "just let them go."

I'm all set to protest that I was only trying cheer up my wife, who already felt bad enough about the disaster without a further scolding from Norbu. But before I can say a word, Ah-loong hastens to thank him for his "deep teaching." A bracing dose of Asian stoicism was just what she needed to snap her out of her disingenuous self-absorption, she now realizes.

I hold my tongue, since that's the order of the day. Maybe I'm too obtuse and Western to really grasp Norbu's Eastern wisdom. Maybe I'm still casting him in the role of my old Beijing buddy, rather than Amdo's own Living Buddha. But all he *seemed* to be saying, as far as I could hear, was that any bad news you can't change, you might as well just forget. Fair enough, I guess, and sane in its way. But couldn't such fatalism just as readily serve to simply wish away any awkwardness, from a marital spat to the Tiananmen massacre?

WE DRESS UP (i.e., change our socks) for dinner, since tonight we're invited for a lofty state occasion: a face-to-face summit conference between two incarnate lamas. Our host is little Tsultrim Drakpa, Choeling's Living Buddha in residence. I'm hoping the encounter will help shed some light on what remains for me the core mystery of this trip: our friend's midlife conversion. How can a normal, sublunary human—someone you dine and joke with—suddenly turn into a Buddha in his own eyes and the eyes of others?

Such deities are made, not born, my common sense insists. The process must begin in childhood and last throughout life. If all your closest intimates take you for a 2,500-year-old superenlightened consciousness, sooner or later you'll start believing it yourself. By the time of Norbu's investiture, he'd already had thirty-plus years of brainwashing. Even in his playboy days, the idea of his lama identity would have loomed large in his mind, if only as something to resist. So, when he finally succumbed, his deity status was already a fully formed concept that he could swallow whole. On the other hand, Tsultrim's conditioning is still a work-in-progress. Maybe by watching him and his handlers we can get some sense of how a Buddha gets incubated.

I imagine the fledgling lama as some sort of Little Lord Fauntleroy—a random boy plucked up in midchildhood and surrounded by inescapable flunkies. But Tsultrim's hardly the heir to an opulent estate. He and all his retinue occupy a simple, cozy *khamtsen*, or dormitory, in the shadow of the Dialectic College. A dozen monks work, sleep, and eat together here in a single, large, L-shaped room with a throne platform at one end. For a household of young men, the place exudes domesticity—no wonder, as nearly half of Tsultrim's attendants are butler-monks who tend full-time to his grooming. There's also a cook who turns in as appetizing a GRYMY as any in Amdo.

A trio of star debaters stay in the *khamtsen* to act as Tsultrim's forensic sparring partners. The majordomo of the establishment is his chief tutor, a stoop-shouldered dialectician in his early thirties. To round out the household, Tsultrim's elder brother also stays here, having taken monastic orders just to keep his sibling company. The brother is a ringer for the Living Buddha, only bigger and graver. Focusing on the difference between the two brothers, though, offers a first inkling of what's so special about the little lama.

For one thing, there's his size. At age fourteen, he's smaller than our nine-year-old back home. But his gestures and expressions are so intense that, when concentrated in his compact person, they take on an extra vividity that commands attention. His smile, for instance: so wide it tries to spread beyond the tight little face. He throws far more into it than just his full sparkling dentition. His tiny eyes light up and dance and crinkle smaller than ever. His eyebrows try to meet his shaved hairline. His forehead beams and reddens. Even his ears prick up minutely, so that sitting behind him we can still tell when he's smiling.

This comes in handy for us, since Tsultrim spends most of the dinner with his back turned to us. He and Norbu face each other across a low table, desultorily working their way through course after course of GRYMY. They don't say much to each other—just the occasional murmured quip, inaudible to us. Yet their "conversation" never drags and their attention never wavers from each other. They eat with ceremonious deliberation, but no strain of formality. They seem hugely amused simply to find themselves in each other's presence. And, somehow, the rest of us also share in the geniality of the two lamas' mutual absorption. I'm at a loss, though, to say just what we find so mesmerizing about their slow-motion, semisilent repast— some inexplicable eloquence of gesture peculiar to Living Buddhas?

It's only after the dessert course that the two lamas turn away from the table and even acknowledge that there's anybody else present in the room. Norbu strikes up a chat with the chief tutor and debating partners. Tsultrim smiles a lot and says little, but tracks every phrase and gesture. Now and then, he replays something he's picked up with uncanny drollery and accuracy. It turns out that he's a brilliant and compulsive imitator, as though born with some crazily benign form of Tourette's syndrome.

From Ah-loong he picks up the knack of nodding encouragement to everything anyone says. Each time his eyes alight on Felix, he takes on a myopic blink and intermittently pushes imaginary spectacles up the bridge of his nose. An attendant monk brings us a plate of after-dinner walnuts and I crack one open for Tsultrim, using a special heel-of-the-hand pressure point trick I learned from my uncle Moe at some long-ago Thanksgiving dinner. After watching me once, the little lama opens walnut after walnut with perfect Moe technique, right down to the comic twist of the eyebrows my uncle used to affect to make his feat more mysterious. Now and then he parrots whole random snatches of our talk in English or Chinese, languages in which he has no speaking fluency at all. But as to just what we may be talking about, Tsultrim shows not a trace of interest. He simply can't help aping people, no matter *what* they're saying. He's a born copycat, just as Norbu's a born ad-libber; a mimic by nature, not nurture.

Not that there's any shortage of attention paid to Tsultrim's nurture, either. Aside from his battery of cooks and grooms, half a dozen intellectual valets devote themselves full-time to getting the little lama through his demanding course of studies. Ideally, a Living Buddha (like any other serious monastic) should pursue the full thirteen-year course of the *geyshe* degree, a kind of Buddhist doctorate of divinity. This is a bit of a sore point with Norbu, since he's none too assiduous academically. Nevertheless, when I ask about it, he translates the curriculum for me as spelled out by Tsultrim's tutor. By the time he attains his *geyshe*, a monk must have memorized and explicated reams of sutras, mastered debate, and become adept in Tantric meditation techniques. Astrology, medicine, and music are optional "electives."

Only a small proportion of the monks ever get as far as *geyshe*, the tutor admits. The rest make themselves useful through domestic service in the monastic establishment and by performing ceremonials for the people. A few monks lapse back into the laity (including some of the brightest, Norbu adds as an aside). Many ex-monks wind up doing

Buddhist social work. Other students, the most fervent ones, try to smuggle themselves over to India to enroll in the learning centers of the Tibetan diaspora under the Dalai Lama's aegis.

I'd heard about refugee traffic from the western reaches of Tibet into India, but I wasn't aware that monks fled from this far east. Plenty try, one of the debating partners assures me, but few of them make it all the way through. The journey is longer and harder from Amdo than from the Lhasa valley. Still, six monks from Choeling are studying in India right now. Another score have made it over the border, but were caught in Nepal and returned to the Chinese authorities, who "kindly minister" to them in labor camps before returning them eventually to Amdo. ("Kindly minister," the little lama parrots Norbu's translation, with just the right note of irony.)

The Choeling monks keep abreast of His Holiness and the exile community through the Voice of America's Amdo dialect service nightly at eleven P.M., the chief tutor adds. Hard to stay up that late when your day begins with four-A.M. chants, but they regard the newscast as simply part of *vinaya*, their monastic discipline. They care only for the diaspora stories, however. The rest of the program, the foreign and Chinese news, doesn't mean much to them. By the same token, they're not all that interested in outside reading or in the sort of secular learning that government schools offer.

Have the monks been exposed to much government schooling? I ask. Mostly not. A family or a village considers it an honor to send its more promising sons to the monastery instead of the schoolhouse. The monks are dead set against any attempt to change this by law. Then, I ask, do they regard the government schools as a challenge to their way of life? Not a challenge. Just irrelevant.

Can a community really afford such parochialism in the modern age? "How can you ask that?" Norbu scolds me. ("How can you," the little lama echoes, sternly, then breaks into another grin.) Such questions help no one, Norbu points out. Just like our earlier maunderings about the Nikon: gratuitous. "After all, what do you expect him to answer?" Nevertheless, he duly translates my question and the reply:

We don't feel our focus is narrow, the chief tutor assures me. We seek depth, not breadth. Maybe in places like Thailand or Japan, they need to work out some modern form of Buddhism. For us, the so-called modern age presents itself as nothing but a vicious assault, something to resist. Reclaiming what has been lost in our time is more than enough to challenge this generation of Amdo monks. Why complicate the task any more than we need to?

BUT MODERN COMPLEXITIES HAVE a way of intruding even in Choeling, as we discover on our post-prandial walk home. Norbu and Pema proceed ahead, while Felix and I detour to drop off Ah-loong and stop at Yuan's Salon to pick up our photo proofs. Just as we approach the shop, two young monks slip out from under the Italian pastoral door flap. One carries some sort of bundle.

"Hi!" Felix booms in Chinese with a sudden access of bonhomie. "Whatcha got there? Oh, videos? Let's see!" He helps himself to the two cassettes and squints at the titles. "Hmmm. Karaoke tapes, huh?" The monks smile sheepishly as he hands back the tapes. "Have fun!" As they hurry on their way, Felix clues me in that the monks had actually just rented a pair of "super triple-X-rated" videos. The box-top blurbs promised "Red Hot Russian Girls."

We brush aside the canvas curtain of the shop and find Yuan inside, waiting for more late-night customers. The photographer hands over our contact sheets, together with a critique of our consistent underexposure.

"So you're in the entertainment industry, too?" Felix inquires, businessman-to-businessman.

"You want some tapes?" Yuan replies, smiling back warily.

"Nah, we're just passing through. But it looks like you've got an okay market here with . . . them."

Better than you'd think, Yuan allows. "Naturally they're curious. And this is about all that most of them can get hold of."

Yeah, but what do they watch it on?

Yuan sighs indulgently at Felix's naïveté. "What do you suppose they live in, caves? Some of these holy men have got it fixed up all right in there: videos, stereos, nice furniture, and all that."

"Yeah? Where do they get the money?"

Well, a few come from rich families, nomads. But even the poor ones find a way. "They've got stuff to sell in there."

"Like what?" Felix wonders nonchalantly. Oh, pictures, bowls, religious trinkets, Yuan replies. You know, *stuff*.

"No kidding? You got any here?"

Yuan suddenly turns wary: "Well, not exactly here . . . What are you interested in, anyway?"

"You know, *stuff*, like you say," Felix presses ahead. "Pictures, *tangkas*. Real old ones, with the lama's handprint on the back. Or skullcups, the kind made out of human bones, with silver tracery. You got anything like that?"

Yuan's clearly getting edgy as Felix starts coming on strong. At the same time, he smells the possibility of turning a quick profit off this avid outsider with his foreign attire and overseas Chinese accent. "Well, maybe tomorrow . . ." the photographer starts to demur.

"Look, I'm leaving tomorrow," Felix cuts in. "If you've got something at home, let's go to your home. If you've got friends who have stuff, let's go to your friends' place. Okay?" Yuan looks at his watch, dubiously. Nearly eleven P.M. "Don't worry, they'll all be up. Listening to the radio, you know," Felix sagely reassures him. "I'm *very* serious. Okay?"

Yuan wavers a moment more, then nods. Felix turns and starts working on me to join in the safari. I want no part of it, but I'm troubled to note that I can't come up with a persuasive reason why not. Granted, I'm not in the market for purloined hieratic art, but is that a reason to stifle my native nosiness? Could Norbu be getting to me, after all, with his sermons against self-indulgence and idle curiosity? Am I just chicken? Or tired? Anyway, I beg off, to Felix's manifest disgust. He and Yuan launch out into the night, taking our only flashlight along with them. I'm left to grope my way along the pitch-black monastery lanes.

Halfway home, a huge wind suddenly kicks up, filling the air with dust and the clatter of unlatched shutters. Back at the embassy, the old beams of the house creak with the gale. To account for my solo return, I stammer out that Felix felt like an evening stroll. Lame as this explanation must sound amid the howling gusts outside, Norbu lets it pass without comment. Abashed by his unquestioning acceptance of my fib, I apologize, after an awkward pause, for my earlier pushiness back at Tsultrim's *khamtsen*.

"Sorry about my gratuitous questions," I offer, "but, you know, probing into stories is, after all, my particular *mandala*."

"That's all right," he yawns. "You do what you have to. Just make sure it's positive."

The gale shows no sign of abating, and I'm starting to worry about Felix. After a few minutes, however, he blows in from the courtyard and makes straight for his bed. "A bit breezy out there," he ventures. Norbu, half-asleep, just grunts. I peer quizzically over to the pallet next to mine: So? Felix just shrugs and shakes his head; apparently he found no worthy *stuff*.

THE STORM'S STILL RAGING the next morning and the creaking of the house wakes me up before anybody else. I let myself out into the courtyard and sit on the stoop, wrapped in my dusty blanket. A couple of *khatags* have escaped from their hook by the door and now chase each other around the tractor. The prayer flags on the gate tower ripple vigorously, like the wings of a manta ray flailing through a heavy undersea current.

Maybe it's the weather, or maybe it's yesterday's discords, but I'm feeling way too restless to wait in bed for our morning meditation. I'm not used to being told to shut up. Even granting the vanity of my vaunted curiosity, I don't know how to *begin* to learn self-effacement. As though on cue to edify me, the very paradigm of modesty comes somersaulting out the window just above my head: old Chogyal, Norbu's man Friday, father of his main acolyte, Pema.

Waking up on his pallet by the kitchen stove, Chogyal's so solicitous of all the other sleepers in the house that he won't risk disturbing them by going out through the main door. He vaults through the kitchen window instead and heads straight for the outhouse. He remains oblivious to me, having no particular reason to glance behind him at the stoop.

As he passes by the front gate of the courtyard, he notices something that's been lobbed over the transom from the street outside. He picks up a wadded piece of paper, unfolds it and scans the print, his brow furrowing deeper with each line of text. Halfway down from the top, he carefully refolds the paper on its original creases and tucks it into the branches of the flowering almond tree against the back wall.

He continues to the outhouse and emerges a few minutes later mumbling mantras. He shows no surprise when he sees me, but tosses me a smile and a nod without interrupting his prayers. As the sound of chanting arises from neighboring courtyards, Chogyal heads on into the house to busy himself with breakfast, leaving the mysterious message in the tree.

THE CHANTING GAINS momentum; time for morning meditation. I follow Chogyal inside to find Norbu and Felix already seated on their pallets, wrapped in their quilts. I settle into place and try to compose my rankled mind. Much the same scene as yesterday—same *tangka* light, same undertone of chanting—but there's some jarring incongruity that I can't quite place.

It's the sound, I realize after a moment. One strand of the sonic web is raveled tight. Cutting athwart the trumpets and bells, the basso drone and tenor canticle, there's a jagged singsong line in nasal falsetto. Multiplication tables? In Chinese?

When I ask Norbu about it he confirms that the county administration has installed a primary school right inside the Choeling complex. In his view it's an assault on Tibetan culture. Come *on*, I tease him—multiplication tables? Well, sure, he allows, nothing wrong with arithmetic; but at *this* hour, and in *this* place?

Would it be any different, I ask, if the kids were reciting their sums in Tibetan instead of Chinese? Still unacceptable; village class-rooms are one thing, but a government school in the middle of the monastery is quite another matter. And at the same time, the Communists are preparing to enforce rules making government schooling compulsory and barring youngsters under eighteen from taking monastic orders.

This kind of "mixing around in our education system" is a direct affront, Norbu insists. It's just like letting the Muslims open a mosque across the street from a Buddhist monastery with an electronically amplified muezzin blaring straight into the temple courtyards. This was actually done in Gansu, sparking riots.

Still, I persist, multiplication tables are not only harmless but actually necessary for a people that hopes to hold its own in the twenty-first century. So who *needs* the county administration to teach us multiplication? he retorts. All of that is already in the sutras that we've been teaching in our monasteries for centuries. And not just basic arithmetic, either; any sort of advanced science you can name—plasma physics, molecular biology. We're only now beginning to realize what's been in the sutras all along.

Wouldn't that suggest, I ask, that these concepts might be buried in the sutras in some arcane form that people can't really use? "*Use*," he snorts. "Always *use*. 'What's the *use* of this, of that? What's in it for *me*?' "

He sighs. "What grasping animals we are. Did you ever watch a newborn baby? From the moment of birth, the first thing, the hands go like this, nonstop." He pantomimes clutching movements in the air.

"Let *go*, for once, will you?

"Look, today, maybe, just *maybe* we'll have your *Mani* initiation. If the timing is right. If the signs add up. If"—imitating NASA's Mission Control—"all conditions are 'go.'

"Now, don't get attached, don't get *married* to the idea of an initiation today. That's one sure way to abort the mission. Just be ready. Be available. Take it as it comes. That means be patient and be neutral.

"Neutral . . ." He draws out the word again for our consideration.

"Think of your mother, your teacher, your lover, your child—someone dearest to you. And then think of your worst enemy. And try to think of them both in the same way. After all, you learn a lot from your enemy, don't you? He's a kind of teacher, right? And aren't you also a prisoner in a way to your dear one—your jailer, your trap?"

He pauses to let us conjure up our own imagery and establish this counterintuitive symmetry between our banes and our benefactors.

"Got it?" he asks after a moment. "Now try to think in that same way about a total stranger, just any random person on the street, or maybe somebody you never even see. After all, even if you don't know that person, there must be a whole world of teaching in him and a whole world of traps. Whether you know somebody or not is just a matter of *yuan*." (He uses the Chinese word for fate, or karma.)

"Not that *yuan* is anything less than absolutely real," he adds, "nor can you dismiss it as mere coincidence. There *are* no coincidences. Every effect has a cause. But the causes and the effects are always changing, always shifting. And your dear one, your enemy, and every total stranger in the world exist on their own terms, not yours. Only when you know that—really *know* it—can you be neutral and see clearly.

"So today, we try to see clearly, look lightly, and"—pointedly to me—"don't get bogged down with questions. Keep neutral, take the initiation if it comes; be patient if it doesn't. And remember, whatever happens, I'm here for you. We've got *yuan*."

ALL VERY WELL to accept your *yuan* with equanimity, come what may, but Norbu's still not above checking signs and portents for even so prosaic a matter as the weather forecast. After morning meditation, he steps out into the courtyard to sniff the air and scan the sky. Will the storm permit today's trip to Thekchen Dhargye Dzong monastery, high in the nomadic reaches of Rui-an? I follow him out and present him with one of the wind-tossed *khatags*, then pluck the folded missive out of the almond tree: "Look what else the gale blew in."

The mimeographed message is all in cursive Tibetan script. It's emblazoned with a round vermilion stamp on the bottom, showing five mountain peaks (symbolizing the five regions that comprise the original territory of Tibet, Norbu explains). The seal identifies the pamphleteers, simply and grandiloquently, as "The True Press."

He scans the text, translating subheads for my benefit: international jurists' conference on Tibet in New Delhi . . . His Holiness' speech . . . nonviolence . . . visas denied . . . protests by opposition members in Indian parliament—all fairly stale news that's already moved on the international wires a couple of weeks ago. But here in Amdo, these are hot stories.

With a mixture of worry and a kind of pride, Norbu points out "you see why the government's so tense about this place? Look at this bulletin. Listen to the way those monks talked last night. This district and this monastery have minds of their own. No wonder the Chinese don't want Choeling to flourish. Wait until you see Labrang, over in Gansu. Very nice, very fancy. Beautiful icons, temples all covered with gold, lots of monks. That's the reward for toeing the line. But none of that here."

As we head back inside for breakfast, he hands the pamphlet wordlessly to Pema, who's unsurprised. Oh sure, the acolyte says, we get something like this every week or two. He nips into the kitchen and comes back with a wad of True Press bulletins. Norbu glosses over them, page by page: meeting in Frankfurt, Dalai Lama with European parliamentarians, Nobel Laureates' conference and so on. Hmm, here's one that stands out from the rest: plague to descend on China next year, three Great Snakes from outer space, epidemics, war. Husband and wife can't even look at each other, parents don't recognize children. "*Wah!*" Norbu exclaims, in Hindi. "*Kya bat hai!*"—Good show!

Before he has a chance to elaborate, though, Pema quickly spirits away the stack of handbills. We have an early visitor: our driver for the day strides into the room while we're still finishing breakfast. He's a puffy, lank-haired Han who billows over the low stool Norbu's acolyte gives him to sit on. He casts an eye about the room and announces, "I used to live here."

Really? And when was that? "In the sixties. Part of the seventies. Still looks about the same." Norbu decides to let this comment ride. He just thanks the driver for his efforts today. "Part payment of back rent," he adds with a laugh.

We set out on the same blacktop that brought us here from Xining, but before we reach Menya we jog off to the West, fording the river without benefit of any bridge. On the other side, we come upon a robed and sunburnt figure loping purposefully along the stony track, his chin tucked into his neck, his eyes, beneath overhanging brows, fixed upon the distant rampart of mountains: it's Jigshed, right at home in his natural element.

Norbu rolls down the window to ask his friend where he's heading. Lengthy peregrinations in the outback are the norm for an itinerant charm-peddler like Jigshed. Just now, the monk is on his way to seal sutras into a wind-driven prayer wheel for one of the mountain farmers who's been losing sheep. Felix, Ah-loong, and I squeeze over in the backseat to make room. But when Norbu asks the driver if we can take another passenger, the answer is no.

Jigshed seems unfazed, but we're taken aback. Those mountains look steep. Can't we simply *tell* the driver to accommodate our friend? Not in China, Norbu explains. Here, the chauffeur is king. He's a Proletarian in control of the Means of Production. Plus, he's a Han. Besides, the road ahead is really so steep and twisty that a reasonable driver might well balk at tackling it with an overloaded vehicle.

JUST WHAT HE MEANS soon becomes clear enough as we head up the hill. The well-watered valley gives way to a hardscrabble cliff face that seems held in place by no more than the cross-webbing of goat tracks. The fields below look miniaturized, as though seen from a low-flying turbo-prop, and our jeep sways as sickeningly as one of those planes. At each turn, the car crouches expectantly and then pounces around the bend with an audible clatter of gravel spun off the roadbed into the void. No telling when a tractor or a shambling yak herd might suddenly heave into sight coming right at us.

If this driver sees himself as a kinglet, at least he earns his crown with real effort and skill. Even in the backseat, the swerving ascent leaves me queasy enough to propose "a convenience stop, please, Comrade Driver—any time or place that suits you, of course."

The chauffeur just grunts and clutches his wheel all the tighter for the next dozen switchbacks. He doesn't even think of stopping—how could he?—until we're off the cliff face. Then he pulls over into a barley terrace at the top of the ridge.

It's too high up here for planting this early in the year, but green wildflowers nestle among the barley stubble and swallows wheel about the skies, diving now and then for seeds. After the cramped and tense ascent, we're grateful for the chance to stretch our legs and clear our heads with mountain air.

At the edge of the terrace, Felix has spotted a cairn of pilgrim stones, each emblazoned with a carving of the *Mani* mantra. He wants a closer look, so we walk along the line of the terrace until, just over a gentle rise, we all at once take in the entire prospect of the next valley: a whorl of terraces, yak-studded pastures, gully-scored cliffs, and distant snowcaps. The whole composition of the vista converges on one particular rock spur, hardly higher than the rest, but denser, furred with pine forest and crowned with temple roofs.

We catch our breaths at this intensely focused scene. "Not bad, for a 'convenience stop,' " Norbu parodies me, simperingly imitating my plea to the driver, "any time, any place . . ." He takes in the whole panorama with a sweep of his crimson sleeve, then homes in on the temple-crowned bluff at the center. *That*, Norbu announces, is Choeling Tashikyil monastery, our first destination today. "*Some* time, *some* place. Intensely specific and exacting. It takes concentration to make a really powerful *mandala*. You need to be all there."

Getting there, however, turns out to be a painstaking process of mincing by jeep over pocked and rutted tracks. Not until the final stretch does the road finally smooth out and widen—only to truncate abruptly in a mound of dirt taller than our vehicle. A work gang lounges on the wayside, smoking. Their cotton hajj caps identify them as Hui. Norbu sucks in a deep breath but says nothing.

Our driver rolls down his window and hails over the nearest road-builder, a slack-jawed teenager. So what to do? The youth scratches his head for a moment and then suggests we back up and skirt the mound through the barley terraces. We execute this maneuver—yet another display of driverly virtuosity—only to find ourselves perched atop the dirt pile with no way to get down the other side.

The chauffeur climbs out and just stands there, hands on hips, confounded. Norbu keeps his seat and holds his peace. The Hui mosey over and watch us blankly. A perfect standoff. Nobody on the scene has the ordained responsibility of getting us out of this fix, so we might as well stay here forever. We're balked by taboos as insurmountable as Hindu caste barriers.

As aliens exempt from this particular caste nexus, it falls to Felix and me to break the logjam. We hop down from the jeep and ask the road crew if we might borrow a couple of their spades. By the time we've turned over the first few shovelfuls, the Hui all fall to with a will, smoothing out the downslope of the mound for us with great verve and professionalism.

The wiry graybeard next to me guffaws at my dainty spadework, spits once on his hands and churns up a veritable geyser of dirt to show me how it's supposed to be done. Ah-loong capers about with her camera, cheering us on. The driver magisterially directs us—a little more here, smooth it out there. Norbu stares impassive through the windshield, like an idol in its niche.

In minutes, we're rolling again to the cheers of the Hui and the visible relief of the driver. Ah-loong, Felix, and I collapse into the backseat, sweating and panting and laughing. Only Norbu seems put off. How bad an omen was this obstacle, I wonder, under his scheme of auguries?

One more hairpin turn and we're into the Choeling Tashikyil forest. The contrast is dizzyingly abrupt from the parched, sun-dazzled barley terraces to this world of filtered light and stream-slicked stones. Massive tree stumps punctuate the boggy, fern-carpeted glades and hummocks of moss, dwarfing the present crop of foot-thick second-growth pines. Norbu swears that the tree-cover here was once so thick that the forest was "black as night, even at noon." Such forests, he adds, used to cover all the slopes we've navigated on our way here—grim testament to how human habitation, even as thinly spread as Qinghai's, can transform "immutable" mountains. Just how Norbu knows all this I'm not sure. Maybe by recalling his prior incarnations.

ONE ASPECT OF the forest, at least, may not have changed much over several of Norbu's incarnations: the peasants who thread their way through the trees, lugging bundles of twigs or jugs of water. When they see our jeep, with its lama pennants, they drop whatever they're carrying and bow while we pass. The forest road is so narrow that their brows practically brush the windows of the car.

It's not in the forest, though, but at the Choeling Tashikyil construction site that we really grasp the medieval underpinnings of the monastic order. The temple that looked so solid from across the valley turns out, from close up, to be no more than a skeletal framework of columns, rafters, and plinths. The scaffolding swarms with corvée labor: carpenters, hod-carriers, masons.

To this work-in-progress, the monks of Choeling Tashikyil welcome us with conch shells and trumpet blasts. Norbu directs us to take as many pictures as we can. He wants the temple reconstruction well-documented, to show his Beijing donors just what it is they're backing.

The scores of women laborers stop long enough to wail us a *Mani* chant. Then they shoulder again their backpack-baskets full of mortar and resume their scurrying up the ramps and ladders of the scaffolding. The carpenters get back to work. One man planes a beam, another chisels ornamental carvings in a doorjamb. An axman splits pegs to secure the doweled joints. Roofers lay green ceramic tile on the latticework of rafters.

Following Norbu, we pick our way through curlicues of wood shavings into the middle of the temple-to-be. Sunlight pours in through the struts and joists where the walls are yet unsealed. The unfinished beams and columns lay bare the hearts of the pine logs, golden and fragrant. Through the gaps in the tiling, the mountain sky glows so blue it's almost purple.

For all the bustle of activity, the construction site is oddly silent. No whine of power tools (no electricity), nor even the banging of a hammer (no nails in the entire structure). No shouted orders, no curses or laughter. Just the padding of bare feet on the scaffolding, the rasp of chisels and the scrape of trowels.

In a few months, this space will be all sealed up and carpeted, gilt and lacquer-daubed, smoke-cured with incense and festooned with *tangkas*. But right now it's storing up the daylight and air, the footfalls and mantras of the work teams that account for the power of the temple. It's hard to imagine how a building could more elegantly or harmoniously present a collective expression of its builders.

Yet at the same time, my mind reels at the idea of a cheerful, functioning feudalism here and now, at the start of the new millennium. This site is the moral equivalent of Chartres Cathedral, aswarm with artisans and serfs donating weeks and months of their life and their labor, ostensibly out of sheer devotion to their Church and its Princes.

NORBU INTRODUCES the two senior Princes of his Church at Choeling Tashikyil, monks well into their eighties. "This one's older than the Pope," he boasts. Evidently in far better shape, too; the two old men lead us all on a circumambulation of the whole monastery compound, a good half-kilometer stroll over steep and twisty mountain trails. This hike gives us a sense of the size of the erstwhile monastery, and also the extent of devastation. Most of the perimeter is now marked by no more than half-melted mud walls. A thousand monks once lived here. Now there are fewer than a hundred, many of them children.

There's something childlike about these two octogenarians, themselves; hand in hand, kindergarten-style, they lead Norbu along the sunlit path, relaying episodes of the monastery's tragedy in the comforting rote cadences of a well-memorized fable. As per instructions,

Ah-loong, Felix, and I scramble up and down the path with our cameras, snapping as much as we can of the ruins, the reconstruction, and the denizens of Choeling Tashikyil.

Halfway around the circuit, Norbu stops and doubles back to inform us that we won't do the initiation here after all. Things just haven't fallen into place. The auguries aren't right. And besides, Norbu needs to concentrate, just now, on the people here—people like these old monks, whose time is, after all, limited—rather than on the three of us. Maybe at our next stop.

Felix looks downcast. Ah-loong just clicks pictures all the more assiduously as Norbu rejoins his two senior guides. As for me, I'm left wondering why the initiation was called off so abruptly. Was it something we did? Some hideous gaffe made worse by our obliviousness? Or some drama we're unaware of among the Tashikyil *sangha* that's preempted his attention?

Or was it the driver and the road crew? I'd been feeling rather cocky about how we'd literally dug our way out of our own problem, appealing to the common humanity of those who were blocking us. Perhaps Norbu put a very different spin on it, brooking no obstruction at all on such an important occasion. Or were the intrusions of Han and Muslims enough to pollute the occasion entirely? If so, it would call for a pretty basic reassessment on our part of Norbu and Lamaist religiosity in general. Anyway, for now I'm as much relieved as disappointed; I'm by no means sure that I can muster the composure for an initiation.

How far I have yet to go is brought home all the more sharply by the chanting that follows our GRYMY. We file into the refectory, which doubles as a prayer hall while the main temple is under construction. We sit cross-legged in facing rows. Norbu perches on his throne to my right. Directly opposite sit the two octogenarians who led us on our circuit of the monastery. The chanting fills the hall. A couple of young monks establish the bass line, with voices so deep they're almost subliminal. They drive the chorale like coxswains, the rest of the *sangha* joining in on cue to propel the prayer through successive changes. Each chant they take up gathers to a head in about a quarter of an hour and then fades with a dying fall, the bass line dropping even lower until it seems to just fade out of the audible range. The effect is like a Doppler shift—it's not as though the just-chanted sutra is finished. It simply sails off on its own orbit and a new sutra spins into our ken—or so it seems to me as I squeeze my eyes shut and gamely try to meditate. I even fancy once or twice I'm almost getting into the swim of things, but each time my concentration wavers. Uncannily, whenever this happens, Norbu, beside me, chimes in with his own line of chanting that helps me regain my stride.

Once, I blink for an instant and register the faces of the two elders opposite. One of them is ivory-smooth, with skin drawn so tight that the ears seem to stand out from the head, straining to catch subtle, unheard resonances. The other, grizzled and wizened, stares right through me with cataracted eyes, a cross-hatch of wrinkles etching his face into a gentle smile. Even after I close my eyes again, these faces remain imprinted on my meditation.

But then my focus blurs, my legs kink up, my nose starts to itch, my GRYMY curdles in my stomach. I shift my weight, trying to regain mental balance. Wonder how the kids are doing back home? What would Mrs. Stein, my old Hebrew school teacher, think if she saw me now? Probably be pretty steamed. Unless, of course, she's already reincarnated into some more ecumenical milieu. How in the world am I ever going to write this up, anyway?

. . . and, before I know it, whatever scintilla of concentration I'd managed to muster succumbs under waves of ambient static. As we're taking our leave, however, one of the two old monks I'd been visualizing—the ivory one—goes out of his way to leave an imprint. I'm nodding my farewell to him, hands pressed together at my chest as per Buddhist protocol. And he takes one step closer to me, enfolds my hands in his and presses his brow to mine.

The move catches me off guard. In the unmediated noonday glare of the high mountain sunlight, his dry, soft skin has collected a surprising amount of heat. I feel it radiating through my forehead and my palms, and I inhale the sunbaked, dusty smell of him. Then he moves on to bless Felix and Ah-loong.

WE RETRACE our route as far as the road crew. Sure enough, they've carefully re-created the mound in all its glory. Same standoff all over again, and the same resolution—the whole charade played out just as though none of us had ever encountered such a situation before. With the help of the Hui, we overcome the obstacle, *Alhamdulillah*.

We keep on ascending until we reach a whole new plateau, with its own distinctive light and perspectives. Here, the scale is so much grander that it dwarfs the daunting slopes we've just come through. Our dizzying top-of-the-world swoon gives way now to a sense of concavity as we realize we're in a basin ringed by distant snowcaps. On this vast prairie, human passersby are few and far between—the occasional horseman, now and then a woman herding goats or a lone child romping with a dog. The solitary figures loom up on the raised shoulder of the road, crisp and vivid against the brilliant blue of the Himalayan sky. The nomad costumes are even gaudier than those of the agrarian Tibetans in the farming valleys below: women jangling with bangles, pendants and silver sashes, the men bearded and wildly tonsured with matted plaits or half-shaven pates.

Even the animals roam freer up here. Each yak herd includes a few old animals with ribbons braided in their tails. In order to earn merit, Norbu explains, the nomads have set these yaks aside as exempt from slaughter, "de-marketized" and assured a natural death. He invites us to free one ourselves. We can buy a yak on this basis from the nomads, who would not only free the beast but also, very likely, contribute the proceeds to the temples. Outside philanthropy, like all other wealth flowing into Amdo, has to enter via the nomads, it seems. Perched at the apex of the Tibetan food chain, all windfalls in the traditional economy must pass through them.

Yet nomad life hardly looks plush, even compared with that of the peasants closer to the valley. At the district headquarters, we lunch at the home of a tribal headman, as substantial a burgher as any in these parts. His two-room mud-and-wattle hut would rate as a miserable shack by the standards of Menya, the first of Norbu's villages that we visited. Nevertheless, the headman has clearly been at pains to maintain a certain gentility in his decor. We're served our GRYMY under an icon cabinet festooned with blinking Christmas lights and flanked by inflatable beach-toy deer. Next to a Dalai Lama rotogravure, a framed certificate proclaims the younger son's membership in the Communist Youth League.

Beyond the headman's house the road dwindles and then virtually disappears, so that we're jeeping straight across country alongside the canyon of a rushing stream. Far below us, at the edge of the gorge, a ring of boulders stakes out a pattern as mysterious as Stonehenge. That, Norbu explains, was some arcane corral system that the Communist Party in its wisdom ordained for the collective herding of animals back in the days of People's Communes. The nomads labored mightily to heave the stones into place, but never could figure out a use for the structure. So the corral has been a ruin for decades, virtually since it was built.

The canyon narrows. The wide open spaces of the morning give way to a jumble of hills and cypress forests. We ford back and forth across the same ice-clear creekbed nine times before rising up the flank of a final hillock. One more bend and the vista of Thekchen Dhargye Dzong opens before us.

Its green tile roofs nestle at the base of an enormous cliff, the sheared-off face of the cypress-clad ridge we've just rounded. Far from a clean break, however, the rock face fractures into spires and spindles, whorls, slabs, and buttresses—a jumbled cubism highlighted by the iridescent greens and grays of the granite. The temple and its white outbuildings settle into the niches of the rock with the inevitability of snowbanks dropped from heaven. One meditation chapel perches halfway up the cliff face, reserved, as it would seem, for the exclusive use of levitating monks. As we approach the cliff, the flat escarpment takes on more relief. Shadows pick out the crags. Crows and swallows swoop from peak to peak.

The entire *sangha*, nearly fifty strong, lines the track as our jeep draws up into the middle of a conch-shell *mandala* that's been chalked for us in the temple forecourt. The monks turn out in full regalia,

with fringed yellow coxcomb hats that render each man a head taller than his natural height, and correspondingly more solemn. The basso profundo chanting and the blast of three-meter-long trumpets gain extra resonance from the wall of rock behind. Conspicuous by its absence is the high-pitched *Mani* wail—no women here to sing it, no village or households, no one in sight but monastics.

WE'RE BUNDLED into the refectory to wash off the road dust and take some tea. The ranked majesty of the *sangha* resolves itself into individual faces—shy nomad adolescents; tittering preteens who hang back in the doorways; a slow-smiling, stocky young man who, in premonastic life, used to be a wrestling champ, we're told; a crinkly elder whose shaven pate makes him look younger than his putative ninety years.

Most of the talking is left to Lobsang, a tall, middle-aged monk whose clever face is framed in bushy sideburns. Norbu jokingly introduces him as Sun Wu-kong, the Monkey King of China's classic Buddhist parable, *Journey to the West*. As taciturn as Lobsang is garrulous, the eighty-six-year-old abbot Aku Kuba glowers at the head of the table.

We ask how the monks knew to chalk the *mandala* and line the forecourt in preparation for our arrival. This place has no electricity, much less any phone for us to ring ahead. Oh, we had plenty of advance notice, Lobsang assures us: this morning the cypress trees shook, so we sent some monks up to the top of the ridge to find out why. And sure enough, they spotted a car far off with yellow *khatag*s tied to the fenders. We knew then it must be our Living Buddha, and so we made ready.

Shaking cypresses? Oh yes, it happens every year. In the spring, after the long cold, the trees one day just suddenly tremble and shake off the dust that has accumulated over the winter. The whole tree all at once shivers like a dog (Lobsang pantomimes) and the dust shakes off in a puff of smoke, leaving the cypress shiny and green. One tree starts it and the next picks it up and soon the whole mountain is shimmering in a chain reaction while the dust rises in a cloud.

It's the first time any of us, including Norbu, ever heard of such a thing, but Lobsang finds the whole phenomenon prosaic, a routine harbinger of spring. The only odd aspect of today's frisson was that it came more than a month ahead of its usual season, so the monks knew something special was afoot.

Highly auspicious, Norbu beams. Proceed straightaway with the initiation. And with that, the three of us are swept into the main prayer hall too suddenly for any quaver of doubt to break our momentum.

I'm not supposed to relate what went on in the initiation. So I won't, except to pronounce that the ceremony—after all that buildup—turned out to be surprisingly simple and wholly affecting. An experience unattainable through any amount of solo study or meditation. Just as Norbu says, it requires both a teacher and a *sangha* to solemnize vows.

Afterward, in the drawn-out chanting, I'm beset with the same creaks and crotchets and charley-horse as before. But this time, these irritants somehow don't matter, they can't touch my concentration. To keep my focus, I once again visualize the face of the monk opposite me. This time it's the abbot, Aku Kuba.

And what a face it is. Bullet-headed and bullnecked, with outsized features crammed into the narrow space between his bulbous brow and his jutting jaw. A flattened boxer's nose plastered down over the thin, pursed, perpetually frowning lips.

A domino of shadow, just perceptibly darker than the rest of the face, masks the eyes—sunburn? The eyelids strain open wide, leaving a micron of white under the iris. The gaze would almost seem truculent but for a light frosting of cataracts that lend a luster of world-weary sympathy.

HAVING MEDITATED on this face in the chill echo-box of the prayer hall, it's a little disconcerting to find myself later that evening sitting right next to it by the wood stove in the lama's snug little chamber at Thekchen Dhargye Dzong. But here's the abbot, for all his forbidding mien, chatting affably enough with our Living Buddha.

Aku Kuba, Norbu tells us, is another Yamantaka initiate. Not surprising, somehow, although it's hard to pinpoint the "family resemblance" between this man and someone like Jigshed. Is it the vigor, the density? Or just some quirk of posture and pigmentation and the upcast, beetle-browed gaze?

The abbot is feeling expansive tonight—unprecedented for him, Norbu assures us. We should take any reminiscences he offers as Aku Kuba's gruff gift for our initiation, the lama suggests. "But don't keep dragging him back to negative things"—Norbu directs this warning straight at me. "The man is old. It's time for healing. Help him to laugh a little, if you can."

When Norbu first met him back in 1986, he says, Aku Kuba could not even speak, much less laugh. He just wept continuously over what he had seen and known and lost during the Cultural Revolution decade. Tonight, with hardly any prompting from us, he keeps returning to the same decade. No weeping now, though, at least not openly. He even manages a kind of laugh in the end.

"I think the great lamas, like your uncle, saw what was coming," he tells Norbu. "Even our teachers up here, when I look back on it now, were trying to get us ready for hard times. They kept telling us, 'Someday you'll need all this.' So when the soldiers came, I knew just what to hide—which relics, vessels, sutras.

"But these things were the least of it. What the Chinese were out to break was *us*, the monks. The buildings were easy to destroy. What they were really after was our *vinaya*, our discipline. I thought, 'These soldiers have come the whole length of China and all the way up these mountains just to smash us. That's crazy, fanatical.' And the only way for us to meet it was to be just as fanatical on our side as they were about our faith.

"They would parade women before us to make us break our vows. I said my mantras. They'd beat me. I'd pray until I fainted and then still pray in my swoon. My teachers here at the monastery long ago taught me how to die. They told me I'd be killed. So I was ready.

"The soldiers beat me and left me for dead. I'd wake up praying. They'd beat me all over again, kill me once more. I'd wake up again with mantras on my lips. Every time they'd see your lips move they'd say, 'You're praying,' and beat you. You couldn't even move your lips.

"Hearing it now, you must think, 'How can this be?' I could tell you more and more of this, but the more I told the less you'd believe.

"Monks fell away. Of all the monks that came with me here as a young man, only I am left. People said, 'Take a wife, the Chinese will leave you alone. What difference does it make? After all, you are who you are.' And that was correct advice—at least for the advice-givers. But not for me.

"Finally, our own Tibetan people couldn't even talk to me. Our own Tibetan people had to beat me when they were told to. What else could they do? For all of us, it was a great teaching.

"The Chinese told me to hunt game for them, to trap some birds and groundhogs because there was no meat. But I wouldn't hunt, wouldn't kill. They beat me, but I wouldn't.

"So they made me a shepherd, and part of my job was to cull the old sheep in the herd for slaughter. Not to kill them, just to set aside the ones that had to die. As I did it, I prayed for the old sheep, I said mantras to help them across. But again it was 'Your lips are moving' and . . ." He pantomimes a couple of sharp rabbit punches.

"In the end, they could only declare that I was simply crazy. It was all they could do with me, the only way to fit me into their 'Cultural Revolution.' Nothing else for it but to shun me as a madman. And after that, I was untouchable, free."

So you won? I ask. Here's where he laughs. It's a perfectly mirthless laugh, but by no means bitter. The thin, pursed lips abruptly draw into a grin and he sucks his gums a couple of times, eyes dancing. Triumphant? Ironic? A laugh, at any rate, that nobody else in the room can share. No one else has the right.

IT'S TOO DARK to see anymore in Norbu's cell, so we adjourn to the courtyard. Watching the gloaming, we all wind up turning away from the setting sun itself and facing north, toward the cliff, where the waning light rings kaleidoscopic changes on the rock face.

Felix wonders if it would be sacrilegious to help himself to a fragment of the mountain. At a nod from Lobsang, one of the monks slips off behind the temple. Next thing we know, there he is way up by the levitating pavilion. A minute later he's back in the forecourt, presenting each of us with a rock fragment wrapped in a *khatag*.

And when our driver grumbles something about no wine with dinner, a little novice is sent off to produce, from somewhere, a bottle of *erh guo tou*. To each his own.

The night takes on an edge of chill far sharper than that down in the valley. Supper is served by candlelight, of a necessity: no electricity. Nevertheless, what works in Montparnasse also works in Thekchen Dhargye Dzong—the romantic ambiance makes even GRYMY taste better. Lobsang and a half-dozen younger monks remain in the room to keep the tea bowls topped up and the stove well-stoked. The yak-butter tea is thick, salty, and invigorating, more like a blood transfusion than a genteel British cuppa.

Hopped up as we all are on bowl after bowl of this highly caffeinated brew, we sit up late around the wood stove and talk of

Thekchen Dhargye Dzong's *vinaya*. The study curriculum here is more limited than Choeling's. For instance, Lobsang wistfully notes, there's no dialectics teacher—an area in which he'd clearly shine if it were offered in his monastery.

For the most part, the monks spend their days in sutra study and meditation. For relaxation, wrestling matches in summer. Plus lots of plain hard chores about the monastery. They don't mind work: tough nomad kids, he adds, throwing an affectionate arm around the bare shoulder of the monk next to him, who's been tending the fire so assiduously all evening. Lobsang introduces a diffident middle-aged monk who is the chief disciplinarian of the temple. Checks beds at night and such. So what does he check for, I wonder. Is there a problem with monks jumping into each other's beds? Norbu throws me a look: You really want me to ask that? I shrug: Why not try? He sighs, then launches into a translation that seems somehow much longer than my original question.

The Monkey King looks crestfallen. Why, he wants to know, does the visitor ask about dirty things? If anybody here had such impulses, he'd simply control them. If he couldn't, he'd have to leave. And that would be very sad, because this place is so special.

Whereupon, he launches into a catalogue of Thekchen Dhargye Dzong's special powers. The monastery's founding adepts were first led here by a *dakini*, a sort of Tantric muse. The rock face behind the temple is alive with *mandalas* and deity images, he assures us, if you know how to look for them. One early teacher here attained such heights of meditation that he could jump at a single bound from the top of the cliff face to the other side of the river. You can still see the footprints where he landed. Lobsang offers to take us there tomorrow to see for ourselves.

Ah-loong, Felix, and I retire for the night, three on a *kang*, in a cell off the monastery forecourt. A monk stokes our woodstove until it practically glows, and we each have a thick wedding eiderdown, silk-covered with embroidered phoenixes. The austerities of *vinaya* sit lightly enough on the monastery's guests.

But our suite has no attached bath, so in the middle of the night, when all that tea catches up with me, I have to make my way to the outhouse clear across the temple's forecourt. I pause in the yard on my way back to bed.

It's icy cold, subfreezing for sure, but still and windless. The only sound is the purl of merging waters from the confluence of two streams in the apron of grass before the temple. It's a chill, crisp sound, like the gnashing of ice shards. The three-quarter moon, now at its zenith, fills the meadow and picks out every spur and spindle of the rock wall.

If I don't move at all, I persuade myself, I can suspend the Third Law of Thermodynamics and retain the warmth of my bed indefinitely. I stand so still that I fancy I can feel the tidal tug of the moon on my still semi-sleeping brain. I strain to read the moon-limned *mandala*s on the rock. That virgule of shadow, there—could it be the curve of a Yamantaka horn?

The air's so cold that I imagine I can trace my every breath on its journey through my lungs out to my narrowest capillaries and back. The first breath is cleansing. The second breath is calming. The third breath is searing, freezing. All at once thermodynamics reasserts itself and I scurry back to bed, teeth rattling, without having quite deciphered any of the cliff-face deities.

MY EIDERDOWN IS so comforting, after this adventure, that I oversleep the following morning. By the time I roll out to Norbu's cell, the sun is high, the tea is steaming, and Aku Kuba is on a roll again. This time he's reminiscing not about the "hard time" but about its aftermath.

"*Really* busy, then. I can't remember when else I've ever been so busy. Everybody needed prayers, everybody had a backlog. People who hadn't talked to me for years suddenly came looking for me. And if they *didn't* come, I'd have to go looking for *them*.

"One man, a Communist—his mother was dying. This man had beaten me, accused me, tried to break me. And now he felt he couldn't approach me. I only learned of it through others. But the old lady was *dying*, you see. How could I not pray for her? So I just prayed. Nobody could stop me from praying. They couldn't during the hard time, and they certainly couldn't now.

"So this Communist found out about it, and he came to me, weeping, afterward, and he said, 'How can I repay you?' And I said, 'Repay me for what? It's I who must repay *you*.'

"Because, you see, he'd been my teacher, although he never meant to be. And to any teacher, devotion is due. That man went on to become a very sincere practitioner. They're all teachers—the beaters, the tormenters. The Chinese, too. The Chinese especially.

"You ask, 'Why now? Why Tibetans? Why this generation?' Call it karma, collective karma. But what a chance it has been for us all to clear our *samsara*," the backlog of karmic debt owed from lifetimes of earthly entanglement. "And what a chance for each one of us to perfect our practice.

"Just as suddenly as it had all begun, the Chinese told us one day it was over: we could go back to our temples. As though it was all a mistake and they'd never really meant it after all.

"So I came back here and there was nothing. Not a *thing*, just rubble. An empty field. *This*, then, was what it all came down to? If so, then what had it ever really *been* in the first place? And what had these past years been for, this hard time? That was when I knew—really *knew*—the Emptiness Meditation.

"So what to do, then? Don't rebuild? Let it go? Impossible. We must start again. But now, I build with meditations, not with hands. I'm old. I mainly stay in my chamber, by the river. I only come out when there are visitors. And somehow, every time I come out now, this place gets bigger and bigger. It's getting so I don't even know who lives *where* anymore."

There's one denizen of Thekchen Dhargye Dzong that nobody knows where to look for anymore: the monastery's patron bird. A couple of old monks at Aku Kuba's side recount the story in relays. They tell how, in a dream, the former abbot saw a *dakini* who promised him a pair of white cranes to watch over the temple and the *sangha*.

And, sure enough, the birds promptly appeared and nested someplace on the cliff face, although nobody could ever find quite where.

They hovered daily around the monastery until, during the "hard time," a Rui-an Communist Party secretary came up on a hunting junket and shot one of the two cranes.

"Wanton," Norbu mutters to us. "Pointless. You've seen this road—how far, how hard. Why would anyone, let alone an official, a busy servant of the people, trek all the way up here just to kill a bird? Can you imagine?"

The dead crane's mate still appears, but only very rarely and unpredictably, alone on the rock or down by the streams in the meadow. Or so the younger novices report; the old monk who's telling the story admits that his own eyes have grown too feeble for bird-watching anymore. But if the pair of cranes were somehow restored, the other one adds eagerly, Thekchen Dhargye Dzong would have its guardians again.

"Ayah, that . . ." Norbu mulls the question, passing a reflective hand over the stubble of his tonsure. Then he hits on an improvisation: "You two, you old white heads. *You're* the two white cranes. With a pair of guardians like you, the monastery couldn't be safer."

The two of them smile at this conceit, flattered. Norbu rubs his pate again, chuckles along with the old monks, and nods. Aside, to us, he murmurs, "Gently, ease them gently. Give them a chance to laugh."

MORE MATERIAL SOLUTIONS ARE required, though, for the ongoing, practical demands of the temple, as set forth by Lobsang and the younger cohort of monks. Norbu pulls out of his flight bag a fat wad of renminbi notes, more tens than hundreds. The assorted functionaries of Thekchen Dhargye Dzong, one by one, recount their needs and receive a portion of the money, together with detailed directions.

As this reckoning drags on, Felix, Ah-loong, and I excuse ourselves and go out for a stretch. Norbu tells us to be back in an hour. We work our way up behind the temple. A few young monks trail after us. Two of them lead stocky, soft-eyed white horses. Ah-loong snaps pictures and Felix struggles in vain to strike up a conversation with a ten-year-old about his Tibetan-language comic book.

Aku Kuba's stories lend a palimpsest effect to the pastoral scene: the searing past blazes through the smiling present. I leave the others perched on a rock spur at the base of the cliff and take off to climb to the top.

Norbu's deadline goads me to hurry. In the thin air, I pant and sweat my way up a series of clefts and channels in the rock that are invisible from down below in the courtyard. I tack from noonday mountain sunlight into purple cliff shadows and back out into the glare again, my nape prickling at each shift of temperature. I dodge brambles and scatter scree down the steep slope.

After half a week largely spent sitting cross-legged among congregations of monks, this solitary burst of heart-pounding exertion comes as a relief. For half the climb I'm on all fours. I note snake tracks, bird tracks, a myriad of small, brave herbs that flourish in rock crags. No time for taxonomy, though: I press on. Still, my worm's-eye view of the cliff face offers a gritty counterpoint to last night's ethereal, moonlit *mandalas*. I start to see how generations of studious men could live full, rich lives without ever straying from this encyclopedic mountain.

As I near the top, inch-square charm papers fleck the bracken. They're block-printed with prayers and flying-horse images. The paper snowfall gets thicker as I emerge through a rock cleft onto a giddy perch staked out with prayer flags.

I clutch at the flag-staves, gasping. The perspective plays scale tricks. The rooftops of the nearby hermitage huts "rhyme" with the green tiles of the main prayer hall way down there; the little *Mani* stones at my feet mimic the massive boulders I've just skirted on my trail up.

Facile conflations. Next I suppose I'll be ready to hop-skip-and-jump through thin air down to the meadow below, leaving nothing behind here but holy footprints. I try out my new *mantra* and find it steadying. The birds, for their part, provide a scaling factor to the vista, soaring from buttress to spire. Crows, swallows, doves, partridges, a hawk—but no cranes.

With a quarter hour left to go, I skid and scramble down the same trail I took up. By the time I reach the jeep, it's already loaded and ready to go. No chants or trumpets to send us on our way, but plenty of *khatags* and smiles from Lobsang and company. Felix presents himself to Aku Kuba, apparently expecting another brow-to-brow blessing as at Choeling Tashikyil. Nothing doing, this time. Duly warned, I content myself with a formal half-bow, my two palms pressed together at chest level. I receive a glowering nod in reply. Norbu settles himself into the front seat, straightens his winged hat, and we roll past the chalked *mandala*.

Midway through the nine fords, Norbu and Ah-loong both swear they actually see one of the cypress trees "shaking off dust." I happen to be looking the other way at the time, and no matter how closely I scan the slopes afterward, the trees refuse to oblige me with a repeat performance. "Let it go," Norbu advises. "Only then might one shake for you."

ON THE WAY DOWN, we call again at the same nomad headman's house. A horse capers in the yard where the headman's shy nephew has just dismounted. Norbu decides that it's time for me to have a ride. The nephew dutifully holds the halter for me, although he looks a bit dubious about the prospect.

So am I. It's been fully seven years since the last time I rode a horse. My entire equestrian experience adds up to a couple of years' membership in a predawn riding club at Mahalakshmi Race Course in Bombay. We rode the racetrack's rejects and has-beens—light, sweet thoroughbreds too laid-back for the jockeys. Each animal had its own *syce*, a member of a hereditary caste of grooms and horse-handlers. In jodhpurs and riding helmets, we would trot around a well-trodden ring, our personal *syce* riding alongside to make sure that nothing untoward happened. With unfailing politesse, our riding master, a mustachioed ex–Indian Army major, would patiently correct our egregious posture.

But this Tibetan horse Norbu's inveigled me onto is a far cry from those docile mounts—that much I can sense as soon as I climb aboard.

Under the tubular wooden saddle, the stubby little animal crackles with cranky energy, more like a turbo-mule than my idea of a horse. Nor, for that matter, is the headman's nephew much like a servile Mahalakshmi *syce*, either.

Freshly dismounted, he's still unkempt and windblown from galloping across these high plains. His cult-mark coiffure alternates bristling dreadlocks with blue-shaved swathes. He walks with a rolling swagger, upturned toes of his mud-spattered boots splayed out. It may be no more than iodine deficiency, but his protuberant eyes show white all around the irises. He ogles in amazement as I fidget about in the stirrups, trying to remember my riding master's pointers. He mutters something that prompts a worried "Uh-oh" from Norbu, who then turns and tells me, with studied nonchalance, "By the way, he says this horse can be just a bit naughty."

With two hands hanging onto the halter-rope like a kite string, the nephew leads my mount in a tight semicircle. For every step the horse takes, I can feel thirty scatter-foot possibilities racing through his tight-coiled little golf ball of a brain. After five paces we halt. The nephew and I exchange nervous, courtly little grins of relief. Then we carefully pace off another semicircle, and another—five times in all. I'm peripherally aware of Norbu as a stiff red-and-yellow semaphore way off on the horizon. But mainly my focus is riveted on a fly buzzing my horse's close-cropped, twitchy mane.

What am I doing up here, anyway? Just losing face in front of a whole paddock of born-in-the-saddle nomads. As soon as it seems decently permissible, I signal the nephew that I'm ready to dismount. Safely on the ground, though, my Bombay equestrian manners don't desert me altogether. I thank my mount with a pat on the neck, just as my riding-master taught me to, repeatedly murmuring *"Gedinche"*— "Thanks," my sole word in Amdo dialect.

AFTER THIS ADVENTURE, I have little stomach for another GRYMY. On the ride home, I doze most of the way. By the time I wake, our jeep is already whipping past whitish-green El Greco pastures. Back in the mountains we've come from, behind Thekchen Dhargye Dzong, the sky has bricked in with clouds. A driving wind from the valley floor below stirs dust devils in our path. The creek willows flail and show their blanched leaf-backs. Lightning flits about the corners of the sky, but so far no thunder. We arrive at Norbu's door in Choeling just as the first swollen raindrops spatter the courtyard dust.

Thubten is waiting for us inside. He's dapper as ever in the same old double-breasted suit he habitually uses for "plainclothes" detail, but something's ruffling his usual cool. As soon as Norbu steps in, he voices his worry. For the past couple of days, his boss has been questioning him about us.

It seems word has gotten out that the lama is harboring unregistered foreign guests. Now the head of the local constabulary's foreign affairs department wants to come over and register us. This news appears to flap Norbu almost as much as Thubten. Not that he's worried about anything the police might do or say. But he wonders aloud who in the monastery or the villages might be reporting on our comings and goings.

Norbu's nervousness infects us in turn, and we start casting ourselves in the appropriate roles for the coming charade. Felix will be the star, a Taiwan Compatriot hi-tech investor, here in Qinghai on a quest for his Buddhist roots in the motherland. By accompanying him, Ah-loong, the dutiful female relative, is simply meeting the requirements of Chinese hospitality. And, true to life, I'll just play my customary bit-part in China as an oblivious foreign tag-along.

By the time the police official finally shows up in the early evening, we're thoroughly prepped for our performances. Felix blithers on about software export zones and Buddhist theme parks, while Ah-loong flutters around the kitchen with motherly solicitude. As for me, I just snap my *"Ni hao"* ("How d'you do") at the cop in an accusatory bark, rather than the appropriate singsong wheedle, like a fresh-off-the-plane tourist who has never heard of a tonal language before. Thubten gapes at me, shocked, but his Han boss seems perfectly satisfied that we're all talking just the way we're *supposed* to sound. He simply asks us to fill in a set of the same registration forms that foreigners must submit at any hotel check-in counter in China.

Clearly, the policeman's focus is not on us, but on Norbu. Encountering an incarnate lama, evidently, so unnerves him that he breaks out in a sweat, despite the cool rain that's come down steadily ever since our return to Choeling. Norbu hands him a napkin to daub his brow, and the two of them make wincingly polite small talk. Amdo born and bred, the Han officer nevertheless speaks hardly any Tibetan. In the normal line of duty in Rui-an he'd rarely run into a Living Buddha and seems uncertain whether to bluster or defer. He tries both at once, peremptorily quizzing Norbu in curt imperatives, yet sticking to the honorific "*Nin*" form of address throughout. As soon as he can get away with it, he scoops up the completed forms, perfunctorily flips through our passports, and beats a retreat.

BUOYED BY OUR RELIEF at coming off so easily in our brush with the police, we repair in high spirits to Thubten's house. Tomorrow, Norbu begins a week-long silent retreat at Choeling and the three of us head back to Beijing. So tonight is our farewell dinner. To reinforce our expansive mood, we're granted a reprieve from having to face yet another GRYMY. Instead, the camp-chef uncle has rustled up a five-star banquet, complete with salads and cold cuts and sugary Darjeeling-style tea. Norbu sings for our supper, regaling our chef, Thubten, and Rinchen with a spirited account of our mountain foray.

Abandoning the sacerdotal gravity with which he'd entertained the police chief, Norbu squints and mugs his way through his recital, now slouching in his chair and then snapping to attention with a comically martial glare. I can't follow a word he's saying as it's all in Tibetan. But the drollery of his gestures and the mounting mirth of his relatives sets the rest of us laughing along with them.

Midway through the story he switches over to Chinese: ". . . so he grabs the pommel and hoists himself aboard, without so much as picking up the reins. Well, the kid takes one look at that and just wraps an extra loop of rope around his hand, muttering something about a 'temperamental animal.'

"The horse, of course, immediately stiffens and casts an eye back over his shoulder"—Norbu mimes this—"and his ears, you know, start going this way and that." He brings his wrists together and flips his cupped hands back and forth menacingly. The smile freezes on my face as I realize I've seen those ears before.

"So I quietly mention, 'By the way, this horse can be naughty.' And you can see him just freeze right away in the saddle up there. The kid leads him a few paces and they stop. He smiles, the boy smiles." He imitates the nephew's stilted grin and my own. "A few paces farther, and again." More grins. "And the horse, all the while twitching his ears and rolling his eyes and wondering what to make of it all."

He mimes the animal so comically that my smile unfreezes and I find myself laughing again along with the others at the absurdity of the scene Norbu's re-created. "But that's not all. When he finally slides down from the saddle, he's so relieved that what does he do? He goes up to the horse and pats him like this"—a brisk stroking gesture—" 'gedinche, gedinche.' And that kid just looks at him, like, 'What? No gedinche for me?' "

Everybody's practically falling off their chairs laughing by now, and so am I. So, too, must be all the nomads for leagues around, Norbu assures me, "because they love a funny story like nothing else." My renown in these parts is assured for a long time to come.

The evening rides to a close on a general tide of hilarity. Norbu, Felix, and I take our leave and laugh our way back to the Choeling gatehouse. We're still too ebullient to settle right down to sleep, so Felix tries out on Norbu a new and potentially profitable scheme he's hatched.

"Rinpoche," he ventures, "can I ask you about those mandalas we saw? You know, it's hard for us to hang on to so many details at once and keep everything straight in our heads—all those doors and passageways and who stands where holding what. Now, I'm a computer guy, and I've been thinking: Why not make a virtual-reality *mandala* to help people find their way around?"

He launches into an explanation of virtual reality; how, with only a screen, a mouse, and some software, "you can take yourself anywhere you want, clear outta this *world*. It'd save you no end of outlay on painting and sculpture and stuff. Latest thing," Felix assures the lama. "State of the art. Cutting-*edge*."

Norbu hears him out with mounting alarm, then gently suggests that such technology might not be appropriate for a *mandala*. "Very dangerous to turn people loose in a *mandala* without a guru or an initiation. A serious copyright violation. What if people start thinking of the computer as their guru?"

Felix, as a seasoned salesman, knows when a prospect's too cold to bother pursuing. But I'm still not ready to accept Norbu's latest Buddhist Luddite outburst. After all, if you can make a *mandala* out of yak fat, why not out of electrons? When it comes to enlightenment, the medium is decidedly *not* the message, is it? There always remains, anyway, that last unbridgeable gap between virtuality and reality, the crib sheet and the exam.

I keep my doubts to myself, however, as per Norbu's earlier admonitions. Why spoil the easygoing mood of our cozy little Pullman on our last night in Rui-an? Norbu smiles benignly over the two of us, framed in the black window behind him. Fleeting flashes of lightning intermittently light up the night outside as the residue of this afternoon's storm still nips at the edges of the horizon. Bats wheel in the waning moon about the *mandala* gatehouse. Dogs bark contrapuntally in the distance.

As a bedtime story, I ask Norbu for a detailed translation of the handbill about the Great Snakes from Space. He has Pema fish out the broadside to indulge me. Half the text relates the origin of the prophecy: how a Tibetan third-grader from Sichuan received a parchment from her late mother's ghost and handed it over to her teacher. The schoolmaster at first suppressed the prophecy until the mysterious death of his own sons scared him into promulgating the jeremiads.

After this wind-up comes the pitch, a sizzling spitball. "Heed and live right! Pray to Tara the Compassionate! Three Snakes will emerge to upend the globe." The handbill gives a timetable of millennial plagues and disasters, starting in China and affecting the whole world.

In those days, the text warns, "man and wife must not even look on each other with desire. Don't sit on the threshold of your house. Eat no food that is cold or raw. Drink no water, only tea." I edge closer to Norbu's platform as he drops his voice to shift from ringing injunctions to dire prophecy. "Parents will deny their children and neighbor will not know neighbor. Returning to your own home you will feel like a stranger. Your horse will shy from you. Dogs will bark . . ."

Whereupon the actual curs of Choeling set up a howl outside. I glance apprehensively at the door, and Norbu uses my momentary distraction to reach down from his platform and clutch me behind the knee. *Yeow!* I levitate, quivering, a half-foot into the air. This time, the lama literally falls down laughing. He sprawls on his bed, helpless with mirth.

"Wah-*du*!" he gasps. "A quivering tree. A cypress, shaking off the dust."

I WAKE, still quivering, to a murky, curdled dawn. Norbu's already sitting rootedly on his throne, eyes closed, with an indrawn smile. No such contemplative interlude for Felix and me this morning. Chogyal's already clattering kettles in the kitchen even as the chants still resound from the neighboring courtyards.

Before we're done brushing our teeth, Ah-loong blows in to goad us through our rushed breakfast and preside over the divvying up of our winter gear. We've got a seven-o'clock bus to catch for Labrang. Since we're heading down the mountain, where spring is already well advanced, we'll no longer need our sweaters, socks, and windbreakers, the theory goes. So, as a self-administered lesson in detachment, we hand over our woolens to Pema and Chogyal, who will be staying up here in the cold.

Lessons in detachment come thick and fast all morning. We scramble out the door and head for Thubten's. Halfway down the main street of Rui-an, I realize I've left my glasses at Norbu's, which means no reading for the duration. Just as well, I try to convince myself. After all, I've read not a word all week, I realize with surprise, and hardly even missed it.

At Thubten's, we barely have a chance to consolidate our backpacks and say a hurried goodbye and *gedinche* to Norbu and Rinchen. Seems pretty cursory, considering. Doesn't our vivid week in Qinghai call for a bit more concluding fanfare? But there's simply no time for ceremony. And besides, I'm hard-pressed to imagine just what sort of gesture *could* appropriately wrap up our Rui-an experience. I guess a *mandala*'s not a linear progression, building up to a final crescendo. Rather, it's a radial composition, revolving around its own vortex. At the edges, it just frays or fades away.

These meditations of mine have to be mused on the run as we trot along behind Thubten to the depot, packs thumping against our backs. We arrive at the bus station, winded, only to find our departure delayed after all. The bus is there in the parking lot, all right, but the driver's nowhere to be seen. Thubten helps us stow our bags under our reserved seats. Then he waits in the parking lot to see us off, with nothing to do but cool his heels—literally, as it turns out, for it presently starts to snow.

The driver finally appears and revs the sputtering engine a few times by way of warm-up. I crane out my window for a last glimpse of Thubten. He strokes the tin flanks of our bus, murmuring "*Gedinche, gedinche*," then cracks up at the memory of my horse etiquette.

THE SNOWFALL THICKENS beyond the Rui-an bridge. As we gather momentum, the fat flakes outside the bus window blur into white streaks against the roadside willows and poplars. Snow collects on the cliffs above, highlighting the ledges and the scrub vegetation.

Just before Menya, we roll to our first flag stop. Two men climb aboard carrying a twenty-foot-long scroll on their shoulders. This village, Norbu has told us, is famous for its *tangka*s, including the giant outdoor icons that are spread out on hillside meadows for the Buddhist equivalent of evangelical camp meetings.

Before the bus even starts rolling again, Felix is already out of his seat, antennae atwitch. He helps the newcomers lash their scroll to the overhead luggage rack, plying them all the while with rapid-fire questions: "Are you guys painters? What's that you've got there, a *tangka*? How long did it take to make? How big? You sell these things? How much? Got anything smaller?"

I wish I could shift emotional gears that smoothly. Here I am, still maundering over the lack of closure in our overhasty leave-taking from Rui-an, while Felix is all set to cut fresh deals. Clearly his is the better-adapted temperament, for the *tangka* painters show themselves more than ready to do business with him. Ah-loong and I yield up our seats to them, the better to facilitate Felix's negotiations.

Standing in the aisle, though, we begin to regret having surrendered our warm clothes. Even the press of fellow strap-hangers is not enough to buffer the mountain cold. An icy draft washes over the floorboards of the bus, freezing our sockless toes. My head fills up with the palpable onset of sniffles. We worm our way up to the front of the bus and perch ourselves precariously on the engine hump next to the driver. It may be cramped up here, but at least it's warm.

Through the windshield, we glimpse our first ice-rainbow—an arc so tight it almost closes in on itself. The colors strike me as unnaturally crisp: "More like an etching than a watercolor," I suggest to Ah-loong. "You mean intaglio versus aquatint," she dryly corrects me, drawing on her fine-arts training.

Such distinctions may be lost on our eavesdropping driver, but he can make out at least that we're talking about the rainbow. He offers a critique of his own, in Henan-accented Chinese: "Not much of a show, eh? Now a *real* rainbow should fill up half the sky, like they used to back in Kaifeng."

That's where he grew up, he wants us to know, proud of his Yangtze delta urbanity. Orphaned early on in Japan's World War II occupation, he was left to shift for himself, living by his wits as a hanger-on in Kaifeng's railway station. Taking stock of my five-day stubble and my droopy nose, he ventures to inquire: "*Bist a yid?*"—a common Kaifeng gambit upon meeting any Westerner. Like every railway tout in the city, he claims to be a descendant of the Jewish traders who migrated to the Song dynasty capital from the Levant a thousand years ago.

Kaifeng's Jewish population has been completely assimilated for at least a century. Still, the presumption of kinship might have earned him some patronage from American GIs during the city's brief post-Japanese interlude before the Red Army swept in. His touting technique proved less ingratiating to the Communists, however; he was rounded up as a "bad element" and exiled here to Gansu in 1958.

He hasn't seen Kaifeng since. He'd go back there like a shot if he could only manage to transfer his residence permit. But, meanwhile, it's not so bad out here, he admits. Plenty of other internal exiles here from the cities—a whole social microcosm unto itself. Together with other "reeducation" alumni, he has set up this Rui-an-to-Labrang bus line as a cooperative venture. And since "reform and opening," he even runs into a fair sprinkling of foreign tourists at Labrang to try out his "*Bist a yid?*"

That turns out to be his only phrase of Yiddish. But at least it's more than he knows of the local dialect, despite having lived over forty years in Amdo. So we infer, anyway, from his blank incomprehension when Tibetan passengers try to request out-of-the-way flag stops or ask for change when they tender their bus fares.

The snubbed Tibetans just shrug and hunker glumly in the aisle—a far cry from the purposeful bustle of the Tashikyil construction site, the confident swagger of the nomad horsemen, or the worshipful alertness of a massed *sangha*. Traveling with Norbu, the Amdo people we've encountered have seemed so self-assured, basking in the presence of their own Living Buddha. Here on this bus, though, the Tibetans are out of their element, at loose ends. They fret about their bundles, mumble alien words and shift footing uneasily as we swerve down the mountain passes.

I'm still feeling a bit off-balance, myself, wrenched so abruptly out of Norbu's orbit. All week long, we've been dependents of a deity, part of a retinue. It's been illuminating, but not without its frustrations: the mediated dialogues, the endless GRYMY, the protocol minefields, the godly tongue-lashings.

And now, here's this garrulous driver—my putative long-lost kinsman, no less—conveying us closer, mile by mile, to the world of bathtubs and fresh vegetables and independence and anonymity; my home base, my news beat, my own milieu. Shouldn't there be at least a glimmer of anticipation or relief? Yet all I can muster is a vague sense of apathy and anticlimax. Is this the kind of detachment that Norbu would have us cultivate?

A POLICE CHECKPOINT MARKS the border into Gansu province. The snow lets up. Our driver orders all the passengers in the aisle to crouch down below the window-line. Gansu cops, he explains, enrich themselves by fining errant drivers for overpacked buses—yet another benchmark of our passage out of Rui-an's ambit and into a whole different matrix here, with rules of its own.

This new *mandala* unfolds its grand geometry before us as we swoop out of the high, barren scrubland down to the banks of the Daxia River. The gleaming spires of Labrang seem to float directly on the sleek surface of the water. The narrow village, wedged between the river and the monastery, intrudes as no more than an incidental interposition—gray, jumbled, and insubstantial as a passing cloud of smoke.

And, indeed, when we pull into Xiahe town, the whole, long riverfront strip turns out to be wreathed in a smog of bus exhaust and fry-oil fumes. The acrid stench is relieved by faint whiffs of patchouli and sandalwood emanating from the head shops that line the sole thoroughfare, interspersed with budget pensions and restaurants. Psychedelic signboards enliven the gimcrack concrete façades.

As soon as we roll into the depot, the Tibetans burst out of the bus like schoolchildren sprung from detention hall. Descending after everybody else, we spot Felix already halfway down the block shouldering the twenty-foot *tangka* together with his newfound friends.

Never mind; we'll catch up with him later. Besides, there's no hope of giving chase right now as our path is immediately blocked by a phalanx of touts.

"Cheap room?" A Hui in a skullcap presses a calling card upon us. A harlequin clone of Norbu's friend Tashi invites us to his shop: "Antiques? Gemstones? Roach-clips? What's your pleasure? Book of the Dead? Only look; no need to buy." Failing to get a rise out of us in English, he switches over to German, then Japanese, and finally what I take to be Hebrew. A strapping Tibetan matron proposes an "herbal massage." A furtive Uighur sidles up offering to change dollars, then hisses, sotto voce, "Hashishashishashishashish."

We flee the depot and join the stream of camera-toting Europeans along the main drag. Sidewalk cafés advertise banana fritters, chocolate pancakes, hummus, milkshakes, gnocchi (usually misspelled "knockie" or "nookie")—the same fare that's on offer the whole length of the backpack tourist archipelago, from Bali to Katmandu.

As we're pondering our luncheon options, a wizened hunchback darts out of a doorway and thrusts in our faces some sort of mummified giblet—purportedly a deer's musk gland. Before he has a chance to follow up with bear claws or tiger penises, we duck for refuge into an unassuming noodle shop. There we come upon Katie Brogan, an anthropology graduate student, poring over her Amdo dialect grammar text with the help of a sardonic middle-aged waiter.

She's been here more than two years already, mastering the language in preparation for her Ph.D. research on the rapport between Buddhist values and economic development. When she hears we've been a week in Rui-an district, she's impressed by our foolhardiness: that place is supposed to be pretty rough, she says, from the standpoint of crime and politics. She generously agrees to guide us on a circumambulation of the Labrang complex, following the route Tibetan pilgrims take around the shrine.

Few foreign tourists make their way to the circumambulation track, where we find ourselves aswim in a steady stream of the devout: monks and nuns and peasant families, hobbling cripples and capering children, abject beggars and bejeweled nomads. A couple of pilgrims measure out the perimeter of Labrang in prostrate body lengths, their knees and palms protected by wooden roundels that clack against the stones each time they fall prone.

The buildings are every bit as magnificent as Norbu had promised—testimony, he'd say, to Labrang's willingness to cooperate with the Chinese authorities. Indeed, Katie relates, the monastery's current lama-in-chief is supposed to be so compliant that even his own monks have lost faith in him, suspecting him to be a bogus incarnation.

The current head lama's predecessor once twitted his acolytes that "If I were to be reborn as a foreign prince, you'd probably not even recognize me." On the basis of this hint, and a few other signs and portents, they have divined the lama's true present incarnation, who ought to be well along in his fifties by now. Deep meditations have revealed to them the real identity of their present spiritual leader: William Jefferson Clinton. As far as a sizable number of Labrang monks are concerned, Katie relates, the ex-president may come here anytime he's free to assume his true calling to Living Buddhahood.

As she's telling this story, a monk comes running out of one of the prayer halls and beckons us in with the greatest urgency. In all her time here, this is something new to Katie's experience. Usually, if anything, the monastics are at pains to keep tourists out of their sancta.

We enter to find a procession of pilgrims crowding around a couple of Ping-Pong-table-sized platforms mounted on trestles. Joining the crush, we inch our way to the front to see what's the big attraction. It turns out to be the apotheosis of all sand castles: a fantastically intricate *mandala*, fifteen feet across and perhaps half a foot high, meticulously sculpted in vividly colored grains of sand.

So lavish is the ornamentation that the eye can hardly make out the underlying architecture of walls and crenellations and gates and balustrades. The composition practically writhes with multiarmed deities and fantastic animals. Arabesques and lotuses and little rosettes fill in all the corners. A moat of sand-sculpted deep-blue "water" surrounds the whole. From every angle, new axes of symmetry present themselves.

The pilgrims shuffle around the *mandala*, silently. An old lady cries—tears, but no sobs. One teenager has stained his brow blue by prostrating right into the sand moat. A young monk, in passable Chinese, explains that this is the *kalachakra*, the "wheel of time," transmitted by the Buddha on his deathbed. It has more than seven hundred deities. Our informant and a dozen other monks spent eight days making it—not to mention the years of study that prepared them for this labor.

I bring my eye level with the table to mentally trace a path from the periphery to the central tetrahedron. Not a sand-grain seems to stir in the *mandala*, unlike a normal sandcastle, which is constantly acrawl with mini-landslides. No matter how I approach it, the architecture of the *mandala* dictates an oblique pathway to the center. Passages bifurcate or dead-end, and every ramp or gate runs into a wall sooner or later.

All at once, without fanfare, an elderly monk with a goiter and a coxcomb hat strides through the crowd and broaches the *mandala* with a trowel-tipped yardstick. A younger acolyte, diametrically opposite on the other side of the table, guides the trowel with a string attached to its shank. Together they plow a hairline furrow from the moat right through to the hub. Slow and deliberate as their gestures are, the sheer straightness of the trench is such a violation of the *mandala*'s curvilinear involution that I catch my breath at the violence of it. They repeat the same move from all four cardinal points, leaving the *kalachakra* rent with jagged fissures, like the aftermath of an earthquake.

Then the old man uses his trowel to meticulously spoon out the rosettes and lotuses that stud the design. He smears the colored sand onto a porcelain palette like so many discarded pinches of Kool-Aid. These are the deities, our young monk says. They have to be removed first.

Our informant squints at my gasping reaction and chuckles. "It's only sand, don't forget. That's why we make it out of sand, you see. Impermanence."

The goitered monk continues scooping sand rosettes, as though he were plucking rubies from a clockwork. It only remains to sweep the rest of the parti-colored sand into a melded grayish heap, shovel it into gunnysacks, and release it into the Daxia River.